The Life of
JOHN
MILNE

My covenant was with him life and peace;
And I gave them to him
For the fear wherewith he feared me,
And stood in awe of my name.

The law of truth was in his mouth,
And iniquity was not found in his lips:
In peace and uprightness he walked with me,
And many did he turn from iniquity.

(Mal. 2:5.)

The Life of
JOHN MILNE
of Perth

Horatius Bonar

For my name's sake thou hast laboured and hast not fainted.
Revelation 2:3

THE BANNER OF TRUTH TRUST

THE BANNER OF TRUTH TRUST

3 Murrayfield Road, Edinburgh EH12 6EL, UK
P.O. Box 621, Carlisle, PA 17013, USA

*

First published 1869
First Banner of Truth edition 2010

*

ISBN-13: 978 0 85151 961 6

*

Typeset in Adobe Caslon Pro 11/15 at
the Banner of Truth Trust, Edinburgh

Printed in the U.S.A. by
Versa Press, Inc.,
East Peoria, IL

Preface

*I*t is not a eulogy that I wish to write, but a record. I should like to show the man, not to execute a piece of sculpture.

In doing this, it will be needful to introduce 'companions in labour', — from him who died first, Robert Murray M'Cheyne, to him who went last, William Chalmers Burns; with others still serving here below. Some names may have been left out; but it was found impossible to make mention of all. The religious history of the last forty years in Scotland remains to be written. Biographies, like the present, are contributions to this.

I fear I may not have been quite accurate chronologically at times; but the narrative is not at all affected by this. As very few of Mr Milne's letters are fully dated, I was occasionally at a loss in regard to order and time.[1] Several things have been thrown in purposely out of order, because needing to be grouped, for the illustration of some particular feature of character.

I have to thank the brethren who have so kindly trusted me with their correspondence, and thereby enabled me to sketch the course of one so 'greatly beloved' by us all.

In a day of bustle and whirl, like ours, it may be well to study the life of one who stood in the midst of all this, yet was not of it;

---

[1] In going over a pretty large correspondence, I am surprised to find how many letters of various men in various positions, especially ministers, are undated; their date being only ascertainable by the post-office mark. I notice that all M'Cheyne's are very carefully dated.

who was never for an hour drawn into it; but sought all his days to draw others out of it, into the calm and joy which he himself so fully knew.

In an age of false ideals and hero-worship, it will be found good, also, to mark one who took, as his great model, both in service and suffering, the Son of God; who knew, above most, what intimacy with him could do, in moulding character, and in producing a true and telling life.

HORATIUS BONAR
THE GRANGE,
EDINBURGH,
OCTOBER 1868.

Contents

A Plan of the City of Perth, 1858

Chapter 1

1807 – 1839
Birth – Studies – Removal
to Perth

*W*ithin six months of each other died three men whom the Church could ill spare, and whom some of us will long miss and mourn.

On the 27th of November 1867, died James Hamilton; on the 4th of April 1868, died William Chalmers Burns; on the 31st of May 1868, died John Milne. Twenty-nine years ago they were fellow-labourers in Scotland, and 'true yoke-fellows'. Their after-work drew them into different fields; their later life was spent in different lands; and their graves are far asunder. London holds the first, Newchwang the second, Edinburgh the last.

Along with the above, I would name other four who left us many years ago, but who were at one time associated with these three in heart and work; I mean Robert Murray M'Cheyne of Dundee, Daniel Cormick of Kirriemuir, William Hewitson of Dirleton, and Patrick Miller of Newcastle. As St Augustine said of his early friends, so I may say of these seven: *'Me multum diligebant ... et ego illos, propter magnam virtutis indolem, quae in non magno aetate satis eminebat.'*[1]

---

[1] 'They loved me much ... and I them, on account of their great excellence of character, which was sufficiently evident at no great age.' From Augustine, *Confessions*, 6.7.11., *Ed.*

'These all died in faith', resting from their labours. The work of each was a true one and a great, though not very long. Their lives were not failures, bringing forth nothing; nor contradictions, one part neutralizing the other. They were debtors to the age while in it (*Rom.* 1:14); and now the age is their debtor. The period which, by their holy bearing and bold testimony, they helped to mould, is a very notable one in the history of the Church of God. The work they did was real, and their footprints are still visible. They so lived and spoke as to tell upon the world; giving a deeper tone both to the religion and the theology of their time. They were men of 'large views', in the sense in which the Lord and his apostles were such; seeking to be neither narrower nor broader than they. They were men of progress; 'adding to their faith, virtue, and to virtue, knowledge; and to knowledge, temperance; and to temperance, patience; and to patience, godliness' (*2 Pet.* 1:6). They knew what they believed, and they believed it nobly; nor did they find any necessity to unsay or undo, in their later years, what they said and did in their earlier. They died as they lived, tenacious of the old gospel, suspicious of 'advanced theologies', and jealous for the divine accuracy of the Scriptures.

Christianity has no weak points. Other systems have. It has none. In the inconsistencies of Christians some have professed to see the weak side of Christianity. But the lives of Christians are not Christianity. Yet, in the cases above noted, Christianity was not put to shame by its friends. Their light shone steadily to the last. It did not wax dim with years, nor hide itself in mist. Living in an age that is oscillating between universal belief and universal unbelief, they were not ashamed of having a fixed creed, and a Bible that never grows old.

Birth, School-life, Fall

John Milne was born at Peterhead, in Aberdeenshire, on the 26th of April 1807. He died at Spring Valley, Morningside, near Edinburgh, on Sabbath the 31st of May 1868.

His father held office in the Custom-house at Peterhead. John was sent, when a boy of five years old, to school in his native town. On his first school-day he met with a serious accident, which told upon his whole after life, and which for a time threatened to prove fatal. The school was held in a room above the Tolbooth, and there was a long outside stone-stair leading up to it At the close of school-hours the children poured out in a mass, to get to play, or to get home as quickly as possible. In the rush John was thrown down, and fell the whole length of the stair, striking his head severely. He was taken up and carried home insensible. After some little time he recovered, and returned to school; still for many years the pain in his head was so violent, that he was obliged, by medical advice, to keep it shaved.

His physicians, in after years, traced to this fall those fits of depression into which he sometimes sank. The brain had been injured, and the effects of the concussion never entirely disappeared; or rather, they reappeared at certain intervals, sometimes producing lowness of spirits, and a feeling of unfitness for work, and sometimes leading him to act fitfully and wilfully; yet never betraying him into inconsistency, nor into timidity; for he was throughout not only one of the most consistent, but one of the *boldest of men,* — a man utterly devoid of fear, and insensible of danger in any shape; a man who would have led a forlorn hope up the breach as calmly as he would have ascended his own pulpit steps, or climbed Kinnoul Hill. In this perfect fearlessness he had only one equal that I knew, and that was William Burns. 'Had I been a worldly man' (I remember Milne saying one day as we were wandering over Dunsinnane Hill), 'I would have certainly been a soldier; and nothing would have given me such delight as charging at the head of my regiment the very thickest of the enemy.' He suited the action to the utterance, and showed how he would have done.

The school to which he went at Peterhead was taught by a Mr Donald, who afterwards became minister of the parish. It was his church that John attended, till he left his native town for Aberdeen; and he does not seem to have found interest or profit in what he heard. I never heard him speak specially of his minister; but I remember him referring more than once to the religious dreariness of these times. Not many days before his death, he came along from Morningside to call for me at the Grange. After some pleasant conversation in the house, we went out together for a walk; and as we sauntered along Strathearn Road, he alluded to his boyhood. He asked me about Edinburgh days some forty or fifty years ago, congratulating me that I had enjoyed such a ministry as that of Dr Jones.[1] He referred sorrowfully to his own religious training in Aberdeenshire, and spoke as one who throughout life had been feeling the evil influence of these bleak and barren years.

Donald was succeeded in the school by Mr Imrie, and under his teaching John made great progress. His health continued to improve, and he was able to study more than he had done. He was generally first in every class; and often, when his companions were at play, he was found busy at his books. He was always a thoughtful, good boy; and from his childhood he expressed a wish to be a 'minister'.

When about thirteen, he was asked by Imrie to give some assistance in the school. This he did for some little time; and when he left for college, Imrie made him a present of a small sum, the first

[1] Dr Jones was upwards of fifty years minister of Lady Glenorchy's Chapel in Edinburgh; a vigorous, earnest preacher, to whom multitudes from many parts resorted in those days. He was born in Wales in 1754, came to Edinburgh in 1779, and died in 1837.

money he had earned. At this time he does not appear to have had any deep religious feelings, though morally correct and pure.

Education — College

In 1821 he left Peterhead for Aberdeen; entering Marischal College, and continuing in the undergraduate classes for the usual four sessions. He used sometimes to mention an impression made on him the first night of his arrival in Aberdeen, where he stayed in the house of Mr James Edmond for a short time. When in the bedroom, Edmond said to him, that 'he hoped he was not afraid nor ashamed to say his prayers.' The word was not lost, though it issued in nothing at the time. It is generally not out of one word or one impression, but many, and these often at intervals, that the Spirit of God brings about the great decision.

At college he distinguished himself highly in different departments of study, especially mathematics. Dr Cruickshanks, who was his professor in that branch, speaks of him as one of the best students he ever had. In the junior mathematical class he gained the second prize in session 1822–23. Next session he gained the first prize in the senior mathematical class, which that year was one of considerable value, being given by the Lord Rector of the University. He also obtained, by competition, Gray's Mathematical Bursary of £30 a year, for two years, the highest honour which the college then had to bestow. On the competition day he lost his portfolio, with all the notes and papers requisite for his work, and did not miss it till he was in the class-room, and the doors shut. To most, competition in such a case would have seemed hopeless. But having obtained paper from the porter, and being thoroughly 'read up' in his subjects, he set to work, wrote his 'versions', and won the prize. This he used to refer to in after years, wondering how it was that he succeeded. His fellow-students speak of his extraordinary perseverance and application, by means of which he mastered everything that was given him to do. This indomitable determination was one of his characteristics through life. He went through with everything that he set his face to. He is spoken of also with much love by those who knew him then, as gentle and kind in manner; polite and affable even from his youth.

Studies and Scholarship

He took his degree of M.A. in March 1825, though I am not aware that he was in the habit of appending it to his name.

During part of his university course he lodged with the celebrated Latinist, Dr James Melvin, who was afterwards Rector of the Aberdeen Grammar School. His own attainments in Latin were considerable; and his classical predilections were as decided as his mathematical. His ready memory supplied him, in after years, with many a Greek and Latin quotation; and often, when the exact word escaped him, his accurate scholarship supplied its place with some equivalent which he knew how to insert, without any breach of prosody or grammar. Dr Longmuir of Aberdeen, who was one of his class-fellows, mentions that when separated during the long summer vacations (which John always spent at Peterhead), a correspondence was kept up between the two students in Latin; Milne's letters being dated from 'Petri Promontorium', the classical designation of his native town, 'Peterhead'.[1]

[1] He did not cease to be a scholar when he became a minister; though, from his great modesty, few had a right idea of his attainments. Yet in some of his letters to Mr Somerville, several years after his settlement in Perth, we find him arranging studies thus: 'I used to read largely in the Septuagint, but I have somehow lost my copy. I do not think it would repay us. What say you to ten lines of Homer's *Iliad* and an ode of Horace on alternate days? You must brush up your classics for the sake of the rising generation. Ten minutes or less will do it. I shall begin Deuteronomy on Monday, five verses; and read critically. It is a pity you have not the points; but it is more a matter of *sound* than of *sense*, and you cannot now help it. *Miserable Moderates*, to teach Hebrew in a way that made our knowledge of it of no use if we wished to hold intercourse with living Jews! Luckily my teacher, Dr Kidd, got his knowledge of it from a Rabbi. Well, shall it be Deuteronomy and Horace on Monday; ditto and Homer on Tuesday, and so on? I am reading, writing,

It was during his stay at Aberdeen that he became acquainted with the Rev. Andrew Gray, who was in subsequent years his co-presbyter and much esteemed fellow-labourer in Perth. In many aspects these two were unlike each other; yet, in spite of dissimilarities, few men have so thoroughly appreciated each other's worth. Gray was the year before Milne at Marischal College; and they, after their graduation, attended the same classes at the Divinity Hall.

Having completed his theological course, he left college and went as tutor to Mr Irvine of Drum, where he remained several years. A brother of Irvine was the first who spoke to him directly about his spiritual state; and in 1856, when that gentleman died, Milne, on hearing of the death, wrote thus respecting him: 'He was the first that ever spoke to me about real religion. I was then as blind as a beetle, yet I remember it. He gave me Guthrie's *Trial of a Saving Interest in Christ.*'

From Drum he went to Hatton Castle, and was licensed while there by the Presbytery of Turriff.

Sojourn in England

In 1834 he went to England, where he taught, first in an academy, and afterwards in a private family, though longing all the while to enter on his proper work. The following extract from a letter of his to Francis Edmond, Esq., Aberdeen, dated Lower Dunstable House, Richmond, October 1834, will show his state of mind at this time:

I have been living here for some months as tutor in the family of the

---

and working a good deal; and more really using and enjoying life since I was with you, than I had done for a good while before. Have you seen the last number of the *North British Review?* The first article, on Ethics, struck me as exceedingly good, and would interest you, as bearing on the subject indirectly of some of your late researches. You will find a fair estimate of Paley as a moralist. I should like to know who wrote it. James Hamilton on Doddridge is interesting and good. But the times are getting too earnest for that kind of style.'

Rev. Mr Snow. The situation is tolerably comfortable. Mr S. is a good preacher, and an extremely pious man. I feel it a very great advantage to enjoy so much of his society. I remember complaining of it to you as a great misfortune, that from the circumstances of my life I had been unable to fix upon one particular thing, and devote myself entirely to it; but I would fain hope that religion is now beginning to assume such a place in my heart and thoughts as will probably move me by and by to give up everything here, and seek for usefulness in any sphere, however humble, connected with my profession.

It was under Snow's ministry that his impressions grew deeper; and it was at Richmond that he passed from darkness to light.[1] It was one special verse of Scripture in which he found the light and peace which he had been for some time groping for: 1 John 4:10, 'Herein is love, not that we loved God, but that he loved us, and sent his Son to be the propitiation for our sins.'

For the first year after his conversion he read no book but the Bible. All relish for other books seemed to have left him. With a divine volume lying beside him, human writings took an inferior place; or rather, at first, no place at all, till he learned, as he did soon, that all which is true, whether in a divine or human volume, is precious, and 'nothing to be refused' (οὐδὲν ἀποβλητον, *1 Tim.* 4:4), but only to be kept in its proper level. With his mathematical tastes and classical accomplishments, he could have 'kept abreast' of the age; but the higher relish absorbed the lower; he dreaded the distracting influence of excessive secular reading; and when he did engage in it, he was always on the watch for something to illustrate Scripture or help his preaching.

Though his theological training had been Presbyterian, yet he does not seem at first to have been very decided in his ecclesiastical

---

[1] It is interesting to know that she who was one day to be his wife, and who now survives him, was at that time in Richmond under the same ministry, and impressed with eternal things. They were, however, quite strangers to each other, not meeting till they met in Calcutta.

views. At one time he thought of entering the English Church. But being led from circumstances to study the subject of church polity, he became a very decided Presbyterian, and began to turn his eye back to the land of Presbytery.

Yet he did not in after years forget the land in which for a season he had been a stranger, nor the Church with which, through one of her many good men, he had been brought into fellowship. Writing to a servant in England, who had formerly been a member of his congregation in Perth, he thus speaks:

> Oh, do not think that our heavenly Father neglects his children, or that our brother Joseph forgets his brethren and sisters. You must not despise the Church of England. If I know the Lord at all, it was in her that He was first revealed to me. You are kindly remembered by many friends here. I have a letter from Mr Burns. He is still at Newcastle, but finds himself much opposed; but he is persevering in the work of the Lord. He seeks to be remembered before the Lord. — *Perth, 20th Sept. 1841.*

Appointed Lecturer in Aberdeen

In 1835 he was appointed lecturer on the Sabbath evenings in Gilcomston Church, Aberdeen, of which the late Dr Bryce was at that time the minister. After he accepted, but before he entered on his duty, he became depressed in spirit, afraid to undertake the work. It was with great difficulty that he was persuaded to go on. But when fully commenced, he proceeded vigorously, and gave great satisfaction to all concerned, especially as a visitor.[1] He remained there till he went to Perth, and on leaving Gilcomston he received

---

[1] It was at this time (in 1836) that his father died; and the reader will be interested in the following sentence from a recent letter of John's sister to her brother, William Milne of Perth, regarding the funeral. 'I often think of the evening of papa's funeral, when we were left alone, how he (John) took your hand and mine, and led us into his study, kneeled down, and committed us to the care of his heavenly Father.'

a handsome testimonial in token of esteem and gratitude. It was during this period that he had a severe attack of typhus fever, so that his life was despaired of. But many years were before him, and much work for God, though at that time men knew it not.

The above building, erected in 1834, was one of Dr Thomas Chalmers' Church Extension charges. Opened in 1835 as St Leonard's *Quoad Sacra* Parish Church, its first minister, Rev. George Miller, remained only three years. It was to this church that John Milne was ordained in 1839. It stands in King Street, Perth, and is now used by a furniture auctioneer.

Chapter 2

1839–40
Settlement in Perth

*J*ohn Milne left Aberdeen in 1839, and was settled in St Leonard's, Perth, on the 7th of November of that year. In that settlement no one rejoiced more than his old friend Andrew Gray, who, at the first meeting of Presbytery after the return of the Palestine deputation in the end of the same year, introduced him to my brother of Collace, with the remark, 'Now, I'm sure you two will be friends.' And so indeed they were from that day forward. In a letter, some sixteen years after, from India, which will be found in full in another place (see p. 422), he refers to this:

> I still remember our first meeting in the Old Presbytery, and where I was sitting when you came in and shook hands; and then R. M'Cheyne and you coming in to me at 14 Rose Terrace, and laughing at my *carte blanche* to Miss — to collect a staff of lady Sabbath-school teachers; and then our next meeting in the vestry of Kinnoul Street Church.

The following letters, as having reference to this period, may be quoted here, as giving us a glimpse of himself by himself:

> To FRANCIS EDMOND, Esq., Advocate, Aberdeen.
> *Perth, 2d Oct. 1839.* — MY DEAR SIR, — I have only this moment received your letter, having been for a few days in the country. I am

ashamed to think that I should have been so long in writing to you. But this arose in some measure from the peculiar circumstances in which I was placed. On arriving here, just a week ago, I found my friends waiting for me, and expecting me to go before the Presbytery; which I did, and went through this part of the customary trials, and had this day fixed for the remainder. I then took up my abode with Mr Gray, with whom I lived till Sunday, when I went out to officiate for another Aberdeenshire man, Mr Noble of St Madoes. I did not come to town till today, which was the reason of my not getting your letter sooner.

Today I met the Presbytery, and finished my trials, when they fixed the 7th of November for my ordination. It might have taken place sooner, but I rather wished it to be put off till after the Sacrament, which takes place on the 3d of that month.

I am sorry to say that, till today, I gave way too much to the unhappy depression under which I had so long laboured. It was very foolish, for I found every one here very kind. I have just been looking for lodgings, but have not yet fixed upon a place, though I shall probably do so tomorrow. It would not, I find, answer to take up house at present, as the expense of house-keeping would, I fear, be more than my income could well afford. I think it will be better therefore to get rid, as soon as possible, of the furniture which I have in Aberdeen. Perhaps you will add to your many former kindnesses, that of assisting my aunt in doing so, and in getting my books packed and forwarded as soon as possible. I shall not feel at home till I have them about me. Mr Gray, who is now sitting beside me, says he will call upon you when he is in Aberdeen, whither he is going to assist at Mr Primrose's Sacrament. I shall expect to hear from you by him, or sooner if convenient. The truth is, I am almost ashamed to write, after all the sin and obstinacy and absurdity of which I have been guilty. I must endeavour now to redeem the time, and by diligence and devotedness to make what amends I can for past unstedfastness and vacillation. I had sat down to write to you this day week, but was called away to something else; and on the following day, I felt again so dispirited, that I put *off* writing from time to time. — Believe me, my dear Sir, very sincerely yours, — JOHN MILNE.

P.S. — You were right in thinking that preaching would do me good. I have felt better ever since, and now hope that all will go forward prosperously.

A few weeks later, he thus writes to the same esteemed friend and correspondent:

Perth, 14 Rose Terrace, 30th Oct. 1839. — MY DEAR SIR, — I was duly favoured with your letter in immediate answer to my own; and I feel ashamed when I think how long a period I have suffered to elapse without answering it. You are, however, aware what a dilatory correspondent I am, and will find an explanation, if not an excuse, for the delay, in my perverse and inveterate habit of procrastination. I have heard repeatedly from my aunt, and have learned from her the kind regard which you have expressed for me, and the great trouble which you have taken about my affairs; and when I add to this all the kindness I personally experienced before I came away, I feel myself at a loss how to express my thankfulness. I shall only say that the conduct which you have on this occasion pursued towards me makes me think better of our common nature, and also strengthens my faith in the love of God; for, if we receive such constant and ill-requited regard from the creature, may we not expect as much from him who gives to all liberally, and upbraideth not? I trust that what has passed between us will lay the foundation of an intimate and abiding friendship.

I am now settled in Rose Terrace, in the family of a Mr M'Naughton, and think I shall find myself very comfortable. The situation is, I think, the best about Perth, facing the North Inch; and you will be delighted with the prospect from the windows. I received my books in safety, and have to thank you for your kind care in getting them packed and forwarded. I felt rather at a loss till they arrived. I have not, however, been doing much in a ministerial capacity since I came here. It was only last Sabbath that I began preaching in St Leonard's, having hitherto been engaged in officiating for the country brethren. I have, however, visited some of the congregation, and found them ready to receive me with a hearty welcome. I have not yet met with any of those difficulties which so much alarmed me; and I cannot help looking back upon this part as on a troubled dream, the origin of which I find it difficult to explain ... Let me remind you that my ordination takes place on the 7th November, tomorrow week, when I expect to have the pleasure of seeing you, notwithstanding the doubt which you expressed regarding it.

Letters — Ordination Services

Some days after his ordination, he writes again to the same:

The proceedings of Thursday went off very comfortably. The ordination service was conducted by Mr Duncan of Abernethy. His text was 2 Corinthians 4:5, 'Ourselves your servants for Jesus' sake.' The sermon, though long and heavily delivered, was faithful, for he is a good man. In the evening a large party met, and spent a very pleasant evening. There was a great deal of speechifying, and I am happy to say that our Aberdeen friends made a very favourable impression on the people of Perth, by the displays they made of this kind of eloquence. Yesterday Mr Bryce and I preached; and now I trust I have plain sailing before me, save that I must look for the usual difficulties from without, incident to this office and the peculiar hindrances which I know I shall experience from my own indolence and unbelief. It is, however, as you have often told me, a good work; and I trust we shall have no reason to regret what we have done: you, that you have urged me to enter on it; and I, that I have yielded to your entreaties — let me add, your tears. My dear sir, my heart will always warm at the thought of you, and I hope we shall soon have the pleasure of meeting. — *Perth, 11th Nov. 1839.*

The Thorn in the Flesh

The depressions referred to in the above letters seem to have rather increased in intensity as he grew older; as ministerial work pressed upon him; as annoyances troubled him, or sorrow weighed upon his tender and loving spirit. During his first residence in Perth they were of frequent occurrence (sometimes brought on by very trivial causes), but not to such a degree as afterwards. After the death of his first wife and second child he sank much; and then came the thought of India. In India he had occasional depressions; but none very severe till 1856, when alone. In 1857 one seemed coming, but passed off. That in 1859 was very severe; but when it passed off he had not another, not even in the slightest degree, till the last in 1867, which was the severest of all. Mysteriously did that stroke upon his head in boyhood develop its effects in his subsequent life. How it told upon his mental energies and spiritual health, we cannot here determine. How it helped or how it hindered; how it roused or how it paralyzed; what it made him learn or unlearn; how it softened and subdued, and moulded and mellowed, can only be known hereafter. Without these sharps and flats, the full compass of his life's music could not have been brought out. It was that stroke (called accident or calamity by man) which gave to the weapon that edge and point, that temper and polish, without which it would not have done its proper work. If the great adversary sought by that bruise to mar or destroy a chosen instrument, he was certainly disappointed; and if he thought, by thus making the Lord's servant often go heavily, to arrest his work, he was foiled. These clouds, though they sometimes intercepted his joy, did not lead him to question his heavenly sonship, or rob him of the Spirit of adoption. He might at times think himself a broken vessel, cast out as useless; but he could still stand beneath the shadow of the cross, as a sinner who had accepted God's testimony to the finished work of his Son. These recurring burdens kept him low and docile; thus magnifying the grace of God in him, and leading him to give the glory of what was done through him, to him who did it all. And does not that singular experience of the apostle teach us much? — 'Lest I should be exalted above measure through the abundance of the revelations, there was given to me A THORN IN THE FLESH, the messenger of Satan to buffet me' (*2 Cor.* 12:7).

It was soon after his settlement in Perth that he became the friend of Robert M'Cheyne, with whom he wrought so congenially during the interesting years that followed. It was regarding this acquaintanceship that he made one day a statement in the pulpit, which one would not like to forget: 'When I was in Dundee, I went to the house of a man prosperous in the world. The family spoke to me of a strange minister there who had said, "That he would rather depart and be with Christ." "Did you ever hear of such a thing?" said the worldly man.' 'Need I say', added Milne, that from that time my heart was glued to that man?' 'That man' was Robert M'Cheyne.

From the beginning to the end of his ministry, he held fast that which he had received, both in doctrine and practice; preaching the one old gospel, and walking in the simplicity of old ways. The constant study of the word kept him from the deflections of the age; nor did he require novelties, either ecclesiastical or theological, to excite his spiritual system.

Religion in a soul or a church must be sick and ready to die, when it requires the use of stimulants to restore it, — the stimulants of music, and dresses, and postures, and ceremonies; or the stimulants of speculation and mysticism, and the 'enticing words of man's wisdom'. Rather, we may say, that it is *dead;* and these are galvanic appliances to make a dead man look, and stare, and roll his eyes like a living one.

Yet, after all, 'that which is born of the flesh is flesh; and that which is born of the Spirit is spirit.' Milne's ministry was to be a testimony to all this; his life was to be an exhibition of it. He knew that what the world needs is 'regeneration'; nothing short of this. He understood that what God had sent was 'salvation'; nothing less than this. His life and ministry were the embodiment of these mighty truths. He did not trifle with the souls of men, nor with the cross of Christ, nor with the work of the Holy Ghost.

His Way of Preaching

His mind, as we shall see, was one of great vigour and versatility; his style was lucid and pointed. If the test of talent be, as some seem to think, the power of mystifying the simple, he had it not; but if it consist, as surely it does, in the power of simplifying the abstruse, he was no ordinary man.

He was not a theologian in the strict sense of the word. The structure of his mind was not theological, and his spiritual experience had not drawn him into system. But he was not the less clear in his enunciation of the faith once delivered to the saints. The church needs both the theological and the non-theological mind; the one to preserve and define truth in its integrity, the other to prevent that integrity from freezing into the stiffness of unimpressive abstractions. That eminent divine and man of God, Dr John 'Rabbi' Duncan, mentioned to me that he had heard Milne, many years ago, in Moody Stuart's church, and that he did not altogether assent to some of his opening statements, thinking them not quite theologically correct. 'But', said he, 'I heard the whole sermon to the end, and I soon felt that I was listening to a man that loved Christ better than I did myself.' In the course of conversation, Duncan made some remarks on two of our well-known men, which are worth preserving. 'Dr Chalmers', he said, 'had a more theological mind than Dr Cunningham, but Dr Cunningham was the better theologian. The mind of the former was a great manufactory, that of the latter a great warehouse.'

Chapter 3

1840–1842
First Years in Perth

*J*ohn Milne began his ministry in Perth with great earnestness; though his preaching at first was not so marked and full as in after years. He had been sent to do a work for God, and he began it with fear and trembling, as one conscious of insufficiency (2 Cor. 2:16). The work he had come to do soon became apparent.

Blessing and Opposition

On the 10th of February 1840, he thus writes to Edmond:

I have been busy, very busy, almost unceasingly, night and day for the last six weeks; and the result of the labour is, I trust, one of the most hopeful and widest revivals that has as yet taken place in Scotland. The person chiefly instrumental in beginning and carrying on this is Mr Burns, lately of Dundee, who is living with me; and we are very happy, working without intermission. We are in a great degree alone, having only got help occasionally from Mr Cumming of Dunbarney, and Mr Bonar of Collace. You can form no idea what a thirst there is on the part of the people to hear; and we have already much fruit in numerous cases of hopeful conversion. I have every day fresh reason to bless God that I was sent here, and to remember you with gratitude and affection for being helpful in sending me. I find cases where my preaching was blest from the very beginning. We have much opposition, and it is getting more violent as the work goes on.[1] Mr Gray is the only town minister that stands by us, though he takes no active part in the services, *as* he is occupied with the non-intrusion question, of which he is the great champion. I find fresh opportunities of usefulness opening up every day; so you must rejoice with me.

Some time after he thus writes to the same: 'I see you all active on the patronage question. Let me know the general state of feeling. I have been co-operating as far as I was able on the right side. Let me hear from you soon, or, still better, let me see you. I used to envy your being so constantly employed; but I have enough of it now. But *labor ipse voluptas.*[2] Are you growing in grace, and in the knowledge of Christ? That is the only desirable advancement.'

I have given these two extracts together, though their dates are separated by some ten months, in order to show how the church questions of that day were interwoven with the highest spiritual work.

---

[1] I remember that at one time the walls of Milne's church, and other places, were scrawled over in chalk with figures and sentences; some ridiculous, some abusive and vile; in mockery of the men and the work. The two names occurring in these inscriptions were those of William Burns and John Milne. The opposition was great. Some calling themselves evangelicals stood quite aloof. They honoured routine, and condemned what they reckoned disorder and excitement. Some, afraid to unite in the 'moderate' charge of 'fanaticism', fell back upon the cry of 'more evil than good'. Often, in different parts of Scotland, have we heard this as the 'sum of the whole matter' in regard to the evangelists of these years, 'They are doing more harm than good'; an expression which might have come well enough from the lips of a zealous workman, but which from those of a lukewarm one sounded ill. At one time the managers of Milne's church resolved to attempt to exercise their authority in refusing the use of the church to Burns. On the following Sabbath Milne made the following announcement: 'The day that my pulpit is closed against Mr Burns will be the day of my farewell to Perth.' A letter to myself, from Andrew Bonar of Collace, dated Jan. 24, 1840, speaks thus: 'In Perth there is a real work of the Spirit under Mr Burns' preaching. I have been once or twice assisting; the meetings during the week are in St Leonard's Church almost daily. The whole town is stirred; everybody is talking of the movement; worldly men are outrageous in their opposition; newspapers also misrepresenting and vilifying those concerned in it, ministers and people.'

[2] 'The labour is itself a delight', *Ed.*

In one of Milne's notebooks we find the following entry:

Most of the existing body and soul of New England churches originated in revivals; and hence a danger of fancying that little advance is to be expected or laboured for when there is no special work of God going on. Who can tell whether these occasional periodic showers or a continual down-dropping dew would be best? But let us seek directness of aim; expect conversions, even when not aware that the Spirit is at work, in the way of prayerfulness and inquiry. In revival times there is expectation of being heard; earnestness and determination of mind commensurate. At other times there is a general faith of God's willingness to answer; but *now* (in revival times) there is a fervour kindled by a distinct grasp of its object as present and immediately attainable. The hearer now comes expecting that we shall call him to repent immediately and turn to God; conversion is in the mind both of preacher and hearer. Hence we find in America short seasons of energetic fruitful nature, and then long dead vacations. God's love, interest in his church, faithfulness, never change; and he puts special honour upon those who are stedfast, and go on against discouragements and opposing currents. There are instances of revival going on through a whole ministry. Let revival effort be used even when revival does not exist.

What are Revivals?

The above paragraph lets us know the state of Milne's mind, in reference to what are called 'Revivals'. It prepares us for understanding the part which he took in them, both in his own congregation and those of the brethren with whom he was associated. Like many of us, he did not trouble himself about the word 'revival'. He did not feel concerned either to defend it or to take offence at it. It was the *thing* which lay underneath the word that he regarded. That thing which occurred in Jerusalem at Pentecost (*Acts* 2:41); in Samaria some short time afterwards (*Acts* 8:8); again at Antioch

(*Acts* 11:21); again at Iconium (*Acts* 14:1); again at Thessalonica (*Acts* 17:4); again at Corinth (*Acts* 18:8); that *thing*, call it by what name we please, seemed to him to be the very end and object of the ministry. A minister of Christ is not an essayist, nor an orator, nor a lecturer, nor a philosopher, but 'an ambassador for Christ' (*2 Cor.* 5:20); a 'fisher of men' (*Matt.* 4:19). His work is not in the first place that of improving morals, or elevating character, or rectifying social evils, or redressing material wrongs, — but of SAVING. As the Apostle of the Gentiles said, 'Christ sent me not to baptize, but to preach the gospel', so we have still to say, as servants of the same Master, 'Christ sent me not to civilise, but to preach the gospel.' It is that gospel which is 'the power of God unto SALVATION' (*Rom.* 1:16); a gospel not depending for its efficacy on the 'enticing words of man's wisdom', but on the 'demonstration of the Spirit and [on his] power' (*1 Cor.* 2:4); for 'after that, in the wisdom of God, the world by [its] wisdom knew not God, it pleased (εὐδόκησεν, it was 'well-pleasing') God by the foolishness of preaching (του κηρυγματος, *this* preaching, *i.e.* of the cross) to SAVE them that believe' (*1 Cor.* 1:21).

The spiritual movement in which Milne took so deep an interest, began, as the first of the above letters indicates, very soon after his settlement in Perth. In December 1839, Burns came for one night; but found such encouragement that he remained for several months, having meetings, chiefly along with Milne, but also with the assistance of some others.

The first night that the church was lighted with gas, Bonar of Collace came to town to help, and found (in the afternoon when he arrived) Milne and Burns sitting together. As soon as Burns saw the two brethren, ready for the evening work, he started up, looked at his watch, and said that he must be off for Dundee to hold a meeting there that night. It was in vain urged that he was advertised to preach, and that crowds would be gathering. He snatched up his carpetbag, and set off for Dundee. The two brethren, thus abruptly left, conducted the meeting, which was a very crowded one; and it is believed that much good was done on that occasion. One individual afterwards gave this testimony concerning it: 'The first sermon convinced me of sin, and the second brought me to Christ.'

Continuous Fruit

The spiritual work went on during January and February with manifest results for good, both in the town and neighbourhood. The crowds were great, both on Sabbaths and week-days. Many were, during that time, 'turned from darkness to light'. Milne's sermon on the barren fig-tree, in Gray's church, is still remembered for its solemnity and power. During the day crowds of inquirers flocked to Milne's house for conversation with him and Burns. Every seat in the church was let;[1] the aisle, the lobby, the vestry (a small flat-roofed room behind the pulpit) were filled at every meeting. After every seat was let a list of seventy was made up, who were waiting for the first vacancies. Many of these did not get seats till after the Disruption. At Milne's first communion, in April 1840, there were one hundred and forty young communicants. For some years afterwards great life and warmth exhibited themselves in the congregation.[2] The members were set aworking vigorously, in different ways; various agencies sprung up, connected with both old and young — Milne himself at the head of all of them, full of faith and fervour. A weekly prayer-meeting was begun, which has continued to this day. The Perth Young Men's Tract Society was commenced. At first three of its members were sent out by Milne with their first distribution of tracts; now there are forty. St Leonard's became noted in the neighbourhood. It became a centre of blessing. To it

[1] This refers to the old practice in Scotland of paying a yearly rent for a pew in the church, *Ed.*

[2] 'Our best days in St Leonard's', writes Milne, nearly twenty years afterwards, 'were when William Burns, and afterwards A. Bonar and Mr Cumming, used to take part, and work side by side.'

was traced much good or evil, by those who either liked or disliked the proceedings there. 'You'll be from St Leonard's', was the answer given by more than one, to an individual who was dealing faithfully with his fellow-travellers. One family was signally blest. Several daughters were converted, along with the mother, who, though she had been long a professing Christian, used to say that never till then had she 'lost her grip of the world'. One son continued unchanged. He soon after left Perth for another place, and Milne gave him a note of introduction to a minister there. The young man saw through the paper his own name, and read these words: 'Others of the family have got the blessing, but he is left.' The words smote him to the heart, and he returned to Perth, seeking the Lord, and has long been a child of God. The father was much opposed to the work and to Milne; but before his death he too was changed; and hearing of Milne, after his return from India, being in the place in which he lived, he sent for him and welcomed him with joy.

Letter from M'Cheyne

An additional communion was kept on the first Sabbath of January 1842;[1] and, some time after, it was resolved to have the communion four times a year. The Presbytery, however, interfered, and the session, for the time, gave way for the sake of peace. Milne seems to have felt this interference of the Presbytery. It depressed him as well as wounded him. Robert M'Cheyne thus wrote to him on the occasion:

> MY DEAR BROTHER, — Your distress has afflicted me. If one mem-
> ber suffer, all the other members suffer. I fear that, like my own case,
> unbelief and sin mingle with your bodily unhingement, and retard
> your recovery. Tell me how you are; you know I feel along with you.

[1] At the same time there was the communion in St Peter's, Dundee, regarding which M'Cheyne writes to him: 'We had a sweet communion season. I never enjoyed one more. It is a milestone nearer heaven. Perhaps I may never see another. It was like the gate of heaven.'

I am weak like you, sinful like you, and now suffering like you. We
have both our Elder Brother, who knows our sin and sorrow, and can
save from both. Oh that he may come speedily! I feel for you also in
regard to your communion. I differ *toto coelo*[1] from the speeches of
your brethren in Presbytery. Had I been in your place, I would have
carried the case to the Synod and Assembly. It may yet be remedied.
I intend to assail Mr Grierson and Andrew Gray the first time I meet
them. I think you should move for four communions in the town. At
the same time, I think you have let go a valuable privilege of an individual session to appoint a communion at any time, taking the peculiar
circumstances of the particular congregation into view. For example,
when I came from abroad we had a special communion season, and it
was greatly blessed. This power should not be taken from sessions …
I have not preached yet, and am only to preach once a Sabbath. Oh
that I could improve affliction! This I have learned more than ever,
that I am a worm. Bear me on your afflicted heart before the throne,
and accept the sympathy and prayers of a suffering brother in Jesus.
— Robt. M. M'Cheyne.

About this time missionary boxes were placed at the doors of
Milne's church, that the zeal and liberality of the people might
have a weekly channel through which to pour themselves abroad.
There are few such missionary boxes at our church doors now. It
is well that our local funds should prosper, and no less so that our
offerings for the poor should be constant. But it is desirable that
the missionary box, with its missionary inscription, should meet the
eye of our people every time they enter the house of God, lest they
forget the words, 'Freely ye have received, freely give.'

We shall see how close, in after years, was Milne's connection
with missions, and how deep his interest in them. In these missionary boxes we see how his mind was already occupied with foreign
work, and his eye turning to the foreign field. To trace a connection

[1] 'Diametrically', *Ed.*

between these boxes and Milne's important step in 1853 might be going too far; but it is not the less interesting to note the fact of his thus early calling the attention of his people to missions, asking their liberality in behalf of the missionary cause; especially in connection with the great work of God then going on at home.

14 Rose Terrace, John Milne's first residence in Perth, which he shared with the family of Mr M'Naughton. 'The situation is, I think, the best about Perth, facing the North Inch; and you will be delighted with the prospect from the windows' (p. 13).

Chapter 4

1840–1842
Letters And Reminiscences

*W*illiam Burns, after his successful labours in Perth, left that city to preach elsewhere. But, wherever he went, he kept up a correspondence with the places where he had been, either by private letter, or printed epistle. From Kilsyth, Aug. 11, 1840, he wrote to the 'disciples' in Perth a long and fervent communication, which was printed and widely circulated. Instead of counting this an 'interference', Milne greatly rejoiced in it, and helped the circulation with all alacrity. In sending a copy to Bonar of Collace, on the 30th of September (1840), he thus writes on the outside of the printed document, 'What, think you, is this official-looking document? It is on the *King's* business.' And on the inside blank page he adds:

MY DEAR BROTHER, — I have just laid my hand upon the preceding, which I somehow overlooked on Monday. I advised its publication, because I thought it would do good. I was a little annoyed to find a blind man on the bridge the other day selling a republication at a penny. But it will give him a morsel of bread, and may give the better food to others. I met — the other day, and had a tilting match upon the subject. He said the old gentleman had written from Kilsyth that William was an evangelist. 'Now', said —, 'when I look into Ephesians, I find evangelist placed higher than pastor. But not content with this superiority, he is now sending his apostolic letters.' However, our friend, I believe, will do good, whether it please or displease. He writes, asking me to make inquiry if the magistrates would allow him to preach tomorrow (the Fair day) on the Inch. I feel with you that if souls may be saved, I shall not be the man to hinder it. Nobody but himself could or would do it. I shall see the provost today and inquire. When Satan is busiest, Christ is most needed. A. C. has just left me. She says, the first thing that disturbed her was the earthquake; she could not sleep for three nights. Then she heard you in the East Church, when you asked whether our earthquake had brought any to Christ. Every word came home to her. I love to trace your footsteps, brother; and rejoice that the Lord makes love a duty. It is a pleasant yoke. I find the Lord gives me a word from time to time. He is the interpreter, one of a thousand. Oh for a closer, humbler walk!

In a note from Milne to Somerville, Burns is thus referred to: 'I found our friend William Burns waiting for me. He is to continue for a few days with me. He has been preaching tonight in the open air, — rather cold work, you will say, but he prefers it; and I rejoice that he should do good in any way he likes best.'

Not Perth only, but many parts of Scotland shared the blessing. There was an earnestness in various quarters which was at times most touching; one village, and another, and another sending Macedonian messages to men of God in other places, 'Come over and help us.'

Letter from W. C. Burns

In a letter from Burns to myself, dated, 'Lawers Manse, Breadalbane, Sept. 20, 1840', there is the following statement:

We have been wondrously visited in the upper parts of Perthshire during the past six weeks. During that time I have been at Lawers and Ardeonaig, in Breadalbane; at Glenlyon and Fortingall; at Aberfeldy, Grandtully, and Logierait, in Strathtay; in Dowally, Moulin, and Tenandry in Athol; and at Kirkmichael and Percy; and in almost all these places there have been decided tokens of the presence and power of the Holy Ghost. Indeed, these weeks have been as remarkable as any that I ever spent since I began to preach the gospel. In some places, the people seem as if they were flying 'like a cloud, and as doves to their windows'. The glory be the Lord's, and the Lord's alone! You will be surprised to hear that I have been in the pulpits of *three* Moderate ministers in this quarter, and that they all, but especially two of them, seemed very friendly, and seriously disposed. Tomorrow I am to be, *D.V.*, at Fortingall; and the following Sabbath in Aberdeen. — I am, dear brother, yours in Immanuel, — W. C. B.

On the 13th of June of the same year, he wrote to me from Kettle, thus: 'There are good signs in some places here, especially at Strathmiglo a few days ago. I think there were unequivocal marks of the Lord's power. The converts at Perth seem numerous and lively, and the public mind seems preparing for another great movement. I was there on Thursday, along with your dear brother from Collace.'

From Milnathort he writes, June 6, 1841. 'There are many openings here. We had, I think I may safely say, a great day here yesterday in the fields. The Lord was with us of a truth.'

From Grandtully, June 15, 1841, he writes: 'We had an amazing assembly here on Sabbath at the tent, and a solemn day. Hardly an individual among five thousand moved for five hours. Much seems to have been done here.'

M'Cheyne's Letters

The following letter from M'Cheyne alludes to the wide-spread quickening over Scotland:

Dundee, 25th Dec. 1839. — My dear Horace, — Come over and help us. A number of the best of my flock have petitioned the session to grant us another communion season, hoping that the Good Shepherd may visit us again, and cause us to rest at noon. The spring of this movement was in the meetings for prayer; so that we may fairly hope that it is heaven-sent, and that it may issue in a full stream of living waters. The presence of the Comforter seems still to be felt in our assemblies, though the sound of his going is not heard as in days past. Still, let him take his own way of gathering in souls, and we will rejoice. The sunbeams that call out all the beauty and fragrance of the flowers, do it without any noise. Come over and help us. The day fixed by the session is Sabbath, the 19th of January. The next day is to be devoted entirely to solemn and joyful thanksgiving. We propose to have sermons only on the evenings of Thursday, Friday, and Saturday, that we may not give cause of offence to any, as if we minded not the temporal benefit of the people. You will preach on the Sabbath evening. You will also have tables to serve. If there be many strangers, we may have service also in both the schoolrooms; and if the Lord send us a plentiful rain, you have more work to do than I can tell you of. As for myself, I must submit to be a weak, left-handed labourer. I hope for great grace to my own soul, and also to all that help me. Bid your people pray for us. I dare say Andrew and Mr Cumming and R. M'Donald may be induced to come also to help us.

Tell me how God's work is going on in Kelso. Oh, let us pray that what is past may be but the beginning of days to our thirsty land! Let us stretch out our souls for more. Anderston, Kirkfield, and Wellpark are decidedly quickened from on high. I also visited a school in St George's parish, and preached to many weeping children. In Carmylie, it is said, several old people are awakened, and weep bitterly. I have also great hopes of Perth. It is a very dead place; but the people in Mr Gray's church are stilled as if waiting for something. The attendance at his week meeting has doubled. Andrew preached in the Middle Church to an immense assembly last Sabbath night. Tell me all you know. I rejoice to hear of Jedburgh. Tell me particulars that I may tell my people. Would it not be greatly for Immanuel's honour to come and reveal himself in such a way that no man could take any of the praise? Oh to be humble and believing and expecting! The cause of Israel is still advancing in the midst. Pray that the Lord would make it sink deep into the hearts of his children. I am persuaded that much of the blessing from on high is connected with it. Pray for me, body, and soul, and flock.

On the 4th of February 1840, he writes to me:

My dear H., — May we come to you in the fullness of the blessing of the gospel of Christ! You must not speak of rest to me as long as I have any strength remaining. The more I do, I find I am the more able. I shall gladly meet you at the footstool of our Father's throne. Oh to seek him alone! My flesh and heart cry out for thee. The Lord has great work for us here, if I had strength and faith to go through with it. I believe that souls are still being saved. But we must not give him rest till all Scotland glow with the rays of the Sun of Righteousness, and till poor deserted Judah arise from the dust and sing. W. Burns is with me today. The Lord is doing great things in Perth. He is to feed my flock during my absence. *Fare thee well, in soul and body.* Ever yours, — R. M. M'C.

Again he says:

Dundee, 19th March 1840. — My dear H., — Grace, mercy, and peace be to thee and thine. I long to hear from you how the vine flourishes and the pomegranate buds in Kelso. Do you see increasing marks that Immanuel in his grace and beauty is with you, attracting souls by his loveliness and fitness, and transforming his own people into his own lovely image? … Meet with me as we did before your communion, every night for a little, about half-past ten, at our Father's footstool, praying for a blessing from on high. Now I commend you to the God on whom you believe. Ever yours in firmest bonds, — R. M. M'C.

Afterwards, on the 16th February 1841, he writes:

My dear H., — If the Lord will, I shall be with you on Tuesday the 23d; and pray that I may receive something from above to enable me to preach with power. We have unspeakable cause to be ashamed of our coldness and unprofitableness in the Lord's service. On the Sabbath I hope to spend a blessed day in the North Church of Kelso. May the Lord the Spirit direct our hearts into the love of God! May the word run and be glorified! Surely there is something wrong about us, or the Lord would make his mighty arm to light down with greater power among us. Patrick Miller comes with me. He is a true disciple. I shall try to remember you till we meet. Wednesday next, William Burns, P. Miller, and another have agreed to fast and humble ourselves before God, especially from 8 till 9, and 11 till 12 morning.

Again, on the 27th March 1841:

I am better, but have not got my strength back. I am not to preach tomorrow. William Burns is to preach for me. This will be his last Sabbath in Dundee for a time. He goes to Breadalbane, where the Lord's work is still going on. Have any souls been added to the church at your late communion? Oh for drops from heaven! Soon our last sermon shall be ended.

Once more, on 29th December 1841:

This is a dark time; but it makes us keep our heads above the flood. Oh for the presence of Jesus with the soul!

Letters and Work

I have quoted more of these letters than is strictly applicable to the exact events before us. But I was unwilling to let such fragments lie buried, and it was easier to quote them all together. They bear very directly upon the contents both of this chapter and the following.

A letter of December 14, 1841, from a Christian friend, contains the following sentence:

A. went this forenoon to Abernyte. In the evening he goes to Blair-gowrie, and then next morning into the Highlands. A request from the poor people of Glenshee came, and was so urgent that he could not refuse. It *is* nearly twenty miles north of Blairgowrie. He promised to spend two days among them, and will not return till Saturday. I enclose a note from —, from which you will see in what an interesting state these poor people are, and how irresistible was their request.

One part was touching, in which they mention that they had set apart half a day for fasting and prayer for a blessing on his visit. He is also to be on Sabbath at Errol instead of Mr M'Cheyne, who could not be from home at present. Mr Milne is to be out here (Collace) tomorrow, though I don't know that he will stay. I go to Dundee next day, though I should more gladly have gone over, a fortnight later, to the communion. Mr Milne is to have his quarterly communion on the same day. His Presbytery called him to account for having it without consulting his brethren but they did not prevent it.

In October 1841 the first prayer union services took place. *Ten* days were arranged for special prayer; and those who remember that time can bear witness that they were remarkable days. There was a violent storm of wind during the whole time, which tended to lessen the gatherings; but in spite of this, the meetings, all over Scotland at least, were crowded. These seasons of prayer have been continued yearly, ever since, though the time was altered to January. Several ministers issued addresses to their people, which were widely circulated. M'Cheyne thus writes to Milne:

God has really given us a few drops of the spirit of unity, the precious ointment that comes down from the head of our Aaron to the skirts of his garments (*Psalm* 133), uniting all in one sweet fragrance. I hope for some good fruit. Our first meeting was quite filled. We meet in St Peter's tonight. I enclose heads of prayer drawn up by myself. Unless the people be guided some way, they will lose interest. I am thinking of trying a meeting in the church every morning at eight; reading a few verses, and expounding for a quarter of an hour; praying and singing the rest. Kirkpatrick in Dublin is to do the same. In the evening I will get good men to conduct little meetings, and all will be enjoined to spend the time in secret who have places of retirement. Pray for us. There is a lull just now.

After this prayer union, M'Cheyne thus writes to Milne:

May the Lord the Spirit do much for you at this ensuing communion in answer to prayer! I think you had too much preaching during the concert for prayer; still, I trust your words were blessed to save and feed many. I trust you will come to me richly laden from your communion table. Oh for more grace, and light, and love! I trust to see you face to face soon. I will pray for you next Sabbath.

Prayer Union

In reference to this time of prayer, as observed in Perth, the following sentence of a letter to myself may be added:

The concert week was, I think, a time of refreshing. I was obliged for your address. The idea of finding time for so many things, but not for prayer, seemed to go home. I look forward with comfort to the commencing half-year. There are some stirrings among the people, and in the minister.

Respecting this prayer union, M'Cheyne writes thus to myself:

MY DEAR H., — Have you a heart to come to us on the last Sabbath of October? My only reasons for asking you are these: Andrew was with me last communion, and I do not like to take him away another Sabbath. But far more. I expect a time of remarkable blessing. This concert for prayer has taken hold of the people, and I think God is opening the windows of heaven. I did not mean to ask you to come so far, but this latter determined me. Lay it before God, and, if he bids you, then come. We have met in the church every morning at eight, eight or nine hundred people, and on Sabbath about a thousand. We are waiting for an answer, and I believe it will come. Some drops have fallen. One soul, weary and heavy laden for four years, was brought, I trust, to saving rest in Jesus on the first evening during the hour of prayer, and in secret. Ever yours till he come, — ROBT. MURRAY M'CHEYNE.

I may be allowed to quote a letter from my friend Somerville, of date Oct. 7, 1841, on the same subject:

What a blessed thing this union is! Never has there been such a one. We may rest assured that good results will flow from it. Our church has been open every evening since the concert began, and is to be so while it continues. I am enjoying the morning hour especially, spending it in devotional exercises of various kinds with my family, and feel the Lord drawing our souls after the glory of Christ Jesus, the precious Saviour whose name shall endure for ever.

In February 1842 Milne was with us in Kelso at our communion, remarkably full of energy, and dealing out largely to the people the gospel of God's free love. He came to us on Tuesday the 22d, and remained till Wednesday, March 2, preaching every night, and on some occasions during the day. His Sabbath services were peculiarly striking. He spoke on the Monday some most memorable words. Referring to ministers beseeching men in Christ's stead to be reconciled, he said:

> Must I go up to heaven and ask the glorious Trinity, 'Art thou willing to be the covenant-God of the people of this church?' Do I need to ascend with this question, and stand before the throne to get it answered? Ah, I need not do that. God has answered it already. I am commissioned to tell you he is willing. Are there no hands stretched out to take hold of the covenant? Oh, what has not the Holy Spirit been doing to win you? This time and that time visiting you; whispering that all was not right; making you say to yourselves, I should not like to die thus; I should not like to die in the theatre, or at the card-table, or in the ballroom. And he invites all sinners freely. This is the last night of the feast. There are no *lasts* in heaven; no last look at the Lamb. There are no *lasts* in hell. All is for ever.

On some of the above occasions, Milne's sermons were long; much beyond an hour. Yet the power with which they came made all feel them short. As on a similar occasion at Collace, when he preached for nearly two hours on the three wells; the dry well, the half-filled well, and the overflowing well. It was a time to be remembered. No one moved. Every eye was fixed, and every heart melted. Many such seasons and sermons could be enumerated; so many, that time and space would fail.

Milne's Sermons — Personal Reminiscences

Some reminiscences, chiefly of this period, may here be introduced. They are by Mr Mackie of the *Warrington Guardian*, one who was attracted by Milne's preaching, and heard him gladly:

My remembrance of Mr Milne dates to 1840, after the revivals had begun. Being then but fifteen, and connected with Dr Thomson's church, I had not many opportunities of knowing him personally. My first decided remembrance of him was noticing him cross George Street to talk and shake hands with a journeyman baker connected with St Leonard's, who was then carrying his bread-board on his head. I had never seen it on that fashion, and was much impressed. My second remembrance is hearing him, in a crowd who surrounded a new convert, say, 'I shall be so glad to tell Mr Gray that it was a sermon of his which first impressed you.' My third decided impression of him is hearing him in his own pulpit say that, though having our common infirmity and feelings, when he saw the crowds go to the church in which Mr Burns was preaching, he had endeavoured to rejoice if the Lord's work was done, whoever was the instrument.

My most decided and pleasant reminiscences of Mr Milne are connected with his Bible class in the old vestry, where now stands the City Hall. He succeeded Mr Lewis, on his call to St David's, Dundee, and at once a crowded class was the result. He commenced with the Book of Exodus, and got on but slowly, owing to the many illustrations he gave us with a view to making us *men* as we grew up. I nearly always sat on a stool at his feet, being generally late, and was literally brought up at the feet of Mr Milne.

I well remember his remarks on the career of Moses — forty years at court, forty years at school in the wilderness, and forty years at work as the Leader. The two first forties fitted him for the last. He was *ready* when wanted. Not being so was the common fault. Most men were unfit for the chance which, some time or other, came to make men of them.

Decision. — I well remember him urging on us this. Search into the grounds of your belief; take nothing on hearsay, and, when satisfied, put the question on the shelf, labelled, 'Examined, and found correct.'

Although not a member of St Leonard's, I usually went there on Sundays, and have the most pleasing memories. Mr Milne inaugurated a new style of preaching. There was no reading of a MS., and no perfunctory dividing every subject into three. Often would he seize an idea evidently on the moment, and extract from it beauties of which one never would have dreamt.

His texts were often very original. Well do I remember him preaching on 'Thy Maker is thy husband', *etc.*; and, 'Blessed are ye that sow beside all waters, who send forth thither the feet of the ox and the ass.' In the latter text his knowledge of the original tongues, and eastern customs, was easily to be recognised.

Mr Milne's manner in prayer, and in the preaching, was most remarkable. He held up the right hand in prayer, and kept it somewhat in advance of him in preaching. His every tone was a tone of earnestness. How he used to emphasize the Master's long-suffering, by quoting that 'His locks were wet with the dews of the night!' In prayer, his power of using Scripture was most telling and remarkable. 'O hope of Israel, and Saviour thereof in time of trouble, *why*' *etc*. It is said that Whitefield's way of pronouncing 'Mesopotamia' was as good as some sermons; and in Mr Milne's WHY, in the passage quoted, there was a depth and meaning we never saw when used by others. To some extent was this the same in his, 'Come into my garden', 'Awake, O north wind, and come', *etc.*

The standing at the singing of the last psalm was, I think, introduced by Mr Milne, as was also the quarterly sacraments.

It is difficult to say how far Mr Milne's preaching affected the people of Perth during the revivals, or how far it effected the wondrous changes then observed. His labours and those of Mr Burns were so blended, that at that time they should not be divided in noticing results. To them, certainly, mainly is due the fact that some thirty to fifty prayer-meetings were commenced in private houses, and the Young Men's Tract Society, still existing, as well as one in connection with Dr Thomson and the Middle Church. I remember the meetings in connection with the latter, and the Doctor's lamentation at the coldness of his people in not having gone their first round, and his joy when I was able to tell him I had been round and well received. That fire in me had most certainly been kindled at St Leonard's.

The present generation can scarcely tell the excitement of the revival period in Perth. Revival, or even lively preaching, was little known. But Mr Burns inaugurated a new era. His solemn, slow, and sober appeals told at once. The first man of note who fell under the word as preached by Mr Burns was Mr Campbell, predecessor to Mr Peter Palmer. He publicly cried out in the church for mercy. Crowds began to attend St Leonard's every night in the week. Mr Burns would preach until nine o'clock; then conclude in the usual way, and retire into the vestry. But he retired in vain. The people would sit still, and out the preacher would have to come, re-ascend the pulpit, and go on till ten or even eleven o'clock. The Perth papers bitterly opposed him, and in their columns of those days some facts and much fiction may be found worth looking at — say, 1839-40.

Several ministers from neighbouring parishes came — I had almost said to mock, but remained to pray. During all the time Mr Burns was, as it were, the leading man in the movement. Mr Milne was doing the building up. In his parish, and out of it, he was ever at work. I remember obtaining almost my first donation to the Bridgend Tract Society from him, and his attendance at two prayer-meetings there, one of them more a family than a public one. The then minister of Kinnoul, after many importunities, refused either to attend our prayer-meetings, or have anything to do with our tract society.

For some ten or fifteen years we were separated — Mr Milne most of the time in India, I in England. I had never forgotten him;

often preached from his favourite texts, and been encouraged by my remembrance of his humble mind, his zeal, and devotion. When he required to return home, it afforded me infinite pleasure to write about him to one of the local papers, and I often looked forward to enjoying his society when I became once more a resident of Perth. We met, in 1859,[1] most unexpectedly. It was at a narrow part of the footpath round the Great Orme's Head. We recognised each other, and the meeting led to a written correspondence by which I much profited, and one or two visits to Perth. I can never forget the kind way in which he alluded to my lectures at Perth (and myself) in giving notice of it on the Sunday morning, and also his introduction of me to the audience, he being chairman. On returning home after the lecture, he spoke of it in a way which made my heart bound with joy. I was busy lecturing to the working men of Warrington at the time of our meetings, and had been so for some years, every Sunday evening. To Mr Milne is due most of the preparation, and all the ambition, which moved and sustained me in the work. He took a deep interest in it, and sent me several donations in money.

Early Years of Ministry

Such were the early years of his ministry; years of faith, and prayer, and work. They were earnests of the years to come. The following lines, written by him at a much later time, when toiling in India, may be introduced here, as the expression of his mind from the first to the last:

I am Thy Levite, Lord; Thou art my lot alone.
Give me a will in sweet accord with all that is Thine own.
Great things I will not seek; they only prove a snare:
Enough if Thou my spirit keep, unhurt by sin and care.
Too long I've lived for time; too long have walked by sight
Let me now leave this earthly slime, for things all great and bright.

---

[1] Milne, in a private letter, dated 16th of September 1859, alludes to 'a walk all round the Great Orme.'

Give me that unction pure, which opes the blinded eye,
And let me see, right clear and sure, the things that are on high.
Oh! clothe me with Thy righteousness, and make me clean within,
That I may see Thy blessed face, Thy grace and mercy win.
Lead me within the veil, where stands Thy glorious throne,
And let my Saviour's plea prevail, as if it were mine own.
Here I Thy name will praise, Thine anger's turned away;
And Thou wilt magnify Thy grace, and all Thy love display.
What wilt Thou, Lord, that I for Thee should do or bear?
My heart will joyfully comply to serve Thee everywhere.
To battle forth I go; Jehovah is my strength:
I will not fear though strong the foe; I shall prevail at length.

Chapter 5

1840–1841
Times of Refreshing

*B*ut it is desirable to gather up the records of this revival. In the *Memoirs of Robert Murray M'Cheyne*[1] will be found some references to it. We must not, however, pass it over with a general statement. Both as important in itself, and as connected with Milne's life and ministry, it claims special notice.

Opposition to Revivals in the Aberdeen Presbytery

In the end of 1840, the Presbytery of Aberdeen took up the subject of 'revivals', and appointed a committee to make inquiry. Though this investigation had primary reference to Aberdeen, yet it embraced other places; among others, Perth. The bias of some members of committee and of Presbytery was very strong against revival work, and especially against W. C. Burns, who had been preaching in Aberdeen as well as in Dundee and Perth. Judging from the statements in the public press, he had turned the world upside down, and had come to do a like work for Aberdeen. He is designated 'A young preacher, named Burns'; 'A silly-looking lad with a sort of meaningless simper on his face'; and he is represented as attempting 'to get up in this city a sort of religious excitement,

---

[1] Andrew A. Bonar, *Memoirs and Remains of R. M. M'Cheyne* (Edinburgh: Banner of Truth, 2009), cloth, 664 pp., ISBN: 978 0 85151 084 2.

in imitation of the revivals which he had originated in the south'. One of the Aberdeen meetings is described in detail; and Burns is represented as standing in the precentor's desk, gazing in silence on his excited audience; dropping down on his knees; covering his face with his hands, and looking through his fingers; 'jumping up like a jack-in-a-box', looking on with a self-complacent smile. His words are called 'daring blasphemy', and his conduct 'a scandal on religion, and a disgrace to our city'. The writer goes on thus:

> There is something in his manner which, whatever it may be now, must originally have been pure affectation. His drawling, unearthly voice, his theatrical attitude, his *outré* expression of countenance, seem as if they were all put on for a purpose. Then a person who, like him, acknowledges that he spent a very wicked early life, cannot be so ignorant of the world as not to know that the effects he produces on the silly females who flock after him can all be fully accounted for on natural principles, without any necessity for a supernatural interference of the Holy Spirit. The lower animals (and ignorant women, when they allow themselves to be led away entirely by their feelings in matters of religion, are little above the lower animals in intellect) can be made to imitate any inarticulate sound. Go into a dog kennel and raise a peculiar whine, and the chance is that you are soon joined by the whole pack, especially if there are many puppies present. Burns must know these things, and be well acquainted with the character and temperament of the women who chiefly follow him; yet he persists in attributing the wails and cries of excited and hysteric females to the direct operation of the Deity ... Had our Saviour been alive, might he not have emphatically said to Burns and his followers, '*Be not as the hypocrites?*'

These are specimens of the mind of the public press, being some of its comments on 'one of the most deplorable exhibitions of misguided enthusiasm and moral insanity which could possibly be imagined'. They are quoted here to show the fierceness of the opposition then encountered by those who did the revival work of these days. They remind us of the scoffer's taunt in reference to the Pentecostal scene, 'These men are full of new wine.' But they are also quoted to give Burns an opportunity of speaking for himself. He wrote thus to me respecting these public charges, and others contained in private letters to myself:

Newcastle, 27th Sept. 1841. — Mr — states as an admitted fact, in his letter, what is wholly without foundation, that it is my practice frequently to stop during my sermon, lay my head on my hands, and leaning on the front of the desk, or kneeling in the pulpit, to engage in secret prayer. The only case in which I ever paused to pray secretly in public was when, in solemn circumstances, I have appointed that all the audience should spend a few minutes in secret prayer. This you may remember was done in the famous meeting of Commission in 1596, when Mr Davidson preached to 400 ministers and elders, and allowed them a quarter of an hour for such searching of heart, and when the silence was only broken by the sighs and groans of men who felt the blood of souls lying on them. Neither have I made it a practice to kneel in the pulpit. I have hardly ever done so, and never, in the middle of the sermon, when the people were waiting for the continuance of the services; this whole imagination has arisen from a statement made by the editor of the *Herald*, who neither knew the circumstances nor what I was really doing. My reason for pausing on the occasion was, that the audience were in so tender a frame that they needed but little said to them, and that I was afraid of exciting them, as it would have been easy to do by a continued and forcible address; and as to dropping down upon my knees, the whole matter was this, that I leant upon the desk, and as it was rather low, I, of course, relaxed my limbs, and might seem to be kneeling to one who did not notice the real depth of the desk. I should like you to notice, on my authority, the charge of kneeling, *etc.*, as there is an air of affectation, singularity, and enthusiasm about the whole statement, which may do injury where I am not known.

The rest of the letter I think I may give, though it refers to Newcastle.

> Join with us in giving praise to God for visiting us with tokens of his presence and power. Last Thursday we had a very large and solemn meeting in the open air, and last night I had an immense audience, who stood solemnly engaged and impressed, under a harvest moon, from five o'clock to half-past eight, and would have remained much longer. I was enabled at last to speak out, I believe, in the power of God, about the sins which are murdering thousands here. Oh, entreat the chosen of God among you to plead for us now in the crisis of the war.

But it is not with the presbyterial report at large that we have here to do; but merely with the record which is preserved in it regarding the work at Perth. It is an official and authentic document, worthy of being studied now, though nearly thirty years have gone by since the events occurred.

Record of Revival at Perth — Andrew Gray

It may be well to set in the foreground the statements of Andrew Gray, one of the ministers of Perth, whose calmness, cautiousness, and honesty will be, to those who remember him, a security for the strict and unexaggerated accuracy of his testimony.[1]

---

[1] We subjoin the queries of the Committee, to which the statements of the different ministers were answers.

1. Have revivals taken place in your parish or district, and if so, to what extent?

2. By what instrumentality and means have the revivals been effected?

3. What special circumstances, in the preaching or ministrations of the instruments, appear to have produced the results in each particular case which may have come under your notice?

4. Did the person or persons, whom you describe as the instruments in producing the effects above adverted to, address children? — at what hours? — in what special terms? — and what might be the age of the youngest of them?

5. Do you know what was the previous character and habits of the persons converted or awakened?

1. A considerable awakening took place about a year ago in this city, and the benefit was partially experienced in my own congregation.

2. The chief instrument in the work was Mr W. Burns, and the means consisted of the preaching of the word, and of devotional exercises. The labours of Mr Milne of St Leonard's, and Mr Bonar of Collace, were also much blessed.

3. The special circumstances referred to were the solemnity and affectionate earnestness of the appeals, the eminently close, searching, and powerful character of the addresses to the conscience, the simplicity and singular clearness with which the distinctive and fundamental doctrines of the gospel were exhibited, and the unwearying perseverance and Christian ardour with which the means of grace were kept in operation.

---

6. Have any who were notorious for drunkenness or other immoralities, neglect of family duties or public ordinances, abandoned these evil practices, and become remarkable for their diligence in the use of the means of grace?

7. Could you condescend on the number of such cases?

8. Has the conduct of any of the parties been hitherto consistent, and how long has it lasted?

9. Have the means to which the revivals are ascribed been attended with beneficial effects on the religious condition of the people at large?

10. Were there public manifestations of physical excitement, as in audible sobs, groans, cries, screams, *etc.*?

11. Did any of the parties throw themselves into unusual postures?

12. Were there any parties who fainted, fell into convulsions, or were ill in other respects?

13. How late have you ever known revival meetings to last?

14. Do you approve or disapprove of such meetings upon the whole? — In either case, have the goodness to state why.

15. Was any death occasioned, or said to be occasioned, by overexcitement, in any such case? — and if so, state the circumstances in so far as you know them.

16. State any other circumstances connected with revivals in your parish or district, which, though not involved in the foregoing queries, may tend to throw light upon the subject.

4. I never knew of any particular dealings with children. There was a strong impression produced upon many of tender age connected with my own schools, and I am happy to say that the good effect of it is still apparent; but I do not believe that any special or peculiar means were taken for causing a religious excitement among the very young.

5. There are persons known to me who, I hope, experienced a saving change, and who were previously given to Sabbath-breaking and neglect of Christian ordinances, and were devoid of any serious concern about the well-being of their souls in the future world.

6. I have no doubt of this.

7. It is quite impossible for me to do so.

8. The conduct of many has been consistent from the time of the awakening, about a year ago, to the present date.

9. Decidedly. There has been a marked general improvement. I have been much struck with this among my own flock.

10. There were, on several occasions, in St Leonard's Church.

11., 12. I understand that this also was the case.

13. There were one or two meetings, I believe, which were prolonged till two o'clock in the morning.

14. On the whole, I disapprove of them strongly; not, however, *so* strongly as I do of our Perth fashionable assemblies, where dancing is frequently kept up till three, four, and five o'clock in the morning. While I say that I disapprove very strongly of religious meetings protracted far into the night, I would not be understood to speak without exception, for then I should condemn Paul's meeting at Troas (*Acts* 20:7-11), which continued much longer than any meeting of the sort in modern times that I have ever heard of.

15. Two deaths occurred, which I have heard attributed to the excitement connected with the awakenings. One of the individuals was thought to have caught cold at the meetings, fever ensued, and she

died. I am not aware of the particulars of the other case; nor do I know how far there is good reason to believe that the parties in question would have been now in life if we had had no revivals. I may add, although the point is not mentioned in the queries, that there have been a few cases of mental derangement apparently connected with the awakenings.

I may here observe that queries 10, 11, 12, 15, seem to me to mean substantially this: Docs the excitement which vivid discourses of the truths, both alarming and consolatory, embraced in religion, necessarily produce, exhibit similar physical phenomena to what are exhibited by excitement arising from any other cause? And I answer that it does.

16. The only other circumstance which it occurs to me to state, is that, in the month of February, last year, sixteen young persons applied to me for admission to the Lord's Table. I saw them twelve or fifteen times; had private conversation with them; and had, therefore, the fullest opportunity of knowing their state of mind. I found that no fewer than ten of their number were under deep and solemn impressions of a religious nature, which had been derived from the ministrations of Mr Burns; and eight of these, at least, I could not but judge, were truly converted from sin to holiness, 'from the power of Satan unto God'. Never had I so interesting and delightful a class of catechumens as on that occasion. It may be supposed that I have anxiously watched their subsequent deportment. I have done so; and I rejoice to state, that all I have observed is confirmatory of the reality of that change which seemed to have taken place.

ANDREW GRAY,
Minister of the West Church of Perth.
PERTH, *29th January* 1841.

Milne's Account of Revival at Perth

We give next Milne's own statement. It does not enter into particulars; but, brief as it is, it is very satisfactory.

1. There has been a revival to a considerable extent in my congregation, and in the town generally.

2. Chiefly through the instrumentality of Mr W. Burns. I believe there are also several persons who consider themselves indebted to my own preaching, and that of Mr Bonar of Collace, and Mr Cumming of Dumbarney, who took part occasionally in preaching and conversing with the people.

3. I had abundant opportunity of becoming intimately acquainted with Mr Burns, as he lived and laboured with me constantly for between three and four months. I never knew any one who so fully and unfalteringly obeyed the apostolic precept: 'Meditate upon these things; give thyself *wholly* to them.' I was struck with his close walk with God, his much and earnest prayer, his habitual seriousness, the solemnizing effect which his presence seemed to have wherever he went, and his success in leading those with whom he conversed to anxious, practical, heart-searching concern about their state in God's sight. In public, his ministrations were chiefly of an awakening nature, addressed to the unconverted. With this view, his subjects were always wisely selected, being such as included fundamental points: man's lost state as a sinner; its marks and consequences; man's helplessness as a sinner; the vanity of all his endeavours to justify or sanctify himself, and the certain and everlasting ruin of all who should persevere in such attempts; Christ Jesus, his righteousness, its *alone* sufficiency, its *perfect* freeness, its *immediate* gift to all who believe; the blessed effects of such faith; the Holy Spirit, his work in convincing and converting, and the danger of resisting him. These subjects were treated more subjectively than objectively, which Mr Burns was the better enabled to do, from having much intercourse with people under concern, who had fully opened up their minds to him. The effect of his preaching was also aided by the unusual earnestness and solemnity of his delivery, as well as by

the densely-crowded state of the church, and the spirit of prayer and expectation in which very many came to the meetings. In compliance with the language of the query, I have spoken of the chief human instrument; but I am persuaded, both from what I saw and felt at the time, and from what I have since known of the permanent and blessed results, that a greater than man was among us: 'Not by power, nor by might, but by my Spirit.' I never witnessed before, nor have I since, such manifest tokens of God's gracious presence as were vouchsafed us during several of the first months of last year. I can only say, in the words of Jonathan Edwards, 'The goings of God were then seen in his sanctuary, God's day was a delight, and his tabernacles were amiable. Our public assemblies were then beautiful; the congregation was alive in God's service, every one earnestly intent on the public worship, every hearer eager to drink in the words of the minister as they came from his mouth.' What he also mentions of the much weeping and deep concern manifested under the preaching of the word, is also true in regard to the meetings here, but is noticed in a subsequent query.

4. There was no address specially to children, though a considerable number attended the meetings, and seemed deeply affected. Some of them, on being questioned, were found to possess correct views of their state as sinners. They had prayer-meetings among themselves in several parts of the town; and though these, as was perhaps desirable, were soon relinquished, yet I would hope that some on these occasions received impressions, which God will acknowledge as his own work.

5. I had only been settled here a few weeks when the revival began, and, consequently, had little previous knowledge of the people. I have since, however, had intercourse with many; some were godly persons before, but on these occasions they seemed to have been literally revived and stirred up. They received enlarged and more realizing and influential views of their privileges and duties as Christians. The generality, how-ever, were persons who had either been greatly careless of religion, or had been resting self-satisfied in a form of godliness, though destitute of its power. The language frequently used was, 'We always thought we were well enough, we had no idea we were such sinners.

6. Yes, though I cannot condescend upon particulars.

7. Impossible, as the persons awakened belonged more or less to all the different congregations.

8. Many are to this day *growingly* adorning the gospel of God their Saviour in all things, and gradually forming a peculiar people, zealous of good works. I am acquainted with families where all, or almost all, the members seem to have been savingly converted.

9. Decidedly; during the time the awakening continued the state of the town was greatly changed. The watchmen at night often remarked that they had little now comparatively to do, the streets were so quiet. At some of the manufactories and large workshops the improvement was very marked. Of course this does not now continue to the same extent; but still there is a sensible improvement within the last twelve months on the general state of the town, as various circumstances show.

10. There were.

11. Some did.

12. There were various instances of this.

13. Once or twice till one or two o'clock; they were generally, however, concluded about ten o'clock, or a little later. It was often exceedingly difficult to prevail on the people to go away.

14. I disapprove, because they interfere with family arrangements, and with family and private devotions; they may occasion disquiet in families where some of the members attend them, while others dislike them; they are apt to produce a kind of spiritual dissipation, that causes disrelish for ordinary ministrations, and they may lead to a violent revulsion into the opposite extreme. Still there are circumstances in which I should feel no hesitation in prolonging such meetings till morning, as we know the Apostle Paul did on one occasion. It is only when there is much of the divine presence and blessing attending our ministrations, that the people will come out to week-evening exercises, far less continue to a late hour.

15. There was one young lady, whose death was attributed to cold caught in attending these meetings at the beginning of the season. Another young lady died during the summer, whose death was thought to have been hastened by the same cause. She was one of the earliest converts; but one of the most decided and most hopeful, and died in great peace. There were also some cases of mental derangement, and others who, for a time, bordered on this state; but they are all long ago restored, and are walking consistently as believers.

16. I would remark the unusual and long-continued thirsting for the word which the people manifested. Night after night, for many weeks, the church was one dense mass of human beings, all the passages being crowded with persons, who remained standing for hours together, and seemingly inaccessible to weariness and fatigue. I would remark, also, the deep, solemn, almost awful attention which they maintained during the whole of the services. I would observe, also, that the awakening extended to many miles round. Persons frequently came in considerable numbers from great distances to attend the meetings, and returned home through the night. I may also remark, that one of the things which was most to be regretted, during the awakening, was the want of a sufficient number of judicious experienced Christians to take charge of prayer-meetings, which were, therefore, necessarily entrusted to young men. And now, though it was to me a time of much labour and anxiety, I look back with thankfulness that I was privileged to see such a season; and it is my desire and prayer that I may yet see similar days of the right hand of the Most High.

But we have other documents, laid before another Church Court. In the same year the Synod of Merse and Teviotdale took up the subject, and, in answer to queries, received statements which it may be well to preserve, as they have not, like the Aberdeen report, been published. From this unpublished record I make the two following extracts. First, I give Milne's evidence:

Perth, 25th October 1841. — I was favoured with your letter of queries regarding the work of God in this quarter. I regret much that I did not make an effort to answer it immediately. My reason for not doing so was my hope that I should find time to do it at some length. The engagements, however, connected with the concert for prayer, followed by those of our communion season, which occurred yesterday, rendered, or seemed to render, this impossible. I this morning write rather for the purpose of acknowledging your letter, than with the hope of being able to communicate any information that will conduce to accomplish the end of your inquiry. You are probably aware that I formerly furnished a short account of God's work here to the Presbytery of Aberdeen. That account, however, was written hurriedly, without the idea that it would be published, and the questions were not perhaps fitted to elicit a full and fair view of the subject. I subjoin a note or two, passingly, in answer to your queries.

Previous state of the people, — I can say little on this subject, having been only settled here about two months when the revival began.

First symptoms of change, and circumstances preparing the way. — Perhaps the settlement of a new minister may have been of some use, at least in my own congregation. Indeed, I know of cases where it was so. There was also a longing, anxious expectation among the praying people — a kind of ἀποκαραδοξια.[1] Their hearts had been stirred by what had occurred at Kilsyth, and still more by what was doing at Dundee, almost at their own door. They felt a kind of godly and humbling jealousy that the Lord should visit other places, and yet pass by them. As is said of Israel in the days of John, not a few were in expectation, and mused in their hearts. I mention this because I believe it to be an important element in preparing the way for him who usually stands at the door, and will not force his way, but waits till he is invited or constrained to come in. On the last Sabbath of the year, Mr W. Burns preached for me in the afternoon. He asked those who wished to converse concerning the state of their souls, to come into the vestry after the service. I had been preaching in another church that afternoon, and when I reached the vestry, found four or five persons there. It was late, and I proposed that they should go home

---

[1] ἀποκαραδοξια: to wait in anxious expectation, *Ed.*

for a little, and return at seven o'clock, when we would meet with them. They went accordingly; and when we returned at seven, instead of the few we expected, we found a considerable number of persons assembled in the lower part of the church. Mr Burns prayed, and sung psalms and paraphrases, making remarks before singing, especially on the 51st Psalm and 44th Paraphrase. There was deep solemnity, which gradually almost awfully increased; many began to shed tears, and to throw themselves on their knees at prayer, in the seats and passages. Mr B. was speaking plainly, simply, without the slightest effort; and yet perhaps at no time during the whole season of revival was there more of the effectual presence and power of the Lord than on that night. Most of those, I have reason to believe, who were present, were either quickened or lastingly impressed. Hour after hour passed, and still they would not or could not go away. It was near midnight ere they all retired. Next day there was a full meeting at twelve o'clock, and another, very much crowded, in the evening at seven, which lasted for several hours. Next day it was the same, and the next, and the next; and thus for nearly three months these daily double meetings continued without interruption, the evening ones always densely, oppressively crowded, and continuing usually for three or more hours — the passages within and without being completely filled with people standing all the time. During this season there were all the marks of a work of God which we see in the account given of the preaching of the gospel by the apostles. The multitude was divided, families were divided; the people of God were knit together, they were filled with zeal and joy and heavenly mindedness; they continued stedfast, and increased in doctrine and fellowship, being daily in church and in prayer-meetings; and numbers were constantly turning to the Lord.

Nature and amount of change. — God's people quickened; backsliders restored; doubting and uncertain brought to decision and assurance; hidden ones, who for years had walked solitarily, brought to light, and united to a family of brothers and sisters; and a large number of the worldly, thoughtless, ignorant, self-righteous turned to the Lord. We have a peculiar people growing up among us, who are separate from the world; know and love one another; watch over, exhort, and aid one another; they seem to grow in humility and zeal, and entertain frequent and endearing intercourse, both by letter and mutual visits, with the good people of Dundee, Aberdeen, and other places.

Facts illustrating. — Had I time, I could, with Mr Burns' help, who kept a record of cases from the beginning, furnish many interesting facts relating to the first impressions and subsequent progress of different individuals. I mention only one, that of more than two hundred young persons whom I have admitted to communion, and of very many of whom I have reason to hope there was a real heart-work, almost all dated the origin, or deepening and perfecting, of their convictions from this season.

Means employed. — The means chiefly honoured in this work was the preaching and conversation of Mr Burns. I regard his appearance as a kind of era in our Church affairs. I know how dear he is to the heart of *multitudes* here, and in the country many miles around. On the Tuesday after the work began, Mr Cumming joined us, and on the Friday, Mr A. Bonar; and their preaching and conversation were also much blessed, and their names are very dear to the hearts of our people. There were numerous *open* and private prayer-meetings. The zealous exhortations, example, and prayers of those who had themselves been awakened, were a most important means of alarming and bringing in others.

Kind of preaching. — Solemn, earnest, affectionate, beseeching; never losing sight, or rather never thinking of anything but the conviction and conversion of sinners, and thinking nothing done if this was not accomplished. The ministers preached after much prayer, and with the almost assured expectation of getting the blessing. The people came believing that they would meet with God. The subject was Christ Jesus in his fullness, freeness, offers; and privilege and duty of immediate acceptance, and danger and present guilt of delay or refusal. Christ's grace and kindness to even the vilest sinners seemed to break the hearts of many. Such passages as the woman that was a sinner;

beginning at Jerusalem; Ethiopian eunuch; washed their robes and made them white in the blood of the Lamb; he was made sin for us, and he righteousness; barren fig-tree; washing disciples' feet. I should say that the holding forth the priestly office and work of Christ was specially blessed. But the goings of Jehovah were then in his sanctuary. None could help feeling this is Bethel. The most careless were awed. There was something unspeakably solemn, sweet, and exhilarating in the services. After exercises of several hours' continuance there was no feeling of weariness or satiety. People who were worldly then, and who are worldly now, were drawn and kept, as by a charm, night after night, in the house of God, instead of straggling about the streets, or haunting places of amusement and dissipation. I felt as if the presence of God were resting on the whole town; and the country round was shaken for many miles.

My time is gone. I do not know if I should send these hurried lines. If you wished, I would try to draw up an account befitting, as much as I could, the momentousness of the subject. The season of which I have been speaking is pleasant to my memory, and its fruits *remain*. I like the queries you propose; they comprehend the subject. I have often heard of you from my dear friend and brother, A. Bonar. Accept my prayers and best wishes. May grace, mercy, and peace be multiplied to you and your Synod.

Andrew Bonar's Report

I give next the evidence of Andrew Bonar, then of Collace, who enters a little more into detail.

Collace, October 20, 1841. — In the autumn of 1838, I came to be assistant minister of Collace, a parish of less than eight hundred souls. There was not much of open or gross vice among the people, but there had been a silent and perpetual flow of worldliness, secret vice, and lax morality, in which each countenanced his neighbour. Many who belonged to the Parish Church had good acquaintance with Scripture doctrine, but their religion was decency and formality. The season of

Handsel Monday was a day of unchecked and open sin, and many really believed that drunkenness, riot, and folly at that time were no way sinful. There were scarcely any, even among those looked upon as superior to others in piety, who reckoned dances, songs, merry-makings, and occasional drinkings, as at all inconsistent with real religion. There were some among them who kept up the orthodoxy of the truth, but had almost totally lost its vitality; most of them resting contented with knowledge and intelligence, even denying that it was the duty of a believer to be sure of his conversion, and attain to a full assurance of his interest in Christ.

During the first eight months of my settlement among them, the people began to manifest a great relish for ordinances, and a great anxiety to be visited and catechised. The attendance at church became very regular and full, and Sabbath profanation very rare. A Sabbath school held in the church for younger children, and a morning class for those above fifteen, were both attended by almost all in the parish of the specified ages. I began a weekly prayer-meeting, which I conducted without any formality or system, expounding Scripture, and familiarly laying before them topics connected with revivals and spread of religion, or similar subjects. To this the people flocked in crowds, even during the severest nights of winter. Still I saw nothing of a real work of the Spirit. During the eight months I knew of no soul converted, though I afterwards had reason to believe that there were two or three who, during that time, did get the first drops of grace. But the general state of feeling might be accurately expressed by the saying of an elderly woman, who stated her mind thus to a neighbour: 'If Mr B. goes away now, he will leave us worse than he found us; for we are halting between two opinions.'

It was at the end of these eight months that I received the call to be one of the deputation to Palestine and the Jews. Circumstances prevented me having it in my power to supply my place during my absence in the manner I desired, and on my return the parish seemed to be in the very state in which I left it. They had read the letters sent to them from abroad with much interest, and cordially welcomed our return. I immediately resumed the weekly prayer-meeting, with more hope of blessing than ever, as the Spirit had that year been poured out on other places. We hoped too, that, because of our love to Israel, God would remember us. I preached, as formerly, the plain doctrines of grace — the sinner *utterly lost,* requiring to be *wholly saved* by the Redeemer; the Holy Spirit's work in opening the soul of the sinner to receive these truths; and the sure and present forgiveness that *is* conveyed to him that believeth. I had occasion also to dwell much upon the necessity of a man being so thoroughly changed that he could not fail to know that old things were passed away; because, while the doctrine of conversion was admitted in the parish, it was at the same time a prevailing and obstinate error that a man might be a regenerated creature, though he was not himself aware of having undergone any change. This form of error was silencing the anxieties and fears of a vast number. I began now to hear of one or two meeting together for prayer; and the regular attendance at the weekly meetings was so remarkable that more than once I heard people say, "that surely there was something felt by them, or they would not come so often to hear the gospel on a week night." There was a great backwardness on the part of individuals to tell their state of mind. Two or three, however, came to me in distress of mind; one of whom, in telling me her case, said: 'It was before you went to Jerusalem that I was struck; you said at a prayer-meeting that a soul must be pure, without a spot, if it is to enter heaven; and all the time you were away I thought on that, and how it could be, and this led me to seek the Saviour.'

I was in the habit of getting those of my brethren, with whom I was most intimate, to assist me, such as Mr M'Cheyne of St Peter's, Dundee, and Mr MacDonald of Blairgowrie. In the middle of April 1840, at one of our ordinary meetings on Wednesday evening, Mr Cumming of Dumbarney, and my brother, Mr Horatius Bonar, from Kelso, were assisting me. The night before we had kept a fast appointed by the Presbytery for the state of the Church, which had been attended with very solemn effects, and this night the meeting was fuller than ever. After Mr Cumming had prayed and spoken upon the scapegoat as a type of Christ, Mr Bonar followed, and took the woman of Samaria as his subject. While he was pressing on all present the immediate reception of the offer of the living waters, many burst into tears, old and young, and among the rest, several boys of twelve or fourteen years of age. A deep and awful solemnity spread over the whole meeting, and, after the blessing was pronounced, fifty or sixty people remained in their seats, most of them in tears. Two or three old people came along the passage to speak with us, their faces wet with weeping; and this was the most affecting sight of all. We appointed another meeting for the following evening, and there the same scene occurred again; some were even more awfully impressed, and one cried aloud after the meeting was over. On the Friday evening all was deeply solemn; but that night nothing external appeared. The results of this week were such as proved this to be a visit of the Holy Spirit — some drops of a shower. From this date onwards, I found the hearts of anxious people in a manner burst open. They would now freely tell their feelings, and ask counsel and direction. This was not confined to persons of any particular age; several aged persons were among the number of the awakened; one of these said, in deep distress, 'I have gone all my life thoughtlessly to the Lord's Table, and nobody ever warned me'; and another said, 'Oh, if I had come to Christ sooner!' Of the young people who were that night very deeply awakened, I know three or four instances in which the impression has completely faded away; and the same is true of one or two elderly people. In some others the impressions of that season often to this day recur to mind, and they speak of it as a thing they cannot account for. In these cases there has been no saving result. But there are many others, in whose cases the work of grace is evident and undoubted; and in this number there are as many heads of families as young people. The general impression also, on the whole parish, has been very marked. At the communion, that same season, very many were alarmed and made anxious by having their attention directed to the truth that men ought to come to Christ before they come to his table; and that those considering themselves unconverted ought to stay away.

The work of the Spirit has not ceased among us, though it has not spread to the extent we longed for and hoped. Many persons in neighbouring parishes have shared in our blessings. At the same time, we see verified among *us* the words of our Lord, 'I came not to send peace, but a sword.' We meet with scoffing, and such like opposition, from the profane in all the country-side, and not unfrequently from cold and dry professors. Indeed, to these last I believe is to be ascribed a great check that the work received, as they used their influence and example to prejudice and cool the anxieties of many, and even led them to conform to the world. Nevertheless, there is now among us a godly seed, small in number, but decided on the Lord's side, rejoicing in the glad tidings.

I could mention many individual cases that would illustrate the nature of the work among us. The mother of a family, who had long been anxious, was brought to peace one Sabbath while I was preaching on John 3:16, 'God so loved the world'. She saw the love of God to sinners, and was filled with such joy, that it seemed to her the most wonderful sermon she had ever heard. In coming out of church she inquired of others what they thought of the sermon, and then of her own husband, and could not understand how they were not all as fully occupied with it as she was, for 'it did seem to her the most wonderful she ever heard.' A young woman, who is a striking example of free grace, and who came to peace after dreadful distress, said to me, 'I often wished to die since I found Christ, for I am afraid of sinning; but one day I remembered Christ's words, "I pray not that thou shouldst take them out of the world, but that thou shouldst keep them from the evil."' The same person underwent a great change in regard to her temper after she got peace, being ever after, as she said, able to be quiet and not hasty when provoked. Another, a mother of a family, who in her agony of soul was on the point of setting out to visit me at midnight, came to sudden peace while reading Mark 16:14: 'He upbraided them with their unbelief' — perceiving that she was not pleasing Christ but resisting him, by not venturing to believe. A sense of Christ's love filled her heart. The father of a large family, who had been long outwardly respectable, became more and more concerned. One evening he asked me to visit him after he came in from his work; and when I went, showed me a chapter in Guthrie's *Saving Interest,* 'which', said he, 'I could not have understood a few weeks ago, but which, I feel, just describes me now.' That night he was quite unable to see the truth; but long after, at a prayer-meeting, when I preached upon Abraham's believing God, the Spirit opened his heart, and, as the meeting dismissed, he told me he had found what he sought. For several days after he was in some measure upset with joy; but that soon passed. He has continued to manifest a remarkable and most satisfactory change. His own account of the source of his joy to one who asked him to explain it, was this: he turned to 1 John 5:11: 'God hath given us eternal life; and this life is in his Son'; and said, 'Now I believe that, and it fills me with joy.' Another man, who has now reached very clear and scriptural views of salvation, when he became deeply concerned about his soul, was so conscientious that he gave up family worship, which he had formerly observed occasionally, 'because he thought he was making his family suppose that he knew the truth, while, in fact, he only saw and knew his want of it.'

Such is a brief narrative of what the Lord has done among us during these three years. It was his word alone which his Spirit blessed, — 'the word that God sent preaching peace by Jesus Christ', accompanied by prayer in public and in secret. We have seen the steps of our God and King in his sanctuary, and we expect him again. 'O the Hope of Israel, the Saviour thereof in time of trouble, why shouldest thou be as a stranger in the land!'

The above extracts will give a better idea of that extraordinary work, which affected the whole town of Perth and its neighbourhood, than any description of my own could do. Having seen a good deal of it at the time, and heard of it from those directly concerned, I would only add that the half has not been told, nor indeed can be. In remembering the events of that period, one is stirred up greatly to desire the return of such days. *Then* it was that we knew something of what it was to be ambassadors for Christ; to preach in earnest; to be listened to in earnest; and not to labour in vain.

M'Cheyne's Letters

It was of the work in Perth, as well as of that in Dundee, that M'Cheyne wrote in October 5, 1841:

> I do not think I can lay any more facts before your committee than those contained in the Aberdeen letter. Only this I would say, that half is not told you; no words can describe the scenes that have taken place in this place, when God the Spirit moved on the face of our assemblies. The glory is greatly departed; but the number of saved souls is far beyond my knowledge.[1]

That there were evils connected with all this is possibly true. The good and the evil go together. The day of separation has not yet come. We prayed for a revival of truth and faith. It has come. But with it there has come a revival of error and unbelief; of superstition and rationalism. We were not prepared for this. It has taken many by surprise. Ought it to have done so? Did we expect the enemy to sleep, or think that the time of sowing tares was gone by?

Both truth and falsehood sometimes lie long hidden, like the seeds of flowers and weeds, deep under the soil of an old garden, till some change of temperature, or some trenching of the ground, makes them spring. Then they come up together. That which vitalizes the one, vitalizes the other also. If this be discouragement, we must be prepared for it; we must face it; we must preach and work as men who believe it. It has never been otherwise in the history of the Church of God; nor shall be otherwise till he comes again. Satan is not yet bound.[2]

---

[1] Letter to the Convener of the Committee of the Synod of Merse and Teviotdale.
[2] In reference to the work in Perth we have the following testimony from Burns,

This chapter may now close with some brief extracts from letters relating to the period. They do not give information as to events, but they help to exhibit the *two* men of God. The first I quote is from M'Cheyne to Milne, Nov. 10, 1841:

> MY DEAR BROTHER, — Many thanks for 'Gloomy sad Gethsemane'.[1] How strange that the darkest night in all this world, should give light and peace to the heart! I don't think you are so much with us as I with you. At all events, we are not weary of you. We had a time of blessing. Oh for more! I was preaching last Sabbath on 'So mightily grew the word of God.' William Burns comes to Edinburgh this week. Let us pray for him.[2]

Again, in the same fervent strain M'Cheyne writes:

> Your notes cheer me; for I have much need of it. Nothing damps me so much as being kept from the regular work of my ministry. We had a good day yesterday. I was preaching on family government, Gen. 18-19: 'I know him, that he will command his children.' What will all our preaching do, if family government be not revived in Scotland? Ah! brother, we must cry louder to God and man than we have ever done. See the blasphemies uttered by the railway directors. The *duty* of trampling God's law under their feet! I think all God's people

---

several years afterwards. In a letter to Milne, dated *Hong Kong, Jan. 29,* 1848, he says: — 'How different are my present engagements from those of 1839 and 1840 in Scotland; and yet this is the work to which I at first devoted myself; and all that I have seen and felt of the power of God in times past ought the more to confirm and quicken me amid the difficulties of a Chinese mission. I feel clear about having followed the call of God in coming here, although I know not for what end he is thus leading me. I trust the Lord is still remembering you in Scotland, and confirming his covenant with many. Ah! when I think of Perth and of days gone past, thoughts begin to open to me which are almost too much to bear. What accounts must be rendered by preachers and people of these days of the right hand of the Most High! Pray for me that I may not fall back, but be enabled to go on to the end in the strength of the Lord God.'

[1] Referring to Hart's old and well-known hymn on Gethsemane.

[2] This spirit of intercession comes out very prominently in M'Cheyne's letters. Here is the last sentence of one about this time: — 'I enclose Andrew's note to let you see the state of things. Pray for us, as we for you. May we have gales passing from Perth to this, and from here to you, and from heaven to both!'

should unite in prayer on this subject, that the Scottish Sabbath may be preserved. God will hear when railway directors will not. We had a sweet time last New Year. Of course I cannot be with you. But I expect Somerville to be with me, and he will give you a word in passing. Farewell, brother. Pray for us, especially in reference to our work.

As one needing intercession he writes:

Remember to think kindly of me, and pray for me, for I am poor and needy. Oh that I had the wings of a dove! Oh to be like Jesus, and with him to all eternity! Ever yours till then, — R. M. M'C.

Longing for the day-break, he writes:

I preach tonight at Newtyle, and tomorrow evening at Lintrathen, in a barn, and on Thursday in Kirriemuir. Pray for me, for I am a poor worm, all guilt and all helplessness, but still able to say, 'In the Lord have I righteousness and strength.' When shall 'the day break, and the shadows flee away'? When that which is perfect is come, then that which is in part shall be done away. I long for love without any cold-ness, light without dimness, and purity without spot or wrinkle. I long to lie at Jesus' feet, and tell him I am all his, and ever will be.

Accepting the sympathies of brotherhood, he says once more:

Your kind note was a great refreshment to me. Sympathy from a Christian brother is like 'the wine that goeth down sweetly, causing the lips of them that are asleep to speak'. I had agreed to come out to Collace, where I now am, and therefore was shut up from accepting your more than kind invitation. Another day I may avail myself of your critical powers. I write now to say that I shall gladly preach for you on Sabbath first, if you will go down and preach for me. Now, dear brother, you must not disappoint me in this, because I came up here (Collace) without making any provision. Do go down, like a vessel full of the Spirit, and may you be blessed among the people! I am like a dry reed, scarcely fit for anything. Yet God will get the more glory if he will blow his sweet Spirit through me. Brother Andrew bids me say that you must be here on Monday.

In the following way does the Dundee shepherd transfer one of his flock to the Perth shepherd:

My dear Brother, — I send you another soul to care for, a name to write on your breastplate when you go in before the Lord, I. B. She seems really to have had her heart opened to attend to the voice of Jesus. She goes to a farm near Perth, and is to attend you … Oh that God would rend the heavens and come down, and fill this place with his presence! I add no more; but pray for weary travellers like yours ever, — R. M. M‘C. Faint yet pursuing. — *11th Nov. 1841.* Day of Culsalmond intrusion.

Milne's Letters

To myself Milne writes:

My ever dear Brother, — I am just favoured with your welcome note, and rejoice in the prospect of your coming. You will give Mr Walker part of the fast-day, and me the evening, as last time, and then preach straight on, Friday, Saturday, and Sabbath. I think our people have been growing stronger since you were here. They got an open door to the fountain, and I really feel that they have not misimproved it. So, courage! I have been in the Highlands, and enjoyed it exceedingly. They ask me back; and we may take a run up for a day or two, when you come. There is an open door. But — Saturday, Saturday. So farewell. Yours very affectionately, — J. M.

To Somerville he writes:

We seem to forget that our Master has received the promise of the Father, and that he baptizes with the Holy Ghost. The longer I live I see the more clearly we are saved by grace. Theoretically we readily admit this; but we come slowly to a humbling, realizing, practical, habitual sense of it … Look at Philippians 2:20-21. Have you ever thought this rather severe? When I look at my own heart, and judge even more charitably of others than of myself, I fear it is too true. Hence I fear the absence of the spirit of love. He *honours* Christ, and we have an undercurrent, *self-honour*, which he will not work with or aid. Search us and try us. Yet it needs not diligent search, for I fear we shall find it polluting all we do.

To Bonar of Collace he thus writes in 1840:

I wish you would write me often, for I find it for a long time refreshing, though it were but a few words. You remember the words, 'In the morning sow thy seed', *etc*.? I have just been at the infirmary, and found a little boy, Jamie Thomson, about twelve years old, lying there threatened with blindness. He cannot see except with one eye, and all he knows is the difference between day and night. Poor little fellow! he is surprisingly patient. He says he is sometimes cast down, but he revives again. I am told by his sister that, after the last Sacrament, there was a great change in him; and, on questioning him as to the cause, he said that he never thought about divine things till the evening of the last Sacrament, when he thought what a happy thing it was to be among the people of Jesus, and to be clothed with the white robes! I meet with many, dear brother, to whom that evening seems to have been blessed.

The Truths Preached

The truths preached were 'old and plain'. It was the divine power which went along with them that made them tell. They were preached by men who had got the great question of their own acceptance settled, and knew the meaning of the apostle's words, 'Who hath reconciled us to himself by Jesus Christ, and hath committed to us the ministry of the reconciliation' (*2 Cor.* 5:18).

Immediate forgiveness to the sinner, upon his reception of the divine testimony to the death and resurrection of the Son of God; — this was their message. It did its work, and was life from the dead to multitudes. 'He that believeth that Jesus is the Christ, is born of God.'

'Peace with God', as the *present* result of a believed gospel, was what they presented and pressed; not peace as the issue of a lifetime's struggles, but peace at once, through him who has made peace by the blood of his cross; peace, not flowing from the ascertained excellency of our faith, either as to quantity or quality, but from the ascertained excellency of him on whom the chastisement of our peace was laid. They made each hearer feel that there was nothing between him and the cross, neither barrier nor distance; that distrust was not humility, and that all unbelief was a crucifying the Son of God afresh and putting him to an open shame; that each weary son of man, as such, was entitled, nay, commanded, to rest at once upon God's free love, not as the result of his doing or having done one good thing, but simply in consequence of that one good thing done upon the cross, — the finished work of him who is God manifest in flesh.

Sinners are by some directed to go to Christ; and so far it is well. But, then, it turns out that it is only for *preliminaries* to salvation that they are in the first place to go, and not for salvation itself. They are instructed to keep at preliminaries (such as conviction, faith, repentance) until these have become sufficiently substantial to warrant them to trust Christ implicitly, and to draw the conclusion that they are saved. Milne, and others whom God honoured to do his work in those years, sent the sinner straight to Christ for *salvation*, — for an *immediate* salvation: 'Whoso shall call on the name of the Lord SHALL BE SAVED', — not merely, shall get faith, and godly sorrow, and humility, but, shall be SAVED. That same gospel which warrants a man to go to Christ for anything, or to expect anything, warrants him to go for everything, and to expect everything. God has kept faith with the world. He promised a Saviour; and in due time that Saviour came. So does he keep faith with the sinner. He promises that whosoever consents to be indebted to this Saviour for life shall have it on the spot. He keeps his word.

It was with this free gospel that the men of '39, '40, and '41, went forth to do the work of the ministry. It was with this weapon that they assailed the rebellious heart; not parleying with the conscience, but laying hold of it; not giving place, even for a moment, to the sinner's excuses or reasons for delay, but urging him with the divine demand and claim; calling on him, at the peril of aggravated and augmenting guilt, to receive at once the great salvation.

Another of his hymns written in after years may be here inserted, as suitably closing the chapter:

TO THE SINNER

Open thy doors, O stubborn heart,
Thy gates of stone fling wide apart,
   The Lord of heaven is come!
He left for thee His throne and state,
Intent to take thee for His mate,
   And make thy heart His home.

Long has He tracked thy devious way,
And seen thee wandering far astray,
   Upon destruction bent.
But yet He would not thee forsake,
Nor from thee would his mercy take,
   But oft deliverance sent.

He called: His voice thou wouldst not hear;
He frowned: His wrath thou wouldst not fear;
   His gifts were all misused.
But still He plied His thankless task,
And condescended oft to ask,
   Though oft He was refused.

Look forth, and see who courts thy love,
And longs to take thee for His dove,
   To nestle in His breast.
Fain would He break thy galling chain,
Fain would He all thy foes restrain,
   And lead thee into rest.

What hast thou to be valued more
Than He who stands thy gate before,
   And access seeks to win?
Art thou not wretched, naked, blind,
With unclean heart, distempered mind,
   All darkness and all sin?

Awake, O Spirit of the Son,
Thy olden works again be done,
   In opening closed hearts.
Put in Thy hand, the bars undo,
The carnal mind with grace renew,
   Before the Lord departs.

Without Thee, vain the trumpet's blast,
In vain the summons wide we cast,
   Till Thou Thy help extend.
Our field with precious seed is sown,
But yet with thorns 'tis all o'ergrown
   Till Thou in rain descend.

Praises to Him the Son who gave;
Praises to Him who came to save;
   But praises, too, to Thee
Who goest forth to work unseen
(Tho' soon we know where Thou hast been)
   To set the captive free.'

Chapter 6

1841–1843
Church Movements
and Letters

*I*n the end of 1841, the Christian people of the Church of
Scotland began to unite in defence of their spiritual liberties,
and in maintenance of Christ's regal rights as the Church's Head
and the world's King. These associations multiplied over the whole
land, carrying on their operations, till superseded by the Disruption of 1843.

In these movements Milne took no lukewarm part. Though by
no means an 'ecclesiastic' in the common sense of the word, he was
a thorough Presbyterian, a vigorous maintainer of ancient doctrine
and Reformation discipline. Those who counted upon his laxity in
regard to Church principles, and who were persuaded that a man,
so spiritual, and so silent in Church courts, would take no part in
the struggles of these years, were surprised at the resolute decision
which he showed in adopting, and the energy in maintaining, the
great ecclesiastical principles then battled for. He acted on the
principle which our General Assembly, in 1646, thus stated to the
divines of the Westminster Assembly: 'The smallest of Christ's
truths (if it be lawful to call any of them small) is of greater moment
than all the other businesses that ever have been debated since the
beginning of the world to this day.'

In the midst of the great warfare of these years, and in spite of bustle and distraction, Milne 'in patience possessed his soul.' The ecclesiastical turmoil seemed to elevate, not to depress; to spiritualize, not to secularize. All the brethren whom he loved, and in whose fellowship he delighted, were of one mind on the questions which were dividing the Church courts. Hence they could meet together, confer together, pray together. There was no distance nor misunderstanding nor suspicion. All were of one heart and of one soul. Milne's loving spirit shrunk sensitively from aught like separation, on any point, from those whom he loved. Some years after the Disruption he thus writes: 'I should have been grieved, and surprised far more, if there could have been discordance between dear brother — and myself. I would give up a good deal rather than not agree with you; and I would go, I don't know how far about, rather than lose your company.' During the months before his death, the prospect or possibility of variance among brethren was inexpressible pain to him. But in the years preceding the Disruption, there was entire unity among the evangelical brethren in the Church. As was said by one speaker at the Convocation, in reference to the band who afterwards formed the Free Church: 'Ye are in our hearts, to die and live with you' (*2 Cor.* 7:3). Never, perhaps, had evangelical ministers been so thoroughly and compactly united.

But there was more than unity. There was a manifest quickening throughout Scotland. The Church questions agitated were not those of partisanship or routine, they were vital and spiritual, both in themselves and in their bearings. They centred in Christ himself; Christ the Lawgiver of the Church; Christ the Lawgiver of the realm. Hence, in handling them, Christian men were dealing with the Master and the Master's honour. The questions were summed up in two: 'Shall Christ give laws to the Church, or shall the Church give laws to herself? Shall Christ give laws to the nations, or shall the nations give laws to themselves?' Christian men had not to come down to secularities and externalisms in maintaining these. They felt that they were discussing matters which touched their spiritual interests on every side, and that they were contending for truths which brought their souls in contact with the Lord himself. Hence Milne writes to Somerville: 'Are you going anywhere to speak on the Church question? Or will you go, if asked? R. M'Cheyne goes north, in a week or two, to Ellon and Deer Presbyteries. So we shall have to take St Luke's Communion between us. Accept my prayer that you may inherit Jacob's heritage — Genesis 28:15 — and Abraham's: "I will bless you, and make you blessings." I wish I could give all my foolish heart to Jesus, and seek all my consolation from him.'

The real character of the time, and the true meaning of its events, were well understood by Hewitson when he wrote: 'Now is not a time to cry out, "The *Church* is in danger"; it is a time to cry out, with the voice of warning, "*The State* is in danger." Judgment in this land is beginning with the righteous; what, then, will the end be of those who obey not the gospel of God? This is a critical time for *the world*!' Into this feeling many of us entered; among these, not least, John Milne. The Church, he knew, was all safe, if she failed not in her duty; but what of the *State*, if she failed in hers? 'If we weep', wrote he, 'it is not for ourselves, but for our country, which, by this act of oppression, may fill the cup of her national iniquity, and cause the Lord to withdraw those barriers which have hitherto prevented the floods of error and calamity from breaking in.'[1] 'This country', he writes again,

is interested in this matter: I infer this from a simple Bible principle. It is said by the Apostle Paul, Ephesians 1:22, 'God hath put all things under Christ's feet, and hath given him to be the head over all things to the church.' Here we learn two important truths: First,

[1] Second letter to the people of God in St Leonard's Church, Perth, dated 7th Feb. 1843.

Christ has supreme and universal power — he is the Head over all things in heaven; the angels dwell in his presence and rejoice to do his will. He is the Head over all things in hell; the lost spirits tremble and are constrained to obey. He is the Head also over all things on earth; princes, judges, magistrates, and other powers that be are his subjects, they are ordained by him, they are accountable to him, and will in a little while stand before his great white throne. The time cometh when they shall all remember and turn to the Lord; when the kings of Tarshish and of the isles shall bring presents, when the kings of Sheba and Seba shall offer gifts. A second thing which we learn from these words is,   the use which Christ makes of his vast power. He is Head over all things *to* the Church; that is, he employs the power which he has over all things for the good of the Church, to protect, extend, and perfect it. If such is the use which *he* makes of his supreme and universal power, then surely earthly rulers and judges are bound to make the *same use* of that limited and delegated power which they receive from him. They are set up by him, they are his servants, his stewards; and therefore they plainly ought to employ the power which he gives them, mainly to preserve, and further, and comfort his church; and if they refuse to do so, they are rebels against their heavenly Master, and *probably* bring a curse upon their country, while they *certainly* expose themselves, as individuals, to the condemnation of unrighteous servants in the day of accounts. Brethren, this is a question in which we are interested, not only as Christians, but also as right-hearted Scotchmen, concerned for our country's weal. 'The kingdom and nation that will not serve Christ shall perish, yea those nations shall be utterly wasted' (*Isa.* 60:12).[1]

I do not enter at length into details of the Disruption. Milne had, by letters and otherwise, prepared his people for that event; and when the time came, the great majority went with him, — ten out of fifteen elders, and a still larger proportion of the members.

---

[1] Letter to the people of God in St Leonard's Church, Perth, dated 19th January 1842.

At the last Communion before the crisis there were nearly 900 communicants; and at the first Communion after it there were 843. All the Sabbath-school teachers, with their 300 scholars, quitted the old walls. Free St Leonard's Church was opened before the close of the year, and Milne's first text was Psalm 24:7, 'Lift up your heads, O ye gates.'

There had been several ebullitions of hostility towards him and his work, beginning with the proposal on the part of some of the managers to exclude William Burns. The last and most important was on the 10th of May 1843, when an interdict, on the part of some of these same managers, was served upon Milne, prohibiting him from using the church for meetings in reference to the principles then at stake, and the great crisis of the hour.

Among the few who left him was his beadle, of whom he hoped better things, though that official, in the exercise of his calling, had not done much to help the meetings of 1840. All that Milne said to him, on meeting him, was, 'Oh Joseph, your name should have been Judas, not Joseph.' Little was known of Joseph subsequently. He died, I believe, some years ago; and his wife, upon her deathbed, sent for Milne; as if she could not die without her old minister, whom she and her husband had deserted. There was hope in her death.

Conversing one day with a minister before the Disruption, and finding that he, notwithstanding the professions of former years, was resolved not to let go his hold of the Establishment, Milne turned suddenly round upon him, and said, 'I see how it is. You are just like Issachar. You see that the land is pleasant and rest good, and so you are about to bow your shoulder to bear.' The words were fitly spoken and were true of others besides the minister thus addressed.

In the great gathering in St Andrew's Church, Edinburgh, on the well-known 18th of May 1843, Milne was present, as might have been expected. He and I were together. He lingered a little behind, or rather went back 'to look', as he said, 'at the faces of the Moderates.' He rejoined me immediately; and, along with Thomas Brown, now of the Dean Church, Edinburgh, we walked together to Tanfield.

M'Cheyne's Death

About two months before this, on the 25th of March, Robert M'Cheyne died; and some of us have not yet forgotten him, though he has been absent from us these six-and-twenty years. How Milne felt the removal of one with whom he had been so intimately and lovingly associated, the following letter to Somerville will show:

MY DEAREST BROTHER, I am thankful to find that our hearts answer to one another at this season. I also feel a tenderer, stronger love for the survivors of our now diminished circle. I suppose we both feel like a mother who has had one of her little ones taken away, and startedly clasps the remainder more closely to her heart. I never apprehended danger till our brother was gone; and even now I don't think I have realized the fact that I shall never see him again on earth. I shall not, I suppose, realize it, till I am in Dundee. His being in heaven makes me feel it nearer, dearer, and more familiar. He is another witness; let us lay aside every weight. I think God is, in some degree, answering the prayer, that he would give us a double portion of his Spirit. I think I feel more fixedly crucified and soft than I did. I regard this operation of God's hand as the loudest note we have yet had of the war-trumpet, and the clearest intimation that our help is in the Lord of Hosts. But let us quit us like men. He who overcometh shall inherit all things. And now let us love one another and be more faithful, and pray more frequently and more earnestly. The only real friends I have ever had in the world are the little family of Jacob, of whom Joseph is now away. Nowhere do we open our hearts to one another but at the throne of grace. Oh, unspeakable privilege of knowing and being known! My heart warms and enlarges as I muse. Look at Hosea 5:15, and 5:1–3. These are the texts I am thinking of for tomorrow forenoon and afternoon. Pray for me on Thursday evening. Like you, I was, in speaking with our people, who have been most widely and deeply affected, led to think on the words, 'Our friend Lazarus sleepeth', as conveying the ideas rest, refreshment, awakening, security in Jesus; 'With Christ', and 'will come again'. The two thoughts that occurred were — Is it well with him? and shall we see him again? I ask your prayers. I shall make mention of you tomorrow (Sabbath), and ask that you may find it a day of more abundant life to those who live, and of quickening to those who are still dead. We have one fewer to pray for tonight.[1] I never thought of it till now. I think it will be good if you stay. We may never meet again on earth. Ever yours affectionately, — J. M.

Such were his first thoughts, when the tidings of that heavy stroke reached him. Coming as it did when our sky was dark with clouds, and when man's help had been found vain, the death of one so stedfast threw a deep solemnity over many of us. What had God in store for us? Was it evil or good? Were our feet to be set in a large place, or were we to be broken in pieces? 'The thoughts of many hearts were revealed' by that sudden sorrow. It told widely and efficaciously; it threw us more upon our true prop; it braced us for stormy and laborious days. How far it is still telling on the Church and the ministry we do not seek to determine. The Church is but too ready to forget her best.

The following year the *Memoir of R. M. M'Cheyne* was published, in two small volumes, by Andrew Bonar of Collace. A copy was sent from the author to Milne; and the following is the letter from him acknowledging the gift:

MY DEAR BROTHER, — I have just received your kind gift, which I value, as showing that I have a place in the heart of a friend of Jesus. I think I feel more heart-joy in this love than in thousands of — No, there is no comparison; for such things cannot be weighed with

---

[1] Alluding to the Saturday night concert for prayer among a few brethren, of whom M'Cheyne was one.

balances together. How strange it seems that one with whom we were so intimate is now in such a different state! And yet it seems as if there could not be much change upon his mind, and as if, when we met him, he would be just the same. I find it difficult to think of Jesus thus; and yet, if I could, I think I should be very happy, to feel that he would just say to us the very words that he used to say on earth. Shall we look for a blessing on Sabbath? I am weary and worn; but his grace is sufficient, if we could, or rather would, but cast ourselves wholly, undoubtingly, upon it! How unkind it is to doubt his grace! I am sure there is nothing we shall one day blush at so much as our doubting, suspecting faith; it is almost worse than blind unbelief. I was struck with this verse today when I first opened my Bible, Acts 27:32: 'Then the soldiers cut off the ropes of the boat, and let it fall off.' Oh to have nothing but the ark to look to for happiness as well as safety! But weak and irresolute is man: yet *his* purposes shall stand, and *he* will do all his pleasure. You will be pleased with the appearance of the volumes? They are very handsome, without and within. I am not sublimed enough to disregard these things. I am going to begin the perusal, and trust that, like many of the brethren, I shall find it life from the dead. Let us look for a blessing, in consequence, on Sabbath. I shall expect it, and, meanwhile, am yours very affectionately, — J. M.

The Disruption

After the Disruption, matters went on with vigour, though opposition did not lessen. Wide-spread interest, full churches, a fervent ministry, the preaching of the gospel everywhere, in barns, fields, moors, highways; large and manifest blessing on the word spoken; such things as these marked the latter half of 1843.[1]

---

[1] Let the following extract from the private journal of one now with the Lord, illustrate one of the scenes of that bright and busy summer: — 'Collace, June 25th, 1843. — Today enjoyed the holy feast of Communion in our tent; the first held here by the Free Church. Oh, it seems as if our bands were loosed, as if our feet were enlarged to run the way of God's commandments. It has been a blessed time. The cloud seemed hovering over the tabernacle and filling it with glory. There was a sweet stillness in the air around; all hushed in Sabbath rest, nothing to annoy. The

Before this, and while still in the Established Church, we were in some respects under restraint. The 'Moderate' clergy did not invite us to their pulpits; and we were hindered from preaching in the villages around by the law of 'use and wont', if not by the law of the Church. Souls in earnest, — some newly awakened, some long groping their way to light, — used to come to us from many a parish; and this gave offence. We were warned as to the peril of transgressing parish boundaries, either in visiting or preaching. The people could not, of course, be prevented from coming to us; but we could be prevented, by ecclesiastical censure, from receiving them, at least as members, if not as hearers. Matters were becoming more irksome every week, both for minister and people. Some of us would soon have been embroiled with our brethren, and the courts of the Church. We could not help ourselves. God was awakening human souls. These awakened ones would not and could not remain under lifeless pastors. They would go where they would be fed. The question was becoming serious for many of us.

The severance came, and the difficulty was at an end. They who had denied us their pulpits, could not now shut us out of their parishes. They who, when we were co-presbyters, threatened us, could no longer trouble us. The event, which they had made inevitable, and by which they had hoped to crush us, placed us at once beyond their reach. Interdicts were now out of the question. They had, unwittingly,

---

sun shone brightly over our heads, and a soft breeze played around; and sweetly the notes of the birds sounded as they seemed to blend with the song of praise that ascended from the worshippers within. And then within there was so much of quiet; not a footstep could be heard as they moved to and from the tables, for the soft and tender grass was all our floor. Nothing was heard but the voice of the man of God, telling us of a Saviour's love. Sweet day! Sweet season! Too, too soon over. Oh for the feast above! We will get to the mountain of myrrh, and look for the day-break, when the shadows shall flee away. Make haste, my Beloved, and come. O my Saviour, prepare me for the blessed day!' Not only our Communion Sabbaths, but our Communion *Mondays* were memorable days. The *Monday evenings* were times of remarkable blessing; and with these evenings a sacredness has been associated, which will not soon be broken.

let loose the very evangelists whom they had been labouring to restrain. We went abroad over the length and breadth of the land, preaching the everlasting gospel, not slow to avail ourselves of the many open doors which on every hand invited us to enter.

Evangelistic Labours

That summer and winter were busy months in Scotland. The labour was great, but the interest was greater, and the success was manifest. No one of us has ever grudged the cost, or the weariness, or the self-denial of that never-to-be-forgotten time.

Milne was a most energetic worker, in season and out of season. Perth itself and the villages around were the special scenes of his labour. He spared no toil. He delighted to preach the gospel among the rural population of the district; and his brethren were glad to have his help, though it was often the help of an over-wrought worker. Sometimes he walked, on his preaching expeditions, and the distances which he accomplished were great. Sometimes he rode, or drove; and he was not always considerate toward the beast he made use of, as he was a fearless rider, and rather a reckless driver. Yet he was more merciful to the animal than to himself. One stormy Saturday he had set out for Auchterarder, to assist his friend George Smeaton at his Communion on the Sabbath. Such was the snow that the mail-gig was stopped. Milne tried a horse, but it could not proceed. He did not hesitate; but set out in the deep snow on foot, and after hours of wading and struggling he reached the village, some thirteen miles off.

It was perhaps the remembrance of this that in after days made him write as follows, — when, having missed the train to Anstruther, to which he was proceeding, he had to go on to Dysart: — 'I am pretty well, not very robust; and it is perhaps as well that I have not a meeting on my hands after the journey. I always think now that all is for the best, whereas, long long ago, I should certainly have set out and walked the fifteen or sixteen miles from this to Anstruther.'

On one of these same snowy winter nights he preached at Newtyle, a small village some eighteen miles eastward of Perth, where M'Cheyne had often preached. The meeting was late; it was very deep snow; the night was dark; but he was bent on returning home immediately. He set out on horseback, in spite of remonstrances, and pressed on. The road was quite obliterated by the drift, and he proceeded sometimes in fields, sometimes in ditches, sometimes on the tops of walls, and sometimes on the road itself, endangering both man and beast; reaching Perth between three and four in the morning, utterly exhausted. In our after talks about this imprudent exploit he did not defend himself; but said that he was very anxious to be home that night.

There was never found a lion in *his* way, when he had to go out to visit a sick member, or preach the gospel of Christ, or minister comfort to the bereaved.

Disruption-Days

To some the Disruption was a sacrifice; to others it was simply a deliverance. It was more of the latter than of the former to Milne. Yet those to whom it was a sacrifice, — and to not a few it was so, — were the last to speak of it as such. They bore poverty and hardship without a murmur. It would have been better for us had we, as a Church, forborne some subsequent boasts, and allowed our doings and success to speak for themselves.

The tide of blessing which, from 1837, had been flowing without intermission, had not yet begun to ebb. Many were daily added to our living membership. The Church's true work went on happily in parts where it had already commenced; and it began in many places to which it had not yet reached. We look back on these months with thankful joy. Gladly should we live them over again, with all their tear and wear of body and mind, had we but our former strength, and the hope of like success. No one who passed through them would wish either to forget or under-estimate the privilege of having been one of the 'labourers' in the reaping of that blessed harvest.

It would serve no good purpose to recall the strifes of that post-Disruption time. In these Milne was but little involved, though none could be more resolute in maintaining the principles of the Free Church. When I say that he was a thorough Free Churchman, and not a mere separatist for the sake of company, or consistency, or political liberty, I am simply stating what all who were acquainted with him knew. His name stands among the subscribers of the 'deed of demission'; and no one signed it more heartily or more intelligently than he. In his Indian diary, of date Dec. 2, 1854, this sentence occurs: 'Sin produces sin, and error, error. Thus the Erastianism of Establishments has produced the Voluntaryism of our days. Happy they who keep the right and middle path.'

He was preaching in the south of Scotland, in the open air, about this time, and a rumour went out that in his sermon he had attacked the Duke of Buccleuch, whose refusal of sites for churches had produced great bitterness of feeling, especially on the borders. His text was 'Acquaint thyself with him, and be at peace'; and it was not likely that such a text could have been perverted by such a man for such a purpose. Before I had time to get an explanation from him of what had raised the report, we met at Newcastle on an evangelistic expedition, during which we held meetings in the streets and market-place.[1]

---

[1] We were together for some time during this excursion. Newcastle was our centre; but we endeavoured to find our way into all the neighbouring towns. One day he had gone down the line to make some arrangements as to preaching; and on coming up in the evening, he told me that, as he was walking about, near some station, he saw a large fine school. He went in and saw the working of it. Before coming away he asked leave to speak to the children. The teacher allowed him, and he gave them a full message concerning the way of life, closing with the well-known story of the Highland kitchen-maid and her two prayers: 'Lord, show me

The first text I heard him give out was the above; and he had scarcely begun, when, in order to show what acquaintanceship was, he introduced a well-known name, to illustrate the difference between knowing about a person, and knowing a person. On the border way-side he had named the Duke of Buccleuch; in Newcastle the Duke of Wellington; in neither case with the slightest disrespect. The origin of the rumour became obvious; ignorance and malice had helped to set it agoing. He did not trouble himself to contradict it, and it soon died away.

Strongly as he felt during the Disruption controversy, he did not give way to sharp words. There was, in his strongest statements, a tone of kindliness, and an absence of 'personality', which tended to keep down angry feeling. He sought to give no needless offence. Yet he loved the Free Church, and knew why he loved it.

M'Cheyne and Milne

Between Milne and M'Cheyne there were points of likeness, yet of great unlikeness also. In appearance they were dissimilar. Both, indeed, were shortsighted, and generally wore spectacles; they both walked nimbly and erectly, moving with an agility that spoke of inward joy;[1] but the former was dark, the latter rather fair; the former was under the middle size, the latter considerably above it,[2] which gave him a commanding appearance, especially on one occasion,

---

myself'; 'Lord, show me thyself.' After coming out he made inquiry about the building, and found it was into a *High-Church* school that he had intruded his gospel message.

[1] 'I remember Robert M'Cheyne coming in one morning to a private prophetical reading which some of us had, before he went to Dundee, and saying, "I felt so happy this morning that I could not refrain from skipping as I came along." Like Philip Saphir of Pesth he could say with gladness, "I have got a religion for my whole man."

[2] '*Proceritas corporis, decora facies, demissus capillus; quae licet fortuita et inania putentur, illi tamen plurimum venerationis acquirunt.*' 'His stature, handsome face, long hair — although these things are accidental and empty, yet they win much reverence for him.' This is a quotation from Pliny the Younger in his *Epistles* (1.10.6), describing the philosopher Euphrates, *Ed.*

when not thinking himself high enough to overlook the audience, he mounted the stool which the minister used for kneeling, and on this elevation poured out one of his most energetic sermons to a congregation of some 1,200 people. Both had a pleasant smile; but there was more of severity about the latter than the former, though the laughter of M‘Cheyne was louder and more ringing than that of Milne. In both there was great plainness of speech, and indifference as to polish and ornament. Illustrations were to them not flowers for the fancy, but arrows for the conscience. In both there was an unearthly elevation of spirit, alike in prayer and preaching, which lifted up the hearer unconsciously along with the speaker. In both there was deep solemnity of voice, though in Milne there was more of the natural, — we might almost say the conversational, — tone than in M‘Cheyne. Both were vehement in denouncing sin, the latter never pausing to smooth down his words, as if afraid of calling things by too strong names;[1] the former uttering the same denunciations more courteously, and with less liability to be misunderstood or to call up opposition. Both of them were, at first, long preachers; both, like our Reformers, used homely illustrations; both spoke without manuscript or note before them, easily and plainly, right into their people's eyes; both thoroughly believed the creed which they had subscribed; and both preached the good news concerning the work finished on the cross in all their unconditional freeness. No man ever mistook their calling, or supposed them to be anything but ambassadors for Christ. In public and in private they were felt to be men of God, on the watch for souls.

---

[1] M‘Cheyne's letter to the chairman of the Edinburgh and Glasgow Railway, on the Sabbath-breaking trains, then first run, is very strong in its language, and shows the intensity of feeling under which he was writing. Yet he aimed not at men, but at their sins. '*Insectatur vitia non homines; nec castigat errantes, sed emendat.*' 'He attacks vices, not men, and rather than chastising the erring, corrects them.' This is from Pliny the Younger, *Epistles*, 1.10.7, Ed.

Milne as a Minister of Christ

Milne kept back nothing from his people, but spoke freely and boldly of all current events and controversies. He was one of the few who could, without awkwardness or difficulty, introduce any subject into the pulpit, either in prayer or discourse. The little things of the day, as well as the great things, were all woven into his ministrations from Sabbath to Sabbath, in a way which made one sometimes wonder, sometimes admire, and sometimes smile. You required to be rather careful what you told him before he went into the pulpit; for you were quite sure that the event or topic mentioned would find its way into some part of the service, and your name along with it.

His first morning prayer in church was always very remarkable for the minute fullness with which it entered into the various cases that had come before him; it might be sickness, or pain, or losses, or bereavements, or anxieties, or spiritual trouble; every one was specially indicated and prayed for. This was one of the tenderest and closest of his pastoral bonds; for thus, while his affections were flowing out towards his flock, theirs were drawn towards each other. In many other ways did his ready sympathies get vent to themselves, far beyond his own people. Wherever he heard of sorrow, thither a note from him found its way, or a call was made; and if the parties could not be seen, his card was sent in with John 14:1, or some such text, pencilled on it, and 'love and sympathy' written above or below his name. A friend was setting off by rail to the Edinburgh dentist; the station-master was sent to him with Milne's card and a *British Messenger*, this being added in pencil, 'May your dental Bezaleel get unusual help. Yours ever, — J. M.'

But these characteristics, though now mentioned in connection with this period of his ministry, marked the whole of it down to its close. At no time did he seem to feel the slightest difficulty in referring to all the movements or events around. Yet all was solemn; all was genial and kindly.

He never meddled with politics, though he formed his judgment on all passing events. I dare say he would have supported a Christian man in a parliamentary election if needful; for he did not think, with some in our day, that none but unconverted men should have anything to do with the affairs of the State. But certainly he stood aloof from political partisanship, as secularizing and deteriorating; though he would, I doubt not, have admitted the vast difference between a political Christian and a Christian politician. His private and conversational remarks on men and things showed that he had not shut his eyes to public occurrences, and that he found, in his daily newspaper, materials for thought as well as subjects for thanksgiving and prayer. 'Even when he read literature and the news of the day, he forthwith sought to turn all to use in some department of his ministry, or some form of personal edification.'[1]

Overcoming Evil with Good

He had far more shrewdness and insight into character than many, judging by his kindly simplicity, gave him credit for. He was a most unsuspicious man; and yet with discerning eye. He might not be the best at giving counsel in an emergency; but even then, as well as at other times, his fruitful active mind would suggest thoughts, or bring up a text, out of which you could extract the advice needed. At times hasty in his conclusions, and not seldom impulsive in his plans, he would accept or reject a friend's arguments too readily, as if he were irresolute, when he was not really so. A peacemaker everywhere, he had his own ways of making peace; sometimes he would take hold of the hands of the parties and put them into each other; and sometimes, as in meetings of session or meetings for consultation, when any heat threatened to arise, he would stop and say, let us sing the 133d Psalm: 'Behold how good a thing it is', *etc.* He belonged to that 'candid school' which 'hopeth all things'

[1] Bonar's funeral sermon.

(*1 Cor.* 13:7), but not to that whose charity consists in palliating evil, or pleading for error, or excusing departures from the faith. If any one showed him any slight, or injured him, he made it a matter of conscience to show special kindness to the injurer. Not as if he did not feel the unkindness, for he was acutely sensitive, but as if bent on overcoming evil with good, and on refusing to be affronted in any effort for the welfare of a soul. As he and I were walking together one day, we passed a gentleman, who bowed. Detaching himself from me, Milne went after him and talked kindly to him. Rejoining me, he said, 'That man does not like me, and frequently shows this, but I must win him over.' He frequently bought articles in a shop where the master was surly. He knew that, *durum patientia mollit.*[1] He was asked, 'Why do you go back to a shop when your custom is not desired?' 'I do it on purpose', he said; 'I am trying to soften that man by kindness. He would scarcely speak to me at first; but I'm getting round him, and hope to come to close quarters some day.'

St Leonard's Free Church stood on the corner of Victoria Street and Scott Street, Perth. Opened in October 1843, just five months after the Disruption, it seated 1,400 worshippers.

[1] 'Patience softens what is hard', *Ed.*

Chapter 7

Various Years —
Times of Waiting upon God

*F*or several years a few brethren in different parts of the country had been in the habit of observing some day in each month (generally, though not always, the first Monday), as a day of special private prayer, that they might seek help and wisdom in 'taking heed to themselves and to their ministry'. The practice was suggested and begun by Robert M'Cheyne; and each of us in turn wrote the monthly letter, reminding the brethren of the day, and noting thoughts and subjects that might seem particularly suitable. It was a happy bond; very pleasant to look back on, though many links are now broken, and nearly one half of the original members have left us to be with the Lord. A few of these letters may be given.

The following is Milne's circular, of date February 29, 1844:

My dear Andrew, — I have been requested by Mr Smeaton to write the circular for this month, putting the brethren in remembrance of our special season of prayer and fasting, on Tuesday the 5th of March. It is said, 'When the poor and needy seek water, and their tongue faileth for thirst, I the Lord will hear, I the God of Jacob will not forsake them.' I do not think we have yet been brought to this. Let us therefore next Tuesday meditate on the terribleness of a barren ministry, till our hearts are wrung and broken. See how Jeremiah speaks (*Lam.* 3:49) of his feelings during the withdrawal of God's power and favour.

'Mine eye trickleth down and ceaseth not.' And again, 'Mine eye affecteth mine heart.' Oh, is it not affecting to see the people flocking to ordinances, and waiting so earnestly on the word, and yet so little of the power being present to heal them! I think I feel it beginning to humble me. The apostles gave themselves to prayer, and to the ministry of the word, and that continually. Is it so with us? Let us examine if there is anything wanting in our prayers for the blessing. Are we frequent, constant, fervent, importunate, special, believing, humble in prayer? Is there anything defective in our ministry of the word? Do we seek the conversion of souls? Do we seek messages from God? Do we speak with authority, in the name and through the power of God? Do we set forth tremblingly, yet affectionately, the awful condition of unbelieving, unregenerate men? Do we in Christ's stead beseech them, 'Be ye reconciled to God?' Excuse me, dear brother. I trust this will reach you before Tuesday, and I shall rejoice to think we are bowing the knee before the same throne, though far separate. Write me a word or two, that I may tell our people next Thursday. I went out to Collace on the Wednesday; but, walking out, was tired, and I fear had little life in speaking. On Thursday I rode over to Newtyle, walking the pony all the way, and sometimes walking with it. I hope there might be some good done. I saw manifest tokens of the Lord having been there. I was at Auchterarder on Sabbath. We had a refreshing season. I had to walk on Saturday all the way, it being impossible for horse or vehicle to go, from the depth of the snow. I felt it good to be toiling through. Write me. William Burns is gone to Kilsyth. Grace and peace be with you.

Looking Upward

Of the same date, and for the same purpose, we have another letter, addressed to Somerville. I give it, partly to show the great fertility and versatility of the writer. Most of us, in waiting these monthly circulars, used to send the same letter to each of the brethren. But Milne seems to have written a different one to each.

He was very ready with his pen in such things; and his heart was full.

My dear Brother, — I have been asked to send the circular for this month, to put the brethren in remembrance of our special season for prayer and fasting, on Tuesday next, 5th March. I am satisfied that some such exercise is seasonable at present, and must be profitable. What is the cause of this almost universal and protracted withdrawal of divine power from our ministrations? 'The Lord's hand is not shortened.' Where does the sin, that grieves and lets, lie? Is it in the people, or is it in us? The people wait continually on ordinances, and listen needfully to the word; and it is affecting to think that, when they so willingly receive the word, there should be so little grace and power present to bless them. Let us begin at the sanctuary. The apostles, at the time of their success, gave themselves to prayer and to the ministry of the word.

Is it so with us? Is there anything wanting in our prayers for the blessing? Are we frequent, constant, special, fervent, believing in prayer? Do we honour the work of Jesus by the largeness and confidence of our requests? Is there anything faulty in our ministry? Is the *matter* the whole counsel of God? Is it gotten by prayer, and followed by prayer? Is the *manner* that of ambassadors of God, standing in the stead of Christ? Are we aiming at the conversion of souls, and do we tremble at the thought of a barren ministry?

The best symptom I see at present is, that some are beginning to feel and lay to heart our deserted condition. May this feeling grow and deepen, till our hearts are wrung and broken. What are we if our Master is not with us? The godly will mourn, and the wretched will contemn. What are ordinances, if the Lord is not there? Dry breasts, empty ceremonies. Let us stir one another up faithfully and affectionately to wrestle for the blessing. I have been a different man since I was with you. The people seem to have been quite aware of it the first Sabbath after my return. I got, somehow, a new view of the free grace of God. In our backslidings, as well as at our conversion, the first movement is on his side. You brought this out in the end of your action sermon. I have had more satisfaction in my ministry since then than I had had for months before. I have been eight days in the country, preaching round; being able to get away, from Wm. Burns being with me. I think things are looking more hopeful. There is an evident work of God at a small village, Newtyle, if curious people do not mar it by blazing it abroad.

It may be well to give here one or two more of these reminding circulars from other brethren. They may quicken to faith, and prayer, and zeal. They may suggest similar unions, or prayer-circles, among those who have not yet tried them. We do need some such divine stimulant now; something that will bring us into closer connection with the great Fountain of all power and blessing; something that will enrich our poverty and replenish our emptiness. For certainly it is not eloquence, nor argument, nor vehemence, nor 'fresh thought', nor the enticing words of man's wisdom that we need for the revivification of our ministry; but the power of the Holy Ghost.

Here is Professor Smeaton's circular:

MY DEAR BROTHER, — As subjects to spread before the Lord, the approaching Assembly suggests itself, together with the removal of some of our most honoured witnesses; another call, surely, from the Lord of Hosts to 'weeping and to mourning' (*Isa.* 22:12). But without assuming the office of addressing you in my own words, though the occasion of your permission might supply the warrant, it gives me more pleasure to quote a sentence or two from the recently published memoir of our late holy missionary, Mr M'Donald: 'I am every year feeling myself to be a less important and more insignificant being in God's world, in Christ's Church, in man's affairs.' 'Down, down; bring me down, O God.' 'My desire is to be breathed upon and quickened *by the Spirit from on high,* that, being delivered from animal excitement, fleshly confidence, and spiritual pride, I may devote myself, in heart and soul, to my Lord himself in my work. It is only of late that my eyes have been opened on what has made my knees feeble and my hands to hang down, even *the lack of the Spirit's power within me.'* 'It seems to me that, in a country where you have all so large a field of concert and co-operation as in Scotland, you ought all to agree to devote a month or two, in common concert of all ministers, to preach entirely on the work of the Holy Spirit in its essential relations to the Church, and the salvation of sinners. The subject is not sufficiently taught nor understood, save by a few men in a few places; and who can tell what good might come, when the blessed Agent is thus glorified, and the multitude of minds thus set in order and prepared for his return? For my part, my only comfort in my Indian work is the thought of the Holy Spirit; and I wish I could infect every mind around me with my feelings on that subject.'

Here is another, dated '*Collace, Feb. 26, 1849*':

MY DEAR BROTHER, — Might I suggest for special meditation, in order to put an edge on our spirit on Saturday, that passage in Lam. 3:48-51, and, indeed, Jeremiah's character in general? Let us ask from him who wept over Jerusalem, and of whom the people said, 'He is Jeremiah', such a really tender, pitiful, and compassionate frame of soul; nay, *habit* of soul. Yet, after all, this is but one of a thousand wants. Dear brother, remember our *account*, Heb. 13:17. Remember also our *crown*, 1 Pet. 5:4. But, besides all that concerns us personally, *remember souls*, perishing souls. Who is sufficient for these things? But let us call on the Lord with one accord, and think on Jer. 33:3.

Prayer for the 'Dead'

Here is another from the Rev. J. Y. Walker of Perth, that honoured servant of Christ, whose name has been, with not a few of us, associated with quiet zeal, sound doctrine, and prayerful devotedness to the Master and the Master's work for many a year. It is addressed to Milne, and has a singular title, 'Prayer for the dead'; and thus proceeds:

Perth, 1st Oct. 1849. — DEAR BROTHER, — Are we buckling on the
armour of God for this gloomy day? For it is a gloomy day; such a
day as we have not yet had. The prophet's complaint may well be
ours, 'Lord, who hath believed our report?' But, dear brother, why
is it thus with us? Let there be heart-searching here. There is ever a
cause. See Hosea 5:15. What may the offence be? The Lord give us
light to discern it, and grace to acknowledge it! I need not say, as
I have been saying to the other brethren, 'Remember us in Perth.'
Are we not in the very midst of death? But that is a small matter.
The dead are dying, — dying to die. Oh for bowels of compassion
here! I fear we seldom realize what it is to pray for the dead of our
congregation, and to pray for them *as dead*. We feel we can pray for
them when there is some little life among them. But when there is
no life, as it seems to be at present, to pray for them *then*, that is
gospel-like. It is a praying in faith, apart from all fleshly feelings.
Would there were more such prayer! It would be life from the
dead among all our congregations. We look for life, and complain
that there is none. Well; but are we really praying for our people as
having no life? In praying for the dead, we have much need to be
always crying, 'Lord, increase our faith.' It is no easy matter to pray
for the dead of our congregations. There are mountains of unbelief
to be bounded over; and how? The Lord help us to this thing as he
helped the blessed Ezekiel in the valley of dry bones. Ponder this
well; and may the Lord the Spirit, the alone Quickener of dead souls,
be with your spirit and mine, that we may, all of us, be enabled on
Wednesday to *pray for the dead,* as we have never yet done.

We surely do not err in ascribing much of the blessing of these
years to the many 'concerts for prayer' of various kinds, public and
private, composed of lesser or larger circles, which then existed.
The streams that turn the great mill-wheels of our manufactories
have their sources in the far-up, quiet glens of our land; and so the
great motive-power of these times was to be found in the closet or
the prayer-meeting hall, to which faith, not 'lifting up its voice in

the street', retired as into its stronghold, there to set in motion the divine machinery by which the real good was done in the earth.

There was in this something quite different from mere work. The work was the pipe, but the pipe could not fill itself. The best laid system of pipes could not create the water. That must come from another quarter. The men were but the wires, the electricity must come from heaven; and, without it, the most complete array of wires was useless.

Superhuman

In the constant and combined prayer then made, there was the recognition of a motive-power beyond all human agency; something supernatural, without which the most compact organizations were useless. Confidence in this invisible strength is the secret of power to the worker; and when this confidence in the invisible is supplanted by confidence in the visible, then effort becomes a failure; the machine keeps going, but without producing any results beyond motion and noise.

When brought face to face with human evil, we feel our helplessness. It is too great for us. Outward remedies do not reach the seat of the disease. Laws restrain it; walls hide it; prisons silence it; civilisation refines it; education teaches it to keep within bounds. But there it is, notwithstanding all these appliances; its real nature untouched by either magistrate or minister. We are helpless before the evil of 'this present evil world'.

Be it so. We fall back on God. We ask him to energize the word; to clothe the speaker of it with superhuman power; to do the work which he alone can do, and for the doing of which he will be entreated of us. Sword and spear and armour may have been in vain. We have still the sling and the stone.

In reference to this it was that Milne wrote, about this time, to Somerville:

There are some tokens that the Lord is near us, and I labour in more than hope. My heart rejoices and feels confident with the thought of your being with me. I have had no news from the Assembly; but I have been longing that there may be much of the Spirit with the brethren. I preached on Sabbath on Acts 1:8, 14: 'Ye shall receive power, after that the Holy Ghost is come upon you ... These all continued in prayer.' What constitutes the power of the ministry? It is not personal qualification. This they had in a good degree already. They knew the facts of Christ's history; they had understanding in the Old Testament; they had the determination to go on with their work; they had commission or authority; they had a pledge of divine guidance and help, 'Lo, I am with you.' And yet, after all this, 'Ye shall receive POWER.' What? Ability actually to accomplish the ends of the ministry in converting sinners and edifying saints.

What Milne felt so strongly, both at this time and afterwards, was the need of the Holy Spirit for the ministry and the minister, and the certain failure of all work in the Church without him; the uselessness of the best ecclesiastical organizations or congregational machinery, or even pastoral work, apart from the direct divine energy of that mighty Spirit that wrought wonders at Pentecost, and is ready still to work wonders as great in these latter days. 'Wells without water' will furnish no refreshment; and lamps without oil will give out no light. The Church's danger ever has been to substitute a ministry of the intellect for a ministry of the Spirit; to confide in the human instead of the superhuman; and the indication that she is entangled in this snare is the feeling, conscious or unconscious, that she can do with less prayer now than formerly, on account of the progress of the age, — an age which is supposed not to require the supernatural helps that other ages did.

Thus Milne wrote to a friend some years after: 'I suspect that much of the religion you will meet with has more of the flesh than of the spirit; more of self than of Christ; more of the world than of the closet; more of working than what is more humbling — meek, patient, waiting on the Lord.' And at another time he says: 'Perhaps *working* is more dangerous than *waiting*, though both have their snares.'

The stress which he laid on prayer is well shown in the following anecdote, which, though relating to a subsequent period, fits in here. 'We went up the hill', writes he, 'and through the garden. The gardener was working beside the summer-house. I said, "This is a morning to your mind." "Yes", he said; "but oh, sir, there has been frost; the strawberries were white." I said, "You have always a *but*. Have you been praying for a good season?" "I have been doing what I can", said he; "but I know it is not so much as I should." So we went into the summerhouse and prayed.'

Power with God

He undertook nothing without prayer. He never went out or came in without prayer. Whatever he spoke or wrote, it was with prayer. He felt that the greatest favour he could do for a friend was to pray for him. His desire was, as the Perth conferences show, to stir up the Church of God to prayer. He understood more than most of us these words of the prophet (*Hos.* 12:3) — 'He had POWER with God! Yea, he had POWER over the angel; Yea, he prevailed, he wept and made supplication unto him.'

The following letter, written in his later years, will show how he maintained the same spirit of intercession throughout his ministry; that as he had begun, so he went on; going constantly, and exhorting others to go with him to the one fountainhead of blessing, the one source of ministerial strength. It is dated, '*Free St Leonard's Manse, Perth, 22d Feb. 1863.*' It was printed and circulated largely:

MY DEAR FRIEND, — We are arranging, God willing, for a short series of evangelistic meetings in the City Hall here, from Sabbath

8th to Tuesday 17th February inclusive, that is, ten successive nights. We expect to have some of those with us whom God has used and honoured in this kind of work. But our hope is in the Lord himself, who alone can give the increase, and who, we have reason to believe from several indications, is at this time very near at hand. We earnestly solicit your prayers, both before the meetings and during their continuance. Pray that those employed may be endued with power from on high, that they may forget themselves, and care only for the things of Christ. Pray that there may be a wide, deep interest excited, and that many may at this time pass into the kingdom of God. Pray that our town may at this season be blessed, and that, through it, the blessing may spread all around. Look at Ezekiel 34:26. Take hold of the Lord and constrain him. You know that he loves holy, filial boldness and importunity, and complains of the want of it. Think of the preciousness of souls, their imminent danger, the Lord's joy when poor, heavy laden ones come to him. Think of the influence it would have on the whole year, if there were at this time a very marked, decided work of God; and as you think, let your heart burn, let your desires be stirred, and so let fervent, effectual supplication flow forth. — Believe me very affectionately yours, — J. M.

It was *power* that he sought; power with God for the sake of men. He desired *influence;* but it was influence with God, and, as the result of that, influence with the souls of men. Other power and other influence he cared nothing for. 'I think', he says, 'I feel the want of *power* to speak to men as sinners; to convince them of their lost estate. O my Lord, let not my ministry be a useless, ineffectual one! Let me not be the dumb dog that cannot bark.' And again: 'I see that *useful power* in dealing with souls can only be through the Holy Ghost operating upon them. O Peace of our peace, Life of our life, Light of our light, BE WITH ME!'

The Secret of Success

It was thus that these men, in that critical time, waited on God for his Spirit. They kept in mind the Master's words, 'Ye shall be endued with POWER from on high' (*Luke* 24:49); 'ye shall receive POWER, after that the Holy Ghost is come upon you' (*Acts* 1:8).

I find, some years after this, the following prayer in one of Milne's diaries:

> I pray for a far more energetic thankfulness; to be a whole and a continual burnt-offering. Let all false fire die; but let the flame of love, through the Holy Ghost, keep me spending and being spent. Renew my spiritual strength, O Lord … I see some whose heart seems to be right with God, and yet they do not receive much blessing on their work. Perhaps they are not seeking themselves; but are they honouring the Lord by faith? The soul that is lifted up is not upright; it is cleaving to self instead of God; it is trying to rise by building a Babel instead of taking hold of the Almighty. But there is a dishonouring of the Lord by the want of a large, joyful, practical expectation that goes on in his strength, and surely prevails. Moses had not this at the commencement of his enterprise, but got it afterwards. Many seem never to get it, and to drudge on in an unprofitable routine.

It may not be out of place to mention here, though it might have been noticed earlier, that it was by this waiting on God that both Burns and Milne became what they were. Up till the memorable Kilsyth Communion in 1839, Burns had not been remarkable as a preacher. But those who knew him can tell how, like the disciples before Pentecost, he continued in prayer; and so he 'received the power' which was afterwards so striking in his ministry; the power described by a contemporary writer as possessed by old Henry Venn when 'men fell before him like slaked lime.' So was it with Milne. His first sermons showed nothing remarkable. But when the great work began in 1839, he himself was brought under its power; he rose up to another level both in life and service. From that time he started on a new course, in which he held on to the last. Other ministers at such times have been stirred, and then gone back. He never from that day looked back. His whole after life took its tone from the first months of his ministry.

Having felt what it was to be 'revived', he spoke freely to others. At an interview between himself and a brother minister, the latter had expressed himself strongly against 'revivals'. After a kindly talk, they parted with these words from Milne, 'Take heed you don't become an iceberg, fixed and frozen, while others are moving on in the warm Gulf stream.'

Though he had genuine talent, his ministry was not what is called 'intellectual' by those in whose reckoning goodness is identified with weakness, and zealous love treated as the offspring of a 'soft theology', inconsistent with scholarship or manly breadth of mind. He sought to be 'filled with the Spirit', and so to be a man of progress; for, as he wrote afterwards, 'work, success, praise, all seem dry and worthless, IF THE SOUL IS LEAN.'

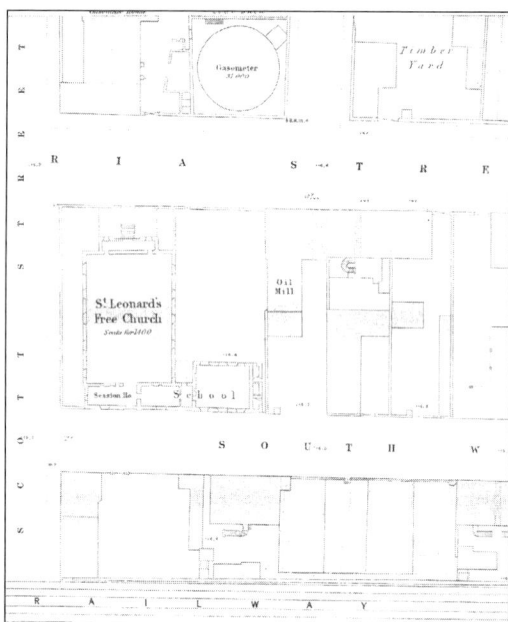

Map showing St Leonard's Free Church and its environs, 1868.

Chapter 8

Various Years —
Evangelistic Tours

For several years the General Assembly set itself in good earnest to do spiritual work for Scotland. Once and again a whole day was set apart for humiliation and prayer. These seasons will never be forgotten, though the number of those who took part in them is diminishing fast. Our children ought to hear of them, and our children's children. 'Ecclesiastical' work was not neglected; but it took its lower and more becoming place. 'WE DID run well; who did hinder us?'

In the memorable Assembly of 1844, after Dr Charles J. Brown's admirable sermon on Tuesday the 17th, and the interesting conversation that ensued, the following motion was unanimously agreed to: 'The General Assembly being deeply impressed, as in the sight of God, with a sense of the sins and shortcomings of the ministers and elders of the Church in their holy callings, and recognising the voice of the Great Head of the Church in his providential dealings with her, and in the Spirit which he has been pouring out upon her, whereby he has been pleased to awaken some measure of concern as regards the past and present fruits of the ministry, as well as longing prayers for the revival of vital godliness in the Church and land, do desire, with profound humiliation, and in reliance on the great strength of Almighty God, solemnly to devote, dedicate, and consecrate anew themselves and their fellow-labourers to the service of God, and his holy purpose of glorifying his great name, in saving souls through the preaching of the truth, and the operation of the Holy Ghost.'

At that time, not an hour, or two hours, but a whole day, nay, two days, were gladly given to this solemn employment. It was in reference to this that Chalmers made the statement, now I fear forgotten, but which, especially as coming from him, ought to be pondered by the Church: 'I was not fully aware of the arrangements of this day, else it might have been altogether spent in accordance with the nature and spirit of the exercises we have now engaged in, that is to say, *altogether sabbatically.* Instead of which I had to pass, by instant transition, from the labours of a committee, engaged in important, no doubt, but still outward business, to the more sacred and spiritual services of the house of God. What a change! What an enlargement! What a felt and immediate translation! As if one had entered into a new country and a new climate, when I came within the precincts of this house of prayer, and breathed its hallowing atmosphere, and joined in its saintly devotions. Let us make it our unceasing endeavour, and cherish it as our fondest hope, that all our external arrangements may be so soon settled and set by, that so the ministers of God may be set free for giving themselves wholly to prayer and the ministry of the word. Oh may the delightful spirit of this meeting wax stronger and stronger amongst us, and be sent forth from our Assembly, as a centre, throughout the Church and throughout the land!'[1]

How far we have fulfilled our vows, it is not here needful to say. Many of our best men have feared that we have come short, and that subsequent years exhibit no reaping worthy of the sowing. 'We

---

[1] See 'Report of the whole Proceedings of the late General Assembly of the Free Church of Scotland, relative to the State of Religion in the Land; with introductory remarks by the Rev. A. Moody Stuart.' Edinburgh, 1844.

have not wrought any deliverance in the earth', have been words often on the lips of brethren who love our Church both wisely and well.

Peculiar Times

Milne seems to have had some thought, both then and afterwards, that the times were peculiar, needing no ordinary faith and grace to enable us, not simply to advance, but even to hold our ground. Thus he writes to Somerville: 'If I mistake not, we are approaching a new era. Common grace will not suffice, for we seem about to enter on new and troublesome times. I fear few of us are willing to believe, or at least to realize this. We like to be quiet and to be let alone, like the Kenite, in our islet nest. But this, I fear, is impossible. When the Lord's time is come, who can stay his hand? Perhaps the Lord is taking you aside to rest awhile before the battle is joined. May it be Tabor and Patmos.'

But it was needful to work for God, as well as to wait upon him. To the *work,* then, the Assembly addressed itself! Selecting those who were deemed fittest for evangelistic service, the Church sent them abroad over the land into the different places considered most needful and populous. Summer after summer these men went out into the towns and villages; some to the southern borders, and some to the *Ultima Thule* of Scotland, — the Shetland Isles; some to the agricultural regions, and some to the mining districts; so that all the needy parts of the land might, as much as possible, be penetrated by this peculiar and stimulating agency. The fruit of these summer evangelistic excursions has not been small. Much of the awakening that has been manifested in different places may be traced to these as the beginning.

Among these summer evangelists was Milne. He was eager for the work. It was quite according to his mind. He threw himself heartily into it, as he had before thrown himself into similar work in Newcastle and the neighbourhood, along with myself and one or two others. 'I am happy', he writes to Somerville, 'you have included me among the evangelists. I should have been sorry if I had shut myself out from such work.'[1]

Evangelistic Tours

Milne's report of his evangelistic tour we shall have to cite in a little. But in a note to Somerville he gives the following sketch of one of these gospel journeys: — 'In answer to your queries, the places where I was were Airdrie, Holytown, and Coatbridge, preaching in and round about. I began on Tuesday, 28th July, and ended on Tuesday, 25th August; being, I think, twenty-nine days. I preached, I find, forty-one times, — twelve of these in church, four or five in schoolhouses, *etc.*, and the rest in the open air.' In another note to the same, he writes of another tour: — 'I feel for that district. I think while there I entered into the expression of the Saviour, "he had compassion on the multitudes." I left my people in good heart, because of all they enjoyed at the Communion. They seem to have been exceedingly strengthened and refreshed. I wish you would interest the committee in the Upper Ward of Lanark. It is so near that it is a shame to overlook it. I am happy that I went out for a short time this summer.'

The Airdrie District 1846

His first gospel tour was in 1846, to what he calls 'the Airdrie district'; and his report of it (dated August 28th) is as follows:

Having just got home, after being a little more than a month out, according to desire I write you a few words about my movements in the

---

[1] From this letter I quote the following sentence, in reference to the events of the day: 'I preached yesterday forenoon, in connection with Dr Chalmers' death, on Matthew 24:44. I felt impressed, and so seemed the people. I have a letter today from William Burns, after putting his things on board. He seems soft and humble; and it tugs my heart-strings to think that we may never meet again on earth.'

Airdrie district. I am not sure that you are acquainted with this quarter of the country, though it is so near you. It is situated in the parishes of Old and New Monkland, and the highway between Edinburgh and Glasgow passes through the heart of Airdrie and Coatbridge. Some thirty years ago, or less, these two places were mere villages on the road-side (occupied by handloom weavers), and a few coal pits. It was found, however, that one of the richest beds of ironstone in the country is in this neighbourhood; and this discovery, combined with the unprecedented demand for iron arising from the introduction of railways, and the application of iron to a variety of new uses, has caused a most rapid and surprising change upon the neighbourhood.

The value of property has increased amazingly, not on account of the surface, but what is beneath. For instance, one estate, which a while ago yielded only a few hundred pounds a year for agricultural purposes, now yields annual rental of £23,000 and more. The feuars sell the iron and coal under their houses and kail-yards, and the church managers sell the minerals under their churches and churchyards, and the magistrates sell the underminings of their streets and squares. In short, the good folks seem to think, speak, and, I presume, dream, of undiscovered *El-Dorados* of ironstone. Don't think all this irrelevant, for I suspect this is the wealthiest rural district we have, and, if well wrought, would yield the sinews of war.

The country has a barren, ill-cultivated appearance, covered with coal and iron mines; each with its machinery, smoking chimney, and railway for the conveyance of the products of the pit. The country is literally cut up with railways. These miners constitute a large portion of the population. They are peculiar in their character and habits. They begin work about four o'clock in the morning, and end, according to their assiduity and skill, about twelve, one, two, three, or four o'clock. I have spoken with many of them coming home from their work in crowds at all these hours. The rest of the day is their own, and is spent in lounging about, and very commonly in playing cards. You see them in large groups, old and young; the old with full-sized, and the juveniles with small packs of cards, about half the size of one's finger.

I called them the Devil's Bible, which they took in good part, and often left their amusement to come and hear sermon … These miners are almost, without exception, joined in an extensive and well-consolidated confederacy. I met it in all directions, and the management of it seems greatly to occupy their attention. The object is to protect themselves from what they call the tyranny of the masters, whom I think they very unjustly suspect. The effect seems to be every way injurious to good order and regular industrious working. They earn every man 5s. a day, the boys from 2s. to 5s. They strike me as in a very low state, both morally and spiritually. They seem unsocial, working *so* much in the dark, and usually with only a single companion. They do not seem to spend their leisure time in reading. I remarked that it was rare to see old men among them; and, on inquiry, found that if they were not cut off by some of the many perils to which they are exposed, yet their life is generally shortened by asthma, *etc.* I went down one of the pits, that I might be able to speak experimentally.

Another feature of the district is the large iron-works for melting the ironstone, called furnaces; and the malleable ironworks for refining and preparing it for various purposes — railways, wheels, *etc.* These are very numerous and extensive around Coatbridge, Holytown, *etc.* In connection with some of these, there are two or three thousand men engaged in the various operations. They are many of them English, and some Welsh; the Scotch and Irish not being skilled in this kind of work. They earn very large wages — 6s., or 7s., or 8s., and more a day. Many of these men work on Sabbath as well as the week-day — the furnaces being kept at work unceasingly night and day, in utter contempt of the requirements of body and soul, and the commands of God's law. These men live in good two-storied houses, very neat and comfortable, and seem, as far as the animal is concerned, to fare well.

I visited two of the largest of these works, the one in daylight, and the other late at night, after preaching, and was very much interested by the huge machinery, the order and regularity, the crowds of half-naked, perspiring men, and the bright lurid flames which blazed in all directions.

The population of the small district which I visited is 70,000 or upwards, not gathered together as in the older part of Glasgow, but scattered over the space of two or three miles; not consisting of the poor and wretched, who, if they have the will, have not the means of debauchery, but consisting of the young and active, earning large wages, free from all control, and having abundance of time at their command. I feel that one cannot overstate the importance of this district, or the necessity there is for our Church dealing energetically with it.

The way in which I sought to be useful was preaching in the open air once a day, and latterly always twice; preaching in the afternoon in the neighbourhood, and then going to the heart of Coatbridge, where there was always an immense concourse of people, and preaching there at seven o'clock in a kind of open space. In going about I distributed tracts, and got into conversation with the people as I went along. I never have had such an opportunity of making proof to the very full of my ministry, and I certainly never spent such a happy month. I lived two weeks in Mr Jackson's house, one week in Mr Jaffrey's, and another in Mr Connel's; being made, by their kindness and hospitality, to feel completely at home, and bringing away with me an abiding and refreshing remembrance of our Christian intercourse. I have reason to believe that the visit has not been without beneficial results in various ways.

I have suggested to the brethren to seek occasional help from you and some of the other Glasgow brethren, which I trust you will give them; also the getting savings banks set on foot, and extended to the various localities and large works. A committee was formed, and they are to commence *arrangements* this week; also that the few brethren who are locally near one another, and have to deal with the same difficulties, should meet occasionally for prayer and conference. I have also written to Mr Bridges to get a cheap edition prepared of a narrative called *Light in Darkness*, which I think peculiarly fitted to be useful to the colliers, *etc.* he has written me that they are to prepare 'a miner's edition of it', and the brethren and other friends have engaged to get it widely circulated.

I preached also one night in Shotts parish, and, ere we left, arrangements were made with the prospect of forming a Free Church congregation in this important and necessitous district. A strong committee was formed on the spot, and I think the thing will go on prosperously.

One other suggestion is, the getting up of good Free Church schools. There is not one yet in the district. In connection with all the large ironworks there is a school for the children of the work-people; but they are the most miserable and inefficient that it is possible to conceive. If each of our congregations had a good school in connection with it, it would be a mighty help to its prosperity, and an unspeakable boon to the district.

I owe the deepest obligation to our brethren, Messrs Jackson, Jaffrey, Connel, and Lawson, who gave up their time and comfort to accompany me in moving about, and in concurring to make the visit useful. I find that their services among my people have been much appreciated.

See what a long epistle I have written! But I cannot express the strong feeling I have of the importance of this district, of the good it may yield if prosperously worked, and the evil it will do if neglected. All kinds of evil are festering here: false doctrine, profligacy, ungodliness, and reckless trampling under foot of God's day. It is an eating sore, and spreading too.

Will you give it your consideration, and make it known to others who may help? I feel thankful for having had this opportunity of teaching and learning, for I have been both an instructor and a scholar.

Lanarkshire 1847

His second tour was in 1847; and from his report (dated 19th August) the following extracts are given:

I then preached at Carmichael. It rained very heavily, but I found a good many people gathered together, and standing under a few trees at the side of the Carlisle highway. I stood upon a little hillock of earth while I preached, and was so pleased with the appearance of the people, that I determined to have another meeting. I accordingly preached in the same place last Sabbath night, and had a large congregation. There were some of the large farmers with their families, and I have no doubt that we might have, and *ought* to have here a strong and prosperous rural congregation. We *must* do something for this district. The people look to us. They are literally perishing for lack of knowledge; and I never was so struck with the needfulness and value of the Disruption movements, as from what I saw here and elsewhere in this country.

South-east from Carnwath is another cluster of Moderate parishes, *Dunsyre, Delphinton,* and *Walston.* I had meetings in all the three. In Walston there is a small Free Church at a little hamlet, Ellsridgehill. It is well set down to rake the *three* parishes as well as the parish of *Biggar,* which adjoins it on the south. It is a miserable place, however, a small Old Light chapel, which the Free Biggar Presbytery have got somehow possession of. They cannot get a site for a manse, else they have the means of building a small one. There are several men who have bits of land in and round the hamlet. I spent nearly two hours in trying to get one of them to give a site, but in vain. Something *must* be done for this place. Either it will have to be given up, or else it must be strengthened, and put upon a right footing, for it would be inhuman to leave one of our ministers in such circumstances. I preached in the small chapel. Also at Dunsyre. Here Mr Patteson has a meeting once a fortnight. Also at Dolphinton. I found the people standing in the open air, amid the rain. We went to one farm, but could not get admission. We went to another, and took possession of the barn. At the end, I asked if the farmer was present. He came forward. I asked if he would give his barn again, and he said he would. Mr Patteson, who was with me, then said that he had long desired to hold meetings in Dolphinton, but had never been able to get a place; but that now the door seemed opened. We fixed that he should go there next Sabbath night, which he accordingly did; and there will henceforth be, I trust, a regular station in Dolphinton.

It was late when we arrived at Abington, about 11 o'clock. We found the inn completely pre-occupied. It is far superior to what one meets with in such a place, having been built by Sir Edward Colebrooke, the chief proprietor in this county, as a residence for his friends, when they come down to shoot. This, unhappily for us, was the evening of the 12th of August, and the house was full. After a time, however, some one, I suppose, had agreed to sleep with a companion, and give us their bed, and so we got housed. Abington is a considerable village. I went to the school and spoke a little to the children, and gave each a tract to take home. This village would be the place for a Free Church for the district, as soon as things are ripe for it. It is of considerable size, situated on the Carlisle road, having the village of Roberton about four miles from it on one side, and the village of Crawford about four miles on the other, and all these having the Carlisle road running through them.

Then, about four miles off, among the hills, is the village of Crawfordjohn, where the parish church and school are. We now crossed the hills to this sequestered village of Crawfordjohn. There were two small public-houses in the place, but neither of them seemed willing to take us in. One of them agreed to give us tea, but would on no account accommodate us for the night. I found there are a few persons who go over occasionally to Douglas, to Mr Jaffrey. One of these is a small farmer named Watson, adjoining the village. I found in one of his fields a few boards nailed together for a minister to stand upon while preaching; and sermon is given here occasionally by Mr Jaffrey, Douglas; Mr Parker, Lesmahagow, *etc*. It was a beautiful evening, and the people were very busy with their hay. The meeting, therefore, was not large. What struck me was that the men and women were all dressed in their best clothes. They spread their plaids on the grass and sat down. A few people came out of the village in their working dress; but they would not come forward and join the little congregation, but stood behind a stone wall.

At the end of the meeting it was beginning to grow dark. I intended to go to Crawford, which is about seven miles off, but found that it would be impossible to find the way at night among the hills. So we set out for Roberton, which is about the same distance, and got there very late. The people were gone to bed, but, after some delay, rose and admitted us. It was a wretched place; but we were glad to get under cover, and passed the night as we best could without putting off our clothes. In the morning we left early, and walked along the Caledonian Railway, speaking with the workmen, and giving them tracts. I asked one of the engineers to explain something to me, which he very civilly did. In speaking, he said something about erecting a bridge over the Danube at Pesth in Hungary. I said, 'Did you know Dr Duncan', *etc* ? His face immediately brightened. He had known the Doctor most intimately, and insisted upon our going with him to see his wife, who had seen much of Mrs Duncan at Pesth. After a long walk we got to Culter Manse, and so ended our journeying, as a gig met us there and took us on to Carnwath.

I am ashamed of this long rambling detail, but am anxious that attention should be drawn to this large and most *destitute* and hitherto neglected district. It will soon be the chief thoroughfare between England and Scotland. It is a great privilege to be permitted to cast the net in places not gospel-beaten.

Let me bring also before you the state of the vast district contained in the parishes Roberton, Crawfordjohn, and Crawford. Scarcely anything has yet been done for them. I should have liked to spend a week here, but you know I have been providentially tied up by family circumstances. In conclusion, I feel, perhaps, more satisfaction in looking back on this service, than perhaps on anything else of the kind in which I have been engaged. I have enjoyed unvaried liberty, and often a good deal of affection in preaching and speaking with the people. They seemed also much solemnized and affected, and I have a strong and thankful conviction that good has been done. There was a good deal of labour in travelling about, and a good deal of exposure from wet, cold nights; but I am better in health and spirits than when I set out. The instrument has not been blunted, but sharpened, and I look forward with hopefulness to my winter home work.

Enduring Hardness

We fear that in these days he did too much. Pastoral, ministerial, and evangelistic work were not meant for one single man. For each of these Milne was admirably fitted, and for each of them he had a fervent and irrepressible desire. He excelled in all of them; and he delighted in them. He loved his work and his Master so well that he would take no holiday. But on looking back on these times, and judging himself in the light of wiser, though not less fervent years, he was not unwilling to admit that he had erred somewhat in denying himself all relaxation, as if his frame could never wear out. 'I feel', he writes in 1859, 'that I am suffering the retribution, the *nemesis* of former years, of unresting, unrelaxing labour; the regular home work without any weekly rest; and then, when summer came, instead of the yearly relaxation, itinerancies of exciting and threefold labour. There was real folly in all this. It was just as it were saying, 'A short life and a merry one'; and yet in the end one finds that there comes a season, neither short nor merry, when the physical, intellectual, emotional, and spiritual all seem expended and worn out, and the unhappy individual becomes a trial and a burden to himself and others.

There is in this a warning to ministers, and a lesson to the people. No man can bear the strain of constant work during the twelve months of the year without a month's rest at least, any more than he can get through the twenty-four hours of the day without the appointed sleep. An over-wrought minister will soon be like an over-wrought workman; he will do inferior work, and in the end he will do no work at all. Our Lord surely taught us this when he said to his disciples, 'Come ye apart into a desert place and rest awhile.' Hence, in May 1847, Milne writes to Somerville, declining work, though he undertook it afterwards in part:

I now fear that it would not be right in me to undertake a month of the kind of work I had last year. I should get through it, I trust, but

I fear it would unfit me for vigorous working among my own people during the winter. I suspect my illness last November arose from getting jaded in the west, and then coming home and attempting for a while to work very hard, making up the leeway of neglected visitation during my absence.

Yet, certainly, it is better to wear out than to rust out. And while the tendency of some, like Milne, is to do too much, perhaps the tendency of the majority is to do too little, both in the way of study and of work.

Eagerness for Work

The first six years after the Disruption were memorable years in many respects; and not least for the amount of evangelistic work done throughout the land. The men who went out to preach felt as Whitefield did when he said, 'I am hunting for lost sinners in these ungospelized wilds'; or when, returning from an evangelistic tour, he exclaimed, 'Another inroad into Satan's kingdom!' and they did not lose their reward. They wore themselves out, perhaps; they were not willing to yield to what some called a prudent regard to health, accounting it a plea for self-indulgence, an excuse for the love of ease; but they did a work which has not been like the morning cloud or the early dew.

During these years he knew no holiday. He, like Robert M'Cheyne, made it a rule never to refuse an invitation to preach, unless unable or pre-engaged. And in these evangelistic excursions he was, as he said, like a pirate on the seas, or a moss-trooper on the moors, eager in pursuit of prey; so that sometimes, he feared, there was as much of the flesh as of the spirit in the eagerness to lay hold of souls, and bear them back as his prize.[1]

[1] What he wrote at a subsequent time may be quoted here in reference to his work in these years: 'I long to learn how I may reach the hearts and consciences of those around me, how to bring the religious spiritual element to bear upon them.' And again he writes: 'I am sure that a living, holy, consistent, earnest, prayerful man must be useful wherever he goes.'

To these summer labours he ascribes, in part, the very severe illness which he had in November 1846. It came on quite suddenly one Sabbath morning with an attack of unconsciousness, from which he did not recover for some time. The most prompt and severe remedies were used; but for a while his recovery was uncertain. It pleased God, however, to answer his people's prayers, and to restore him.

On one of the Sabbaths during which he was laid aside, Moody Stuart preached for him, and through him he sent the following message to his people:

DEAR MOODY, — I avail myself of your kind offer to put my beloved people a little in possession of my experience at this crisis. Say to them that I feel that I belong to them, and that in my affliction they are afflicted; that what I have seen and heard of their sympathy with me has very greatly endeared them; and that, if spared again to go in and out, I trust they will see that the tie between us is deeper, stronger, tenderer than before.

Say to them that, doubtless in answer to their prayers, I am wonderfully acquiescent in this humbling, awakening dispensation; that I am even in some measure thankful and joyful, seeing much of the Lord's goodness in the nature of it, the timing of it, and the measure of it.

Say to them that I am very rapidly recovering, and that I am permitted by my medical friends to say that, if all progresses as heretofore, I shall be worshipping with them next Sabbath, and perhaps taking part in the services of the sanctuary.

Say to them that many things concur to make me feel that the Lord has something yet to do both with them and me. Last Sabbath was the first Sabbath of my eighth year among them. I had finished the seventh, and was without any particular thought going to begin the eighth. But how was it begun? In being prostrated by a stroke, and stripped at once of all that my foolish heart has too often, I fear, made a ground of glorying before God, and of conceit towards man.

What thanks I owe to my gracious Saviour for casting me into such a furnace, ere I began the second stage of my ministry! What thanks I owe him for making me what I am, a broken, emptied worm, having nothing now to hinder me from taking up his yoke and learning of him! Dear brother, my heart is full and soft tonight, but strength is not commensurate. The Lord be with you and with our flocks. — Believe me, very affectionately yours, JOHN MILNE.

Thoughts in Trial

He also wrote in November 1846 to her who had just promised to become his wife:

I see clearly the Lord's hand in this affliction, and feel that in much loving-kindness he has done it. My ministerial life has been a constant moving, — toil, anxiety, temptation without a moment's intermission, and without a loving, sympathizing heart to bear a share of the burden, and soothe under it. Oh, how truly the devil has often bestridden me and spurred me on! I see a new era opening, and am full of hope. It *is* a little trying for me at present to be eating, drinking, sleeping, with nothing to do, no preparation for Sabbath; but I feel more for you than myself. It is a strange beginning for you, dear R.; yet I do trust it is sowing in tears to reap in joy, it is laying the unsightly foundation of a goodly and happy superstructure.

On December 3d of this year (1846) he thus wrote to Somerville:

I am fast recovering, though not going about yet. I *do* hope that I have got permanent good, and that I shall not forget or lose the teaching of my Lord … I have hope that the Lord will so show us the worthiness of his Son that we shall ask, expect, and receive greater things than we have yet known. I feel as if I had been an idler. We should try to keep up continuity of grace. Our good frames are usually like springtides, that swell high and then speedily shrink back, leaving our deformity and feebleness to appear. Would that, having received Christ Jesus, we could walk in him, not after the flesh, but after the Spirit. I am interested by what you say of next Sabbath being the first of your tenth year. May it prove to you a blessed day! On the first Sabbath of my eighth year I was thrown into the furnace.

And about the same time he writes to Collace:

The Lord makes me a little happy. Existence seems a blessing; for the new way is ever open *even to me;* and the Lord is willing that I should follow and serve him.

Through much tribulation he was to enter the kingdom of heaven. The billows which, in their approach, threatened to submerge him, as they came on, lifted him up to the heaven he was bound for.

St Leonard's Bank, Perth as it is today. It appears that after residing with the M'Naughton family at 14 Rose Terrace for some time, a house in 'Leonard Bank', with a beautiful outlook over the South Inch, was provided as a home for the St Leonard's Free Church minister, perhaps not long after his marriage to Robina Stuart of Annat Lodge, Perth, in 1847.

Chapter 9

1847–1853
Marriage and Family Sorrows

On the 26th of January 1847, Milne was married to Robina, second daughter of Kenneth Stuart, Esq. of Annat and Rait. It was truly a union in the Lord, and the source, for a few brief years, of much joy and blessing to him.[1] Yet it was through this that his heaviest trials came to him, fitting him for larger usefulness, and giving a new direction to his ministry. The joy was turned into sorrow; and again the sorrow was turned into joy. 'He leadeth the blind by a way that they knew not', was a text often upon his lips and in his letters. He had tested it himself, and found it true.

Life and Death

The following entries in his family Bible give us the touching outline of his private history, at this time, from his own pen: 'Robina

---

[1] Immediately before his marriage, he thus writes to Somerville: 'I have given orders about banns today, and was offered a reading of the marriage-contract; but as it looked a little long, I did not choose to be troubled with it. I suppose the only thing now is to get a ring. Care is now and then peeping in at the door; but hitherto I have been enabled to thrust the intruder out, and shut the door in his face. But I feel a little tremulous. It seems like a flood that has not yet got through the barrier, but may rise higher, and prove irresistible. May we be kept by the mighty power! What weak, wretched things we are! I almost tremble when I look at the abysses of my nonentity, or rather perversity. But Jehovah is real, and Jehovah is right.' And again, after his severe illness at this time: — 'It is not easy to pay the vows which we have made in trouble. Hezekiah is a startling beacon. The first idea when I awoke to consciousness was, "I am now Jacob, and shall go halting all my days"; and then, "I will make worm Jacob a sharp thrashing instrument."'

Stuart, born at Annat Lodge, Perth, 23d April 1823; married at Annat Lodge, 26th January 1847. Jessie Marie Milne, born at Annat Lodge, 5th August 1848. Robert John Milne, born at Leonard Bank, 12th June 1851. — Robina Milne died at Leonard Bank, on Sabbath, 15th June 1851, in the full blessed view and experience of her gracious Lord and Redeemer. Robert John died 19th August 1852, at Annat Lodge, where Jessie Maria also died. So that mother and children are now before the throne. The Lord setteth the solitary in families, and he makes solitary again. Blessed be his name. "Better to have loved and lost, than never to have loved at all.'"

Among Milne's papers there is a beautiful piece of poetry by a friend, to which Milne appends the following note:

August 21st, 1852. — Written on the funeral day of my little boy, Robert John, who died a few days after the birth of Mrs O.'s infant son. She had very lately seen my little boy, and felt much interest in him.

> 'In these few last summer days,
>   Each of us a child hath given;
> I to tread life's thorny ways,
>   Thou to swell the ranks of heaven.
> Into sin is born *my* boy,
> *Thine* to everlasting joy.
>
> *Mine* a feeble, trembling thing,
>   Scarce his dazzled lid unfolds;
> *Thine* before the Almighty King
>   Constantly his face beholds.
> *Mine* doth wail with fear and pain,
> *Thine* can never weep again.
>
> On *my* infant's baby brow
>   Shades of future errors press;
> *Thine,* beside his Saviour now,
>   Wears the robe of righteousness.
> *Mine* will sin ere he can die,
> *Thine* is purified for aye.

Ah! I hold thee blest in this,
   Who, in spite of grief, can say,
"Lord, it was Thy greeting kiss
   Gently drew my babes away —
Love to them, not wrath to me;
Are they not at home with Thee?"

Pray for me, bereaved friend,
   That when death my children claims,
Like *thy* babes may be their end,
   Without blot upon their names,
Writ in the Redeemer's scrolls,
On the lists of ransomed souls.'

Sunshine

One or two brief extracts from letters during these few happy years will give us a glimpse of the brightness of his married life. They show how little of the morbid there was in him; how thoroughly he enjoyed every good and fair thing about him; how much of the cheerful, the childlike, the playful, and the poetic, there was in his constitution. He writes,

Every day and everything is good, if we take it and use it aright. On Wednesday, I actually enjoyed it. The mists hanging like soft down upon the mountains; hundreds of white hoary streamlets rushing down the hill-sides, the little burnies crossing the road, and glistering out of sight, like little serpents winding away; and then a sheep breaking away from a drove, and thinking it needful to run before the gig, till, being fairly wearied, it jumped aside, and, as we passed, turned up a look of expressive intelligence, as much as to say, 'Haven't I done a clever thing?' And the curlew, and the hawk, and the pee-weet, playing its little maternal tricks to draw us away from its nest; then a word or two with driver, and getting him to sing a psalm; and thoughts now and then of better things; — altogether, one may be worse off than in an open gig, on a cold, down-pouring morning, going through a Highland glen.

Again he writes:

I send you Mary's note, which is very good. I begin to think the Follies are not *a* bad race. There's Mary S — , and Mary S — , and Mary M —. And then there was Mary the mother of Jesus, and Mary Magdalene, and dear Mary of Bethany. But yet Mary is not to ride the water in; for there was Queen Mary, and Bloody Mary, and Mary of Guise.

Then, again, he writes:

I have been very idle today, and am not pleased with myself. But in such moods I try to be pleased with Christ. I am willing to be the black cloud that shall make his righteousness appear in most marked relief. What poor unprofitable things we are, and yet the Lord thinketh upon us!

He was a very happy man, notwithstanding his occasional moods of depression. For as sunshine is the characteristic of summer days, though many a cloud darkens its June and July; so joy was a true feature of his character, though he was sometimes troubled in spirit. Thus, for instance, he would once and again speak out: 'I am brimful of happiness, my earthly cup is running over … We cannot expect such happiness always to last.' At one of his last communions he said that 'Christians should go through the world singing the 103d Psalm.' he thus writes, about this time, to Somerville:

I feel the lapse of time quickening, and begin, I think, a *little* oftener to look across the bourne, and wish that 'present or absent I may be accepted.' What is our busiest work if we are not accepted in it? his favour is life. As time passes, also, I think I am happier. I don't know that I ever was more so than during the last six or seven months. Is this your experience? Does it not sometimes strike you that our hearts ought to be far more lifted up in the ways of the Lord? he is such a Master, and we are so unworthy.

Again, to the same, Jan. 21, 1851:

I was at Collace yesterday, at a little meeting of brethren, which we found refreshing. Andrew is to bring in your eastern gatherings, and I shall bring them on Saturday. You will not object to their paying toll by the way. The little fox seems to have been an object of deep interest, and compensated for the absence of the venerable Tabby. Either the appearance of the creature, or Andrew's showing off, seems amazingly to have wrought upon the natives of Collace. Andrew, when he saw what a hit he had made, carried Reynard with him next day to St Cyrus, where, with Dr Keith, his son, *etc.*, we had a large meeting of old and young; and where the little fox was as great a favourite as at home. When he sat down, the old Doctor whispered into his ear, 'Being crafty, he caught them with guile.' On Thursday evening we are to have a similar meeting of old and young here, to follow up your Monday evenings, which seems really to have interested and instructed rich and poor. So your goods and chattels are not lying idle, but laid out at usury, without hurt to them ... Oh that I might be more pure, more fervent, more consistent! I think I should like to get at the hidden manna, the living water, the Incarnate God! Strange that we can labour after that which is not bread, and neglect the true substance. But the flesh cannot rise above the dust. Oh that he may quicken us according to his word! What answer do you give to this question, 'By whom shall Jacob arise?' A departed friend, when leaving one part of the field, was gladdened when he saw another coming after him with a sharp, sharp sickle. The whole world is guilty before God, — a world of criminals, a world of the condemned, — the far greater part ignorant, heedless of their condition. How can we forget or overlook this?

For a short period after his marriage his life was bright, and his work in Perth went on with unbroken vigour.

Family Breaches

The first breach in his family was by the death of Jessie Maria in 1849, about eight months old. In a letter to his wife some time afterwards, he thus gives vent to his feelings respecting this sorrow:

> There is not a day I don't think of our poor little totty. One still thinks of her as the little smiling thing, though she has far outstripped us already in knowledge and goodness. I don't *regret* her death. The feeling is rather a pleasant thankfulness for her, and an occasional longing to fondle her again. But I think we should so love the Lord that we should be well pleased with all his ways. I see nothing really good now, but to love the Lord, and then all that is his, and then to mourn over what has gone astray and lost his friendship, likeness, and love. I quite feel that a heart loving the Lord is a right and happy heart. The creature is hurtful and ruinous while we are immersed in it, and lie under it, but good when we get above it, for then we look down and love it, and seek its good for its Creator's sake.

The death of this little one was a sore and lasting grief, so that, ten years after, when reading aloud of the death of a little child, he became so affected, that the individual to whom he was reading had to stop him, and gently withdraw the book.

In the introduction to a brief record of his wife's deathbed experience, which was one full of joy and light, he thus writes concerning her: 'Those who knew her are aware how meek, gentle, and loving she was, yet the Lord's dealings with her for years were those of the Refiner and Purifier.' And truly, during the four and half years of their married life, they were scarcely ever out of the furnace. Sickness and bereavement marked nearly the whole course of these years, and then one was taken and the other left. The little boy survived his mother for about a year, and then he, too, was removed. The husband and father was again alone. It was then that his thoughts turned to India.

Faith and Patience

There are one or two letters, illustrative of his state of feeling at this period of trial, which may be quoted here. He writes to Bonar:

> MY DEAR ANDREW, — I write one word. You know that word — 'Ye shall be scattered, every one to his own, and shall leave me alone, and yet I am not alone.' I got this a few days ago, and now it is fulfilling. They are *all* away, and baby with them, to Annat Lodge, and I am left for a little with empty house and empty heart. Poor Naomi! I know what she felt. I was full and am empty. Yet I love my Lord. He has been unspeakably kind and overwhelmingly gracious. I cannot for a moment think the shadow of a thought that he has dealt hardly. Satan has sometimes tried to make me think it, and been saying, how few there are that suffer as you are doing; but he does not get leave to make me draw any conclusion that can darken the wondrous loving-kindness of the Lord. I see that nature must be in the grave, and the flesh upon the cross, and 'the spirit life because of righteousness'. — Your very affectionate brother, JOHN MILNE.

Here is another, to the same, without an exact date, but, from the nature of its contents, about the same time:

> MY VERY DEAR BROTHER, — I was favoured with your kind and welcome note, and desire to reciprocate your brotherly love. You know how much I value it, and thank the Lord for it. What will heaven be, where those who love will never part! I wonder how completely I have been kept in peace, and free from all reflection and unkindness, during this affair of Mr Anderson.[1] On Saturday morning, at breakfast, I got the *Guardian* from A. Somerville, and I was rather annoyed, only, however, because I find he speaks of what he 'saw and heard in my house'. As long as he kept to myself, I really did not care; but this

---

[1] Jonathan Anderson of Glasgow, who had attacked Milne and his preaching. His case came afterwards before the Presbytery of Glasgow and the General Assembly. There are several allusions to the case in M.'s letters; all of them kindly and charitable. But we cannot enter into details.

seems to criminate another dearer than myself … But we must not be overcome of evil, and I only feel pity and regret that he is ruining himself. It was evening on Saturday before I could set myself rightly to prepare, but I was helped; and on Sabbath I must own that our Lord was gracious. Thanks for your 'Mercy of eternity'. Take another in return. You know the children's lines —

> On, then, to glory run,
> Be a crown and kingdom won.

One night last week I lay down, weary and rather discouraged, when these words came into my mind with a strange, peculiar bright reality or glory, which made me start up ere I was aware, and be for a little peripatetic. Yesterday afternoon, in reading in church Acts 22, Paul's defence, the thought struck me, at verses 17-21, that the proximate reason of Paul's want of success among his countrymen was, that he trusted too much in his apparent qualifications for the work. Like Melancthon in his young zeal, he thought nothing could stand before him. 'Everybody will feel that must have been no light matter that has made me thus turn round; who so fit to be a Jewish missionary?' And so he wonders and almost complains of his vain labour. But — go, go. Is this a libel? Last night, in reading Job 39:14-16, I thought I got a blow under the fifth rib; but you know it was from a friendly hand.

He writes to Mr Flockhart, one of his elders:

I feel sad and fearful when, for a moment, the future gets into my mind. Hitherto a vivid sense of the eternal world, and of my glorified one's joy, has been uppermost in my mind; but ever and anon that verse is coming into my mind, 'Ye shall be scattered, every one to his own, and shall leave me alone.' Pray that I may be enabled to add what follows. I feel that the Lord has been very kind in so wondrously crowning his work of sanctification, and in giving us to see it. What a value she set upon your prayers! With what interest she inquired and heard about the Tuesday evening supplications, and what a quiet rest she seemed to feel when told about the feeling there was of the Lord's presence on the Wednesday night, just before the Lord interposed in her behalf! Will you kindly remember me to all the brethren? I feel a shrinking from much meeting, but it will pass by. You will arrange for the meeting tomorrow night. Oh, what a cause of thankfulness it would be if what has emptied my house and heart helped to fill heaven, and to fulfil Christ's joy!

Gifts and Sympathies

To the same he writes:

I was much surprised and affected by your inclosure, which I received last night. I desire to see much of the love of God and man in this most unlooked-for yet considerate and seasonable kindness. Will you find means of expressing to my friends the thankfulness and affection which I feel? They have rejoiced with me in my joy, and grieved with me in my sorrow, and ministered to me in times of difficulty; and I do trust that these are only the indications of a union which will outlive this passing world. I feel some regret that they should have put so large a sum at my disposal; but their abundant care for me will, through grace, make me more instant in prayer for them, that the Lord may enable them to be daily *receiving* Christ Jesus in all his fullness, to bless, and sanctify, and satisfy their souls.

To Edmond he writes, on the 7th of July:

My very dear Friend, — I have at this time had very many brotherly and friendly expressions of sympathy, but none came earlier and none was more welcome than yours. I have lost one who was every way worthy of love and admiration, and fitted to be my ornament and my joy. She was a meek, gentle, loving, lady-like creature, with a superior and beautifully balanced and refined mind. I have an empty house and an empty heart. Yet exceeding comfort has been mingled with the sorrow. The Lord was *very very* kind to her at her departure. I have never read or heard of so wondrous a scene. For two days and nights we sat and stood beside her, and though there was the interchange of light and darkness, conflict and victory, yet for a long time at the end there was *peace*, mounting up to assurance, triumph, transport, ecstasy. I wish I could tell you a little of these wondrous forty-eight hours. I feel that it is 'separated, but not divided; gone before, and following'. All my thoughts are sweet, thankful, softening, elevating. The Lord seems saying now, 'You have nothing now to do but to serve me.'

To the same he writes, after his last sorrow:

MY DEAR FRIEND, — You will be grieved to find that I have again to make a claim upon your sympathy. My dear little boy has just been taken home to meet his mother and sister. The thought oversets me; but I shall not be alone. The Lord still remains, and some dear friends, among whom, though we so seldom meet, I fondly reckon you. — Believe me in time, and I trust in eternity, yours very affectionately, JOHN MILNE.

Tranquillity

On the first anniversary of his great bereavement (15th June 1852), he writes to Somerville:

MY VERY DEAR FRIEND, — I go to Mr Cumming on Thursday week, and I suppose you are to be with him on the Sabbath. What are you going to do for us in passing? Let me hear before Sabbath. We must levy toll and tax, and see that the King's revenue suffer no damage. So there must be no covert or silent passing by. Dear brother, remember me. This is the anniversary of dear Rue's going home. About a quarter before twelve this day year she entered into the *full* glory, for it had already begun. The past year has been a new year to me. The Lord has been strangely kind ("as one whom his mother comforteth"), lifting me up when cast down, and smiling me out of my bad humours, and making me ashamed of myself, and a wonderer at him, when I was beginning to think that I was hardly used.

To the same he writes, about the same time:

Your plan will do admirably. I will go with you to Andrew's, and we shall come back for our Tuesday evening meeting. Collace woods have their memories, so have Arran shores and hills. Our week of fullest happiness was there. I came from my work in Lanarkshire, and stayed a whole week, trotting my dear Rue about on Donald, stubborn, tricky fellow as he was. But he never was rude to her, though he played tricks to all the rest of us, and carried poor Eliza on toward Brodick. These days can never return to me; but I can rejoice in my dear brother's quiet full joy. Tuesday, a quarter before twelve, was the anniversary of her going home. Latterly I have been kept constantly busy and happy in my work, which is very kind, is it not? Mr Cumming will tell me if you are to preach for him on Monday, and if so, I shall come out and join you. Possibly I may get out on Sabbath night. Did we not first become acquainted by my coming out in that way? I remember 'his locks are bushy and black as the raven.'[1] We walked home on the Monday. We inquired ages. You were twenty-eight; I was a little older; and you looked as if you thought, 'How much I shall have done ere I be as old!' These are reminiscences.[2]

Even in these pensive moods and days, he could write thus to his friend:

I found my work easy on Saturday, and had help and buoyancy yesterday. So, thanks. Last Monday I was out with —. It was his communion. He is an 'olive green in the house of our God.' All about seems to prosper. Even the dog, Watch, is an honest, happy-looking beast; and the little olive plant *is* sprouting up most luxuriantly. We remember you when we meet.'

A few brief extracts from letters written about this time may come

[1] The text of Somerville's sermon.
[2] In June 11, 1850, he thus writes to Millar of Clunie, inviting him to his communion: 'We know one another, and therefore it is pleasant and profitable to labour together; for I always find that on such occasions the dew comes down. We are the two persons that have most interest in that congregation; and if at this time the Lord enables you to come, then let us engage, in the grace of the Lord, that we shall be of one mind in seeking very great blessing.'

in here, as forming a link between this chapter and the following:

I wish you could give me some idea of your exercises of mind during seasons of acute pain. It seems a severe trial to lie hour after hour in a state of suffering. It seems to me the only support is to feel that we are then, through Jesus, presenting our body a living sacrifice, and trying to glorify God in the fires. One cannot also help thinking of the lost, who have no hope. It seems to me that acute and long-continued pain, graciously borne, is the most effectual instrument for softening the heart, and making us willing to depart. What could the whole world do for us in the way of making us glad, when we are in a state of bodily anguish?

There was a thought given me last night when I was speaking with some young people: 'Their bodies, being still united to Christ, do rest in their graves.' Our dearest friends soon grow weary of our bodies when life is gone, and put them away; but Jesus holds them fast. Corruption does not make him let go his hold. And then I thought that a dead, corrupt soul is more loathsome than a dead body; and yet Jesus comes and takes hold of us when we are dead in trespasses and sins. He sees not what we were, or what we are, but what we shall be when he has formed us both body and soul to show forth his praise.

We are very happy and comfortable here. But I want to be a pilgrim and sojourner, and hang loose. We should live as at a day's warning, and this should not seem hard.

I feel your thoughts on the family *very* sweet. They are given you by the Lord, and you must not be surprised if sometimes I give to others what you have been the means of giving to me. Let us long and labour for the gathering and completing of that blessed company. What love, what joy, what songs will be there! Some we loved, and still dearly love, are there already, and we, through grace, shall soon join them.

We are wonderfully made, and we must take care of our bodily as well as spiritual health. I think nothing gives me refreshing, strengthening rest, but trying to open my heart to take in the glory and love of the Lord. That fills the heart, and is the bread which satisfies.

Milne had done good work and true in Perth during the first thirteen years of his ministry. He was to do more of such work again during his last ten years. But between these two periods there was to be an interval, which he had little counted on. There was work of another kind to be done elsewhere.

Brotherly Consolation

Perhaps it was during these times of sorrow that he learned to be the comforter, and to enter more deeply into the sorrows of his flock and friends. The following letters, or fragments of letters, written in different years, are thrown together here, as illustrations of his dealings with the sorrowful. They require no introduction nor comment.

> *Free St Leonard's Manse, Perth, 3d April 1860.* — MY DEAR BROTHER, — We got your note this morning at breakfast, and at once feared what was true. We were with you in your waiting on the Lord, when as yet you knew not what might be his will; and now we are with you when you are saying, though with tears, 'It is well with the child; good is the will of the Lord.' I do not know who told me the story; but a gardener, in Wales somewhere, tended carefully a favourite flower, perhaps was a little proud of it. The owner of the garden, one day walking through, espied the flower, plucked it, and put it, for beauty and for pleasure, in his bosom. A friend of the gardener's, observing the blank, said, 'Where's the flower?' 'The master took it', said the gardener. Give him thanks, dear friend, that you have begun to take infeftment[1] of heaven; and let Rachel be comforted with the thought that your little Andrew will come again to his own borders, and will be found in his place when the home circle is again complete.
>
> I think I have noticed that, when the Lord took away something that I valued greatly, he always gave me souls in return. One very

---

[1] *infeftment:* a Scots legal term; to infeft is to invest with heritable property; *infeftment* refers to the symbolical giving possession of land in completion of the title, *Ed.*

special case I could mention; but we can talk of it when you see how many Peters will be given you in the room of your little Andrew. May we both find, next Sabbath, a quickening and growing time! Sabbath week I was at Collace. I am trying not to do anything, or go anywhere, but at the bidding of the Lord. He opened the door to my old resort, so I went and took all the services. It was pleasant to remember and speak much of you at the old fireside, and then to pray for you in your family trial. I enjoyed the day's work very much. Old Mrs Reid, before I came away, said, 'There is no such man in the world as Mr Bonar. Wherever I go, everybody, old and young, loves him more than I can tell; and how did he contrive to be always among them, and always working?' But good-bye. — With much love to Mrs Bonar, believe me, very affectionately yours, JOHN MILNE.

Free St Leonard's Manse, Perth, 17th October 1864. — MY VERY DEAR ANDREW, — We are all greatly grieved and startled by the intimation of this morning. We thought that all was going on well; and she was always so healthy, we never dreamt of such a blow as this. I feel stunned, and sad at heart, for you know the old and tender friendship and love. None on earth can comprehend the sorrows of your heart, and none on earth can fill up the blank and void; but you know well who can do both, and that he is not far off nor uninterested, but has already made provision both for the present and future trial. One almost welcomes these breaches, just to see how skilfully he repairs; one almost welcomes these tears, just to see how tenderly he wipes them away. 'I was dumb, I opened not my mouth, because thou didst it.' 'The Lord gave, and the Lord taketh away'; and 'blessed be the name of the Lord.' That is one side; but there is another. 'I go to prepare a place for you'; and is he not doing it? Your house is less home-like today; but is not heaven become more so? You are now a divided family, and you know which part is safest and happiest. Don't you long for the gathering together, and the rest, and the 'no more death, nor sorrow, nor crying'? It will be a sorrowful communion week, but many will be praying for you. I should have liked to come through, if it had been only to shake hands and say, 'The Lord help you, brother; the Lord be the guide of your motherless children.' But I am tied up this week, and cannot get away. We all unite in much sympathy. — Believe me, very affectionately yours, JOHN MILNE.

Free St Leonard's Manse, Perth, 16th October. — MY VERY DEAR ANDREW, — Mrs Stuart of Annat is living with us just now; and last night, as we all sat together, we were remembering that this is about the time of your great sorrow. I know well that it is only the Elder Brother that can bind up the broken heart and satisfy the longing soul. But I know that you do not undervalue the sympathy and prayers and much love of the younger brethren. Let me tell you a little incident that will cheer you. There has been a little ingathering at Rait through Moody and his sons. A young man, Clarke, is one of the number. He says he was your Sabbath scholar at Collace, though the family did not come to the church. You visited the house one day, and spoke to the boy. You said to him: 'Did you ever read the Bible from beginning to end?' He answered, 'Na, sir; it's sae lang.' You said: 'But if you had a friend in America, and he were to send you a nice long letter, would you read it all?' 'Oh, yes; every word', said the boy. He now says he never forgot this; it made him uneasy; but now it is his guide, and the word of God is the lamp to his feet. He was asked to take part in the meeting, but he drew back, saying, 'I dinna ken grammar.' But young Moody said: 'You have what is more useful: grace is better than grammar.'

But good-bye. I ask myself, Why are you so different from Andrew Bonar in home comforts? But time is short, as Paul said, who, you think, was a widower himself. Love to Miss Bonar and the infantry, especially the Benjie, — much love. — Yours very affectionately, JOHN MILNE.

Free St Leonard's Manse, Perth, 19th Oct. 1866. — MY VERY DEAR ANDREW, — I don't know how to thank you enough, both for Barbara and myself, for all your kindness and helpfulness in this time of trial. Your notes were a great support to us, and the mindful observant

Master will remember in that day. Give our many thanks to the praying bands for all their mindfulness and prayers. It has been a time of exceeding suffering; I do not know that I ever really knew pain before. We both look back with wonder, and almost trembling of heart, upon the ten or eleven days, and especially sleepless nights, of ceaseless, crushing agony. But the Lord was very, very kind. I think he has taught me many lessons, which he will never let me forget. I am still very weak, slowly, surely regaining strength. I think I am enabled growingly to leave all in the Master's hand, and to say in truth and love, Not my will. It is very sweet to feel that we are his, and that he careth for us with such a wise, constant, tender care. Dear Andrew, I thought for a little that I was to get the start of you in the race to the sepulchre. One thing will interest you, I remember it quite distinctly. You know that, like you, I would like to live to welcome the Master back; and yet I recollect that when, on recovering consciousness, I said to Barbara this is the end, and thought it really was, I felt no discomposure, no disquiet, no regret at the disappointment of my desire and hope. Tell Horace, when you go to the opening of the new sanctuary, that I shall be with you in spirit, praying that the glory and power may fill the place, and that the Lord may make them, and the places round about his hill, a blessing, giving the rain in its season, and sending showers of blessing. Love to all my friends in India Street. B. and all of us join in best wishes. — Believe me, yours affectionately, JOHN MILNE.

To Mrs Moody Stuart, after the death of her son:

Free St Leonard's Manse, Perth, Nov. 9th, 1866. — MY VERY DEAR JESSIE, — It was so kind of Moody to write to me before the Communion. Kindly tell him that I was graciously kept from all thought, and enabled to enjoy the quiet season very greatly. The suffering for many days and nights was very fearful; but B. and I look back, and feel that it was a continual communion. We can truly say, that the Lord is a very present help in time of trouble.

And now I trust that the Lord is dealing very kindly with you all, and filling up the blank in house and heart with his own gracious, constant presence, and giving you sweet thoughts of the blessedness of him who has gone before. A favourite thought of mine is, that when Jesus says, 'I go to prepare a place for you', he means, that often this preparation consists in taking our best and dearest there before us. He impoverishes the earthly home to make a heavenly home. I am sure it is more easy now for you all to set your hearts on things above. Happy Andrew! Like James, he has soon got his discharge, and been called up higher; he has been called away from the cross, the bitter cup, and the trial upon trial which accumulate so sadly when the journey is prolonged. I am sure that you and Moody must be thankful now that he had made proof of his ministry, both in public and in private, ere he was taken to his rest. He has not lived in vain; and as time passes, you will learn this more and more. He has not died in vain. You cannot tell what lessons it has taught, what influence it has exerted. Let us thank God, and take courage. The Lord will come, and bring all our dear ones with him. Love to dear Moody, and a happy Sabbath. Love, united and warm, to all the rest. You know who says, 'Be of good cheer, it is I.' — Your very affectionate JOHN.

Free St Leonard's Manse, July 15, 1867. — MY VERY DEAR ANDREW, — We both thank you very much for your loving note. Since we heard of the going home,[1] we have been thinking and speaking and praying for you all, especially the widow. I have been thinking often of heaven since I heard it. This morning I awoke from a deep, sweet sleep with the word in my mouth, 'His name shall be on their forehead.' It seemed as if it had been the answer to the inquiry, 'How shall we know the multitudes whom we shall meet there, but whom we have never known in the flesh?' I think of your brother as one of the most unblameable characters I ever knew. He always seemed as a father among you, looking so benevolent, and taking a quiet placid interest in all that was going on. You have been a very, very happy family; and now that the circle is breaking up on earth, and that long dear 15 York Place will, I fancy, be left desolate, the family circle is

---

[1] The death of my brother James, July 11th, 1867.

re-forming above, never more to be broken. My young friends will feel this very much, especially James. Give our love and sympathy, and take it to yourself, dear brother, for I know the hidden wound bleeds afresh. The Comforter be with you in his own blessed, effectual way. B. joins me in much love, and believe me, ever very affectionately yours, JOHN MILNE.

P.S. — B. asks me to say to you: 'Thy brother shall rise again.' I hope to be with you in heart, though not in presence, when you go to God's acre. May we both get what William Burns got when he went with his uncle's remains to the churchyard.

Skilful Consolation

In after years, we find his chastenings leading to such utterances as the following: — 'Weary, but turning to Christ.' Again: 'O my Lord, I desire to put away all these grave-clothes of unbelief, and to walk with assurance of the perfect love which casteth out fear'; and 'The chief hindrances of spiritual growth are want of spiritual diligence, conformity to the world, and power of unbelief.'

His trials told permanently upon his spiritual growth. They were life-long blessings. He was calm under them; so calm that he could converse about them freely. After the death of his wife, to whom he was fondly attached, he was able to speak of her death-bed from the pulpit, and to narrate her happy departure. His skill in comforting the bereaved, in dealing with the sick, in calming the troubled was great. His words were not spoken at random; he could suit his texts or counsels admirably; while his tone and manner were so kindly and winning that he was fitted to be, above many, a friend in the day of adversity, whose very face spoke consolation, and bid the mourner be of good cheer.

If he met anyone in mourning, he almost invariably went up and spoke to them some kind and suitable words, such as: 'I see you are in distress'; or, 'You have lost some near relative; I sympathize with you, and so does Christ.' Many interesting meetings he has had in this way; some of them with careless people, who were struck with his message of love, and some with Roman Catholics, who listened eagerly, and invited him to their house. The bow was drawn at a venture, but the archer found that the arrow had reached its mark. Some of these casual messages are known to have given comfort to the heavy heart. 'A good word maketh it glad' (*Prov.* 12:25).

Chapter 10

1853
Thoughts of India, and
Correspondence about It

*T*o the loneliness of feeling produced by the death of wife and children, we may trace his first thoughts of India. The following sentences will show this, and will help to connect the last chapter with the present. Link after link was broken, till at last he felt as if he could remain no longer amid this desolation:[1]

> My little boy promises now to live (he writes to Somerville); and his little face begins now and then to peep up in my heart, as I trudge along solitary, alone.

Again, to the same:

> I found my dear little boy very weak and prostrate. It was agreed to move him back to Annat Lodge; and so they all went off, and left my house and heart very desolate. As I sat amid the emptiness, I felt as if I could enjoy a good hearty cry, but was afraid to begin, as I did not know where I might end; the prayer-meeting tonight helped me a

---

[1] The weight of his own sorrows quickens his pastoral sympathies, and thus he writes to Somerville: 'May we have a good day tomorrow. I am preaching on Psalm 46:10: "Be still", *etc*. The last mail from the east and west has, during the week, put four families in mourning — two for sons; one for a son-in-law; and one for a brother. I have very lately had some old and young departing in a sweet and blessed state. How it sweetens the rod!'

little. I am trying neither to have thought nor desire; but just to wait on the Lord.

Again, to the same:

I was with you about this time last year, and remember all your kindness, and the good I got from it. But I am changed since then; and the world seems changed, and this place is changed. Yet there is not, I think, bitterness, but thankfulness for the Lord's kindness to one who loved me.

Then, in a letter to Collace, he says:

I must not any longer hide from you what is in my heart. Nor can I any longer want your prayers and counsel. I think the Lord is drawing my heart to India. It *is* more than possible that you will have to write 'Calcutta', instead of 'Perth'. The thing, as yet, is only in embryo. You will ask guidance for me.

Lastly, in a letter to myself, he says at last:

I am engaged to go to India; and this brought about by dealings in my lot, my soul, and a number of little linked circumstances that look very like the work of God.

The insight which these five scraps give us into the heart of the man, the Christian, the father, the husband, the pastor, is touching; and, besides, they supply the key to what follows. He had now set his face to the foreign field of labour, and from this time he says, in a letter to myself, 'My mind has never wavered. Yet in simplicity I am in the Lord's hand, though I fear there would be more of the cross in *staying* than in *going.*'

He was not long in divulging his purpose. He entered without delay into a correspondence with Dr Duff and Mr Hawkins; who, disappointed and almost despairing because of many failures, were thankful beyond measure at the prospect of obtaining such a labourer for Calcutta.

But opposition, as might have been expected, arose. His people, full of warmest affection, set themselves against it. They thought their own claims to be, if not first in importance, at least foremost in every other respect.

On New Year's Day, 1853, Milne had preached on the text, 'Lord, what wilt thou have me to do?' He spoke strongly, though in general terms as yet.

> The ministers keep their Master's commission to preach the gospel to every creature folded up, or only referred to when some one obeys it, and a new victim is laid on the missionary altar. We are too fond of clustering round the honey-cells of home; deaf to the death-groan of India's perishing millions.

His people were startled. A rumour went out that Milne was minded to leave Perth, and offer himself for missionary work in India. The office-bearers conferred privately; appointed two of their number to wait on him; ascertained the truth of the report; had a meeting of elders and deacons called, who with one accord agreed to entreat him to remain, offering such reasons as the following. They could not see that such a translation was for the greater good of the Church; they thought that the Lord's command to go unto all nations was to be understood under limitations; that Perth and Scotland presented an ample field for a minister; that Milne's present charge (now for thirteen years so successfully occupied), with its 900 communicants, and crowded church, would be endangered by his leaving; that his fitness for the Indian field was very doubtful, especially at his time of life. This was on the 11th January 1853. On the 15th of the same month, the Young Men's Association presented a memorial, considerably briefer, but equally urgent.

Andrew Gray's Dissuasives

Meanwhile a private correspondence had been going on among his personal friends; some dissuading him from, others encouraging him in, his purpose. The following letter, from his friend Gray, will give one view of the subject, — not a very gratifying one to Milne:

27th Dec. 1852. — MY DEAR FRIEND, — On the whole, I lean every day more and more to the opinion that there is no clear call to *you,* and that you ought not to go. My reason is, that I regard it as very doubtful if your temperament would accord with the circumstances in which you would be placed ... You must beware what you do. It is an immense responsibility you must take. The Church is not calling you to go. Dr Duff and Mr Hawkins, although wishing you to go, are scarcely calling you to go. What if you go without any call at all? It was no unequivocal movement of divine providence that set this business agoing. The simple fact is, that *you took it into your head,* and so the thing began. And how did you come to think of it? Why, you happened to be in a low fit. You wanted, naturally and properly, to get out of it. Grant was off; Cumming was on the move; why should not you be jogging too? And was not Calcutta the very place? Catching at the idea, you have got out of your depression for the time. — Ever yours, most affectionately, — ANDREW GRAY.

The above is rather hard on Milne; not quite fair to him, perhaps, nor making due allowance for his trials. Yet it came from a warm and true-hearted friend.

Encouragements

The following contains another view of the subject, though in some respects coincident with the previous:

Collace, Jan. 10, *1853.* — *Monday evening.* — MY DEAR BROTHER, — It may be that my affection for you, and the sort of melancholy that is suggested to my mind by the idea of Perth without you, – it may be that these considerations are influencing my judgment, as your loneliness may have influenced yours. Be this as it may, you want me to state how the matter now looks to me. Well, then, my impressions continue to be these: (1) All plans originating in a time of despondency are to be suspected *prima facie;* — there is so little of faith in low spirits. I find that at the time when the Spirit separated Paul and Barnabas for a mission, they were vigorous and full of work, ministering and fasting, publicly and privately, full of energetic service. And, on the other hand, when Elijah, in low spirits, goes to the desert, and then to Horeb, he is sent back again; so that we soon find him sitting on Carmel once more. (2) Your thoughts about Calcutta did not seem to me to amount to a call made upon you by the Spirit. You were not bent towards Calcutta by any great and preponderating sense of the claims of that field over all others. Was not your feeling rather one of merely decided admission that the sphere was important beyond doubt? In other words, you thought you felt uprooted, and you saw you might as well be planted down in Calcutta as anywhere else. Still, was this a drawing? Is there at this moment a drawing, such as you might, from its peculiar strength and tenacity, interpret to be the result of the Spirit calling you with a Macedonian cry? The brethren with whom I met today prayed for you, asking 'counsel', that you might not mistake, and 'might' (*Isa.* 11:2), that you may execute what you see to be the Lord's will. Perhaps, on the whole, they were more ready than I to admit the probability that our Master may have made use of your very loneliness for shutting your eye on the home field, and opening it on the vast fields of India; for no one felt otherwise than that Calcutta, and all connected with it, is of very peculiar and very vast importance; and that, were *you* there, you might be a most suitable instrument for the work there. Whatever be the result, I can say of you as Paul could, Philippians 1:7: ἐξω σε ἐν τη καρδια μου[1] and will feel, if you go, that I am more a pilgrim than before, waiting for our 'gathering together unto him'.

Again, on the following day, Bonar adds:

You will see I had written to you last night, fully believing that you were not yet decided, and so suggesting to you those aspects of the matter that caused me to feel doubtful in regard to it. If it has got

---

[1] 'I have you in my heart.'

the length today's note seems to imply, I shall say no more, but shall believe that the Lord has overruled your circumstances to bring about his own purposes as to Calcutta, just as he overruled Stephen's death and its results to scatter messengers over many lands. May he be glorified, whatever becomes of his instruments! May souls be won to him!

In a subsequent note to Milne, Bonar says:

I cannot now resist the feeling that you have been guided almost in spite of yourself. I see scenes of wide usefulness rising to view, if the Master see meet to carry you to the shores of India, and already some have been struck by your devoting yourself to the cause. My brother John writes that it was in this light he viewed it; as so likely to suggest self-denial to ministers settled, so to speak, on their lees.

And it was in this spirit that afterwards Bonar of Greenock thus wrote to him:

Greenock, Jan. 28, 1853. —— MY DEAR BROTHER, — I felt a strong inclination to write to you when I first heard from Andrew that you thought of exchanging Perth for Calcutta; but as I should have ministered encouragement and congratulation rather than dissuasion, I could not bring myself to pen even a few lines; — first, because to urge you to persist in the resolution to which you have been so strangely led, must have looked ungracious and harsh. But, second, because I shrink from doing anything to countenance a project that involved the removal, to an immeasurable distance, of a friend so truly and deeply loved, so long as I did not understand that your mind was conclusively made up. From what took place, however, at your Presbytery, I can gather that your purpose is irrevocable; and therefore, though it be with mingled and conflicting feelings, I cannot any longer refrain from assuring you that I rejoice in the grace that has been given you to serve God in the path you mean to follow. I rejoice in your purpose, because, from your peculiar temperament, I doubt if your spirit would soon recover its edge amid the tokens of desolation which your home, no longer a home, presents. Besides, I have a strong conviction that every minister of Christ should vary his sphere of labour, if in his power, once at least in his lifetime; and that, in our Church, the pastor has too much overshadowed the missionary in our estimate of evangelical labour at home. Then you have chosen, — no, — in 'blindness' have been conducted to a field which, in the highest sense, unites promotion with change; for, indeed, all things considered, Calcutta might be viewed as a centre of influence with which no other that we have access to can be compared. But, above all, let me say — say with joy, yet humiliation — that your determination fills me with delight, as setting to us in the ministry, who have too long been settled on the lees of routine, and to our probationers, so devoid of enterprise and magnanimity in the things of Jesus, an awakening example of devotedness and zeal such as our Church truly needed, but which I had wholly despaired of seeing.

I give these as specimens of the way in which Milne's purpose was viewed by his private friends. They show the difficulties that beset him on every side; the arguments which were presented to him both by his own flock and by the Christian friends in whom he trusted most. But 'none of these things moved him.' His heart was set on India. For it he could leave all behind him, and hear voices saying, 'Are we not your flock, whom, for thirteen years, you have loved and fed? And are we not your friends and brethren, your "companions and fellow-soldiers in the Lord?" And are these not your native hills and streams and uplands? And do not your dead lie here, — wife and infants, — with many others in the churchyard, your children in Christ Jesus?' He could answer all such appeals with, 'I must go; the world is dying; India needs help; Calcutta stretches out her hands; the harvest is great, and the labourers are few.' But while some of his private friends hesitated or dissuaded, weighing his purpose in Scottish balances; while some kept silence, afraid of interposing, he had other correspondents who cheered him on, reminding him of India and its stupendous claims.

The Calcutta Call

The Calcutta congregation had sent home a most touching and urgent letter, signed by Dr Ewart, and dated April 7, 1852, to Duff and Hawkins, entrusting to them the responsibility of looking out for a minister in Scotland. It concluded with making mention of the prayers which were going up for good success in this important matter. These two individuals, — too well known in the Church and throughout the world to need notice or eulogy here, — took up the matter with all earnestness, commending it to God, and casting about for someone who would go out in the spirit of an apostle to do an apostle's work. On the 23d of November 1852, Hawkins received the following letter:

> MY DEAR MR HAWKINS, — You remember my little boy, who was brought to my house a fugitive from hooping-cough, the night you kindly came to me. Poor little fellow! it seems he brought the seeds of the disease along with him; and, after a time, he sickened and died. I fear I have not managed the affliction so well as I might. I fear I have fainted under it. I have been feeling a good deal like a tree whose roots are loosened and have no earthly hold, or like a ship whose moorings are cast off. So thoughts have been rife of change of scene and change of work; and there has been a revival of old dreams about India, which, when I was fairly settled down, and prospered, have been overlaid and forgotten. The question occurs, After having laboured part of my life at home, may it not be intended that I am to spend the remainder in the foreign field? I believe in all such cases the right course is to ask the counsel of a judicious Christian brother. It has occurred to me that you could help me to determine whether these thoughts are right and ought to be cherished, or whether they are of the nature of a present temptation and to be refused.'

Of Hawkins' reply we can only give a part:

> *Nov. 27, 1852.* — MY DEAR MR MILNE, — Words would fail to express what I felt on the receipt of yours of the 23d. You are aware that Mr

M'Kail left the congregation of Calcutta some time ago in consequence of bad health. A committee was sent to Dr Duff and myself to look out for a minister. We have applied to more than one, and have thought of others; but in every instance something has occurred to prevent the presentation of a call. My own mind has been much exercised in this matter; but, after looking in one direction and another, I found the path of wisdom to be in standing still and keeping it before the Lord. And now let me say, as I can with perfect truth, that to no one of the ministers of our Church have my thoughts been directed as they have been to yourself. A recent letter from Calcutta constrained me to open my mind to a member of my family, and to say, 'Would that I could get Mr Milne for that congregation!' This was on the day on which your note was written. Hence the feelings with which it was received … Should you ever be pastor of the flock at Calcutta, you will find a congregation very much smaller than that which now gathers round you every Sabbath, — in fact, a mere handful; and even among these few you will meet with worldliness, and much that your spirit will mourn over. On the other hand, you will find a few choice spirits there, some of the Lord's dear children, who will give you a welcome in their Master's name, and uphold your hand by much prayer to God. If you seek to be a partaker in missionary work, there is plenty of that, with our large Missionary Institution, in the heart of a heathen city. Many an opportunity will be found of preaching in your own tongue the unsearchable riches of Christ. But no man will do more missionary work there than by countenancing the mission as pastor of the flock, and by leavening the congregation with the missionary spirit. It is this which I so much long for in that people. Stir up the people there to think much about the mission, and to pray for it, and you will have accomplished a great work for the Lord.

There is another aspect in which I cannot help viewing the subject. I fear there are many, very many of our ministers that shrink from the very thought of India as a field of labour. But let a minister in your position, the pastor of a large congregation, volunteer when others hold back, and let your people as freely give you up for their Lord's sake, and I believe it would go far to break up the apathy of many. It may be the will of the Lord, in this way, to proclaim an alarm in our Zion, to cause many an eye to be turned to himself, inquiring, 'What wilt thou have us to do?' and to lead many to look not upon a parish, a town, a city, or even Scotland itself, but upon the whole world as the scene of evangelistic labour, prescribed and pointed out by infinite love, not merely as a scene to which the whole collective Church of Christ is to come, but as one, also, in which he has allotted to every man his post of duty, and to the occupation of which every man must be willing to go up at the bidding of his Lord.

To this Milne replied:

You know how solemn and complicated such a question is. If I were to go, I should look forward to an early grave. I ran sensible, also, that though feeling at present as if uprooted, I should carry with me many broken and bleeding roots; yet I really do not think that personal considerations will at all enter into the calculation. I think a minister of Christ should stand out among his fellows as a man of self-denial, self-oblivion.

And again Milne writes to Hawkins on the 8th of December. After mentioning that he had consulted friends, he adds:

If we could but see the mind of the Lord with some clearness, we might put all such circumstances aside, because he would, in his own way, make the path plain. I find that the more I keep by the word of God, and reflect upon the spirit of the first preachers, the more I reckon myself as one that is done with the world, and with all contrivances for ease and self-enjoyment; the more I think of advancement in holiness, as the one great aim, the more I seem to feel my heart inclined in this direction. What is the Master's will? I feel that nothing short of this can warrant my leaving my present place, or would bear me up amid the new trials I calculate on meeting, and the occasional seasons of heart-sinking and home-sickness.

Hawkins replies to this at considerable length. His letters are full of interest, and breathe a high Christian spirit. But it is impossible to quote in full either his communications or those of Duff. One letter of the latter, however, I give at length, as it specially refers to the preceding correspondence with Hawkins.

Dr Alexander Duff's Letter

Camberwell, London, 15th Dec. 1852. — MY DEAR MR HAWKINS, — The correspondence between yourself and Mr Milne of Perth I have perused with feelings of no ordinary interest. The case of our church in Calcutta has hung heavily on my mind since May last. The failure, in one or two instances, in obtaining a fitting minister, though tantalized with the temporary prospect of success, and the non-discovery of any more, at once qualified and willing to go, throughout the course of my recent travellings in the north and west of Scotland, all tended to produce a certain feeling of despondency. And so, though the subject has been constantly present to my mind in prayer, it came at last to be a topic of peculiar urgency at the throne of grace. Looking at the date of Mr M.'s first note to you, I am greatly struck with the coincidence, as to time, between its heart revealings and the power of utterance to which I was prompted in prayer, saying, 'Lord, graciously have mercy upon us, and raise up *the* man. Put it into the heart of *the* man, whom thou dost choose to disclose himself to us.' How, then, can I help being struck at the unprompted disclosures of the inner workings of his mind made in Mr M.'s first note? The fact is, that I had often thought of Mr Milne as the man for Calcutta. But the same reasons which appear to have kept you back prevailed with me too. But if Mr M., as before God, declare his own mind on the subject, as Mr M'Donald was led to do, the thing is done. The congregation of Mr M., and the Perth Presbytery, will then not have to consider the question, Whether we have succeeded in making out a case for Calcutta sufficiently strong to warrant their loosing the present pastoral tie, — but, Whether they feel warranted, before God, to interpose between Mr M. and the following out of the conviction of his own mind, as to the path and sphere of duty? But though no case might be made out to *satisfy* a congregation and presbytery at *home*, naturally *biassed in their own favour*, and ignorant of the *peculiar* claims of a place like Calcutta, a very strong case could be made out, sufficient to satisfy an unbiassed mind, fully acquainted with the relative bearings of the services of a minister in Calcutta and Perth.

In Perth there are other four Free Churches, and some very able ministers; and, throughout the country, churches and ministers in abundance. In the whole of Bengal there is but one Free Church. It is there a conspicuous object; and from the character of its ministerial services will a judgment be formed of the character of the Free Church pulpit in Scotland. One of the very best men in the Church ought, therefore, to be placed on so conspicuous a watch-tower. Though the Calcutta congregation be numerically smaller than that of Mr M.'s in Perth, I must solemnly protest against estimating the importance of any charge *merely by numbers*. Account ought to be taken of the position of members in the providential order of things, and their power of influencing others for good. Now, in this respect, the members of a church in Calcutta — at least a fair proportion of them — occupy a position in which, by their conduct and example, they may influence myriads around, favourably, or otherwise, towards the gospel of salvation. It is impossible to exaggerate the importance, in this respect, of a faithful and powerful mainstay of the gospel, in such a mighty focus of emanative influence as Calcutta.

Besides, though at present the congregation be small, it ought not to be forgotten that, as a mere matter of fact, it is, from circumstances (which are well known to you), unhappily a shattered fragment only of what it might have been, and what, under a minister like Mr Milne, it might well be expected soon to become. Besides members of our own Church, there are always, in a place like Calcutta, not a few who, sitting very loose to the peculiarities of their respective systems, would be rejoiced to rally round a man who really fed their souls. What an incalculable blessing, in this respect, would an experienced man like Mr Milne become to many! What a strength would such a man, and such a congregation as he would be sure to gather around him, prove to the mission cause generally, and especially to our own! What an unspeakable comfort to our converts and native preachers, and candidates for the ministry! How far and wide, alike through European and native society, might his own living spirit permeate, diffusing light and life amid the realms of darkness and of death!'

As to Mr M.'s age, he should not think about it, nor his physical frame either. The present Bishop of Calcutta went out at the age of fifty-five, and has laboured now with uncommon vigour for twenty years. Mr M.'s frame may not be strong; but I am not aware of any organic ailment in it. And if not, he ought not to consult with flesh and blood in such a matter, but cast himself at once upon the Lord, in the assurance that, if the Lord has put it into his heart to go, he will accomplish by him the work which he designs. And ought not such assurance to satisfy any loving, and obedient, and dutiful child?

As to Mr M'Donald, I can testify in the strongest manner, that, up to the very end, he felt satisfied that in going to Calcutta he simply yielded to a divine monition, and rejoiced in having so done. May the Lord guide our friend! If he is *the* man, the Lord will give him no rest until he decide to go. — Yours affectionately, ALEXANDER DUFF.

After this there followed a large correspondence between Milne and the brethren connected with the foreign field. There are several most interesting and fervent letters from Duff, Dr Tweedie, and Hawkins. But as they do not contain anything material beyond what the preceding extracts convey, I must, reluctantly, withhold them, lest I should swell this volume unduly, and introduce matter not directly illustrative of Milne himself. Some parts, however, of Milne's answers to these letters may be given, as helping us more accurately and fully to understand his mind, and to appreciate his character, in its true-hearted devotion to his Lord.

Letters to Dr Tweedie

Thus he writes to Tweedie, on the 23d of December 1852:

I think I may tell you that my mind is *fully* made up. I feel that the Lord has gently withdrawn my heart from the home field, and is now making it to embrace India, with that calm, settled, vigorous faith and hope, which I have always found the precursor of joyful, useful working ... I am quietly feeling my way, and endeavouring to prepare my brethren and people for what is now about to take place. I have a fond, perhaps over-sanguine, hope that I shall be able to carry with me their acquiescence, if not their approval. I should like that the hand of the Lord might be seen and acknowledged in the whole matter, and that our parting may be, in sorrow and love, as those should part who love one another much, but who love their Lord and his glory more, and who expect soon to meet again where love to him can be fully exercised and expressed, without those painful severings and acts of self-denial.

I have often wondered and been overwhelmed when I think of the strange and overwhelming prosperity with which I have all along been favoured here. My church, from the very commencement of my ministry, down to the present moment, has always been over-crowded. My people have been strangely affectionate and attached. There is a very large number of ripening, zealous, liberal Christians among them; and I look back to very, very many who have departed in peace, often in triumph, and of whose presence with the Lord I have the fullest assurance. My office-bearers, between 40 and 50 in number, though of very different ranks and habits, have never once known what debate or division is, but have lived and acted in a most strange love and harmony. I have still a very pleasant home, though its light is now quenched and its ornament gone. I have credit for a kind of catholicity of spirit with the other denominations, and I have always had abundant and welcome access to the pulpits of my brethren in several of the surrounding counties. The bones of my wife and children are here; and I think I may say the bones of not a few whom God has given me; and *yet,* I think, in your own words, that the pillar of cloud and of fire has arisen, and my heart bounds to follow.

Your allusion to ten years ago brings back pleasant and sad memories. At that time I thought of nothing less than ever being in any way connected with India. I was rushing into the home work as the horse to the battle, expecting, like many, a great outpouring of the Holy Ghost. Yet, even then, I had a strange impression of the importance of Calcutta; and, in my zeal, often thought and said, 'Oh that Mr Tweedie saw his way to go!'

Thus again he writes to the same; but now it is as to the question of his own fitness:

'*Leonard Bank, December 24, 1852.* — MY DEAR BROTHER, — I have been reading much in M'Donald's life, and am a good deal oppressed. The nature and importance of the Calcutta position is opening up, and becoming more vivid and definite to my mind. There is but one Free Church minister in Bengal — what kind of man, and Christian, and minister should he be? We have been dealing too much with the question, Am I willing? There is another, unspeakably more important, Am I fit? Dear, honoured M'Donald was a noble, holy man; I am a weak, foolish, sinful child. I am amazed that the Lord should have made me, and kept me, so long a minister, and that men have borne with me in such an office. Let this, therefore, now be the matter of inquiry, and let it be fully and honestly dealt with. Let no delicacy to me stand in the way; we can have no desire but for the right filling up of that important post. A man may move on even usefully in a subordinate place, surrounded, supported by those who are wiser, better, and stronger than himself, who would lamentably fail when isolated, and perhaps crushed, by the exigencies of one of the high places of the field. I know that blessed word, 'My grace'; but that does not supersede the wise adaptation of means to ends. My dear brother in the Lord, much of whose mind I have been seeing tonight, deal honestly and fully with this. — Believe me, very affectionately yours, JOHN MILNE.

Leonard Bank, 29th December. — MY DEAR MR TWEEDIE, — I *was* favoured with your prompt, full, and heart-stirring letter. I see the Calcutta kirk-session is a mission college; and if the Lord sends me, he will find some niche or place where I may labour with and among the brethren. It is a great and unlooked-for felicity the thought of being connected with Dr Duff, whom I so greatly admire and love. Feeling deeply the solemnity of the step I take, — for the issues are known only to the Lord, and they must affect eternal interests, — I yet think it better to commit myself, both as a means of relieving my mind, and also stopping the solicitations of my dear friends, such as Andrew Bonar and George Smeaton, who both say they are thunderstruck. Men are too busy at present to be touched much, or touched long by anything; so this, like other things, will have its brief day among my friends, and then pass by. It is likely there will be opposition from my brethren in the Presbytery. The objections will probably be, that the movement is ultroneous on my part; that there is no call of the Lord or the Church. Another would be, that neither Dr Duff, nor Mr Hawkins, nor yourself know me sufficiently to be able to judge of fitness. I feel that my two last notes must have given you at least considerable insight into my character. When Moab is at ease, the sediment lies at the bottom; but when he is stirred, it comes to light. You have seen that I am sensitive, sanguine, impulsive, prone, when the Lord loosens the rein, to run off into pride, or stumble into unbelief, and to pass very fast from the one sin into the other. It is a sad flaw in the earthen vessel; yet I think the Lord sometimes makes it an inlet to self-knowledge, and an outlet for his power. Pray for me that I may be much helped and blessed at present, and that I and my people may rejoice in the Lord alone. This will be the best preparative for whatever he may purpose. May the blessing of him who dwelt in the bush dwell with you and yours! — Very affectionately yours, JOHN MILNE.

Opposition

The matter was not to be so easy as he, with his sometimes too sanguine views and hopes, at one time thought. He was not to be torn from Perth without protest. His roots had struck too deep and spread out too widely to give way without a wrench. He awoke at last to the knowledge of this, though at first he prophesied smooth things. Thus he writes to me:

> I am engaged to go to India, and this brought about by dealings in my lot, my soul, and a number of little linked circumstances, that look very like the work of God. But the opposition is universal, both among my own people and in the town and neighbourhood; and I stand alone in a furnace of delicate, respectful, earnest, loving solicitation. This has taken me by surprise, and made me admire the exceeding kindness of God to man, to a poor unworthy worm, a mere bubble. Of course I have had searchings of heart and inquirings arising out of this unlooked-for expression of affection. Is this a bar in my way? a bar of love? Or is it a trial, to test and prove? As yet I have held to the latter, and my mind has never wavered. Yet in simplicity I am in the Lord's hand, though I fear there would be more of the cross in staying than in going. There is to be a meeting here this week between some of our Edinburgh friends and a deputation of my office-bearers. I trust some light will come out of it. Pray for me; for if I stay or go without the Lord, it will be a great mistake and a great sin.

In a similar way he writes to Hawkins, on the 7th of January 1853:

> MY DEAR MR HAWKINS, — I was favoured with your kind note. You are right. This affair is not going to be so simple as I thought. Yesterday there was a private meeting of office-bearers and friends; and two of the most respected and most gracious of them came and had a long converse.
>
> I think I was enabled to be firm. This afternoon my dear friend Mr Burns, in whom I have much confidence, came, and with expressions

of earnestness and affection, dealt with me. I think he left with the impression that I was unchanged. Tonight there has been a meeting of elders and deacons, more than forty; and a deputation has just been with me. I am still free, and think they feel that my mind is unchanged. On Thursday there is to be a meeting of the congregation. You see, my dear brother, that this is to be martyrdom; for I love this dear people, who have grown with me, borne with me, — we have been often very happy together, never had the slightest difference, — who have loaded me with benefits, gifts, and kindness; and now say, 'Go for a year, two years, but do not break the tie.' I know you will feel for me in this trial. We must fall back on him whose will shall be done.

I dare not say the Lord is not blessing me here. Some new cases have come before me this very day; and a man, whom I had given up for a while as hopeless, has been with me this evening; and when I got him to engage in prayer along with me, I found, to my delighted surprise, that the Lord has made him a humble, contrite, waiting child. Still my heart, I may say my purpose, is unchanged; but it will be a dreadful trial, because I dearly love them all; and how can I bear to *seem* unkind, and harden myself against them? If it be the Lord's will, you know he will bear me through. I think the only way by which you and your dear friend can help me is by prayer. Ask that I may be helped and guided in my public and private intercourse with my people, so that we may all look simply to the Lord. I wish to avoid all direct allusions to the subject, and just try to keep myself and them in the immediate presence of him, where the poor creature dwindles and disappears, and selfish and natural feelings give place to adoring submission to his blessed will.

His Congregation

Again, on the 10th of January, he writes to Hawkins:

MY DEAR MR HAWKINS, — Surely the Lord is in this matter. It really seems as if clouds arose *only* to be dispelled by a gracious Lord. I was a good deal alarmed when I wrote on Friday night. Had it been common opposition, I could have withstood that; but with these successive waves of delicate, respectful, earnest, affectionate solicitations, I was afraid that my firmness would give way. On Saturday I went on as usual preparing for Sabbath, and was almost ready; but toward evening I began to think that you had got my note, and were praying for me. Then a passage was brought before my mind. I rose and looked at it, and saw at a glance that it was just as if it had been made for my case. I thought a little; it opened up; and putting away what I had prepared for the afternoon, I sat down and began to write. Easily, speedily, happily, I went on, and at the end found that I had been led to bring out all the elements and principles that should determine my conduct and that of my dear people. Still I intended no special allusion; but about nine o'clock, a note came down from — , who had been out in her district, and had heard that there was warmth in some quarters, and thought I might explain a little. I sat down again, and prepared a statement. Yesterday, between sermons, my friends came in; but they had been *waylaid* coming out of church, and were completely staggered. They said not a word, and would not so much as by a look implicate themselves. I went to my room, feeling that I was *quite* alone; but though a little stunned, not discouraged. It is a great thing, as our Church court men say, to have possession of the House. Psalms, prayer, sermon, prepared the way, and then I opened up briefly how I had come into my present position, – glancing back at all their kindness, my own trials in lot and soul, my correspondence with you, the drawing of my heart to India, and my engagement to go there. 'And now, what will you do? Would you have me draw back? Would you withhold me, and show that, while ready to give some things, there are others that you will be angry if they are even looked at? The trial has come to you; let it only quicken the graces of the Spirit, making you desirous to know and do the will of the Lord in love and peace. We may differ in opinion; it is unavoidable in this dark world; but we are still one in heart and love.' And so on. I think the Lord was with us, and I felt that I carried my people, though in sorrow, along with me. I scarce know how I could have acted as I did.

I seem like one who has leapt over a fearful ravine in the dark, and then, when he looks at it in the light, wonders how he ventured on what now seems so impossible. How the cup has gone round! First you, then me, now my people! When it comes to my brethren, they will have little to do; and I expect a good scold for having cut the tie, instead of waiting till they loosened it in due Presbyterian order. How kind and gracious is my condescending Lord!

Pray for me that I may be upheld. I feel like that one who said, 'Stay me with flagons, comfort me with apples; for I am sick of love.' The deep and universal regret of this whole town and neighbourhood at the thought of my departure, so variously and unequivocally expressed, quite unmans me, and lays me in the lowest dust. I am learning my favourite text: 'They shall fear the Lord and his goodness in the latter days.' There is only one thing wanting to make me go away singing for joy, and that is, to see my dear people united and harmonious in the choice of my successor.

Preparations for Decision

Again he writes to Hawkins:

MY DEAR MR HAWKINS, — I am favoured with your kind note, and shall be at the station on Tuesday evening to welcome you, thankful and joyful that my gracious Lord has given me such a friend to love and receive. Things are going on here in that smooth, happy tranquillity, which I suppose is meant, when it is said, 'I will give peace like a flowing river.' All minds and hearts seem overawed, or overruled, or graciously turned, so that neither in look, word, or act, has there been anything to pain me.

On Sabbath the 6th, Mr Dymock and I exchanged in the forenoon, and he served the edict. In the afternoon and evening I was with my people, and in the school and classes as usual. On Monday evening, the deacons' court took tea with me, — a very full, delightful meeting, — and they agreed upon a minute, conceived and drawn up in a beautiful, truly Christian spirit, to be carried by their commissioners to the Presbytery. On Tuesday evening, the session met and adopted the same minute. On Wednesday evening, the congregation met and adopted the same. This they will give in as their commission, for the different bodies, and merely add one kindly word or two. They view it as the will of God, and it is only on this ground that I can stand.

I have never, you know, inquired about the Calcutta congregation. I never *curiously* think of it, though my heart is there long ago. I have no tomorrow; the Lord is carrying me, and I *do* know that sweet happy life of faith, nestling in my dear Lord's bosom, to which you alluded in your former note, and which was very sweet to me. I think it would be well if, all through, in answer to humble prayer, the Lord would graciously show himself. My dear people are acting nobly. Do encourage them, and ask dear Dr Duff to do so. They have been in the forefront in liberality, self-denial, and all devotedness from the very first. They worship in a poor, barn-like church, that they may minister to the wants of others. I am in partings many. It is a daily dying, and I like the sweet rehearsal, for the Lord is making it sweet.

These letters bring out the whole history of the case as it stood, before the Presbytery met. From them we learn how the matter ripened for the final issue. Those who knew him only in his gentleness of spirit would have said, 'He will give way before their entreaties of affection'; but those who knew his fearlessness and immobility of purpose where duty seemed leading on, would have said, 'None of these things will move him.' He would give up any plan of his own, and submit to any amount of self-denial, in order to oblige the meanest member of his flock; but not a hairbreadth will he move, in spite of the beseechings of the whole thousand members, when the way of duty is made plain to him.[1] All he could say was, 'What mean ye to weep, and to break mine heart? for I am ready not only to go to India, but also to die there for the name of the Lord Jesus.'

[1] The extract contained in the following note ought to have come in earlier; but as part of it is illustrative of the above remarks, it is given here: 'It is not that I am hopeless here; far from it. I have not been permitted to doubt but that there will be blessing here from on high; perhaps abundant, perhaps soon. Neither is it that my people were ever more numerous or more attached. I believe that we never loved one another more, and it will be a sore pang on both sides when we part. But yet I am changed. My heart is sad and lone. It seems withered like the grass. Husband, father, widower, and childless; and all in fast succession. I feel that I need change of scene and employment, and hope that in another land my poor, weak heart may again open, and begin to find a new and fresh interest in life. My work, and dear friends like you, are now my earthly all. I think the Lord is beginning to smile upon me and help me. Pray for me my own earnest prayer, "that I may recover strength before I go hence and be no more". I should like that my last days were good days.'— *Letter to Somerville.*

Chapter 11

1853
Decision as to India

On the 23d of February the Presbytery were to meet to consider the case. The usual steps were duly taken, and the congregation cited to appear for their interests.

But, meanwhile, Milne was desirous that his people should be of one mind with himself as to this step; and should acknowledge what he believed to be the mind of God in it; and should, though it might be with sorrowful hearts, appear at the Presbytery, not as opposing, but acquiescing to this translation.

The full narrative of all the interviews and correspondence relating to these weeks, would occupy more space than can here be given to it. We content ourselves with a few letters which bring out the state of things, and introduce us to the decisive meeting of Presbytery.

Milne writes to Duff on the 12th of January:

MY DEAR DR DUFF, — I have this day had two new manifestations of my Lord's tender grace, and great considerateness. Last night, when I got home late from a long day of visiting, I found a lengthened paper, containing reasons for my not leaving my present charge, along with two notes, one a medical certificate (from two of my elders), and the other an invitation to a conference this afternoon at three o'clock. Oh, how much I am humbled and laid in the dust by having so much ado made about a poor wretched creature! This morning I was quite comforted by a letter from Mr Hawkins, which I took with me to the meeting. Oh, how painful to be among my dearest and most cherished friends, and constrained to grieve them! After prayer, I said, 'I am not come to reason; how can I fight against such love? I wish merely to state my deliberate conviction of the divine leadings.' They all met me in the same spirit. How kind, respectful, and tender they are with me! I left them, acknowledging on both sides that all we wish is the will of the Lord. I was going home, very sadly, lamenting that you and Mr Hawkins should be so much troubled about one so unworthy, and that I should be forced into publicity. At that moment the postman passed, and looking in his bundle, gave me a letter; it was yours, and my burden fell off, and I was lightened.

I fear Mr Hawkins will be startled, when a huge lawyer-like paper is sent him. I don't like to write again, for he must be weary of seeing this constant dropping. I begin to feel that there is a principle involved, and that something *must* be done to prove that it is not a pastor's will, nor a people's will, that is to determine this arrangement of the forces of Zion; but that it is the will of him who walks among the golden candlesticks. My mind has never wavered; I have had sinkings, but have anon been lifted up again. What would be bitter indeed, would be division between this dear, dear people. If they come to you, try to plead what has ever been my prayer, my teaching, my example, 'That they all may be one in the Lord.' JOHN MILNE.

Looking Eastward

On the 17th of the same month he writes to Hawkins:

MY VERY DEAR MR HAWKINS, — Shall I allow that I look with no little interest to your visit? I suppose, in the first instance, I shall not be permitted to have more intercourse than shaking hands at the terminus, for my dear friends here are jealous of the influence which they think you and Dr Duff exercise over me. I am quite alone in a hot, hot furnace of love. I think I can say to the Hindoo, breaking loose from caste and family, I know it all. Of course all this leads to the inquiry, as I told my people yesterday, 'Is *this* a bar in my way — a bar of love? or is it rather a trial to test and prove, and see if we are those self-abandoned ones whom the Lord loves to use and honour?' I believe the people are in the very state that I prayerfully desire, — softened, loving, waiting on the Lord with one accord. They had a very full meeting on Thursday night, and another most touching meeting for prayer last night. I think all is going on in the way which Paul would call 'Exceeding abundantly, above all that we can ask or think.' Will *you* be firm? I feel the door of usefulness here so very wide, and the ready access to every one I meet, by day and night, that I feel there *is* a most weighty responsibility; and though all my predilections now, and plans, are eastward, and though it would be a real cross to be stopped, yet in my heart I seek to be in entire simplicity at the Lord's disposal. I have *liking*, but desire to have no *willing* till he decide it. I am sorry I cannot get over tomorrow night to the meeting in the New College. The subject is one ever uppermost in my heart. It is our communion week, and we meet in session tomorrow night to confer about the spiritual condition of each district. What is passing here is surely a revival of the Disruption spirit, and as such I hail it. — Believe me, ever very affectionately yours, JOHN MILNE.

Never did worldly man seek after promotion and emolument with such earnestness as Milne set his heart upon missionary work in India. His whole soul seemed to burn with a desire to go forth and labour there. His correspondence shows this. His repeated and unwavering declarations to his brethren show it. Nothing could turn him aside from this purpose.

The meeting of Presbytery was deeply solemn as well as touching. His people nobly gave him up, though with broken hearts. They left the whole matter in the hands of the Presbytery; and the Presbytery, with reluctance in one aspect, and with joy in another, felt constrained to make the sacrifice. He pleaded so fervently. It looked like pleading against Perth, against his people, and against Scotland. Yet it was not so. He pleaded for India; he pleaded for the heathen. He entreated to be allowed to go forth into the field of foreign work for Christ. We give his speech in full. Both from its own power, and from the intensity of soul in delivering it, its effect was overwhelming.

Speech in Presbytery

MODERATOR, — My brethren will not be surprised if I am a good deal oppressed. I crave their sympathy and prayers. I am come to a crisis in my mortal history. If I draw back, as friends desire, I know not what shame may cover me, or what thoughts may haunt and dog me to the grave. And yet, if I go on, I shall do what may, perhaps must, affect me seriously for time and for eternity. If this were all, it would be a small matter, and it would be an unspeakable relief to know that my movements would only affect myself. But I cannot hide from myself the fact that my movement may, perhaps must, affect others both for time and for eternity. This is a burden too heavy for a sinful worm to bear, and I could not endure it, if I had not some realizing sense of a present Jehovah, in whose fulness I see enough to supply the wants of my dear flock who may soon be without a shepherd, and to meet all the exigencies of that new, untried life on which I am about to enter.

I have received many tokens of my Lord's loving-kindness in connection with this affair; and I reckon it not one of the least of them that, through the kindness of our beloved friends, Mr Hawkins and Dr Duff, I am this day spared the necessity of doing much more than simply declaring my unchanged, unwavering, unqualified adherence to the offer which I have made of my services for India. That offer was prompted by feelings and convictions which you have heard very fully detailed, and I know not that I should care to add anything to that statement, were I not most anxious that my brethren, if they cannot approve, should at least acquiesce in the step which I have purposed to take. A linked chain of circumstances, little in themselves, and which it would be impossible to narrate, but which are to me interesting and significant, have led me to a full assurance

that this movement is of the Lord. It may be said that it had its commencement when I was in a state of sorrow and dejection; granted.
But who will say that this was not the Lord emptying and bringing
down my heart that I might be made willing to go whithersoever he
would? It may be said that this offer was made when I was greatly
ignorant of the affection which my dear people felt for me, and of
the amount of spiritual good which I was the means of doing among
them; granted. But who can say that this was not the Lord leading
the blind in a way that he knew not? covering my eyes to what he
saw all the time, that my heart and eye might be irrevocably fixed on
a different field of labour?

My brethren will doubtless see not a little sin and error in what I
have done. But are there any actings of ours that are pure and perfect? And yet a sovereign God takes them and links them into those
chains of providence and grace by which he accomplishes his eternal
purposes. Looking back, I see some things done in ignorance, some
in unbelief, and some with too little consideration and consultation
of my dearest friends; yet I see also a pathway of heaven's own light,
that causes a lively hope that the Lord, out of this movement, will
bring good to my flock and glory to himself. I have found it a good
time for my own soul since this negotiation began. The Lord has come
near, and the world is far away. Long has the word sounded in my ear:
'Leave all and follow me, and I will make you fishers of men.' I have
often coveted the grace to do it, and I do feel as I never did, 'whom
have I in heaven but thee?'

I go in simple faith. I have made no provisions, no conditions, no
comparison of the two fields, no very particular inquiry about difficulties and dangers. I think I have heard a command 'Go', and I wish to
go; 'Follow me', and I wish to follow. And he who calls seems to *be*
breaking up the way. Clouds have arisen, only to vanish; difficulties
have sprung up, only to give way; objections were suggested to my
own mind, but they have been wholly removed. My dear people's deep,
wide, tender interest in the matter seemed at first a bar. My heart
trembled, as wave after wave of delicate, respectful, loving solicitation

broke upon me, and I feared my purpose would give way. I am a wonder to myself when I think how I have stood out; and this, more than anything, makes me believe that it is of the Lord.

My friends here know that I early said, 'If it be of the Lord, everything will give way', and so I have found it. My people are greatly reconciled, and so will be my Presbytery too. Brethren, a bubble on the water, a straw in the gale, are insignificant in themselves, but significant as showing the direction of the wind and the drift of the tide. Such am I, one of the weakest and unworthiest among you. Yet for the moment I occupy an important position; for, from your decision on this matter, it will be seen how your heart is affected to that great command, 'Go ye into all the world.' You have sent away our brother Grant to Australia, Cumming to Glasgow, without a single word of objection or disapproval. If you lay an embargo upon me; — but no, the thought is absurd. We have too long joined in the prayer, 'thy kingdom come, thy will be done on earth.' Here we see and know only in part. We can take in things only in little parcels at a time. It is well that it is so. One scene of this affair is transacting today; another will come by and by. I know this heart will be torn and lacerated in every part when I bid *adieu,* a lasting *adieu,* to my brethren and beloved flock. But I know it will be separation, not division, — we are one in Jesus; we shall still here meet at the throne of grace, and be reunited, ere long, around the throne of glory.

Deal gently with me and my people. Bruised hearts are here. Pour in wine and oil, and exhort and help us to hope that this affliction, which is not joyous but grievous, will yet yield peaceable fruits of righteousness.

I am Debtor

The Presbytery yielded to his pleadings, though some were not fully persuaded in their own minds, and resolved to loose him from his charge in Perth, that he might forthwith proceed to Calcutta to take pastoral charge of the Free Church congregation there.

The desire of his heart was fulfilled. 'I am debtor', he could say, 'both to the Greeks and to the barbarians, both to the wise and to the unwise; so, as much as in me is, I am ready to preach the gospel to you that are at' — *Calcutta* also. He was now setting off to pay the debt. He was doing so with his whole soul. Never did the pale, broken-down exile return from the land of the sun to his native Scotland with half the gladness with which Milne went forth to carry the gospel to these 'regions afar off'.

No minister ever loved his flock more than he did, yet he parted cheerfully from them to fulfil what he conceived to be his more special mission. He was now loosed from home; or, rather, he had found a new home and a new sphere. Thus he writes, in a private journal, on the Sabbath immediately before the meeting of the Presbytery, anticipating its decision.

His 'entry' on that Sabbath was a little premature; the case was not decided, though his own mind was made up. Many things might have hindered. But it was his way. The step which he had resolved to take was counted as already taken, and spoken of or written about as such. His ministerial arrangements were at times somewhat of this kind. He would fix his plans, arrange his meetings, expect you to help, announce you as one of his assistants, and yet his invitation was only on its way to you! he saw no hindrance, and so concluded that there was none. You *must* come, whether you could or not. It was all arranged and advertised! Yet how lovingly he bore the disappointment, when he found that you actually did not come! his earnestness might sometimes make him precipitate, occasionally too urgent; yet it never misconstrued a refusal, but took all in good part. Let us hear his journal.

His Journal — Thoughts and Preparations
  Leonard Bank, Perth, 10th February 1853. — Sabbath night. — This is properly my last Sabbath as minister of St Leonard's. I have been

graciously upheld and supported, been enabled to go on as if, on Wednesday, I was not to have the pastoral tie dissolved. How kind God and men are to me! I am overwhelmed. I fear the Lord and his goodness. Still there is in me the body of sin and death; and though, for the present, it seems graciously subdued, and greatly restrained and kept under, yet may I walk softly, watch and pray always, and diligently use all blessed appointed means of holiness. Lord save and bless!

21st February. — *Monday night.* — Rather wearied, but I always find that a short season of quiet resting in the Lord sets me up again. How sweet to me is that word, 'He restoreth my soul'! It was remarked to me tonight, as a pity, that my last Sabbath here will be the communion Sabbath. But I have had it brought to my mind that thy parting, O my Lord was at the supper table, and that thy servant Paul took leave of his beloved friends with the breaking of bread.

23d February. — *Wednesday morning.* — Dr Duff and Mr Hawkins came last night, and today the Presbytery will separate me from St Leonard's. Thou knowest, Lord, I have but two wishes — thy glory, and good to my flock. 'Yea, what is good the Lord will give.' And that, as the day, so my strength may be. I feel, by long experience, that when I am weak, then I am strong; when I stumble, I am lifted up. Condescend, in thy sovereign mercy, to glorify thyself in me.

Evening. — I am no longer minister of St Leonard's. The meeting of Presbytery was all that could be desired, solemn and affectionate. Surely the Lord smiles on this whole movement. Lord, I am a stranger and sojourner with thee. Keep my heart from resting henceforth on any earthly thing. I am a weak and sinful man; and yet, when I try to be thine, thou takest me.

26th February. — *Saturday evening.* — Went to Edinburgh on Thursday with Dr Duff and Mr Hawkins. Made necessary arrangements in a few minutes, as Mrs Hawkins and Mrs Duff are to arrange all. Oh! how smoothly and easily I am carried on. My God and my fellow-men are loading me with benefits. Make me holy. May I strive after holiness! May Satan's devices disappoint him, and turn back on his own head! Bless what I have been thinking of for tomorrow. I wait on thee.

27th February. — Sabbath night. — This has been a very comfortable day. I went a little earlier to bed last night than usual, and I think that is good. I have greatly enjoyed my work this day. Whether it has been useful in the same degree I cannot tell; but I am thankful for thy help, O my gracious Lord! Guide me in regard to that matter which has struck me in Bunyan. I feel my heart greatly drawn out for my young men. There must be about sixty of them at least, and many are gracious and most hopeful; also my young women; there are as many of them, though I cannot speak with anything like the same certainty, not having seen so much of them. How my heart warms to the simple, gracious, praying lads! How often I have been refreshed among them, and what proofs I have had of their confidence and love! Help me to pray much for my people. Help me to join in the union of the week for prayer. Help me to preach savingly and convertingly while I remain. Last week has been a very busy one; and this day, though pleasant, has been exhausting; but my Lord sustains me. Thou wilt preserve me from *every* snare and evil work. Thou knowest where I am very weak and vulnerable. Oh, save me from all presumption. Humble, holy, I would be.

March 2d. — Wednesday morning. — I have this morning had some gracious longings for a soft, humble, holy heart. O my Lord, give it, continue it, increase it, for thy name's sake. Let thy increasing goodness make me thy humble, holy, adoring, burning lover and servant. My heart, my whole heart, I want to be entirely, eternally thine. Teach me to distinguish between law and thy blessed gospel. May I never look to myself for my warrant to come to thee; but may what I growingly see in myself of all baseness, sin, and vileness, and what I desire growingly to see in thee of all goodness and worthiness, and grace and beauty and desirableness, make me pant and languish, and long and die, of heart-love sickness.

March 3d. — Monday morning. — Overwrought a good deal yesterday. Tried a little during the night, but now restored. Have written a little pastoral letter to the flock at Calcutta. How much I feel the necessity and blessedness of being careful for nothing; but in everything, with thanksgiving, pray! If I look at myself, or at outward things, I become gloomy; but in thee, Blessed One, is no darkness at all. Even a Pilate could say, 'I find no fault.' I desire eternally to cry, 'Chiefest among ten thousand, and altogether lovely!'

March 5th, Glendoich. — Saturday morning. — I see thy goodness, O my Lord, and my own sin. I do desire grace to deny myself in every form. Oh, help me to crush all the desires of this corrupt nature, whether in the form of vanity or pride, or of ease or sense. I do see and feel a little that it is good to die daily. Be thou chief and uppermost. Take us the foxes. I see a merciful deliverance, and thou guidest me with thine eye. Make me thy friend; and may I walk with thee in the fulness of a most transparent and unsuspecting confidence.

Evening. — Arbroath. — Somewhat helped at church. I am overwhelmed with a sense of thy goodness, O Lord. I see sin in what I have now before me, — I fear it began in sin; but I also see more and more thy gentleness and mercy in it. Oh, how kind — how kind — how kind thou hast been. I do desire with all my heart to give myself unreservedly, eternally to thee. I only wonder that thou shouldst care for such a gift. My Lord, — my blessed, glorious, heavenly Lord, — let me every day increasingly fear thee and thy goodness. Deal kindly with all those I am thinking of at present; manifest thyself to them, and let them love thee. I ask a blessing for tomorrow, — not merely help, but *power.* Let souls be awakened and saved, and let me be able, as I journey along, to say, 'Now thanks be to God, who always causeth us to triumph in Christ, and maketh manifest the savour of his knowledge by us.' Let me never trifle, but be always girded up and seeking eternal things.

March 7th, Monday. — Leonard Bank. — On Saturday night a letter from Francis Edmond told me of the impossibility of getting on to Huntly Lodge, Perth, and Elgin, as I intended. This for a little was a trial, and disconcerted all my plans, because I have now little time. But I gave way, and doubt not that I shall yet see good reasons for this disappointment. Enjoyed the Sabbath work both in public and visiting the sick; but felt a wish that I had prayed more on Saturday night. I think I was too much carried away and excited. Happy this morning, and have comfort in all the circumstances of travel. I would seek to remember that every moment we exercise influence. I felt this in read-ing that sentence last night, and I feel it today in the commencement of my converse with Mr Webster. Oh, what a watchful, self-denied, considerate, girded-up life one would need to live, and yet how easy and sweet such a life would be, if we walked in the light, as he is in the light! Lord, make me holy, that is, make me wholly, constantly, heartily thine. I am once more home. I feel that I have never realized yet the final going away. But it will soon come, and thou wilt bear me through. A new home even on earth, if thou seest good, and an eternal one, by and by, above. Have just heard a report of some terrible accident to the Harbours on the railway.[1] Help me to bear them on my heart. Guide my dear people at present.

March 8th. — Tuesday morning. — Went over last night to Spring-land, and found that the rumour was true, and that the reality was worse than the rumour. I feel that thou, Lord, art giving me to bear these sorely afflicted friends upon my mind and heart night and day. Thy will be done. I desire increasingly to count all loss. Make my heart clean. Thou knowest that I have never felt bitterness under my trials, though I have sinfully sunk under them. But what, after all, are mine to theirs? Lord, support and bless them. Guide me in all I have to do today. Let me be thy holy, happy, diligent, simple child and servant.

March 10th. — Thursday night. — Troubled rather on Tuesday, and also Wednesday morning. My Lord, I tried to look to thee, and think I have found relief, though my seeking was poor and weak. Have had much happiness in my journey to the west. I thank thee, Lord, for opportunity of meeting with so many friends in Glasgow — for the kindness of the Presbytery — for opportunities of usefulness on the way to Rothesay — for all that I have learned from the Mackails; for I feel more hope and encouragement than ever, and it is simply in

[1] See p. 170, *Ed.*

looking to thee. May I strive more and more after the work of faith with power. I see a clear ordering of all my steps. I seek the perfect love which casteth out fear. Thou hast also taught me lessons, and I pray that I may not forget, nor neglect them. O my Lord, guide, keep, and bless, and, in thy good time and way, bring me to my new scene of work. Yet let me not expect much on earth, nor seek great things here.

I find my Lord strangely overruling all things. Thou art disappointing my fears, or rather, out of what I feared thou art bringing goodness and blessing. Thou removest my burdens and cares, and makest my dear friends willing to take them up. May I care for thy things, and may my besetting sins be subdued. May pride and self be quickly checked, and greatly abhorred. Help me — help me to quench the fiery darts, and to live a life of faith, walking with God.'

March 12th, Saturday. — *Edinburgh.* — The Lord has been kind today. I have had comfort in preparing for tomorrow. I saw also thy goodness yesterday, and my heart trembles and is enlarged. O my Lord, I long to be wholly and abidingly thine. This body of sin must remain; but may I watch, and pray, and look to thee. This world must remain; but may I think little or nothing of it, but in connection with thee. Bless those I think of. Make them holy.

April 3rd. — *Sabbath evening.* — I desire thankfully to record my gracious Lord's loving-kindness. Life has been flowing on in a pleasant business (*i.e.* busy-ness). I find that my hands are made sufficient for me, and as the day so is my strength. I know no care. Amid constant engagement, and great responsibility, I really know no care. It is a style of life which I have sometimes fancied, but which I never knew before. I am trying to care for the things of the Lord, and he makes many dear, wise friends care for my concerns. I think I do see that he is making me feel an interest in every creature I meet in his providence. I find it a great help not to look at things in the heap, but to take them one by one, hour by hour, day by day. Also I am strangely delivered from care about earthly things. I seem not to seek my happiness in any way in them, but in the Lord; and in him is no darkness, disappointment, or mortification. I almost wonder how I am carried on; but it is the Lord. I feel very much as Simeon: Now lettest thou thy servant depart. My dear people's love overflows like a mighty tide, and I should not know what to make of it; but a voice that brooks no refusal says, 'Be still, and know that I am God.' If he lifts up, who can cast down? I had much pleasure in meeting friends in Aberdeen, especially my dear friend Francis Edmond. Also much pleasant intercourse with the Duchess of Gordon and Mr Rainy at Huntly. I cannot tell how much I owe to that lady. I have found my intercourse with her quickening and elevating. Also with my friends at Perth I have been happy, and I have enjoyed my meeting with Mrs MacDonald and her family at Elgin. Let me record those things to look back upon, and find cheering in future hours of trial. I find my dear people looking to — ; and how will my heart rejoice, if, unitedly and speedily, they invite one to labour among them! Thy will, O Lord, be done. Thou overwhelmest me with kindness, and I have need to say, 'I am oppressed, Lord undertake.' I ask guidance and help for the few remaining days. May I experience thy constant presence and blessing. Remember, O Lord, my young men and women. Thou art making me to remember my evil ways and loathe myself. This morning I felt wearied, poor, and needy, and unable to realize present support. Looked for help, and desired to be simple and earnest, and I have been helped all day, yet feel some regret that I did not make more of my meeting with the young women. I feel as if I had lost an opportunity. I find that no day passes without some slip, often at the very end. Help me to repent. Forgive and guide me to repair.

April 4th. — Monday morning. — I have given away my little almanac to Eliza, and so I shall put my wishings and thoughts here. Awoke pretty early. Felt my need of close, steady, continued seeking thy face, O Lord. May I walk softly, and fear, because of thy goodness. I have the prospect of a very busy week, and in each hour occupied. But I must not look at the whole, but live hour by hour. Thou wilt guide and help. Keep my eyes from tears, and my feet from falling. May I watch and pray more, and be ever guided. This is not the place for relaxation. Help me to be in earnest in all I do, and always doing.'

The Single Eye

In all these transactions and communications the single eye is manifest. His face was set stedfastly to his work, whatever and wherever that might be. He sought not to please himself. Nothing could turn him aside. He was a minister of Christ; nor could anything make him lose sight of that. In the pulpit, or out of it, he was the same. The more you knew him, the oftener you conversed with him or corresponded with him, the longer you lived with him, the more did you learn to admire and love. His house, his study, his closet, his servants, his guests, his nearest relatives, were witnesses of his bright consistency. The farther in you went, the more of Christianity you found, and the more of the image of Christ you saw.

Chapter 12

1853
Farewells – Voyage

*A*mong old letters there turns up the following farewell note to *me* from William Burns. He dates it 'Off Portsmouth, June 9th, 1847, on board the "Mary", — "Bannatyne", for Hong Kong.' It runs thus:

> DEAR BROTHER, — As our pilot is still on board, and will not leave us at least till the morning, I drop a note to thank you for your three unanswered notes. I have often thought of writing, but have wanted an impulse sufficient to move my tardy pen. I have just entered on my field of labour and patience here. We have got worship this evening begun in the cuddy. This *is* something. May the Lord himself come to us, though it should be needful that we be awakened by the stormy wind and tempest. My way seems to have been made very plain in the matter hitherto; and yet you can easily see that it is a dark and solemn dispensation, either to myself or to those I leave behind, when one of the grounds of my departure is the want of any *special* blessing at home. Truly we live in solemn days; and it is much, I think, to be enabled at present to hold fast that which we have already obtained. I must not enlarge, but remain, dear brother, yours ever in JESUS, our hope, W. C. BURNS.

Four years later, Milne writes the following similar farewell memorandum or diary on board ship:

April 27th, 1853. — Much has happened since last entry. It was a busy yet happy week, and the communion on the 10th seemed blessed. On Monday night was our happy farewell meeting; happy, because of the presence of the Lord, the display of mutual love, and the hope that, ere long, we should meet in glory. How my heart fills at the thought of that dear people! and I desire to be stirred up, at the thought, to constant watchfulness, earnestness, and prayer. On Wednesday, set out for Edinburgh; on Friday, for London. I think with pleasure of the journey, and of all the kindness I received from Mr Nisbet, Mr Kinnaird, and Lady Pirie.

W. C. Burns and John Milne

Thus these two friends, companions in labour and in warfare, setting out for different lands and in different years, as they bid farewell to their native shores, speak out in the fulness of their hearts. There had been many changes in their lot since the time that they worked so joyfully together in 1840. Both had been, even in their years of busiest life at home, thinking of the foreign field; by very different processes these thoughts had ripened, till at last, — the one in 1847, and the other in 1853, — they set out, being led in ways that they knew not, for foreign shores, to labour apart for years, and at last to die within two months of each other.

> Already lies my childhood's home behind me,
>   Though still I linger on my native ground;
> And here must soon be loosed the ties that bind me,
>   When moves yon ship, now by her anchor bound.
> Friends of my home! then fare-ye-well, I leave you;
>   The sail is spread, the hoisted flag I see;
> Think, when in prayer, of me, nor let it grieve you;
>   Mourn not, — remember *who* has gone with me.
>   *Missionary Embarkation Hymn (German).*

He thus writes to Somerville, on the 8th of March:

Did you *really* think, now, that I would or could go away without seeing you once more? I trust, for the credit of us both, that no such thought ever was yours. It was only a passing cloud, darkening your love for a moment, and then passing away. I cannot say what day I shall get through, but likely in the week after next. I was going north this week to Banffshire and Morayshire, but have been obliged to return, as the roads are still uncut. This has broken up my plans; but I am quietly believing that God's disposal is better than my proposal. I shall let you know before I come. So far had I gone on, when something said, 'Why put off till then what may be done now?' So, will you wait for me tomorrow at your own house a little after ten? I shall come by the first train. *P.S.* — What sad tidings reached me from Manchester when I got home yesterday! [referring to the railway disaster which brought sorrow to Mr Harbour's family.] I would not believe it till I went over to Springland, and found that reality was worse than rumour. I am much crushed; for it is scarce ten days since I parted with them all at the Grange. I am sick, sick of the world, and should be glad to get away, were it not for a friend or two, and the hope that I may have a little yet to do.

The weeks before Milne's departure were busy weeks, filled up with farewell visits and farewell sermons, and farewell work of other kinds. He preached his last sermon on the evening of Sabbath the 10th of April.[1]

[1] The following paragraph is from a local journal: 'Our readers are aware that, some time ago, Mr Milne accepted a call from the Free Church congregation of Calcutta, addressed to him through Dr Duff and Mr Hawkins. On this account, the pastoral connection between him and his present congregation came to a close, by appointment of the Presbytery, on Sabbath last, the day on which the sacrament of the Lord's Supper was dispensed; and in a few days, we understand, he leaves his native shores for the far distant land, which is to be the scene of his future labours. The removal of such an honoured servant of the Lord from the midst of us has created a deep sensation among all classes of the community, more especially among the members of the Church of which he is a bright ornament. For thirteen years he has been pastor of St Leonard's congregation. During this time he has endeared himself to all by his uniform kindliness of manner and

Farewell Congregational Meeting

Besides this farewell Sabbath's communion services, there was a Monday's meeting in Free St Leonard's Church on the 11th, where there was an immense gathering to bid the final farewell. Of this it will be best to give the newspaper account, as more vividly bringing the scene before us:

On Monday evening a meeting of the congregation of Free St Leonard's Church was held in their own place of worship, for the purpose of taking a public farewell of their late highly respected and beloved pastor, the Rev. Mr Milne, and presenting him with a token of their esteem previous to his leaving his native country to take the pastoral charge of the Free Church congregation at Calcutta. The church was filled to overflow, and great numbers belonging to different persuasions, who were anxious to witness and take part in the proceedings, could not get admittance. John Flockhart, Esq., presided; and upon the platform erected in front of the pulpit, besides Mr Milne, the members of the kirk session, and the deacons' court, we noticed the following members of the Free Church Presbytery of Perth: The Rev. Messrs. Gray, Dymock, Grierson, Bonar, and Walker; the Rev. Mr Moody Stuart, Edinburgh; W. S. Turnbull, Esq. of Huntingtower;

---

singleness of heart, labouring zealously, faithfully, affectionately, and successfully amongst a large, influential, and attached flock, who, holding as he did the scriptural principles for which the Church of Scotland contended during the "Ten Years' Conflict", adhered to him at the Disruption, and continued to enjoy his valued ministrations. We feel deep regret at parting with him. The thought is sorrowful and solemnizing, that we are to see no more his light and rapid step, as he hurried to and fro through the streets of our city, ever engaged in the work of his heavenly Master, to wait at the couches of the sick and dying, and to carry the bread of life from house to house. We sympathize deeply with his bereaved congregation, who are no more to hear in the sanctuary his earnest and glowing appeals, or to receive at his lips, in the time of sickness and sorrow, the consolations of grace, which sustained his own spirit amidst severe domestic trials, and which he knew so well how to apply to others. Long, long will it be before the honoured name of Mr Milne will be pronounced by many in Perth without emotion, or fail to call up in their minds associations of a tenderly, impressive, and very solemn nature. Still, whilst his people and the community of Perth suffer a grievous loss, it is an alleviation to think that his labours will be continued in the same great cause, though in a distant laud. Scotland's loss is India's gain.'

A. Cunningham, *etc. etc.* The solemn and highly interesting proceedings of the evening commenced by singing the 121st Psalm. The Rev. Mr Stuart read the 20th chapter of Acts, from 17th verse to the end, and then offered up a fervid and appropriate prayer, highly suitable indeed to the circumstances in which pastor and people were placed, after which the chairman called upon the Rev. Mr Gray to address the meeting.

The Rev. gentleman, in a short address, alluded to the part he had taken in the ordination of Mr Milne as minister of St Leonard's Church. The thirteen years since did not seem long, and could be easily spanned. The congregation were now in very much the same situation as then; for his personal friend, Mr Milne, with the closing services of a communion Sabbath, was no longer minister of Free St Leonard's. But neither pastor nor people were the same. His dear friend was not the same, for he had had trials and experiences that would go with him to the grave. The congregation were not the same for, after his settlement amongst them, there was a wonderful work of the grace of God manifested. They were not the same, for the faithful labours of Mr Milne had been sanctified to the conversion of not a few, and all had much to answer for the privileges they had enjoyed. After stating that the removal of Mr Milne preached a sermon to the unconverted, Mr Gray proceeded to say that Mr Milne leaving his present sphere of labour was a loss, not only to the Presbytery and his own congregation, but to the city of Perth, the neighbourhood, and to the whole Church.

Mr Bonar of Collace then engaged in prayer, after which a part of the Hundredth Psalm was sung.

Mr Wallace, senior member of session, then addressed Mr Milne, and feelingly alluded to the peace and harmony which had subsisted between him, the session, and congregation. Mr Wallace having exhorted Mr Milne to be courageous in fighting the battles of the Lord in that land of idolatry and spiritual death whither he was bound, affectionately shook him by the hand, and bade him farewell on behalf of the session.

Mr Livingstone, on behalf of the deacons' court, also bade farewell to Mr Milne.

The chairman, in an appropriate address, then presented Mr Milne with an elegant and highly finished spring skeleton clock, with lever escapement, jewelled in five actions, with compensation balance and maintaining power. It strikes the hours on a gong, and the half-hours on a bell. The clock is twenty-five inches by eighteen, and is placed on a marble stand. On a plate of pure gold attached to it is the following inscription: — 'Presented to the Rev. John Milne, minister of Free St Leonard's Church, Perth, on the eve of his departure for India, by the members of his congregation, in token of their high esteem and affection for him, as a faithful and devoted pastor, during the thirteen years he has laboured amongst them. Perth, April 1853.' There was also presented to Mr Milne, by the chairman, a purse of sovereigns, to purchase such books *as* he thought were required by him, or to be applied in any way he thought proper. In presenting the above, the chairman, after adverting to the watchful care and earnest labours of Mr Milne, trusted he would arrive at the future scene of his ministry in peace and safety, and be a blessing to the Church and the world, in the vast region of India.

On receiving the gifts presented by the chairman, Mr Milne said, he felt assured that, on the present occasion, he needed the sympathies of his congregation. He had looked forward to separating from them with much fear and trembling, and it was his original intention to have gone away quietly on the forenoon of Monday, after divine service in the church. But their kindness had detained him, and he was there not their unwilling captive. He might say, looking at his present position, what a man of God said in different circumstances, 'It is the Lord, let him do what seemeth him good.' His congregation had been teaching him divinity after a new fashion. The present gifts were too much for him, and were undeserved; they put the copestone upon their mag- nificent liberality to him. He before had received many an Ebenezer at their hands to humble him in the dust, and the present kindness tended more to do so. He could make no return for such liberality, for he parted with them with no desire to meet face to face, till they met in glory. He should look back upon his present congregation — if he might now call them such — as an united, peaceful, and prosperous people. Mr Milne then returned his fervent thanks to the members of session, the deacons' court, the Sabbath-school teachers, and the district collectors. He then replied to the statement which had been often made to him, Why break up a fellowship which had been so pleasant? He did so on his own responsibility, and he was not afraid to face it. He had considered the matter of leaving his flock in light and in darkness, and he was convinced that God called him so to do. He therefore had no wavering and no fear, and he was persuaded his conviction could not be shaken. Nor was he afraid, in separating from his congregation, but the same brotherly love would continue. There would, he was persuaded, be no change in that respect, but they would be more abundant in the Lord. He should ask three things: first, that as they had received and honoured him, they would receive and honour his Lord and Master; the second request was, that as he had had many sins, failings, and shortcomings, and may have been partial, having the feelings of the man, they would cast the veil of charity over them; and a third request was, that they would give him their supplications; while praying for their pastor, he hoped they would pray for him as their missionary. Mr Milne concluded with praying that the Lord would bless the congregation of which he had been minister.

A part of the 8th Paraphrase was sung, after which the chairman called upon the Rev. Mr Grierson to make a few remarks and engage in prayer.

The Rev. gentleman said that Mr Milne was the first to intimate to his congregation, in 1842, the coming disruption of the Church of Scotland, which took place on the following year. He then said that, come what will, he should go and preach the gospel, as he had no incumbrance. He (Mr Grierson) considered the congregation of St Leonard's an honoured people. They had had the gospel faithfully preached to them. They had been distinguished for love and union, and, as had been stated by the members of session and the deacons' court, no diversity of opinion had prevailed amongst them. Moreover, they had been distinguished amongst the congregations of the Free Church by the liberality with which they had contributed to the cause of Christ. But, above all, they had shown far greater liberality than in giving the gifts that perish, by giving up their minister to labour in the sphere to which the Lord had called him, and that in the spirit of unanimity and love. Mr Grierson concluded his address by exhorting them to continue to be distinguished as they had been, and to look out for a pastor who should be a man of wisdom and of the Holy Ghost.

A portion of the 23d Paraphrase having been sung, Mr Dymock pronounced the benediction, and the vast assemblage, amounting to nearly two thousand persons, then separated, evidently deeply impressed with the solemn and mournful services in which they had been engaged, in separating from a devoted and dearly loved minister of Christ.

The Voyage

He lost little time in making ready to start. If he was not quite so speedy as Burns, who, immediately after his appointment by the Synod for China, took up his carpet bag to set off, he was no less eager to get his work begun. Leaving Perth on Wednesday 13th, he had a day or two in London; and on the following Wednesday (20th) he was on board the steamer, 'ready to depart', and his face set stedfastly towards the East. Thus he briefly journalizes at this time:

On Wednesday (20th), set out with Dr Duff, Mr Hawkins, and Lady Pirie, for Southampton, and embarked. They stood on the shore waving to me till the little steamer went out of sight. I am treated with all kindness and respect here; and after two days of storm and severe sickness, I found myself becoming accustomed to this kind of life. It is a strange life, and yet I feel there are boundless opportunities of usefulness among the many young men who will soon be scattered over the eastern world.

But it needs much watchfulness, prayer, resolute, self-denying effort, and constant supplies from on high. I am now sitting in the saloon; the band is playing, and the young men are scattered about, most variously employed. It may seem often a kind of hopeless labour in such a soil; but God *will* make it to grow. Oh that I might be kept lively, holy, spiritual! Lord, help me much, much! I wait on thee. Give me deliverance and guidance, that I may walk wisely, happily; and that I may help, and not be hurt. I see the danger of sinking; of becoming slothful and self-indulgent. Lord, I am alone, and I look to thee.

He moves on over the waters, sometimes in calm, and sometimes in storm; always, in so far as his strength allows, seeking to sow the eternal seed. He passes through Egypt, down the Red Sea; his face resolutely towards India, like the powerful vessel he sails in. He suffers somewhat in body, both from sickness and from an uncomfortable cabin; heat from the sun by day, and from the boiler by night; visited, too, by cockroaches under his pillow, at which he murmurs not, but accepts all as his Father's will. For, is he not going on his Father's special errand? Is he not rapidly nearing India, to whose mighty capital he is carrying the good news of God's great love in the gift of His Son?

On Wednesday, the 18th of May, he again journalizes:

Much has passed since last entry; Gibraltar, Malta, Alexandria, the Nile, Cairo, the Desert, Aden, have all been passed. We are now stretching into the sea, to Ceylon. I have had few discomforts. I scarcely feel weariness, and would not shorten the voyage, even if I could. Yet I shall be glad, I think, when I get to land, and begin my regular work. Yet thy will be done. I would not be in Calcutta a moment before thy time. Oh that I might, in my Master's spirit, be able to say, 'The hour is come, guide, help, and bless me.' I see that I shall have trials to encounter, in the fewness, the spirit, habits, and frequent changes of my future flock. But all things are possible to thee. Only strengthen me by thy Spirit in my soul unto all patience and longsuffering with joyfulness. I pray for a general, perhaps almost unconscious, preparation for my work. I think thou wilt do it, Lord. I feel it a privilege to have had dealings, however slight, with so many varieties of character. May I humbly, thankfully, earnestly, persever-ingly live and labour on.

Thus he girds himself for his work; taking to himself the whole armour of God. He casts himself, in believing simplicity, on the strength of the Mighty. He approaches India with fear and trem-bling; yet in faith, and 'watching unto prayer'. He has one entry more before he sets his foot on Indian soil:

Saturday Morning, 28th May. — We have the pilot on board, and are making for the river, expecting to reach Calcutta tonight about seven. It has been in many respects a most speedy and prosperous voyage. From being put into a cabin near the boiler, and so intolerably hot, I became ill before we reached Ceylon. I have suffered a good deal; but it is past. At Ceylon I was moved into a better cabin, and began at once to recover. In consequence of this illness, I could neither land at Point de Galle nor at Madras. I felt it a trial to be deprived of the opportunity of meeting the brethren there; but saw at once that it was duty not to attempt it.

Looking back upon the way, I see much cause for thankfulness and humiliation. My fears have been disappointed, my hopes exceeded, promises have been fulfilled, and unlooked-for opportunities of being useful, — studying character, and coming into peaceful contact with other minds of the most various kind, — constantly afforded me. I look back with wonder upon all this intercourse, and leave it with my Lord, assured and confident that, though carried on in much weak-ness, and under diverse disadvantages, it yet has not been in vain. If it be thy will, may I hear of these persons from time to time, or even meet with them. I think the Lord has preserved me not a little from my besetting sins, and enabled me to walk safely amid the temptations and snares of this kind of life. The chief want, perhaps, has been an opportunity for private prayer. The motion of the ship I have found a hindrance. True, if there was much inclination, nothing could prevent.

Thus prayer has too often been meditation. Perhaps the Lord has sent me sickness just to force me nearer to him. At least this is the light in which I like to view his afflictive dealings.

Lord, remember my relatives, friends, and flock at home. I have separated myself from them; but thou art in the midst of them. Cast the skirt over all my sins among them, and may nothing be remembered but what may be in some way useful to them. Lord, teach me to pray. Oh that I might live in the secret place, and put prayers into thy golden censer, O Lord! And now, when I enter on a new sphere, oh that I might be strangely humbled, purified, guided! Lord, leave me not under the known or unknown dominion of any of my sins. Thou wilt subdue our corruptions. I ask deliverance from self-seeking. Take thy right place, O Lord, and be all in all. Let self be growingly eclipsed and forgotten. Let me decrease, and do thou increase. Let me learn to rejoice with them that rejoice, and weep with them that weep. I feel that the serpent's brood are in me; let me watch and pray. There is no more condemnation to Christ's dear ones, who walk not after the flesh … I see that I am entering a scene of trial and a place of the shadow of death. Help me to watch and strive. Save from sloth, from merely enduring life, instead of living to thy glory.

Lord, help me. Thou knowest my heart. Search and try, and lead me in the way everlasting. O my Saviour! a little, helpless, foolish child, I now implicitly commit myself to thee. I know that, by thy grace in the past, I have been brought hitherto. O my Lord! I cast myself on thee. Leave me not, forsake me not, forget me not. Let me never misconstrue or judge hardly of thy dealings. May I trust, and hope, and rejoice. Seek and find thy servant. Let thy strong hand be my help. Graciously use me, bless me; make me willing to learn, and willing to teach; willing to be led, and willing to lead. I am uttering all my words before thee. Thou knowest how stripped and bare I am. I have no idol to bring and kill save this indwelling corruption; and I do think I should like that it were slain; and that, in a new, strange simplicity and godly sincerity, I might serve and honour thee henceforth. This inner war now lies specially before me. I expect in this new land to be hedged up by outward circumstances. But just so much the more may I fight against the evil that is within. O my Lord! to thee I look, on thee I wait. May my character be transparent, and my life blameless, holy, earnest. I commit myself wholly and eternally to thee. I am well pleased with thy person, offices, benefits, cross, rod, and all thy ways. Those whom I have ever truly loved have been thy people, and anything worth the name of joy has been found in thy service. I love to praise thee, and to hear thee praised. Lord, help me! ...

The men are busy cleaning the cabin. It is the end of a voyage, and the preparation for a new one. I accept the lesson. O my Lord! sprinkle me with hyssop; wash me, and I shall be whiter than snow. Give me the peace, the softness, the joy of thy forgiven, gentle, hopeful children. Bless me in my meeting with friends tonight. I have no plans, yet thou knowest my foolish heart. Oh, how great is thy goodness, which thou hast laid up for them that fear thee!

Christian and Minister Always — No Half-Discipleship

He was not idle on board, though unable to do so much as he wished. He found opportunities, from day to day, of doing or speaking something for eternity. His light could not but shine during that voyage, and of this there were found some traces on the vessel's return. A gentleman coming from India in that same year (1853) was surprised to find tracts and little books lying about the steamer. He asked how and by whom this had been done. He was told that, last voyage, a 'curious gentleman' had been on board, going to India. Every evening he used to go among the sailors, talking to them and listening to their stories. When they had done with their talk, he would take out his Bible from his pocket, and read a portion to them. Then he prayed with them. It was he who had given the tracts and books. There was no difficulty in discovering who this 'curious gentleman' was.

On the same voyage, he went about among the cabin-boys, getting hold of them whenever he could. He used to promise them a sixpence or a shilling if they would learn a certain psalm or chapter, and repeat it to him. This was his practice on shore as well as at sea; and his card would frequently be handed in to Mrs Milne by some boy, with this pencilled on it, 'Give the bearer sixpence [or a shilling as it might be] if he repeats the 53d of Isaiah', or 55th, as the case might be. His devices for getting hold of people, or getting a word spoken to them, were as various as his zeal was unflagging. In Perth, or on the road, he might be seen helping a baker to carry his board or basket, or a man with a wheelbarrow, that he might get an opportunity of speaking to them. A Roman Catholic woman, who went about as a hawker, selling plates and dishes, tells that, meeting him once as she was coming down a long stair, he said to her, 'You are looking weak'; and then he insisted on carrying her basket down to the street, dropping a word as he went. These were frequent occurrences; and he would say on such occasions, 'You know we should bear one another's burdens', or some such word.[1] Some would have thought it beneath his dignity to hand his coat to a poor man who complained that he could not get to church for

[1] One is struck with the resemblance between some of Milne's ways and those of Lieutenant Blackmore, as narrated in his *London by Moonlight Mission:* 'At the bottom of Edgware Road', says the Lieutenant, 'I overtook a poor old woman with a large basket of linen. I offered my assistance, which she gladly accepted. As we walked along, she on one side of the basket and I on the other, I had an excellent opportunity of speaking to her of the love of him who said, "Come unto me, and I will give you rest."' Again, the Lieutenant tells us this: 'At the bottom of Holborn Hill, I overtook an old man with a heavy load on a truck. I said, I'll get hold of this man's heart, if I can, and then speak to him of Jesus. "You've got a heavy load there, my friend; I'll give you a lift." I took hold of the pole, while the old man pushed. Arriving at the top, where there is a public house, the old man pulled out a penny, saying, "You'll take a drop of beer, sir." "No, thank you", I said; "but I'll help you a little farther"; and as we walked along we talked of the love of him who, though he was rich, for our sakes became poor. He listened with eagerness; and at parting, held out his hand, with thanks. A gentleman afterwards calling, asked me if I had one day helped to wheel up a truck. "Yes, I remember doing such a thing." "Do you think this worthy of an officer or a gentleman?" "Well, whether it was that or not, it was not unbecoming a Christian." "I believe, sir, you're not quite right in the head." "Perhaps I am not. It's not the first time I have been thought a fool. Good morning."'

want of clothes; or to pat the heads of the ragged children whom he passed on the street, and speak kind words to them; or to rush out of his house one snowy day to the Inch (or public green) to help a poor woman to get down her washingropes; but he never thought of his own comfort or dignity when he could assist another. Whether on shore or on ship-board, in Scotland or in India, his benevolence and obligingness were the same. In one pocket you might find a bottle of wine for some sick person, in another a bunch of grapes, and in another a packet of tracts or books. He was 'ready, aye ready', for every good word and work. He 'called nothing common or unclean' whereby he could serve the Master, or comfort a disciple, or arrest a wanderer.

In his Family Bible there is the following entry, which bears upon the events of this chapter:

> Loosed from my charge of Free St Leonard's on the 23d February 1853, in order to go to Calcutta, according to the will of the Lord, I trust. Pardon and take away what is mine in this matter; stablish and strengthen what is thine own. Goodness and mercy have followed me hitherto — Ebenezer! And I shall be preserved from every snare and evil work — Jehovah-Jireh. Landed at Calcutta, after a speedy and prosperous voyage, on Sabbath, 29th May 1853, and commenced my ministry in the Free Church that evening.

A very important portion of his life now begins. It is to a new work, and in a new country, and among new people, that he is called. But wherever he is, he shows himself the man of God and the servant of Jesus Christ. He is the Christian and the minister always. The salt never loses its savour. His first love never cools. As Luther said of a friend, 'He lives what we preach.'

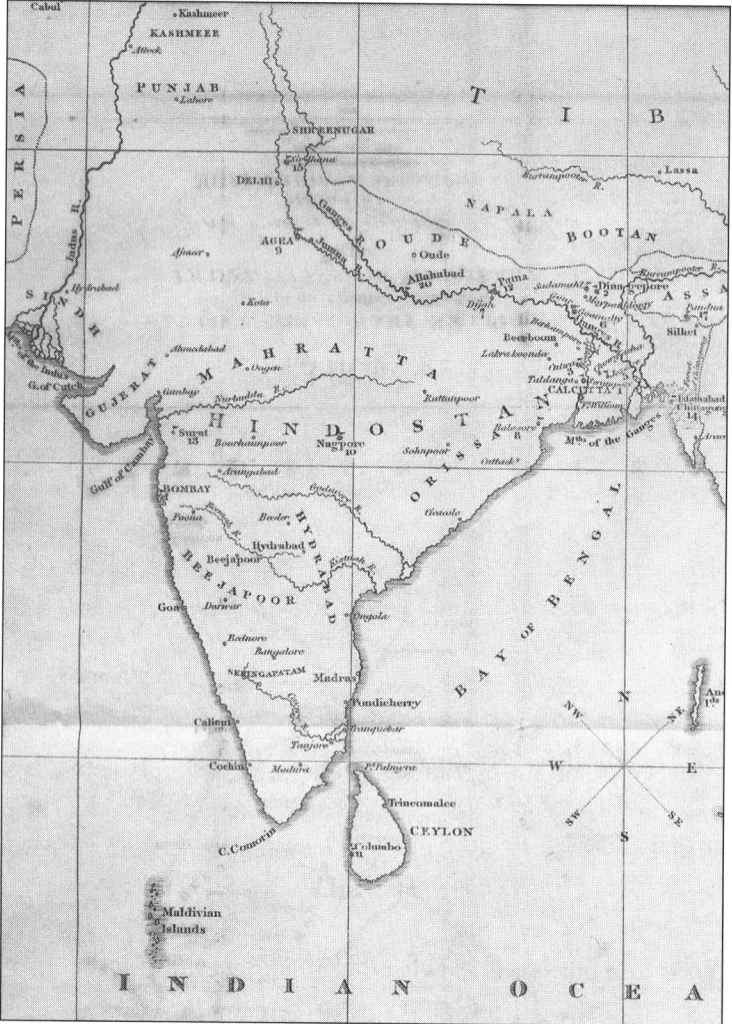

Map of India

Chapter 13

1853–1854
In India

*H*aving reached Calcutta, John Milne lost not an hour in beginning his work. It was on Sabbath, May 29, that he landed, and passing almost from the steamer to the church, he preached in the evening to the congregation, of which he had undertaken the charge, from the text, 'Lord, what wilt thou have me to do?' He was not, however, regularly inducted till the 12th of June.

Looking round him on the mighty India which was now to be his home, and marking the eager worldliness on all sides, he exclaims: 'Poor India! Its cadetships and writerships are sought after; but its schools and pulpits few seem to care for.' How is it, we may ask, that among the thousands of Christians and Christian ministers at home, so many seek their own, and so few the things that are Jesus Christ's? Worldly men rush out in thousands to become rich; Christian men lag behind, when souls only are to be won. For the corruptible gold multitudes compete; for the incorruptible, but a handful.

Thoughts on Work

In the course of a few days Milne had overtaken a considerable amount of work; so that, in a fortnight after his arrival, he could write in his journal:

June 16th. — Chowringhee Road. — Little more than a fortnight, and yet how much has passed! I have visited many of my people, the religious institutions, become acquainted with ministers and missionaries, and am as much at home as if I had lived here for years. I acknowledge thy kindness, O my Lord! in the warm welcome I have received from them, in the large open door that seems set before me, and in the hope and freedom from care which I enjoy. I see that it must be a daily taking up of the cross. The heat, my bodily uneasiness, and the dark heathenism all around, with the distance from beloved friends, make it a real sacrifice to be here. Yet I feel that the truth as it is in Jesus can carry me on. May I daily kindle my dim lamp, and warm my cold heart, and renew my failing strength at this changeless glory, and so go on my way rejoicing. Let me feel increasingly the power of the truth to sanctify, gladden, and animate to all patient suffering and earnest well-doing.

June 17th. — I see more and more that if I am to live in some measure of holy activity here, I must fix my eye on the eternal rest, and press through, quite irrespective of present experiences and events. There is here a bodily irritation from the insects, and a lassitude from the heat. There is the absence of all early friends who knew and were known. There is the impossibility of moving about during part of the day. There is the pain of seeing multitudes perishing, and yet, from ignorance of the language, being unable to speak a single word. How can one bear up in such circumstances, unless, like Abraham, he determine not to look at them, but to press on to the glory which is to follow? Help me to persevere!

Afternoon. — Various frames of mind. But, after all, am setting my face forward; and yet not in a self-seeking or self-rejoicing spirit, but broken and weak. Lord, raise and revive; yet so that I may still be broken and contrite.

June 18th. — Saturday morning. — I have had some thoughts of the blessedness of a complete deliverance from a legal spirit, and a quiet unsuspecting rest and abiding in the free love and faithfulness of God. How slow we are to come to this! And hence all our sinful fears of being overcome by temptation, and failing in duty. Lord, help me to such growing assurance of thy love that I may walk in peace, and especially in the prospect of another Sabbath. Save from the workings of an unpurged, unreconciled heart. Make me fruitful and full of sap, to show that thou art righteous.

June 19th. — Sabbath night. — Varied experiences today. All is new here; and I find that all day there must be the carrying of the cross. I fear, Lord, thou seest me often shrinking, surprised, languid; but thou canst subdue, and quicken, and uphold. Grant me to have a lively, growing sense of thy nearness, and of the seasonable help which thou ministerest. Oh, what a thought it is, if habitually realized, that thou art watching, praying, ministering, upholding! Lord, let me not be brutish to overlook thy benefits. I have been seeking the clean heart. I now seek the tender, heedful, mindful one. O my Lord, how we stand, as it were, on the very brink of the mightiest, most blessed truths, and yet scarce look at them! Draw me; bring it before me again and again. Deal with me as with Peter, — show me again and again; as with Zechariah, — waken me again and again. I have seen my weakness in two affairs today; and yet I think that I have been guided aright in both. O my Lord! let my character be transparent here; and let me be a blessing.

June 20th. — Monday afternoon. — I have moved about a good deal today, and come into contact with minds in many different states. I quite feel that, as minister of Christ, I must be the teacher, the brother, and the preacher. Help me, Lord, to fulfil my office, and not to fall beneath, nor yet strive to go beyond, my calling. 'Let thy covenant be with me of life and peace.' I find the daily cross; but have I not vowed to take it up daily? Let me not forget nor grudge. I do not look back but I do look forward, and heaven brightens and is more attractive.

Transparency and Generosity

All who knew him, or even met with him but once, recognised in him that *transparency* of character, that grace for which, in the above extract, he prays. He had no reserve, no guile; he sought to have a conscience void of offence toward God and man. With great mildness of speech and kindliness of tone, he was honest and straightforward, both in the pulpit and out of it. His conscience was tender, and showed its tenderness in little things as well as great. It troubled him, for instance, as he told me, that during his later months he could not always *kneel* for prayer, on account of the heart-complaint, but felt it necessary to stand, or perhaps walk about. There was no heedlessness about him as to what he did. He considered and weighed everything. He had a purpose in all his doings, even those that looked most hasty and impulsive. He had less of *routine* about him than most; less of stiffness in any part of his life or intercourse with others.

> *June* 21. — *Tuesday morning.* — I see some difficulty before me in money matters. I have been too unheedful of my matters. But, Lord, thou knowest that I have done this in simplicity; and if there is a net here, in which I am caught, I feel sure that thou wilt bring me out. My eyes are ever toward thee, and thou wilt bring my feet out of the net.

Such an entry as the above is quite characteristic, and just what we should have expected. Both in Perth and in Calcutta he showed great carelessness in money matters. It would not be wise to give details; but the instances of his liberality, his generosity, his putting away money when it came to him, of his refusing to be rich, would, if we were at liberty to give them, make some, who think themselves liberal, ashamed of their covetousness.

It is now nearly thirty years ago since a friend was making inquiries about Robert M'Cheyne, of whom he had heard somewhat, but whom he had not seen. 'They tell me', he said, 'that he is immensely generous; that he cares nothing for money, but gives away all he has.' It was a true report, and it added not a little to the influence exercised by that man of God during his brief course among us, that he was known to be so open-handed in all things; for nothing so destroys ministerial weight, either in the pulpit or out of it, as covetousness or penuriousness. Milne was no less known for his liberality than his early friend. His hand was always open; and it was to him 'more blessed to give than to receive'. He was not so fond of receiving gifts as of bestowing them; and we remember well a brotherly talk as to the propriety of his conduct in returning certain gifts which had been sent to him. We could not convince him at the time that he was wrong; but he admitted that there might be pride in such refusals which it was needful to guard against. During his first years in Perth he used (as he told me) to go to the bank at certain times, draw out all the money that had been placed at his credit, pay his bills and give the rest away; thus providing the bags which wax not old, and laying up the 'treasure in the heavens which faileth not'.

Intercessions

In his entry of the 25th of June, he refers to his bodily trials from the new climate; but thinks he is getting out of this 'irritating, feverish condition of body'. Then he adds:

> Deliver me from carefulness. Have I not given all up to thee? Am I not professedly a whole burnt-offering? Help me more and more to walk by faith, and not in bondage in any way to this present world. O my God, bring me more and more under the dominion of the world to come, so that I shall be satisfied with its joy and glory, and be indifferent to things of time. I ask thy blessing this day. Help me to prepare for tomorrow, and to be much in the exercise of supplication. Lord, endear this exercise. May I see that true love will find its chief outlet here.

> *June 29. — Wednesday.* — Varied experiences, yet many loving kindnesses from God and man. My Lord surely 'dawts'[1] his weak, foolish

---

[1] 'Dawts': fondles, caresses; an old Scotch word, often used by Samuel Rutherford.

child … I am conscious of a slight occasional drawing to a closer walk with God. Lord, help me to be thy simple, truthful child, coming to thee in holy familiarity. Bless my friends at home; those whom I have been unable to write to, *etc.*; keep them from wearying or suspecting that I forget them.

July 2d. — *Saturday.* — Give me, O my Lord, heart and activity. How easily I allow religious work, people, plans, exercises to take thy place! (Help me to be alone with thee, near thee, delighting in thee, hoping in thee.) To give way to this is a slow, withering death. All my springs are in thee. Bless my friends at home; in China and these eastern regions; here and in Madras, Bombay, Ceylon, Alexandria, Malta, Gibraltar, London, Liverpool, Newcastle, and all through dear Scotland. Bless my relatives and friends in the West Indies and America. Thou lookest down, and seest all at this moment. Let them be blest more than I can ask. Give some blessing, much blessing tomorrow, and all the week. Thou knowest the engagements, and opportunities, and meetings with friends that lie before me. Pity my weakness, languor, emptiness, dryness, want of power, and give me grace to glorify thee, and to do good.

July 3rd. — *Sabbath.* — I feel in full health today. Give me spiritual strength and grace. I have been thinking of Psalm 132, in connection with Isaiah 61:10: 'Let thy priests be clothed with salvation.' 'I will clothe my priests with salvation.' And now in Isaiah, 'He hath clothed me.' Often what we find only a seed in an early part of the word, we meet with afterwards a full-grown, fruitful tree.

Siftings

The subsequent entries for some weeks are fluctuating in their tone. The heat prostrates him; the climate seems as if sapping his constitution; difficulties confront him; success is small; the enemy is powerful; the mass of idolatry appals; he stands dismayed before that 'vast pile of human mockeries'; the inconsistencies of Christians depress him; his old friends are far away; he seems as if falling into one of his old lownesses. But the cloud passes off; his 'horizon clears', as he expresses it; he gives 'thanks to the Lord for softening of heart'; adding, 'Save me from causing offence, or hindering thy work; rather take me away with a stroke. Give tenderness of heart; love to thee and holy things; grant holiness.' He is not quite delivered. Troubled thoughts force themselves in. He wonders if he is in the right place; whether he has not done wrong in leaving Perth; and then adds, 'I desire to walk in thy light.' Perhaps, in these variations or perturbations, he is not at all unlike his brethren, either in India or at home; but he gives way to what some resist; he speaks out what others repress. The power or habit of self-control is a great thing for a Christian. It helps to steady him, both in feeling and in action; it saves him from hasty plans and inconsistencies. Like the strong hand of the pilot grasping a strong helm, it keeps him from drifting or deviating. Milne often spoke of 'the iron will' of some. He had himself a thoroughly vigorous will, when his health was good; but he sometimes succumbed to his own varying moods, instead of resisting them, when depression for a season had taken the pith out of his natural character. But these many tossings sifted him; drawing out his whole man, both in its strength and weakness, and delivering him from all self-leanings. He needed them to make him what he was, to fit him for the work he had to do, and to make his light shine. *Nil thus, si deficit ignis.*[1]

> *August 24th.* — I was preaching on Sabbath upon that text, 'Take heed, lest there be in any of you an evil heart of unbelief.' I can see that almost all my sorrow has sprung from this. Yet how unwatchful and uncareful to keep my heart! But there is another keeper, Isaiah 40:27-29. Here is the heart of unbelief [saying], God has forgotten me, he does not care for me, he does not deliver me. How does Jehovah-Rophi deal with this sore disease? Why, what reason have you for these hard thoughts of me? Adam, why dost thou think that I have withheld thee

---

[1] 'There is nothing of this if the fire is lacking', *Ed.*

from good? Cain, why is thy countenance fallen? Jonah, why angry? Disciples, why are ye fearful? Examine and see how groundless and sinful. Pride and self-will. The prince of darkness increases gloom, and all is distorted. What damage to our own peace, to the comfort of others, to the glory of God, when thou sayest thy way is hid! But not only, Why dost thou doubt? but, Why dost thou not believe? Hast thou not heard? [He is] *mighty,* — look at his works; not a sparrow falleth; consider the lilies. *Wise,* — how unsearchable his judgments; wait and see his end, that he is very merciful. *Good,* — he giveth liberally unto the evil and unthankful. He does not despise; his bringings down and weakenings are in order to make way for strengthening. Lord, help me to feed on this, and to feed others. Let truth dwell in the heart; let the lip spread it abroad. Pity those who have trials and temptations, and yet who 'have not heard', who 'do not know'. Shall I ever become crucified? Why go I about to build up my own glory? Why not willing to see, and that others should see, that I am nothing? Lord help me! I desire to be poor in spirit, and to take thy yoke, and learn of thee. Bless me this day. Live and walk and work in me.

The Inner Life

Subsequent entries are for some time much of the same cast. Hope and fear, sunlight and dimness, rest and trouble alternate. Yet never once does the question of his own sonship emerge. That was all settled long ago. In all the varying frames which this journal records, doubt has no place. He speaks of God, and to God, as one who knew him and was known of him. He is cast down when confronted with the immensity of wickedness and idolatry and worldliness; he asks if he is the man for such a position; he is weak in body, but his hold of the cross is always the same. It is with him as with the apostle in his work and warfare: 'As unknown, and yet well known; as dying, and, behold, we live; as chastened, and not killed; as sorrowful, yet always rejoicing' (*2 Cor.* 6:9-10). He says calmly, yet sorrowfully, 'There is nothing to cheer here but the favour of the Lord; none know or care what you are doing'; yet, when lying down tired at night, he speaks of 'peaceful days', and a 'sense of the blessed liberty which Christ gives'.

He speaks of his visits to the hospital; of missionary meetings, and his enjoyment of them; of his intercourse with young men; of fellowship with brethren; of work among the heathen. 'Save us', he cries, 'from seeking anything lower than conversion; from falling into mere routine; let us avoid inflating them with the idea of their importance.' And then we find him saying, 'I desire to live for my Lord. Deliver me from lower aims. Let me not seek the honour that cometh from man. Let not my life be a lie.' And then again, 'A peaceful day, though not strong ... Make me prayerful, calm, self-recollected, trustful ... I have been kept, but I have not been watchful; a foolish child. I war not with flesh and blood, but with principalities and powers ... Give me the right, Christian, truly heroic frame of spirit.' At another time he says, in reference to the previous day: 'No entry yesterday; I did not seek my Lord, and so it was a useless and unprofitable day. Lord heal me.' At another time: 'I have had several wounds today, and see that only the shield of faith can save from pain and sorrow. I would be daily putting on the whole armour of God.'

His entry one Monday morning is worth noting: 'Have been to the hospital, and so not enough yet with God ... Peaceful all day.' Again: 'Peaceful, yet not very lively. Would that my soul and heart sprung joyfully to my Lord! ... May I not fear or honour man above my Lord; but may my heart at all times flee to thee.' Again: 'Awoke early, and lay in bed till gunfire. I had not communion; my mind seemed to rove among earthly objects.' Again: 'Refreshed, peaceful, hopeful; yet this joyful hope can only be by the power of the Holy Ghost enabling me to receive and live upon the promises, so that there may be a constant upspringing of peace and joy in believing.' Again: 'Tired at night, yet comforted and kept. I feel that my Lord is increasing my faith, and enabling me more simply to rest on him.' Again: 'Let me feel that I am in my place, and let me not be mindful of the things behind.' Again: 'Much occupied reading letters from home. But thou wilt restore my soul. Bless my dear friends at home, and let not any change in my condition abate their love … Felt the effect of not having my reading before looking at my letters. But I think the Lord helped me and upheld me. Grant me grace in my intercourse with missionaries and ministers, and suffer me not to *settle down* in this dark land; but may I growingly learn, through the mighty power of the Holy Ghost. Deliver me from all the excuses and plausibilities which sloth is wont to produce, and help me to be stedfast and pressing forward.' Again: 'Be with me in meeting the brethren this morning; give me the spirit of prayer and real joy, and spiritual benefit in approaching thee … Evening. — A peaceful day. I found the missionary conference useful and profitable.'

Intercessions for Others

The following entry, of date October 5th, will give some idea of his work:

Have been at the hospital, and am a little fatigued. Looked in at morning prayers in the cathedral; I fear I should soon feel such duty a bondage. But how easy and pleasant would all be, blessed Lord, if we did all from love to thee! Show me how worthless all those acts are which proceed not from love. Strengthen me to look this fairly in the face, even though I should be constrained to acknowledge that I have been walking in vanity, and am an empty voice. Let me think of the glory of thy kingdom, and speak of thy power. Let me make a good confession in the face of this vain, proud, despising world. Thou art my King; thou shalt reign, and unto thee every knee shall bow. Lord, guide and bless me this day. Beginning in weakness, may I end in peace and strength. *Evening.* — The day did end in peace and strength.

Oct. 6. — Thursday morning. — Too late in going to bed last night. Tried a little during the night, and without the softness I had last evening. O Lord, thou seest how unwilling Satan is that I should make progress. Incline and help me to 'pray with all prayer'. This is the chief thing, in putting on the armour, for night or for day. The Lord is our armour, our shield, our helmet, our sandals, our girdle. Help me to live in the spirit of prayer. Give me to mingle in spirit with those above, and to see and feel as they do. It is the Lord. Grant that all difficulties may fly at the sight of thy glory. Bless my flock; feed and advance them. Bless my distant friends. Guide me wisely in a perfect way.

Oct. 7. — *Friday morning.* — Peaceful. Whom have I but thee? May I be prepared for Sabbath. I had opportunity of seeing yesterday how much the world is in the heart of those with whom I have to do. Grant that it may not be in mine; and let men see and acknowledge that it is not. I desire grace to persevere, and then my little meetings will gradually *tell*. I am thankful, Lord, for being able to remain quite cool and collected in dealing with gainsayers, and I see the advantage this gives. Make me wise, yet humble, and may I win souls. O my God, stir me up and quicken me, and fit me to plead thy cause. It strikes me that our missionary friends act too little on the aggressive; but I am also becoming more alive to the difficulties they have to contend with.

In the evening of Friday, October 10th, Milne was married to Barbara, only daughter of Simon Nicolson, Esq., of the Bengal Medical Service. Very frequently in his journal does he refer to this union as the source of joy, and strength, and blessing. The simplicity and tenderness of these allusions are very characteristic, very illustrative of the man; but they are not for the public eye.

After this we have such entries as the following: 'Thou hast graciously repaired thy servant's breach, and healed his wound.' 'I am far from the cares of a distant land. I have few [cares] here, except to care for thy work and glory. O my Lord, I desire to be holiness to thee!' 'A peaceful, happy day, as free from care and full of good as I ever could well look for here, unless, Lord, there were again the raining down of life and righteousness from the opened windows of heaven.' Again: 'Resting, peaceful, happy, and, I trust, preparing for coming action and usefulness.' Again: 'Feel refreshed and solemnized. Take and keep thy place, O Lord, in our house and heart!'

Difficulties Within and Without

He mourns the little amount of work he is able to do. He desires greater aggressiveness in missionary operations. He longs for the coming of the Holy Ghost in fulness and power. He asks if we could not deal more directly with prevailing superstition. He is cheered by the visit of two young natives, seeking their way to the cross. 'This', he adds, 'and some other things today, encourage me to hope that a holy, earnest, kindly aggressiveness, tempered by prudence, will be accepted and blessed of the Lord.' He visits 'the Institution', and rejoices to take part in its work. Again, he is 'pleasantly occupied with tidings from home'. Again, he rises early, a little before four, and walks on the roof, thinking of him who rose a great while before day. He is struck with the longing which these two youths who visit him have for knowledge, as that which would lift their country from degradation. He feels the responsibility which this brings upon our nation and our Church. Another native comes to him, and he is cheered again, though it breaks up his plans; yet he comforts himself by remembering how his Lord, even when he had gone aside for rest, came forth to the multitudes. 'My heart', he says, 'is open to thee, O Lord! I have been thinking that I should like to live a heavenly life on earth. O my God, help me! The element in which my soul thrives is faith and love. Unbelief, cares, frettings, are death. Teach me to *hope,* by the power of the Holy Ghost. Lord, draw me to thy seat! Let me not rest in *saying* that all will be barren till the rain comes; but may I more become *as in an agony* until the shower begins to fall.' He is troubled because of the little access he has to his fellow-men, in comparison with what he had at home. He finds few godly ones; such 'distance, coldness, and isolation'. 'Puseyism, evangelized moderatism, and the strong tide of worldliness' shut him in on every side.

The following more lengthened extract gives us an insight into the workings of his spirit, and shows how he realized in Christ the forgiveness of sin, and in his gospel the good news of a work done once and for ever. It reminds us of Luther's words: 'Christ is no exactor, but the propitiator of sin. Hold this tenaciously (*hoc mordicus tene*, with "tooth and nail"), nor suffer thyself to be plucked away from this most sweet definition of Christ, which gladdens even the angels in heaven, — that Christ is no Moses, no exactor, no executioner, but a propitiator of sin, a bestower of grace, of righteousness, and of life; who gave himself, not for our merits, or holiness, or righteousness, or our holy life, but for our sins' (On *Gal.* 1:4).

Oct. 25th. — I have found repeatedly how little the gospel is known, and how little, Lord Jesus, thou art understood. Men walk with thee as if thou wert a Lawgiver from Sinai, and not a Saviour from Zion; as if they must follow thee and serve thee wholly at their own charges. O my only Wisdom, my only Ability, help me to preach, and teach, and live down this error! May I see springing up a number of humble, believing souls, that feel their poverty and wretchedness, and yet rejoice and glory in thee as their righteousness and strength! Fit me for my work here; save me from all earthly selfish motives and impulses; baptize me with power; and so may I break in upon the preserves of the god of this world, and break through all the cordons of worldly etiquette and carnal ecclesiasticism. Oh that some of my thoughts long ago might now be realized!

Oct. 26th. — *Wednesday morning.* — Refreshed and thankful. Comforted in reading. Let the 91st Psalm dwell with me today. Thou knowest it is not corn and wine, nor gold and silver that I seek, but showers of grace and harvests of conversion ... Guide me in writing to my people at home. I pray that I may be enabled to write what will illustrate and endear thy word, and also what will give an increased interest in this land.

Oct. 29th. — Saturday morning. — Have been at the hospital, and begun what may prove a pleasant acquaintance. Lord, guide in regard to ministering to the soldiers tomorrow; also in getting Bibles for them; also in teaching them to learn to read. Save me from thoughts of self in these things; guide me till I may carry them through. Make me holy, and then use me for Thy purposes … Oh that I had perpetual sunshine in my soul, as we have it in our skies!

Oct. 31st. — Occupied with the Hindoo youths, and have got a lesson in duty with them. I desire to pity them, and to wonder at distinguishing mercy. I would delight myself more in my God, run to thee, and rejoice in thee, and admire thee greatly. There is none like unto thee, and no works like thy works. Draw me this day, for I am feeble. Went down the river with Smith and Behari. Enjoyed much the sail up and down, though the tide was against. Was interested by what I saw of Indian village life. The people are more comfortable and more accessible than I thought. May this be but a beginning of work of this kind!

Nov. 2d. — At the hospital, and a good deal worn out. Also have not had my usual reading. My peace and strength depend on getting hold of the Lord and his word before I go among my fellows or engage in other matters … Have found this day the evil of having mind and heart unfurnished before going out … Vexed at the apathy of the native converts, and their want of interest in the salvation of their countrymen.

Peaceful, Happy Days

Often does this entry recur: 'A peaceful, happy day'; and in one place this is added, 'I have been thinking how good it would be if I were wholly *off my feet,* and carried in the everlasting arms'; and again, 'O my Lord, let me live habitually *with* thee! Was not Jesus ever with thee? Let me now, in him, be with thee. Was I not, in Christ, with thee before? Am I not ever there? Let me realize this from hour to hour … Help me to have no desire but for thy joy and glory, and then nothing can offend me.' These Hindoo youths sometimes cheer and sometimes trouble him; he feels as if they were coming to him as the multitudes did to Jesus, — for the loaves; yet he resolves to set before them the bread of life; he prays that they may be stirred up to think of their countrymen; and adds, 'Bless this small beginning, which seems so unpromising; but of it thou couldst make a native home-mission to spring. MUST NOT INDIA, AFTER ALL, EVANGELIZE INDIA?' The following overflow of feeling with regard to himself is striking; and the picture drawn is not wholly unlike:

> Fit me for this place. I feel that I am rash, impulsive, incautious, inconsiderate of the feelings, views, prejudices, and habits of men; and, moreover, too often forgetful of difficulties that are in the way. Incline and help me to watch and pray. Give me quiet influence. Look upon thy work in this place. It does not prosper as it ought. Draw me to thy seat, for the spirit of power, and of a sound mind. Give this grace also to many here. Use them, and let me follow and sit at their feet. But save from contentment in a low unprofitable state of things. *I do earnestly pray for a living, vigorous, evangelistic native church* … I should like to see a time of revival, a stirring up of the hearts of the converts to love the souls of their countrymen, and labour for their salvation; a great ingathering of souls; and a new unity among the various religious denominations. I should like also to see my country-men beginning to care for the good of this great land, and temporal and spiritual prosperity advancing and keeping pace. Yet let nothing, not even this, turn away my heart from Christ, or take, or keep his place … May I not give unnecessary offence, and yet not fear to offend, if thy work requires it. Be pleased to use us both and prepare us for the coming of thy dear Son. Have visited a good deal, and like to move about among my fellow-creatures. Trials also of various kinds. Yet they are good, for they show both corruption and grace; it is safe to see the first, and it is comforting to see the second. May I hate this evil and abominable thing. May I rejoice more and more that there is

a laver that washes it away, and a cross that kills it. Nothing can thrive into which sin enters. It is a worm at the root; it is rottenness in the foundations. It will blast and wither all.

Thoughts about His Work

Then follow many similar entries: his own peacefulness; the benefit of trial; pleasant intercourse with the young Hindoos; his visit to a native house; his quiet breathing time of domestic joy and sunshine; clouds 'gathering and closing'; his determination more and more to search for truth; his wish in company to lead the conversation to holy things. Then he asks, 'Am I ready for the coming of the Lord? Is there anything in the world that I should like to keep as it is? Would it be painful to have the Master come and supersede my work by his own mighty power? Could I rise up joyfully and welcome him? I have not come to teach mere literature, but to teach sinners the way of life.' The following sentence is worth setting by itself:

> I have desires in my heart which perhaps God will grant me to see fulfilled before I die. (1) A true revival here. (2) A holy, active, numerous church. (3) The native Christians fully awakened, stirred up, and made successful in seeking the conversion of their countrymen. (4) The East Indians raised from their present degradation and put in their proper position.

And not less the following:

> I am quite sure that the word of truth alone will be owned by thee for the conversion and salvation of men. Help me quietly to go on studying and preaching it.
>
> *December 17th. — Saturday morning.* — I am very wearied; rather cast down; but some peace in Psalm 122, and looking forward to the heavenly city. Why am I careful about things on the passage? My citizenship is there. My Elder Brother and friends are there. Let my

affections and interests be all there. Let me walk as they walked. The traveller does not stop because the day looks cloudy or threatening, but presses on. The workman goes to his labour in sunshine and shower; his work must be done. So, Lord, let me go on. Daily trials there must be; daily causes of care and casting down; but let me still trust in thee, and do good.

A quiet day, without much trial ... Lord, I am thine. Thy will be done. Keep my heart and life, and all the outgoings of my soul. Let me forget myself, thinking of thee, and seeking thee ... Fightings and fears, I can scarcely say deliverance. How weak my faith is; how small my submission to thy holy will! Let me begin more truly to take up my cross ... Going to Chinsurah. Lord keep me in all company and engagements; let me not grieve nor dishonour thee. Be my gracious Monitor and Preserver. Let me praise thee at my return ... Disappointed in my plan of journeying at the last moment, and so have hurried back, not doubting, but that it is for good. Quiet rest during the afternoon, and so refreshed and strengthened ... Peaceful, yet need to watch. The flesh waits its opportunity. How great is thy faithfulness, O Lord! What care thou takest! What patience thou exercisest! Yet let me not provoke thee, nor tempt. Quiet day, but not much done ... Make my Wednesday meetings times of great sensible enjoyment (and may the flock thus be built up in the Lord); — make them also times of enlarged, hopeful prayer for all people ... Interested by meeting with Mr — 's family from the Moffussil. People say it is impossible to walk with God and be an indigo planter; but this seems to be a humble Christian. Abraham loved and feared the Lord in Canaan.

December 24th. — I know not what may be doing at Perth. This was the season when we used to look specially for mercy. Yet, Lord, thou canst bless me, and make me a blessing here ... I see more and more that my life here is to be quite different from what it was at home. But it is well to pass through changes, and I shall have larger sympathy and fellow-feeling with those who through faith and patience inherit the promises ... A busy yet very happy day; refreshed at night by F— 's prayer.

December 29th. — I beseech my Lord to put an edge upon my spirit. I think thou art dealing with me for good. Be pleased to put a new edge upon my spirit. Let me feel as one standing between the living and the dead; let my spirit be up to the measure of my position. I will wait on thee for Sabbath.

December 31st. — *Friday.* — What a life mine has been! I can look back on nothing with satisfaction. I have been covered with sin, and have no righteousness. But thou castest out none. I have latterly become more sensible of sins of omission — the want of zeal, life, love; falling into a sluggish, forgetful, cold state of soul. May I be delivered from this in the new year! Also, may I be more drawn to prayer, yea, may I set myself to pray much and often. Also, help me to interest myself more directly in the state and conversion of particular individuals. I desire also to be enabled to walk more evenly, living a life of faith, and not looking so much to the seen and earthly. My eternal interests do not at all depend upon my worldly standing and prosperity. On the contrary, when I am poor, then am I likeliest to be rich. Help me to be more concerned about men's feelings toward *thee,* and not so much to care how they feel, or what they think of me. Oh, how hard it is for my proud heart to be overlooked, lightly esteemed! but I desire to have no will but thine. Lord, undertake for me.

His Birthday

For several months there is no record; and then the following entry stands alone:

April 26th, 1854. — My birthday. I am now far on in life, and have learned and done little. I can scarcely hope to do much in what remains. Visit me, O Lord, this day, with thy good Spirit, that I may wisely consider what I am, where I am, and what I can now do for thee … Nothing would so delight me as to see times of refreshing and abounding spiritual life … I am afraid to think how I should feel if revival were to come by means of others, while I was passed by. Yet, I think, I should acquiesce, perhaps rejoice, and join heartily in helping on the work ... I have left all my dear people and beloved friends, and am now among strangers who do not know me, nor care for me. There are here trials unknown at home: languor arising from the heat; pining of heart for wonted fellowship; the low state of religion generally; and the apathy and unmoveableness of the heathen. Yet thou hast been kind, Lord, in giving me a loving wife, and bringing me into a family, where I am thoroughly domesticated. Thou hast in earthly things compassed me with many comforts. It is and must be a very monotonous life. Lord, undertake for me. I have no access to the general population. They seem settled down in their several encampments, and in determined irreligion ... I have been useful, I believe, to some souls. Though sometimes cast down, the Lord seems to lift me up again. I have had a good deal of intercourse with the English-speaking natives; but as yet none have turned to the Lord, and the door at present is very much closed. Lord, fit me for this work. I pray for tenderness of heart, and a willingness to wait much in quiet, and to pray. Give a time of refreshing. This is a kind of watchtower, where I might see much of the state of the world, and might be useful to brethren at home, in informing and stirring them up. Lord, help me to see what I might do, and enable me, and fit me for it.

A month elapses, and there is another entry to the following effect:

May 31st, 1854. — I have now been a whole year in this place, and can form some correct idea of the nature of my position. I see that I am compassed with difficulties. But I will not look at them. Give me the heritage of those who fear thy name. Give me fitness and heartiness in my work. I look to thee, O Lord; give me utterance and entrance, and zeal and help.

Subjects for Prayer

Such is the substance of the volume in which he records his first year's experiences in India. On a blank leaf at the close of it, there is written the following arrangement of subjects for daily prayer throughout each week:[1]

> *Sabbath.* — Ministers; work of God; refreshing.
> *Monday.* — World. *Tuesday.* – Church.
> *Wednesday.* — India and Calcutta.
> *Thursday.* — Congregation; office-bearers; Sabbath-school classes.
> *Friday.* — Family and friends.
> *Saturday.* — Free Church; missions.

An Eye-Witness Report

The following sketch or narrative from Mr M'Leod Wylie, regarding Milne, will be more effective than any statement that could be given by one not on the spot:

> Before Mr Milne's arrival in 1853, some of us, who were deeply interested in the spiritual welfare of the people, met weekly, to pray that the Lord would send us a man after his own heart; and when we heard some preliminary accounts of our coming minister — that he had been a friend of M'Cheyne's, and that he was (as one letter said) 'one of the best of the revival preachers', — our hearts were gladdened by the hope that we should see days of blessing. I well remember his arrival. It was the Lord's day, and I was detained at home by illness; but I heard the steamer's guns; and soon after the service was finished he came over to see me, and then I found that he had, immediately on landing, hurried to the church, and had reached it in time to see the

---

[1] I have beside me M'Cheyne's jottings of a similar kind. They will interest some, though fragmentary. They are divided into — (1) Confession; (2) Prayer.

Confession. — Sins of natural life. Sins of ministry. Sins under affliction. Sins against Father, Son, and Spirit.

Prayer. — Pray for my health. Pray for my soul; especially submission, — deliverance from envy, love of praise. For thankfulness, humility, brokenness of heart. For my family and friends. For Burns, and other fellow-labourers. For the whole of my people; awakened, believing, backsliding, unconverted. For direction to the prayer-meetings, *etc.* For preparation for the communion to them and me. For help and success on Sabbath. For the Carse [the low-lying plain along the River Tay between Dundee and Perth, *Ed.*]. For the Jews. For the Church in this dark time.

assembled people, and that he was ready to begin his work by preaching in the evening. He was the guest of good old Dr Nicolson; and that family and mine, I can truly say, rejoiced together in the grace we saw in him. Everything seemed to encourage our expectation that we should ourselves be animated to fresh devotedness, and that we should see a revival around us. But while others, I know, were greatly blessed through the ministry of that humble man of God from the first, I soon found Satan very busy; and as the case may not be unprofitably considered by other believers, I will mention the circumstances.

The Christian people in Calcutta had gone on for many years in an easy, contented way, with a name to live, showing a measure of zeal and liberality in mission work, and in many benevolent undertakings; but there was little deep knowledge of the word, and little decisive testimony for the Lord. It was an unusual thing to speak plainly in private to worldly friends and associates, or to have much spiritual communion one with another. Meetings for reading the Scriptures were very little known. There had been a meeting, some years before, at Mr Hawkins' house, at which good Mr M'Donald, the Scotch missionary, expounded; and at Mr M'Donald's house, for a time, a few friends met on Saturday evenings for reading the word; but, on looking back, I can scarcely remember to have learned any truth from others. Mr M'Donald used himself much to dwell on the Puritan divines, and much recommended them; and for some years I was a diligent student of them. But I am sure that it was a rare thing among the believers in Calcutta to help and edify one another with fresh views of truth gained by personal study of the word; and the general state of things was formal and cold. It was the Lord's purpose to send his messenger and his message, and then (as always has been the case when the Lord has drawn near) the thoughts of many hearts were revealed. While many, who had previously made no profession of religion, heard from Mr Milne new, stirring, and affecting appeals, which touched their hearts and roused their consciences, there were others (and I was one) who felt that this kind of religion went beyond their experience, and in effect tested and exposed them.

At times the power of his preaching was irresistible. Such, I remember, was a sermon on the Saviour in the house of Simon the leper, — detecting the true communicant, not in the rich professor, but in the poor abashed suppliant at his feet; and I remember, too, one occasion when Mr Granger (one of the Baptist missionary deputation from the United States) described to me his experience while listening to another sermon before the communion. He said that he sat there overwhelmed, and could only feel the force of such words as 'I am a worm and no man.'

There were many who affected to think lightly of Mr Milne's preaching. It was not 'prepared', it was not learned, and so on; but this was all misconception. The preparation was, in fact, of the best kind. He preached weekly out of a full and exercised soul, which was constantly occupied in applying the word to the hearts of inquirers or mourners; and he gave forth out of the good *treasure*, which his own study of the word was gaining day by day, things new and old. And though there was no show of learning, yet there was learning, and far more, I believe, than would have been displayed by retailing the comments of critical authors. The result was, that he often conveyed vivid impressions of the true, free, and full meaning of many passages of Scripture; so that his hearers often associated for ever afterwards particular portions with recollections of his unfolding of them. I can say this, for instance, of the last chapter of Micah, and of passages in Hosea 14 and John. But there certainly was something unusual in his way of acting and speaking.

He had little concern for the outward business of the house of God, though, I must say, I never saw any sickly and unmanly indifference to really necessary work; and he was anxious to show his interest in all such meetings as those of the Bible Society's Committee and the Missionary Conference. But then he put spiritual and personal work *first*, in a very decided manner. He paid visits which were solely visits of a pastor or a brother in the gospel, and he came therefore only to speak of spiritual things and to pray. He was 'instant in season and out of season'. He spoke with much directness — without ambiguity, and in a searching way, — that often startled and displeased. This often led to rebuffs. But how many can testify, as I can, that they *never* saw him angry or displeased; *never* manifesting the pride of ruffled spirit; *never* treasuring the memory of unkind or harsh treatment! He had, I think, more of the mind of Christ in this respect than any man I ever saw. He was content to be abased if others were exalted; to be accepted 'only in part'; to be treated as an inferior — inferior in judgment and knowledge; and I think, too, I may say that I never saw 1 Corinthians 13 so exemplified as it was in him. How he could suffer long and be kind; how he lived and acted as judging none, and thinking no evil! Of our blessed Lord it is spoken that he was deaf and dumb, and that he suffered not his voice to be heard: he was dumb, he bore the contradiction of sinners; and he opened not his mouth; and how delightful it is to see in one of his followers this meekness and gentleness of Christ! There was much of it in Mr Milne. And then he was entirely unworldly. He cared not for the worldly appearances and human praise, but had that faith which overcomes the world.

His course in India extended from May 1853 to August 1857 — more than four years. Before he left, he had settled down into habits of regular work among his own growing congregation, and was less engaged with others outside. But his work was extending in another way. In Calcutta itself it was chiefly confined to his own people; but he was sought out by Christians who came there, and he was led into correspondence with those who left for other parts of the country. I suppose that, if he had remained, his influence would have rapidly extended; for he was an epistle of Christ, known and read of all men. In some cases his usefulness was very remarkable. A young civilian, for instance, a stranger to him, lived near him, and was suddenly plunged into deep affliction by a bereavement. Mr Milne at once ventured in to see him, with words of comfort; led him to the Saviour; and afterwards, when he left Calcutta for the Upper Provinces, was his friend and counsellor. And certainly he had the gift of ministering to strangers, for his perfect guilelessness removed all annoyance at apparent intrusions. It was impossible to mistake his 'purpose', or 'his manner of life or charity'. He was eminently transparent, and evidently had but one thought and one object; and thus very often he overcame evil with good. Where, at first, he was met with impatience, and even contempt, he won his way by the meekness of wisdom. And, indeed, often have I, in reference to him, thought of the words, 'He that winneth souls is wise.' Much else there is that appears wise, and is highly esteemed among men; but there is one work in which it is truly wise to spend all our strength, and which certainly will abide — the Christ-like work of seeking out, to save, the lost; and to this blessed work our dear friend devoted himself. This one thing he did.

He gave himself wholly to the work of the ministry, and he had special qualifications for the work. He was remarkably self-denying and generous, so that he spared no pains, and would willingly part with everything he had to show his sympathy. He was quite free from jealousy and envy, from secular pursuits and engagements, and from habits of variance and contention. He was full of tender compassion, and could truly weep with them that wept, and rejoice with them that rejoiced. His successor in the ministry in Calcutta, Mr Pourie, told me he had experienced quite a new blessing to his own soul in visiting among those who had been quickened under Mr Milne's ministry.

While in Calcutta, our friend always showed a real and hearty interest in all mission work. He took a class in the Free Church Institution every week to expound the *Pilgrim's Progress,* and I know of other evidences of practical co-operation in mission work, or at least of lively affection to those engaged in it. When such choice missionaries as the late Mr Ingalls, of the American Mission in Burmah; and Mr Jaaske, of the Moravian Mission in Thibet; and the late Dr Ribbentrop of Chupra, were in Calcutta, his heart overflowed with love to them; and after he returned to Scotland, he and his beloved wife ceased not to remit aid for some of the work in India.

As might be supposed, a man of this kind attracted much (and, I may say, more and more) love from those who were most manifestly on the Lord's side, and who were able to appreciate the depth and the fervour of his spiritual life. I may mention particularly the late Colonel

Wheler, who was generally very reserved in his communications, even with old friends. To Mr Milne he opened his heart, and gave records of his work, much more than to others — more, certainly, than he did to me, who had known him and corresponded with him far longer. I remember hearing, through Mr Milne, a wonderful narrative I had never heard from Colonel Wheler himself, of an Afghan convert of his who went forth into his own dark country with his life in his hand, resolved there to speak of Jesus at all hazards, — one of whom the world was not worthy, and whose name will never be known till 'that day', when his work, and perhaps much fruit from it, shall be declared openly.[1]

Mr Milne's departure from India was rendered necessary by the continued illness of his wife. They were separated in 1855 in the hope that she might return to India sufficiently strengthened to bear the climate; and to one so affectionate and so dependent as he was, that separation was no ordinary trial. He was liable to fits of extreme depression, and I recollect one occasion when I went to see him, at a time when he was quite alone, and found him in great darkness and distress. At such times he found no relief except in spiritual work; and if there were but some call on him for counsel, or some case in which there was hope of the Spirit's work, his thoughts seemed instantly diverted from himself, a new song was put into his mouth, and he went on his way again rejoicing.

I might say much more; but I cannot doubt that others, who knew him longer and better, will be able to describe his general course fully; and as he was the same man in India and at home, so the account of his home life will answer the purpose of a more complete sketch of his career abroad. The impression in my own mind, from a review of all my acquaintance and intercourse with him, has been very deep. The simplicity of character, the long-suffering, the willingness to be counted even a fool for Christ's sake, made many think of him as weak and powerless; but he was able to glory in infirmities, that the

---

[1] See that most stirring and remarkable book, *Memoir of Colonel Wheler* (London: 1866).

power of Christ might rest in him; he was strong in his strength; and so, while some thought that he was scarcely to be accounted of, his influence was felt by every man, and his labours were blessed beyond almost all. I read in his life a great lesson, — the lesson that true strength and true power come only from much living communion with the Lord; that he will use and exalt those who are willing, for his sake, to be abased; and that the memory of these is most blessed who here do most truly glorify him by likeness to the lowliness and service of Christ.

We live in days when we hear much of the need of an intellectual ministry, and of preaching to meet the wants of the age; but the career of this dear servant of Christ may serve to show that, if we want to win souls, we must know nothing but Christ and him crucified. While hundreds of elaborate discourses — the products of research and painful labour — have served no purpose whatever but the gratification of so many of the hearers as were able to understand them, the sermons which Mr Milne preached, fresh from the fulness of his own experience, fraught with the spirit of the gospel, directed only to the consciences and hearts of the people, are remembered, and have borne fruit to life eternal. May the Great Head of the Church send forth into his vineyard hundreds of servants qualified with 'like precious faith', and sustained from first to last with a quenchless desire to make full proof of their ministry to the glory of his name only, in the salvation of sinners, and the manifest example of a heavenly mind!

Ere leaving home he had counted the cost, and never for one moment regretted the step he took. Yet he felt the difference between Calcutta and Perth, though he enjoyed the intercourse of his missionary brethren, and speaks of them with great kindness. 'How little', he writes, 'we seem to know, in this land, of the communion of saints! But the life and sweetness of that is the communion of the Lord; and his fellowship can be enjoyed in private as well as in company … How I should like to have Andrew Bonar here, and be able to say all I think and feel, with a sense of reciprocation!'

The following hymn, one of many such found in his note-books, gives expression to his feelings. It is upon Psalm 37:1, and occurs after an entry to this effect: — 'Driven about all day, and no rest. I was away from thee, O Lord, and so I sank; and then sin comes in with resistless power ... My life is passing fast away, and I continue poor and helpless. Undertake for me ... Feel the need of the Lord. Surely he is making me feel my need of him!'

FRET NOT

Lord, help me not to fret, when troubles o'er me flow;
But still before me set the path of toil and woe.
For few Thy comforts were; Thou thoughtest not of ease;
But soughtest still from Satan's snare Thy brethren to release.

Grant me to follow Thee, my self-forgetting Lord!
And when from toil I flee, reward me of Thy word;
For Thou hast said that they, who will Thy service try,
Must ever, day by day, both self and sin deny.

The cross I now uptake; the burden seek to bear;
And for Thy dear name's sake, I would Thy sorrows share.
Deign, Lord, on me to smile; my fainting spirit raise;
And make me, 'mid my toil, lift up the song of praise.

John MacDonald

He delighted to speak of John MacDonald, and of what he had heard of the sayings and doings of that noble missionary, who, in his brief course, gave such a decided testimony for Christ in Calcutta, and shone there as a burning and shining light.[1] Once and again he referred to the deathbed of that man of God, as it had been

---

[1] 'What I miss in some missionaries', he writes, 'is that glow, and warmth, and stirring of spirit which you see in Paul to the very end. May I live fast and get an early grave, if one *must*, after a time, cool down.'

described to him by those who witnessed it; especially recalling the words of Lacroix (a well-known missionary of the London Society), as he stood in the death chamber, ere the spirit had departed, 'There lies the holiest man in India.'

Chapter 14

1854–1857
In India

*H*e took, as we have seen, a very warm interest in all missionary work; and associated himself lovingly with missionaries of different churches. To work for God, to gather in souls, and to keep himself unspotted from the world, was his aim. He was 'debtor' to all; he knew it; he had gone to India to pay that great debt; and in his daily life there he showed his sense of how much he owed. Our Free Church Institution he visited every Monday, often going to it when weary enough with his Sabbath work and the Indian heat. He had a class there, with which he went through the Epistle to the Ephesians, and some other parts of Scripture. On two occasions he wrote to the then Governor-General, Lord Dalhousie, and obtained handsome donations for the Institution. He wrote afterwards to Lady Canning, who responded to his application by sending one of the Government secretaries to inspect Mrs Ewart's school for Jewish and Armenian girls, then under Miss Johnstone's care, and was so pleased with his report that she sent a contribution from herself. In his correspondence with friends up the country, he often urged, and not in vain, the claims of the Free Church Institution and of the Orphanage.

Work and Correspondence

He had regular engagements for almost every day of the week. On Monday evenings he met with some pious soldiers in the fort for reading and prayer. On Wednesday evenings there was the regular congregational prayer-meeting. On Friday mornings he had a Bible reading at his own house; and the evening of that day was devoted to young men; on alternate weeks for natives and for the young men of the congregation. Frequently, on Thursday evenings, he preached to the sailors. On Saturday mornings he had a young ladies' Bible class. All this was in addition to visiting his congregation, the jail, the hospitals, the ships, and every place or person that was accessible; especially in cases of sickness and distress. He kept up a large correspondence with Free Churchmen all over India,[1] not only by letter, but by the transmission of tracts and periodicals regularly.[2] He used to compare his work in Calcutta to that of a man standing in a gateway, and speaking to all who went in and out. They and he might never meet again; but the word spoken might be remembered for ever. This 'sowing beside all waters' was one of the most remarkable features of his Christian life. He never seemed

[1] I should add, not only with Free Churchmen, but with all who loved the Lord Jesus of every Church. Referring to the *Memorials of John Mackintosh*, and his views as to other Churches, he says in one of his Indian journals, 'I like his liberality and charity.' 'Liberality' was not with Milne a word indicating facility in believing anything or nothing; nor indicating dislike of those who believe or disbelieve very earnestly, and who attach great importance to what they believe; nor yet indicating sympathy with every form of opinion or religion: it was to him equivalent with love to all who truly love the Lord. His large-heartedness did not consist in assuming everybody to be right; or in thinking that believed truth and believed error are equally acceptable to God; or in holding it to be a hard thing that one man should be saved for believing what is true, and another lost for not believing it. His liberality was true and deep; and yet it was in thorough accord with the mind of him who said, 'Strait is the gate and narrow is the way that leadeth to life; and FEW THERE BE THAT FIND IT.'

[2] In September 1855, he writes: 'I have sent away this week between thirty and forty packets, besides various *chits* (notes) and letters to many parts of this Indian land.' Again: '*October* 1855. Went to the post-office with a huge bundle of letters and papers I was sending in all directions.'

to be weary in well-doing. He did not sow sparingly, and he did not reap sparingly (2 *Cor.* 9:6); nor is his harvest yet over.

What is to be Done for India?

In letters to a friend in Perth about this time, he speaks of the hindrances and difficulties which arose from the climate, and the native habits, and the shifting population. And he adds: 'How desirable it is that Christians should be lively, consistent, holy, manifest fearers and honourers of the Lord! We are surrounded by native servants night and day, and they mark closely all our on-goings. I am learning many things from observing these poor people, and am determined, through God's help, to do all for them I can.[1] Poor things! they would do anything for us.' He seems never to have looked upon the natives, whether indoors or out of doors, without being stirred to pity. And he goes on to say: 'I rather like to see them moving about, in the spotless white dresses; and sometimes wish they were as white within. If they were as careful to please the Lord as they are to serve and please us, watching night and day, and anticipating every wish, they would be a noble and happy people.' Feeling the responsibility of his position, he asks for special prayer in his behalf. 'Pray for me, that I may be blessed in preaching and visiting the flock; in my classes; in intercourse with strangers passing up and down; in visiting the various institutions; and in intercourse with the missionaries. You see the large, important field that is here; and you know, when your prayers make me a full vessel, we shall, ere long, rejoice together.' In some other letters he asks with pointed earnestness, 'What is to be done for India? Mediocrity, dull routine, cold formality among Christians, and a powerless, apathetic

---

[1] When living in a boarding-house (September 1855) in Calcutta, one Sabbath morning, some native carpenters began erecting a small house in the compound or yard. M. wrote at once to the landlady: 'Don't you think it wrong that men should work on Sabbath? But perhaps you have not power to stop them.' — enclosing the tract, 'The Price of a Soul'. Immediately the work was stopped.

native Christianity make me almost despair. Alas! *our* young men seem to be among the best, and yet how little can we expect from them in the way of evangelizing the land! Only faith, fervour, burning love to souls, and large, generous, self-denying enterprise can do anything for such a land; and where are they to be found?' He then goes on, in the intensity of fervent zeal: 'My heart is sad, yet not dismayed; but rather indignant and jealous. Where is the Esther who will go in and touch the golden sceptre? I cannot help thinking that, if there were one real revival, it might lift the standard up and give a new aim and impulse. Let us keep this in view; for unless the Lord plead his own cause, I cannot see what is to be the end. Poor India! What is to become of it? There is no zeal, no enterprise; but everywhere death, lukewarmness, and worldliness.'

He writes, in July 1855, thus: 'Sometimes I fear that the curse of God lies on this poor land. There seem to be so few generous, large-hearted souls to care for it. I suppose the Lord is shutting us up to himself. Reading Isaiah 45 at worship, I felt for the moment how easily he could remove all difficulties out of the way. "*I will work.*" I suppose I shall end by looking for the coming of the Lord himself to end the Church's long, selfish sleep.'

A little later he writes: 'How little I habitually live as one who is redeemed, accepted, beloved, a citizen of heaven, a friend and follower of Jesus; and how I try to get joy, and find instead only care and sorrow from the world around, when I might get every good and perfect gift from the world above!' And again: 'Why should we not feel so warm in the love of God, that we should not be sensible of the coldness and unkindness of men? Why should we not be so strong and confident in his help, that we should not be much concerned though men stand aloof or oppose? Why should we not be so filled with the earnests of coming glory, that we should not much mind the crooks and holes in our worldly lot?'[1] In another

---

[1] Of this date is the following sentence, so expressive of the man, reminding us of

letter he has this most searching remark, fitted to make us inquire into the reality of these great externalisms and organizations which look well, but may perhaps, after all, be hollow. 'I am feeling more and more that *nothing in the Church is of any value save what is really the work of God.* He builds the house; and much that we build is only *dekna-ke-waste*,[1] or, as Paul says, to "make a fair show in the flesh."'

True State of the World before God

Feeling deeply the evil of this present evil world, and knowing that outward improvements, such as those which are affected by civilisation, or government, or literature, fall short alike of God's purpose and man's need, he thus remarks: 'We are not laying to heart enough the state of the world. God is calling us to mourning and prayer; and we seem to go on much as we would if his terrible judgments were not in the earth. There seems to be a good deal of restlessness and uneasiness in many parts of India. The native mind seems heaving up and down, and very likely we shall have outbreaks in other parts than Rajamahal.' This was written in September 1855; and, at the same time, he remarks on passing events: 'This is the Mohurrum,[2] and yesterday was the great day, so that the town was full of tumult and noise. *We have conquered India for Leadenhall Street, but not for Christ;* and these outbreaks seem as if the devil paraded his votaries, and vaunted of his power. What David will come and kill the giant? For *all here seem at rest, and take it as a*

Paul's 'This one thing I do.' It is a word for all, especially for ministers. *'Let us try to say something to every one we meet. I have been trying it today.'* When in London, among some Government officials, he astonished them by speaking personally to them about eternity, especially one venerable gentleman, who, not at all offended, simply made the remark, 'I was never spoken to in that way before.' It was most pleasant, but somewhat perilous, to have a walk with him. The stoppages were many; — words to be dropped; tracts to be given; kind deeds to be done to passers-by.

[1] Hindostanee; meaning literally, 'Appearance for looking'; fair show; like the apostle's word εὐπροσωπεω (*Gal.* 6:12).

[2] A great Mohammedan festival.

matter of course?' Yet, troubled and almost overwhelmed by the sight of these idolatries, he can say at the same time: 'I am never allowed to think that I did wrong in coming here. I never wish that I had not come. I feel that I shall be to all eternity a different man, in consequence of my Indian experience and trials. There are many to do the work at home; there are few here.' Then he turns from the spectacle of a ruined world, and a benighted India, to a lesson of Christian experience: 'I have been out on my little terrace, and saw a native busy fanning his little fire. I wonder if I could teach him how to "rest" his fire, as they call it in Scotland, and so have only to stir it up when morning comes, and be saved this daily laborious process. But then, I began to think, does the fire keep alive in our souls all the night; and has the Lord no trouble in kindling it again? I wish we had a *continuousness of spirituality.* Watchfulness, self-denial, and separation from the world would help; but, better still, joy in Christ, 1 Thessalonians 5:14-24 shows, I think, how the fire might be kept always burning. Dark, gloomy, unthankful thoughts quench it very much, and they make way for other evils.'

The Master and the Servant

His October letters of that year take the same solemn tone. Here are some extracts:

Changes, changes; but I find our hearts do not change for the better, and only ceaseless, unwearying, omnipotent grace can make us better. We are the clay, and he the potter; and even our stubbornness and unholiness cannot baulk or hinder him in his work, when he puts to his hand … If we could do all things in the secret place, as before the throne, there would be no languor nor want of interest then, but the constant pressing towards the mark; and even the little things, and the trying things, and the humbling things would be the most interesting, as being most fitted to prove our desire to please the Lord. Our life springs out of the death of the flesh; our pleasure out of the denial of our own will; our glory out of a counting ourselves nothing, that the Lord may be all in all. We must be cross-bearers ... We live, I fear, upon our plans and labours, our success, and the standing we have among men.

At another time he writes:

I have just been thinking how contemptible such a life as Christ's would seem to the great mass of the higher class of people here! He went about without any ecclesiastical rank, any government appointment. His friends were the poor, and he ministered to the poor almost wholly. If he could appear now as then, I suppose he would be esteemed as some fanatic preacher. I wonder how he bore up under so many discouragements! But 'He trusted in God.' I wonder also at his hopefulness and thankfulness at any little appearance of success! When Peter said, 'We know and are sure that thou art the Christ', he immediately saw his Father's hand in this, and looks forward to a conquering Church. And yet how soon these dawnings were overcast again, and the truth made manifest, that it will be the interchange of light and darkness, grace and corruption, to the end!

He frequently expresses his interest in his Indian servants; pitying them, grieving over their ignorance, their dishonesty, their idolatry. He wonders why there should be such a difference between one sinner and another, as between himself and them. 'My fellow-creature', he writes, 'pulling the punkah, tries me. Why should it be thus, when I am seeking to approach my God, who is no respecter of persons?'

Letter-Fragments

We shall now give two series of extracts, illustrative of this period of his life — *first,* Fragments from letters written to Mrs Milne during her absence in Scotland; and, *secondly,* Quotations from a diary kept by him during his residence in India with great regularity.

We give the letter-fragments first; and we do so without any order or connection save that of dates, and not always even that. But they are not the less interesting from being so miscellaneous.

I had an interesting evening with old G. After a little conversation about Scotland, we got to better things. I read several of the psalms, and prayed, and he told me a good deal of his history. I spoke to him as an outcast, in love and pity, and he felt it; but assured him, on the ground of the gospel, that his case was not hopeless. He was touched.

How many sad, sweet memories you must have! But as time passes, the sadness will pass, and the sweetness remain; and we shall say, 'He hath led us by the right way.'

I agree with you that Psalm 65 is a missionary or millenarian hymn. There is a little cluster — 65, 66, 67, 68, — like a nest of honey, put in before Psalm 69, for the comfort of the man of sorrows.

Tonight our old friends, Mohendra and Nobin, with another young man, came in; and we have been for nearly two hours beating up and down, I fear to little purpose, except that one feels a comfort in think-ing they have heard a good deal of the word of God.

June 1855. — Mrs Mullens asked me if I would go and visit a friend of hers, Mrs H., in Park Street, who is dying of consumption. She had met me somewhere, and wished to see me … I found Mrs H., and read and prayed. They entreated me to come again. She seems startled; but up to this time has lived a worldly life … Mrs H. I found worse … Went to Mrs H., and found a complete change. Her face was bright, and she was full of joy and thankfulness. She said the Lord had opened and softened her heart, and that she now saw the Lord. She said it was during the night; her husband was with her, and was praying, when the light, as she said, broke in on her mind, and she began to see the truth, and broke forth in praise. She blessed me very much for having come and spoken to her, and her husband came with tears, and said, 'All this change is since you came.' I cautioned her that her present feelings might not last; that Satan would tempt her. She seemed at first amazed, but at once acquiesced, when I said, he is the murderer from the beginning. It will be a great encouragement if this is indeed another instance of redeeming grace ... Mrs H., I found, had not the same light and joy as before; but was peaceful, and says I was right in what I told her. She says she is always praying. I have seen her twice since then, and really hope that the Lord has visited her soul. A great many are now gathering round her of the church to which she belongs, and they all seem to see the change ... Mrs H. still lingers ... When at dinner, a note came from Mr H., asking me to go and see his wife, as she seemed dying, and wished to see me. I have been there a good while, and hope that, though a sad wreck in body, she will die in peace.

A note has just come to say that Mrs H. has died very peacefully. Her husband wished me to take the funeral service; but I answered, her own minister should take it, but I would attend.

A Mrs S. joined at this communion. She belonged to the English Church, but has been attending with us for a good while. Our acquaintance began when she called me in from the street to see her sister, whose husband had died on his way from Rangoon. I have seen a wonderful progress in both sisters, and in one brother and his wife quite a little bundle of grace. But they have one brother who still does not feel the truth. He never went to church, but now comes pretty regularly to our church, and they say they pray for him night and day. How salvation refines and elevates! It seems I had twice spoken with the brother, not knowing who he was. I went to see Mr M., who is soon to get the command of the 'Spy', a surveying vessel. I suppose he and his wife will join us. God has begun already, I should think, in her. She had met me when I was visiting, and sent to ask me if I would call on them.

Last night, went to visit sick people — walking. Among others the person M., about whom Mr Ferguson wrote to me. I had the coachman with me, and he tracked his way through lanes and gullies, in the moonlight, like a hound. I found the poor youth almost gone — apparently the very last stage of consumption.

Went again to visit sick, first M. I found him dying. A good man was there, a Baptist, who knew him. We could make nothing of him. He said he could not attend. He asked how long he would have to suffer. Altogether it was the most hopeless, melancholy deathbed I have ever seen. I took Mr C, the Baptist, who is a good man, out to the door, and asked what he knew of the poor young man. He said, he had destroyed himself with low debauchery. I went in again, and tried in various ways to awaken and interest; but in vain. After prayer, I had to go to others.

Today, Sabbath, it has been fearfully hot, — the church very full, and oppressively hot. At the Sabbath school; several of the teachers absent; but we made out. The children came in rather late, apparently waiting till the sun had a little lessened his blaze. In the evening church thin. This has been a happy day, though I have been several times drenched as if I had been passed through a river ... In the evening, went to the fort, and liked the meeting. One of the soldiers of the 98th, who volunteered, and used to come to us, spoke with me. His wife has gone home with the little Russels. She had gone to see him at Dum-Dum before leaving, and on the way home had been attacked by two artillerymen, brutally treated and robbed. The poor fellow was on guard when he heard it, and, without waiting for leave, he ran and broke out of barracks. He had been seized and punished, and all this had fairly overset him, so that, though a true child of God, he had, like Job, begun to repine against God and man. He was worn to a shadow. I walked up and down with him, and he seemed to get light and comfort a little again ... I have been visiting a good deal, and at night went to see a Mr L., in Government Place, who is dying of consumption. He is a merchant, and has a young wife and child. The doctor says he can only linger a very short time. His father, in England, is a good man, they say ... I have just been seeing Mr L. He is dying. He seems full of peace and joy; in the middle of the night he broke forth in thanksgiving. He said, 'God has led me by a strange way; but it is the right one', and went on admiring and glorifying the grace of God to one who had sinned so much. He said, 'Tell my father that I shall be waiting for him'; and to his partner, when he went in, in the morning, he said, 'I thought I should have been in glory ere now; but I shall soon be there.' How different such a house is from those which, I fear, are too common here!

Mr M., the chief officer of the ship, is very ill, I suspect dying. I have seen him two or three times; but have not been able to get near his mind as yet … I have been a long time with poor M., now captain of the 'Spy'. They had sent for me; but I had not got the note, having gone out early. But I called on my way, and found him sinking fast. He said, 'I have neglected Christ too much, and too long.' He is quite calm and collected, though weak, and I think the Lord is touching his heart. He spoke of the hardness of his heart, the difficulty of believing; but assented when I spoke of the dying thief. He must have long been a sufferer, as no one knew what was the matter; now they say cancer. I trust it is to be a case like that of L. There is something interesting in the candour and honesty of these men. When fairly brought to a stand, they confess their sin and lost estate, and so are ready to hear of the Saviour. They are not truth proof. It is a kind of new thing to them. I have left the doctor, who is a friend of his, to read to him. I said, 'You see his state of mind. He feels that Christ alone can help him now.' He said, 'Yes', and undertook to sit by him and read a little as he is able to bear it. The doctor took me to see another officer of the little squadron who is ill. He will succeed M. if he dies. Is it not curious how one is led on from one person to another? It will be a great comfort if this poor fellow gives evidence, before he dies, that he has found the Lord.

Hospital Visitations

On Thursday morning, ere daybreak, I was awakened to receive a note, saying Captain M. was dying, and wished to see me. I went. He was quite calm and self-possessed. Rallied again, and continued in this state till Friday morning, when he gently died, and, I trust, in the Lord … Last night I went to the hospital, and went among the soldiers. It is a sad scene; quite crowded, and doolies coming constantly in with sick men. I found Private Jliffe, who has been the beginning of good in the regiment, lying very ill. He was quite well on Monday night at the meeting, went on duty on Tuesday morning, and was brought in in the course of the day. Sergeant Hunter I found very ill. In the woman's hospital was one of the saddest sights I have ever seen. Near the door, Sergeant Hunter's wife was dying. The place was crowded with women more or less ill, their children round them, and in many cases their husbands. They cried, 'You are welcome; it is you we need here.' They say the fort is like an oven, and they are falling by tens and twenties. Coming out I met a fine-looking man, Sergeant D. W. He was almost crying. He said, 'I am the only sergeant fit for duty in my company, and am worked night and day. My wife is here ill, and I have no one to take care of my three young children', and he struck his staff on the ground in a kind of desperation. I have promised to go back this forenoon. Were we but full of grace and truth, there is abundant room here for going about continually doing good.

The natives say yesterday was the most oppressive day we have had. Curious enough, I was much out and enjoyed it; but I mean to rest today … About twelve, I went to the hospital. Mrs Hunter died about a quarter of an hour after I left last night. Many of the women were Papists; but they seemed all glad that I should read and pray with them. Then I went to the other hospital. Jliffe seemed a little better. He said he had been delirious during the night, and dreaming of my sermon on Monday night. I went from bed to bed. All welcome me, even the Papists. One was reading the Douay Bible. I took it, and read to him a little. Another was reading A Kempis' *Imitation of Christ*, with Popish blazonries and notes. I read a little of the text, and spoke to him, and one or two more near. Then up to the third storey. Several had died since I was there last night. One man was dying and quite unconscious. I tried to speak to him, but in vain. So two or three of them came, and I prayed beside him. A little crowd gathered, and I read and spoke a good deal. Then went to poor Hunter. He was much cast down. They had only told him a little before of his wife's death.

His little boy of four years old, or less, was standing beside his bed. What desolation! I am going back today. I think it a most hopeful field; and even if all one could do was merely to soothe and comfort, I would go; but I think the Lord is at work.

The following extracts are from letters:

July 1855. — I rose early and walked out. An old man came out of a carriage. I walked with him a little, and spoke about seeking the Lord in the morning. He assented, but said the world took such hold of him ... A note came today, asking me to go and see a Mrs P., whose husband, a pilot, was drowned yesterday. A telegraph message came up of his death. I found her a young creature with two children. My *James' Widows* are all gone, but I still have some *Cecil's Visits*[1] ... I have seen the —. They were not out on Sabbath, for their horses were ill, and they were knocked up, being at work on Saturday from 6 a.m. till 9 p.m. I said, 'You look oppressed; tell me if anything is troubling you, not what it is; for, of course, I do not pry into your private matters, but that I may sympathize with you.' He told me that they had lost money, and are in trouble with their Australian trade, as many now are. I, of course, exhorted him to cast his burden on the Lord.

Aug. 1855. — Last night a buggy [a gig] was overthrown near the gate with a great crash. I went down to see if I could help. One of the gentlemen was swearing. After sympathy, and offer of my carriage, I softly said, 'You are wrong. You have had a most providential escape; is it right thus to dishonour your Deliverer?' He stopped and thanked me, and became quite quiet ... At night went to the sailors in Lal Bazaar. I went into the street and brought different parties in and gave them hymn-books, and read till the service began. Mr Chill was doing the same, and the place was nearly full ... Have been a little round with the beadle to hunt up for the Sabbath school. After that I went to the sailors' meeting in Lal Bazaar. There was a good number. I took 'Ye were as sheep going astray' — the lost sinner, the saved sinner. There was a good deal of impression. When we finished, for

[1] One of these books he generally sent to everyone in sorrow.

I made Chill pray and close, none rose to go away. I spoke a little to them, and said, 'You have encouraged others to go astray; try to bring your companions here; — for they all said they would come back next night. You have been the devil's tools, now try to be Christ's helpers in well-doing.' One old boatswain said, 'I have been the wanderingest sheep of all." … I have had a visit just now from Mohendra and Nobin. We have had a really affecting, interesting meeting. Mohendra asked me to read something that I thought suited him. I read the last half of what is said to the Ephesian church: 'Nevertheless I have somewhat against thee, because thou hast left thy first love.' He said it cut him to the heart, and he acknowledged that he had fallen. He again asked me to read, which I did in Jeremiah. I made him observe the passage in Revelation that it was not indiscriminate censure, for it said, 'Thou hatest the deeds', *etc.*, and that this corresponded with what he had told me, that he could not go in with the ways of many of the medical students. It turns out that the present movement about re-marriage of widows originated at our meeting in his house.

Nov. 1855. — The ceaseless changes of Indian society try me; but I wish to go quietly on. A few cases such as that of dear A. would make me think years of labour and trial well spent.

You will remember the — s we used to meet out driving. She is just dead and her baby expected to follow … I have sent Mr — a little book, and have a note from him … Have found Mr — 's card on the table.

Called on Mr A., and have had a very long, interesting conversation with him, going over passage after passage, and trying to explain difficulties. He is in a very interesting state, and is anxious that it may not pass without saving benefit; but he is, as you may suppose, very dark. We have gone over a good deal today, and I have sent for the *Anxious Inquirer,* which begins with 'Impressions, and the danger of losing them.' …

Looked in on Mr A. He took me to his own room. He said he was coming to see the truth. He is in a most interesting state; I should say converted. He says, he has got great good from the *Anxious Inquirer,* which just met him at the point where he was, and then led him on, removing his difficulties and errors. He said it was all new to him that we must be justified before we can be sanctified. He always thought, 'I must try to be good, and so get peace with God.' He finds the Bible a new book; and, altogether, I think the Lord is leading him on in much love. He asked me to pray, and then I asked him, which he did without hesitation; but was, as I expected, all in the first person, and very affecting and full, thanking God for not cutting him off during the past twenty-two years of sin and carelessness. He seems being amiable and candid. He says he wishes to come to the Free Church tomorrow.

Mr A. came in this morning. He is in a beautiful state of mind; the Lord is carrying him on without cloud or interruption. You would be delighted with much that he says; for instance, that if he had not passed his examinations (which he had just done) he would not have been surprised, for that those who fear God have glory waiting them, and therefore if they have less of this world's good, it would be no wonder. He is to join at the communion with us ...

A. called today. He is a fine example of the Spirit's teaching, and I trust the Lord will use him. We prayed together, each in turn. There is great freshness about all his views, and yet he is but a boy ... In the afternoon Mr — came in, and we have had much pleasant and happy conversation. What a world it would be if all were converted!

Nov. 1855. — Mr — came in, and we went to the graveyard to see the tomb he has erected over the grave of his wife. On returning, he remained with me for a little, and we both prayed, and then he left. I feel as if I had lost a brother.[1] ...

Nov. 1855. — I am sometimes inclined to murmur at the strange isolation I feel; but I am checked by the thought how many are in the same condition, scattered up and down this vast land, and cut off, in youth, and for many years from their friends. So I am not going

[1] Milne and Mr A. never met again. For many years they kept up a close correspondence; and last year, when Mr A. had the prospect of being in Scotland, Milne looked forward with great desire to see him again; but on several occasions was disappointed.

to give Satan a song by idle complaint. Besides, you know, faith, if it were lively, would soon bring us into good company; 'Ye are come to Mount Zion, and to the city of the living God.' There is the family beneath and the family above ...

Nov. 1855. — I trust that, wherever we are, the Lord will give us grace to love and serve and live for him. I think my views are becoming more settled in seeing only two objects on earth — the kingdom of grace and the kingdom of darkness. The one I should like to live in and to see advancing, and help it on; the other I should like to leave wholly and for ever, and to see its diminution and decay ... I am passing through a good deal of trial in my own soul, but I think the Lord will bring forth judgment unto victory ... I am crushed under a sense of unworthiness; everything about me and around me seems so unlike the great salvation, little, selfish, earthly. Who will be the first to awake and live and speak as a child of light and heir of glory? I have a strange feeling of uselessness, which is sometimes quite oppressive; but I trust I shall be enabled to wait quietly till the clouds break and pass away.

Leanings to Millenarianism

December 1855. — I have been reading the Lent Lectures for 1854 in St George's Church, Bloomsbury. They are feeble; but that does not repel or disincline me from Millenarianism, because I believe that it is seen not by any eminence of talent, but by the illumination of God. I think Jerusalem will be the metropolis of the Christian world, and that, as many now go from superstition there from year to year, so all nations will then go in love and thankfulness to worship the Lord. But whether Christ will be visibly present and accessible there, I do not know, and dare not give a decided opinion; but all my sympathies are with you.

January 1856. — Called on Mrs M., who is in great distress about her son at Peshawur, who is ill, and her husband will not show her the letter about it. I said, 'The way in which you can best help him, is by putting away your cares and fears, and trying to pray in strong faith and hope.' ... Should we not observe little things? When I was at the funeral yesterday, I saw a man looking about as if the burial service were not intended to be followed and felt. I turned towards him, and he became attentive; but I thought I should like to speak to him. I lost sight of him, however, in the crowd. Well, yesterday, when I went into L.'s shop, I found my friend; so I said, 'You were at the funeral last night'; and then put my hand on his shoulder, and spoke seriously and kindly to him ... I have had a visit from two Baboos.[1] One is one of those of whom we several times had hopes. I said, 'Are you still sticking in the mire?' He said, he thought he was advancing a little. The other seemed a flippant, self-complacent fellow. I said, 'Are you a Christian?' He said, 'No; I am sorry to say I am not a Christian.' I said, 'You are not sorry; I wish you were, for then there might be some hope.' And I felt checked, when I remembered the young ruler.

March 1856. — I am not sure that the J.s have regular family worship; so, what do you think I did when I called today? I made his boy turn up Ephesians 6:1-3, and read it. Then asked, 'What is nurture?' 'Food.' 'What was baby's food?' 'Milk.' 'Well, that's for the body; but what is nurture for the soul?' We turned to 1 Peter 2:1, 'The word of God.' 'Well', I said, 'your father labours, and he gives you nurture for the body, — how often?' 'Breakfast, *etc.*' 'And how often nurture for the soul?' 'Morning and evening.' 'Does he not read and pray with you?' The boy looked at the father, and the mother looked, and I did not look, but went on speaking a little ... I have been to see Mrs M. She said, 'Neither I nor my husband are very pious; but we think it wrong to profess what we do not feel, as many do.' I said, 'Right, madam, in that; but it is very wrong not to feel pious. You and your husband ought to fear God, and trust Christ, and repent.' She looked rather taken aback, but was peculiarly friendly ...

Called on — [the husband of the lady to whom the previous extract refers. Both were Episcopalians]. Spoke of various matters. After a little I brought in religion, and felt my way. Had he never had deeper convictions than at present? He looked very sharply; but I looked at

[1] *Baboo:* a Hindu clerk who is literate in English, *Ed.*

him, and so he went on, and said he had, but business had carried him away. I said religion did not require long research. It brings us a heavenly Friend, who is willing and able to support us under those crushing responsibilities and perplexities of which we had been speaking. 'Hear, and your soul shall live.' He said he had been originally intended for the Church, and would have got a living in Ireland.' 'But', I said, 'you know I have a roving commission, — "every creature", and so count you as a patient.' He said, 'You are right; I am obliged, and could not be offended.' We parted very kindly.

May 1856. — Dr K. has been in. He is of an inquiring, speculative turn of mind, and says he feels in doubt about many of the truths of God. I think he will be led on.

July 1856. — I have been writing to Dr K., sending him Miss Graham's memoir. I ask that our intercourse yesterday may be the beginning of an open, brotherly correspondence, which, I trust, will end in his saying, 'My Lord, and my God!' I say that I have little faith in men's reasonings; that a true Christian is God's own creation, born again of God; that the doubts and questionings he feels are no cause for pride, but for sorrow and humiliation; that they are a fruit of sin, and only found among men on earth, — devils believe and tremble, and even infidels drawing near to eternity distrust their former doubts; that I think the Bible is our best witness when it is read prayerfully; that many things may seem at first mysterious and unaccountable, but postpone seeking the explanation till you are more fully acquainted with divine truth. There are many things in your own profession which you did not comprehend at the commencement, and if you had insisted on getting an explanation you would never have been Dr K.

August 1856. — *On board the steamer going to Benares.* — There is a young man on board, exceedingly clever and well informed, who has been, and still is, very ill. I should think he may not live long, but it is difficult to get access to his mind. He shrinks from any allusion that might make him think himself in any danger. Perhaps I may get an opening ere we part … We were conversing on deck last night, when the others gradually dropped away and left me alone with H., the sick young man, and I had an opportunity of speaking to him, which I had scarcely looked for. He took it in good part, and we parted shaking hands heartily.

Sabbath Morning, August 1856. — On board the steamer. — At breakfast I prayed that we might have a little of the Sabbath rest and Sabbath spirit. The captain, beside whom I sit, said, 'I have never been so happy in any voyage before; and when we reach Monghyr, about 1 o'clock, I shall stop for the day, and get and give the Sabbath rest.'

Each day during this trip he had a little meeting for reading the Bible and prayer in his cabin. It began with young men, but gradually others joined; even the captain. At one of the stations on the way up the river, the judge read the English service, and asked Milne to preach, which he did.

September 1856. — Coming down the river to Calcutta. — I had beside me today a person who says he has wandered over most of the world, except Australia, and he is going there. I said, 'What have you learned?' He answered, 'To be a fool.' I looked at him, and said, 'It is time for you now to learn to be wise', and then spoke to him … Yesterday I gave tracts, and they have been handed about the ship. The captain took me to his cabin last night and seemed much affected. This morning he has been reading on deck, and came and sat beside me, and I read little bits to him out of my Bible … We have had at dinner a debate about keeping the Sabbath. Of course it came to little; and I don't think that is the way to do much good. In the evening I got into talk with the chief malcontents, first speaking about tiger-hunting and then the Sabbath. I said, 'The question should not be about this way or that way of keeping the Sabbath, but, are we converted men? If we loved God, and had our citizenship in heaven, would we weary of the spiritual employments of the Sabbath and pant for worldly amusements?' They quite went along with me … Captain G. has been speaking a good deal to me, and says he was much affected last Sabbath during sermon … C. came also and said much the same, that he would have cried but for shame. He told me of his wife's death, and other trials. I spoke a little to him, and then asked him to lean over the gunwale of the vessel, and I prayed shortly.

October 1856. — As a minister I feel I have a right to speak to every creature, and usually I don't allow it to lie idle … I have just been thinking that Christ's coming is a definite, and distinct, and comprehensible object. Put this away, and then death, heaven, and a kind of dreamy idea of lengthened life is all that people have to occupy the future. All along, since it was said, 'The seed of the woman', *etc.*, there has been a looking forward to the coming of a Person …

Calcutta. — I went in last night to see Mr W., an Oxford man, a civilian. We talked first about general matters, then about his religious state; and we got into a frank, open-hearted conversation, going over a great deal of ground, and ending with the Bible … I have just been thinking how strangely the Lord has brought us into acquaintance with His people all over this land! I gave eleven notes to the B — s; for I found that I could introduce them to children of God in every place they went to on their way to Bareilly. But we must not rejoice in this, but only, and constantly, and greatly in the Lord. I find that, whenever I begin *to feed* on any earthly thing, and to roll it as a sweet morsel under my tongue, it invariably becomes bitter, and the idol is turned into a cross …

Last night, I went to see the D — s, and stopped a little. For the first time, there was an indication of life in D — . After reading and prayer, he was telling me about a little nephew, who went to Southampton to meet his mother, and met only her corpse, she having died during the voyage. He said, 'The scene was heart-rending.' I said, 'The saddest scene in all the world was Calvary, and this opened his heart.' I think he got good on Sabbath. We had real talk, and parted with the look you know. I fear he is a dying man, and may be carried off at any time, and it would be so nice to see him on the Rock …

At the missionary breakfast, the question was, 'Should missionaries, after being a number of years in India, have a furlough, even though they are not ill?' Some nice remarks were made. When it came to me, I said, 'I thought they were very naturally looking at one side of the

question — their own; but that there was another. What was good
for the Church? Did not the people at home require that missionaries
should go among them, and tell them what the Lord was doing, and
kindle the flame of missionary zeal? At present, when they went home
only in bad health, they either were unfit for this, or it injured them.
But that the furlough at the end of some years, might send strong
men who would do good service at home; that a dreary, interminable
prospect sunk a man's spirit; but that, if he saw a little way before him
rest and change, he was quickened and reanimated.' ...

A gentlemanly man called with a note from J. G., an old friend in
Perth. We talked about various things pleasantly, and he rose to go. I
said, 'I will read a little', and he sat down. I read Psalm 34, and prayed.
He thanked me. He is looking out for employment, and I prayed that
he might be guided. In a moment or two he opened up, and we had a
most delightful conversation. It was very touching. He is to join with
us on Sabbath. He is living in the house with young G. I told him
what trouble I had had in vain, trying to get that young man to church,
and said, 'You must help me.' He is to watch, and try what he can do.
His face quivered as I spoke of the responsibility of those who knew
the truth. As we shook hands, I said, 'Well now, if I had not proposed
prayer, we should have parted, and never thought of one another any
more; now I hope we are friends for ever.' ...

I had a long walk and talk last night with Colonel B. He says he
is over-wrought — fourteen hours a day, — and he cannot stand it.
I spoke of the rest, and Hezekiah's prayer, 'Lord, I am oppressed.' It
was very nice ... A Prussian, and one of the leading merchants in
the Straits, has been to lunch. He opened his mind to me. I read and
prayed with him, and he seemed affected.

March 1857. — I think it likely that God will break up all existing
organizations of the visible Church; he will thresh the barn-floor, and
gather out His own. But *he* will do it, not man ... We should have no
glory but Christ's. It is a miserable thing to be esteemed and praised
by those who despise and neglect Christ. Hence I should think that
to be popular with worldly men should make people very anxious

about themselves. True, Christ was followed, but that arose from curiosity, self-interest, and misconception. When they really knew him,
and his doctrine, and his aim, they went away and crucified him …
There would seem to be a dotage as well as an infancy in human science. Long ago, when men knew little of nature, they thought matter
and motion enough to account for all. And now, when centuries of
observation and experiment have accumulated stores of true knowledge, they still come to the same sad conclusion, that dead matter,
and blind, necessary laws, without a designing, overruling God, can
account for all.

March 1856. — In speaking on the ten virgins, I said that there was
no painter like Christ. Here was a picture of the Church in all places
and ages. She slumbers and sleeps. Her normal state ought to be life
and activity; but it was not so. Now and then a spasmodic galvanic
upstarting, and a promise of doing great things; but soon the head
begins to nod, the eyelids to droop, the limbs are relaxed, and down
she sinks. Was it not so in Calcutta? I had been told there had been
better times; but where now were the men with loins girt and lamps
burning? where the line of demarcation? where are the godly? You
say, In church. Right. You say, At the committees of religious societies
tomorrow or next day. But where were they last night, or the night
before? Was it at the masquerade, the fancy ball, the idle meeting of
frivolity and worldliness; and there up to twelve o'clock, or perhaps
beyond? The worldly go to church with the godly, and the godly go
to Vanity Fair with the worldly, and thus they alternate; they are just
in one cradle, and the devil is rocking it. And so the rich man with
his large barns, is not his name Legion? Might we not say to almost
any man we meet, 'Friend, did you not sit for your portrait more than
1,800 years ago?' … If you write to Andrew Bonar, tell him I am greatly
enjoying Baumgarten on the Acts, and that, if anything human will
make me a millenarian brother, I think it will.

His Calcutta Journal

We now give the journal-fragments, which will, we think, greatly interest the reader, as illustrations of the writer's own mind, and as a record of his work. With his feet consciously upon the rock, he looks within and around.

Calcutta, 31st October 1854. — Lord, thou knowest all things; search me and try me. I desire, through thy blood and Spirit, and word and providence, deliverance from my besetting sins, many of which I know, many I do not know. Make me like thyself, a lover of righteousness and a hater of iniquity. I read that 'the Spirit of the Lord should rest on thee, and make thee of quick understanding in the fear of the Lord.' Lord, I covet this. Change me, and I shall be changed. I desire the fleshly tablet of the heart, which will be ever alive to the intimations of thy will, and so receive and retain thy teachings from moment to moment. I desire henceforth to live unto thee. Make me see thy glory and thy loveliness, that I may rejoice in my portion, and that my weak heart may wander no more. Forgive the sins of yesterday, sins known to thee and to my own heart, and keep me this day, that I may no more grieve and wrong thee. How foolish, how miserable, to be pleasing men, and displeasing thee! Having such promises, I would cleanse myself from all filthiness of the flesh and spirit, and walk with thee in a filial, loving, honest spirit.

I have now been a year and five months in this country. I find it too true, *coelos non animos mutant qui trans mare currunt.*[1] The sins that clave to me in Scotland cleave to me here. Lord, give me deliverance! I seek it by faith, and not by the works of the law. Teach me how to perfect holiness in the fear of God, and then, my heart no more condemning me, I shall have boldness before God and man. I see an exceeding proneness to legalism in my heart, a wish to value myself, and to rejoice in efforts made and success attained. It seems utter death to give this up; yet help me, Lord, from this moment, through thy grace,

---

[1] 'They change their skies, not their minds, who cross the sea.' That is, travel changes our surroundings, not ourselves; this is a quotation from Horace, *Epistulae*, I, II, v. 27, *Ed.*

to do so. May I rejoice in Christ Jesus, and have no confidence in the flesh. My soul, think not, speak not of thyself, but make thy boast in the Lord. I desire to do my daily work heartily and carefully, and leave the issues with the Lord. I should like to look, not at the things that are seen, whether prosperous or adverse, but to the things that are not seen. I think I see a hope of being useful in my ministerial work, though there will be difficulties and disappointments to the end. But I feel that I am differently situated here from what I was at home. There the eye was fixed on my own sphere almost exclusively; here I look at the whole country, and look and labour for its elevation. I think I feel my heart drawn increasingly to India, so that it would be a kind of death now to leave it. I am disappointed both in the character of missionary work here, and also in the amount and value of its results. Perhaps I have too little considered the difficulties, and been too apt to blame. Let me rejoice that there are Christian instrumentalities at work, even though I think they are in some things in error, and less efficient than they might be. Lord, arise and plead thine own cause.

November 4th. — I see that we can only overcome by the blood of the Lamb. There is a great tendency here to yield to external circumstances, and sink down; and yet the only safety is in a continual watchfulness and girding up. I must work the work of God. Lord, help me to be pitiful with others, but stern with myself.

November 29th. — I have been thinking of the certainty of the punishment of sin. We never doubt that to go contrary to material laws will bring evil; for instance, he who throws himself into the fire will be burned; much more he who breaks any moral law shall die. Fire is only a creature, and God may change and restrain its properties, as he has often done; but the law is an expression of God's holy, essential nature, and ere it can be prevented from carrying its sanctions into effect, God's own nature must be changed. But he changeth not — he cannot deny himself. How overwhelming the thought that, living in sin, we have been in greater danger than if we had been plunging into a sevenfold heated furnace!

November 30th. — I desire this day to seek, and find, and hold fast my Lord. How empty are my days and nights of thee, O blessed One, who alone canst fill all in all! ... I have been reading the life of young M'Intosh; — sadly interesting. It may be good that, now and then, such an instance may be given of the result of study carried on under the most favourable circumstances; but I think I would rather be the earnest worker than the earnest student. I think the two should go hand in hand, else we shall become mere *literateurs* and sentimentalists, or sink into the dull rut of regular, mechanical, unthinking labour, I think he got the good of such a life, passing from land to land, and examining many shades of opinion, true and false. I should like to get to my Lord's standpoint, and see as he sees, and feel as he feels. It is a dangerous experiment, however, to sit in judgment upon divers opinions; and there is a risk of becoming ultimately unfixed and drifting about without any anchorage. M.'s safety, if he did escape the danger, arose from his hold of Christ, and his having got beyond the doctrinal to the personal truth. I think I can see, as he drew near the close of life, that the *mare magnum*[1] of inquiry and investigation was still opening up to him, and that the time was still far off when he would have cried, 'Stop, it is enough.'

December 3d. — Sabbath night. — I have been helped in my work, and found it a pleasant day. My comforts at present are very many. May these loving-kindnesses sink down into my heart, and prepare me for times of darkness and trial. I have had some risings of the flesh today at the lukewarmness, selfishness, and want of hearty cooperation on the part of those who should be friends; but trust not in a friend, but trust in the Lord; blessed are they that wait on him. Faith can carry through all. The quiet mornings here are invaluable. One feels fresh after the repose of the night, and gives to the Lord what progress he may make in good, and what preparation he may receive for the trials and requirements of the day. But too often they are lost. There is the morning walk; the meeting with friends, and weariness; there is the morning lounge; the silly, worthless newspaper, laid often on the bed ere they are awake. I have been trying tonight to warn against these. Lord, give thy blessing, and grant me to keep myself unspotted.

[1] 'Great sea', *Ed.*

December 5th. — Tuesday night. — Busy yesterday. The mail arrived, and our tidings were pleasant. Busy again today. Many mercies, and yet evil return. It is not truth in the mind, but in the heart, that will influence the heart. There is no perfection or real trustworthiness but in Christ. He is the Rock; but, looking to him, we should aim at perfection, even to cleanse ourselves from all filthiness of the flesh and spirit.

December 7th. — Thursday morning. — Some help and comfort yesterday. I feel that my calling is to walk in love, not returning evil for evil, but, contrariwise, blessing. Lord, make my heart soft today. I cannot learn, and I cannot do others good, while my heart is hard and wilful. Lord, make me tender and contrite now, and let me take my motives from thee, and receive my joy from thee, and be the servant of God and not of men.

December 9th. — Saturday morning. — Passing on; busy, and yet not much seems to be done. *Thursday evening.* — Meeting of Presbytery, to arrange for Mr Mackay going to Scotland, and Mr Millar to Australia. *Friday.* — Various trials, which serve to show me what I am. Lord, help me to live in thee and on thee. The evil that is within me is unspeakable. Save me from its eruptions, and from its indwelling dominion and power. I see the duty of watching and resisting at once, and discovering all its motions and beginnings. Lord, help me. Make my heart right with thee, and let me no more identify myself with the work of the devil. I find in this place strange undercurrents of evil, causing unlooked-for umbrage and alienation, so that I am often out in my calculations. But why am I more discontented at this than the mariner on the deep, when he finds himself frustrated by adverse tides and winds? Surely the children of this world are wiser than the children of light. They are more practical, more reasonable; they hold on their way. Help me, Lord; my hope is in thee. Grant times of blessing, and then there will be union. I fear it would often be hard for some to rejoice if the Lord were to give the blessing to others. How selfish we are, seeking each our own things, and not the things of Christ! Enable me to rejoice in all that is the joy of Christ. I am affected by that word, 'My soul shall have no pleasure in him.' God may still remain by his providential, upholding presence, but he finds no delight, and he expects no gladness. He was still with the men of the world before the Deluge, but it grieved him at his heart to be among them.

December 12th. — Tuesday morning. — Went to Chinsurah on Saturday evening. Preached on Sabbath, and in the afternoon went among the natives and villages which have lately been almost de-populated by infectious disease. Sad scenes of misery. Dying like the beast, and not knowing nor caring what after becomes of them. I have been kept during these days. Lord, help me to possess my soul in patience. Make me to dwell on high, and ever to rejoice in God my Saviour. I desire guidance and blessing this day as to the places I visit, and my conduct and converse there. Lord, hide me in the secret of thy presence.

December 13th. — Wednesday evening. — Many blessings, and slight trials. Sense of the danger of losing my Lord. Have been trying to seek much this night at the prayer-meeting. I desire to seek the good of all men. Grant me the charity which flows out of a pure heart and a good conscience. Help me, Lord, to rise above little, proud, selfish feelings, and to love and care for all, and that for thy blessed sake.

December 23d. — Saturday morning. — I think I feel, Lord, that thou art softening my heart, and revealing to me more and more of the evil of sin. I think I see more the need of a broken heart, and a soft, tender, watchful walk. Grant that this may be abiding and growing. I desire to make use of the lessons I am learning from Mr Morgan's — as far as man could judge — deadly illness, and now the beginning of hope and restoration. Lord, prepare me for all thy will. Grant me to do from day to day, with my might, all I have to do. I desire to put away all partialities, envies, jealousies, and to love all, and to seek their whole good, earnestly, continually, and by all means. Grant me grace daily to walk with thee, my Lord; and then, when all else fails, this fellowship will remain, and brighten, and deepen.

December 24th. — Sabbath morning. — My friend Mr Morgan died suddenly last night. He sunk all at once, most unexpectedly. It is a sore disappointment, and, as far as I can judge, an almost irreparable loss, for he seemed just the man for his work. Lord, help! I have been a good deal tried during the night; but my hope is in thee, O Lord. Forgive me, and aid me, and let all thy will become my will.

December 26th. — Tuesday morning. — Busy yesterday. How easily the over-engrossed heart slides away from the Lord; and yet how willingly and and unresistingly it yields to the temptation, and even rejoices, and prides itself upon these, too often self-sought and self-wrought, activities! Met my old friend, Mr Anderson, formerly of Banchory, who has come to be a Professor in one of the Government colleges in the N.W. Provinces. Met also the new head of the Martiniere, at Mr Woodrow's. Long conversation on metaphysics. Persuaded that all these discussions are unprofitable and hurtful. It is striving to explain what God has left in mystery, and to set aside the supernatural faith which God gives to his elect. Lord, I bless thee for thy word. Help me to learn all it teaches, believe all it announces, obey all it commands.

True Power

In the beginning of the next year (1855) he gives utterance to both hope and fear. He looks the obstacles right in the face, and casts himself on God. He mourns over High Church sectarianism; asks for the breaking down of 'the walls of partition with which these Judaizers encompass themselves'; prays for times of unity and mutual appreciation, and to be kept, meanwhile, from despondency and from bitterness. He takes everything to God; he looks at everything in the light of the divine glory; he records his joys and sorrows; and, above all, his confidence in the living God, both for himself and for his work. He grieves over his weaknesses and unfitnesses, and adds, 'I feel the more need to cultivate close fellowship with my Lord.' There is the prospect of his beloved wife having to leave for England on account of health; and he asks for help for both in this long separation. There seem clouds rising over the land, and he says, 'We may be on the verge of great events; guide me in reference to public affairs.' He gets down very deep into self-humiliation, and his utterances are like those of David Brainerd. Yet his faith fails not. His eye is always on the cross; and so he moves on, feeling the conflict within and the opposition without, but not succumbing. He looks round, he calls up those over whom he is yearning, and adds, 'Pity, Lord, those I think of as I write, and give a time of salvation ere they leave this land or die.'

Jan. 12th. — *Thursday.* — I think God is leading me more into the mystery of the kingdom, and making me see that it begins inwardly and *works out*. The word and Spirit in the soul makes one a member of the kingdom, and fits for service in it. Let me cease from putting much trust in outward working and management. 'Ye shall receive POWER'; and then build. But it was not the power of wealth, or mere eloquence, or fashion, or state endowment, or organization, or machinery. Lord, keep my eye upon the rock whence thy church has been dug. Make me deaf, and blind, and dead to all the contempt, and indifference, and carnal neglect with which thy cause meets, and enable me to labour on in hope, without bitterness. Save me from vain thoughts and sad thoughts, and enable me to seek and proclaim thy truth in growing simplicity and power. I feel what a hindrance the bigotry, Popery, Judaism, and earthly power of the High Church Episcopalians in this land present.[1] I shall need much grace to bear and wait. Arise, O Lord, and bring down this pride and dispel this darkness ... Make me mindful of the nature of thy kingdom; that it comes not with observation; that it is not outward organization; that it does not bulk large in the world's eye, but is the gathering together of the poor, the babes, the broken-hearted. Even while really seeking the salvation of souls, and feeling that nothing short of this can benefit them, how apt am I to seek mere congregational prosperity! Lord, in mercy lift me up; bring me into the secret of thy presence; make to

[1] An Episcopalian clergyman, not High Church, called on him one day, and said, 'I am walking in your footsteps, and going into all the lanes and gullies; but you know far more of this work than I do, and you must guide and help me.' Afterwards M. wrote to him encouragingly, and received a most cordial reply, expressing the earnest hope that they might work in love side by side.

seek, find, and feed on truth … Bless the daily reading of the word, and all the events of life. I scarce know how I may be conformed to thee in heart; it probably must be by means most painful and distasteful to the flesh; but do Thou save me in whatever way. Show me thy cross, and teach me to glory therein, and to enter into all the sentiments it suggests and the motives it produces. Let me be a crucified man; yet let me live because thou livest in me.

The rest of this month is filled up with happy entries. 'A truly good and peaceful day … Much peace and comfort today … Much peace.' February is strewed over with little tranquil notices. His peace was like a river.[1] March comes; and though he had been sorely tried by parting with his beloved wife for a two years' residence in England for her health, yet his records are still bright. 'Life has been passing on quietly and smoothly; some trials, though slight and brief, and many more mercies.' He speaks, too, of encouragement in his work, but mourns that he has been 'too little with God'; and feels a 'dryness and distance creeping over his soul'.

March 24th. — Saturday morning. — I think the Lord is leading me to live a good deal above the world; not to think how this or that might have been better or more comfortable, but to get away from it altogether and seek HIMSELF … Once or twice the thought has tried to get entrance, what life would be if anything were to befall B., and I were left to wander on alone? But I desire to resist and put away such thoughts. Mrs Morgan left behind at Cairo, dangerously ill; Mrs Fordyce sinking; so that, if I begin to think, I see I should give way, and therefore I desire to hope continually.

Birthday Thoughts

The most of April passes by unnoticed, till he comes to his birthday, and then he resumes:

---

[1] These are memorable words: 'I see clearly that I can only be useful in this land by striving to attain and introduce a higher spirituality both in life and work.'

April 26th. — Thursday. — My birthday. How many, O Lord, have been thy tender mercies! Thou hast borne with me more years than thou didst with Israel in the wilderness. Thou hast led me about, emptied me from vessel to vessel, brought me into acquaintance and tender friendship with some of the best and dearest saints; and thou hast showed me not a little of thy glorious and gracious working in the souls of men. Thou hast twice united me in the tenderest relation to women of God, the beloved of the Lord. How many have been thy mercies! I desire this day to commend to thy loving care my dear wife. Guide, and keep, and bless, and sanctify, and use her; and then unite us again, that together we may try to serve and honour thee. I commend to thee all my relations scattered up and down the earth. Let them be precious in thy sight … My dear wife is far away. Bear me up in her absence. I stand much alone in this place and land; for I find none like-minded to whom I can pour out my heart. All seem to seek their own, or to be tied up in their own little circles … Let me have growing trust in thy love and care. I desire never to rest even on a work of real grace within; but to know that it was advancing, might encourage and give me confidence.

In his July entries he speaks of clouds, and depressions, and languors; yet he also speaks of 'some glancings into his heart of *the joy of life, as an opportunity of living with and to God!*' His home-letters comfort him in some respects; but he is cast down at the intelligence that his beloved wife will not be able to rejoin him till the end of next year. The long array of weary months stretching out in prospective, almost sinks his heart. Yet he does not give way and this petition is still uppermost: 'Lord, give me to see thy work'; and this also: 'Enable me to go on calmly and holily.'

He meets with Dr Anderson from America, and more than once gets refreshment from conversation with him. 'He has been brought to see that it is only an election that will be gathered in; and therefore we should go on hopefully and yet self-deniedly, having no will of our own, but watching and waiting to see what is the will of the Lord.' He works heartily at our institutions, and takes pleasure in missionary conferences; yet longs for higher things than he sees. 'Secular education has too much taken the place of preaching Christ.' He feels 'burdened'. The converts are too dependent on us for support, and are not men of zeal and energy. He would like to try the apostolic procedure, and go to the old as much as to the young. He is afraid of a compromise with unbelief, and would like to see more simple trust in Jehovah and in his gospel as the power of God unto salvation.

His entry on the 14th of August (1855) notices his watching the deathbed of Mrs Milne's father; and on Sabbath, the 19th, he writes:

> Papa has gone from us. He sunk softly and peacefully, and on Friday morning died without even a sigh. I have every hope that it is well with him now. Grant us, Lord, the use of what we have been passing through, and be our support and portion in what is before us. Prepare my own B. for what will be to her such sad tidings. The funeral quiet and solemn last night. Bless me and aunt, and guide us in all our arrangements, and bring B. in due time again to us. I desire to live in thee. It has been a dreary, sleepless night, and I feel feeble; but, Lord, do thou use me, and all will be well.

Thoughts of Old Times in Perth

On the 8th of November 1855, he writes to Mrs Sandeman:

> MY VERY DEAR MRS SANDEMAN, — I have been far too long in acknowledging your very touching letter, and in thanking you for all your kindness to my dear wife, whose heart seems much drawn to you. Perhaps you may be able to write her a few words, now that she *is* in sorrow herself from the loss of her dear father. He died in much peace, full of days and of general esteem. I was deeply affected by all your details of the last hours and experience of Alexander and Hugh. I call that letter your 'way home'. And now last mail brought me Mrs

Barbour's 'way home'. Strange, indeed, have been the Lord's dealings with you; but he knows what is best, and I am sure you trust him, and think well of him still. I remember quite freshly the first call I ever made at Spring-land. It seems like yesterday; and at this moment I can recall every object and every feeling. How much has passed since then! But we are going on. We cannot and would not turn back. You must now seek grace for Charles and Frank. It is a great thing to have children and children's children in heaven. I hear most gratifying accounts of David and Frederick as preachers. May the Lord greatly use them! It will be a trial parting with David; but he goes to a great work, and he is the only one I know fitted to be a coadjutor to William Burns. I met the Bishop of Victoria here lately, who knew Mr B., and spoke of him with great admiration.

His diary then proceeds for some days much in the same strain as before; a record of peace and help, and conflict and work, interspersed with thoughts on Scripture:

August 24th. — Friday morning. — Let me follow out the thought of being dead with Christ. What manner of person should I be? I have nothing to do with things below in the way of being anxious about them, or vexed, or over-glad. What does a dead man care for these things? Though a man buffet him on the cheek, trample on him, what does he mind? Alive with Christ! Let me live where he is, and have heart and mind there. Yet he looks down on men, and dwells among them to pity and save. So let me be in the world, but not of the world. Here for the good of others, to do my Father's will; but not for any expectation of good.

Hymns

He refers to his lonely circumstances; — wife and relatives dead or far away; yet he goes on, acquiescent in the heavenly will; accepting his position here; looking upwards, and willing even to fail, if such be the purpose of God. 'Only let me love and enjoy thee, and let all else go.' Yet he feels he is of 'some use' here; 'learning what he could not have done amid the privileges and prosperity of home'. He is ever recording petitions in behalf of his dear wife, and longing for her return; yet working on contentedly; 'life passing on quietly, without much trial', and with 'Jehovah alone his salvation'; desiring 'to please him in all things'; 'ashamed of his unbelieving fears'; 'becoming more and more alive to the difficulties of a holy life'. Thus he sings: —

> Revive, O Lord, this sluggish soul,
>   And give me back salvation's joy;
> Let grace my sinful lusts control,
>   And send me forth in Thy employ.
> My hands hang down, my feet are slow,
>   My lips are dumb, my heart is cold;
> Let Thy free Spirit on me blow,
>   Let fresh forgiveness make me bold.
>
> See, Lord, these fields are ripening fast,
>   And sin and death their sickles ply:
> Oh send me forth the net to cast;
>   Oh stir up men from wrath to fly!
> I know that poor and weak I am,
>   A very babe, with stammering tongue;
> Be Thou my helper, gracious Lamb,
>   And in Thy strength let me be strong.

I may notice, that the pieces quoted here and elsewhere are interspersed throughout his Indian diary; as if his soul, in that land of strangers, loved to pour itself out in these strains. He seems to have written them with great ease and rapidity, walking to and fro on the verandah, I believe; yet they are singularly correct in rhythm; some of them very beautiful. Here is another:

Give me, O Lord, Thy changeless peace,
    And calm, I pray, this troubled mind;
That I from bitterness may cease,
    And 'mid unkindness, still be kind.

Thy sun his ceaseless course pursues,
    And shines alike on good and ill;
May I, like him, to stop refuse,
    When thankless souls my spirit chill.

Give me the strong, untiring love,
    Which hopes, endures, and never fails;
But, daily strengthened from above,
    At length o'er all who hate prevails.

Contrasting the obedience of creation to its Creator's laws, with the disorder and conflict of his own inner man, he thus writes:

My God, the kingdom's Thine; all things should Thee obey;
    But this rebellious will of mine resists Thy gracious sway.
The sun fails not to shine, the moon holds on her way;
    But this rebellious heart of mine resists Thy gracious sway.
The seasons know Thy sign, and come without delay;
    But this rebellious heart of mine resists Thy gracious sway.
The winds and waves combine to do what Thou wilt say;
    But this rebellious heart of mine resists Thy gracious sway.
Thy word comes line on line, Thy mercies day by day;
    But this rebellious heart of mine resists Thy gracious sway.
In weariness I pine, for succour oft I pray;
    Yet this rebellious will of mine resists Thy gracious sway.
Work in me what is Thine, and teach me to obey;
    Then this renewed will of mine will love Thy gracious sway.

I add another here, in another strain. A few more will be cited, farther on. But the pieces are too numerous, and some of them too long, to find a place in this memoir:

Open my blinded eyes, and make me clearly see
The loveliness that hidden lies, O Lamb of God, in Thee.
Let Thy mild beauties win the mastery of my soul,
And turn my carnal heart from sin, and all its thoughts control.
The fathers from afar beheld Thy day of old,
They saw Thee, bright and morning Star, Thy distant rays unfold.
And as they marked Thy rise, and felt Thy healing beams,
Their hearts, o'erwhelmed with glad surprise, forgot all meaner themes.
All things seemed full of Thee, God's fair and lowly flower!
They saw Thee growing in the tree, and dropping in the shower.
And oft they wondered how, and asked the question when,
The Lord on high His heavens would bow, and dwell with sinful men?
Why, then, am I so slow, more favoured far than they,
My great Incarnate Lord to know, and follow in His way?
Awake, my soul, from sleep, betake thyself to prayer,
And search and learn the mysteries deep that save from endless care.

Changes Within and Without; Benares

Intermingled with these artless, yet not commonplace effusions, the journal goes on: 'A comfortable day in church and Sabbath school.' 'Another peaceful day.' 'A good day this has been; quiet and peaceful; yet I have felt the old enemy within, and the old enemy without.' He asks 'guidance and self-command'. He goes to various places, 'meeting with much kindness, and finding opportunities of doing good.' 'Helped, and happy.' He wants to 'love the low estate, and to lose his life that he may find it unto life eternal'. 'A pleasant and encouraging day'; but he must 'watch lest he lose all'. 'A pleasant peaceful day; fellowship with God; one or two trials to humble.' 'A busy and encouraging day.' He asks more 'simplicity of nature, and habitual, entire leaning on the Lord'. 'Dr Duff in the morning [preaching]; full of truth and power.' 'An unsatisfactory day; hurried, and needing special mercy.' 'Feeble, and no strength in myself, yet a very pleasant and comfortable day.' 'Home letters, full of mercy.' 'Bless my own B.' 'A busy working day, yet peaceful.' 'Much driven about, distracted, and worn out and tried; I cast myself on thee.' 'A pleasant, happy day; help, and power.' 'Make me holy to thyself.' 'Poor and sinful.' 'A busy, but quiet day.' 'I seek grace this day to live in and on Christ.' 'Rainy at night, and prayer-meeting thin; home letters full of mercy.' 'A very toilsome day; wandering from place to place.' 'Upon the whole, a peaceful day; a little tired at night; but if self were given up, I should not have felt it.' 'Some searchings and humblings of heart, and some longings for the Lord.' 'Not much done, yet kindness from the Lord.' 'Poor and needy, unable to lift myself up; yet a good day.' 'Barrackpore: a good day.' 'Tried and failed; help.' 'I long to love thee, Lord. A good day; helped to walk softly.' 'Seeking a fixed heart; feeble all day, but kept.' 'A good day; tried, but enabled to take it as part of the crucifixion.' *August 10th.* — Communion. Dr Duff served the table. He seemed helped, and I feel refreshed.'

Towards the end of August he went to Benares for change and rest, as his health was failing; and there is a record of his journey, his work, the places he saw, and missionaries he had intercourse with. He speaks strongly of the evil done by the Government schools, in 'raising up a race of atheists, who have no fear nor principle'. On the 19th September he records his return: 'On my way home. I have spent a very happy time at Benares, and feel thankful for all the fellowship I have had with Mr Tucker and his family.' He had spent six weeks there, and returned to Calcutta quite invigorated. *'September 26th.* — Letters from home last night. One from Mrs Stuart from Paris. Eliza is going home to die. Help me, O Lord, to bear her on my heart. *29th.* — Eliza Stuart in London, on her way home to die. Lord, be with her in giving light and peace.'

During the following months there is a great amount of remarks on various topics, chiefly on passages of Scripture, both in the Old and New Testaments; the notices regarding himself being fewer. Occasionally, however, we have, 'A very happy day; I enjoyed my work, and desire to thank the Lord for all his goodness.' 'A quiet day, though weary; mercies and loving-kindnesses. I need constant keeping, guidance, and also constant watching, and an unceasing intercession.' 'I long to be rivers of water; to have that fulness of Christ and heavenly things that will not be restrained, but will urge and make way for itself.' 'I feel the blessedness of waiting on the Lord, and not fretting because things seem not to be going right.' 'I feel as if I had been slipping away from the Lord, and suffering many things to come between him and me.' 'Dec. 31st. — My dear wife and her aunt arrived in safety; many mercies.'

After this comes a blank, or, rather, many blanks, for the entries are fewer:[1]

> May 27th. — We are in the midst of defection and revolt. Every mail brings tidings of regiments casting off their allegiance. Delhi is in the possession of the mutineers; much bloodshed, and many barbarities committed. It is a crisis in Indian history; but I trust we shall be brought through it. I think I am learning something from the state of the times. Oh to live in nearness and growing oneness with the Lord!

[1] Here is an extract from a note to David Sandeman, that noble and honoured servant of Christ, who, after a few years of labour in China, passed to his reward. His name is strongly linked with that of John Milne and William Burns. It is a note introducing some friends, and asking Sandeman to 'encourage them in seeking the Lord': — 'I had a long letter from your dear mother, telling me the particulars of your last visit to Perth; also from Mr Ogilvie. I wish you could have come round this way; but the Lord otherwise ordered it. But we must try to keep up some interchange of brotherly affection by letter. How much of this mutual interest in one another there seems to have been among the early Christians! Paul seems so anxious that his friends at a distance should know all his concerns, and that he should know all that was befalling them. I think there is reason for this. We cannot think of one another, nor pray for one another aright, unless we know one another's condition. Don't you think these intercommunications are like the gales of the Spirit that keep the atmosphere, or like the tides which keep the seas, from stagnation? Without occasional hearing from one another, our love will languish and decay. I trust the Lord is upholding and comforting you, and giving you earnests of a large and abundant harvest.' — *Calcutta, 19th Jan. 1857.*

The Indian Mutiny

In May 1857, about the time of the beginning of the mutiny, he and Mrs Milne went to visit some friends a little way out of Calcutta, near a gun manufactory. Other guests were in the house as well as themselves. In the course of the evening a message came from the officer in charge of the manufactory, to say there were so many rumours of risings among the native troops in the neighbouring stations, and he could put so little confidence in the sentries posted round his own house, that he intended to send his own wife and child on board a steamer in the river for the night; and he thought any ladies or civilians in the house in which they were should go on board also. Some of the party present laughed at the idea of danger; but Milne was very decided that such a message should not be neglected, and insisted that they should go at once to the officer's house, and embark with his family. Accordingly, they did go to his house; and when parties from other quarters had all gathered there, they got into boats to go to the steamer. Most of the gentlemen went with them; and when all the ladies had got on board, they did so too, Milne amongst them. They remained there all night; but as soon as Milne had seen his wife into the cabin, and in safety, he put his Bible into her hand, and said, Good-bye; and in one moment was over the side of the steamer, in the boat, and off to the shore again. When he got back to the commandant's house, the officer said, 'What's the matter? Why have *you* come back?' 'Oh!' said he, 'wherever there is danger, there the minister of Christ should be.' And there he remained till dawn, when danger for that night was past.

Gloom and Terror

May 29th. — This day four years I had just landed in Calcutta, and gone to church. How much have I gone through since then! . . .

May 31st. — Sabbath afternoon. — This Sabbath four years was the beginning of my sojourn and ministry in this place. *June 11th.* — Every mail brings tidings of fresh mutinies and violence and murder. All is dark, with very little to cheer in passing events. Here and there courage and promptitude and ability have appeared; but, generally, there has been great want of foresight and energy. European troops are arriving, and proceeding in small bands up the country. Had there been combination and united action on the part of the enemy, we must have been overwhelmed in all directions. But the power that has been able to raise this flame has not been able to actuate and direct it. Hence the outbreaks, though fierce and disastrous, have been local and successive, and have been, in leading places, resisted and put down. Delhi, their headquarters, must soon be reached, and then there will be an aggressive movement all over the countries. I have letters from many places, speaking of the dangers and sufferings which are endured almost over all the land. Here we have only an occasional alarm. Leadenhall Street, with its narrow, selfish policy, its time-serving, and truckling to error and idolatry, will now, I trust, be superseded, and a larger and more liberal system introduced. I feel my heart drawn out in pity for the many sufferers; a longing that our rulers may be decided and energetic; and a hope that many may be led to decision, and true faith in the Lord.

June 12th. — Still gloomy tidings from up-country. The conspiracy seems to have been universal, and must have succeeded had it not broken out prematurely. We wait for news from Delhi, which, as it is the heart, so it may have been the source of the evil. Precautions are taken here, for we have a considerable Mohammedan population. Not too soon. But the dream of peace and safety, which has brought sorrow on so much of India, may also bring ruin on the capital itself. I feel quietness of spirit, looking to the Lord. There is not much to care for here.

June 13th. — The tidings from up-country still gloomy; but European troops are fast flowing in, and arrangements are made for the protection of the town ...

June 14th. — Just as I was going into the pulpit, a letter was brought from a missionary, saying, on most reliable authority, that two native regiments, 43d and 70th, had broken loose from Barrackpore, and were approaching the town, strongly urging and entreating that there should be no morning service. He and others had fled on shipboard. I knew last night that these regiments were ready for revolt, and thought it probable that the report might be true. I felt the responsibility of keeping the people together in such circumstances, especially in a Mohammedan district like that in which our church stands. However, I determined to go on, and we were carried through in peace; though I felt anxious, knowing what would be the consequence of any panic in the church, even though there were no real danger. We seem, however, to be on the eve of an *émeute*;[1] but the authorities are aware and prepared.

Such is his own brief reference to a proceeding on which it is not easy for us at a distance to form any opinion. Many will pronounce it imprudent; and most ministers in such circumstances would have yielded to the threatening danger, and not proceeded to church, nor allowed the congregation to assemble. The simple explanation of his 'imprudence', as some may call it, is to be found in his own natural fearlessness, which made him quite unable to comprehend danger to himself. We may give a slightly fuller account of the matter, which will confirm our view of his character.

Alarms in Calcutta

On the Sabbath that the troops at Barrackpore were disarmed, and when it was feared they might rise and come down on Calcutta, when he went into the vestry, two gentlemen begged him to have no service on account of the danger of attack, and one showed him a letter he had had from a missionary who had taken refuge on board ship. But he said, 'No, it was duty; only he would be brief.' In the closing prayer,

---

[1] *émeute:* a seditious tumult; an outbreak, *Ed.*

he thanked God there had been no interruption to the service. Then, having taken his wife home, he went to visit a sick friend, and on the table he found a revolver! In the evening, when he and his wife were again going to church, a friend called to say that the troops had been quietly disarmed, and all danger was, for the time, over. That evening there were just five-and-twenty in church.

June 20th. — European troops arriving. The inhabitants are embodied to defend the town. Still, there is a possibility that the Mohammedans, in blind rage, may make some outbreak.

June 22d. — Yesterday I found a good day, being helped. Today I have been at the Institution, and afterwards visiting. Many seem disturbed and alarmed. Some I find trusting simply in the Lord, and believing that he will protect them. There seems a rather general fancy that some outbreak will take place tomorrow, as it is the anniversary of the battle of Plassey and the festival of Juggernaut, when there will be crowds in the streets. The panic-fear of so many must encourage the enemy, and lead them to suppose that they are stronger, and we more defenceless than we are. The tidings from up-country are still disastrous, — death, and violence, and fresh outbreaks. The missionaries are fleeing. We are not judges for one another, but I feel inclined to ask, Where is your faith? Such has been the faithlessness, deceit, and brutality of these wretched and bloody men, that it is difficult to avoid feeling a sinful indignation, and longing for severest retribution. Yet what they have done is the natural fruit of their perverse and dark religion. What have we done to turn them from their errors?

June 24th, — Yesterday passed quietly here, but we have still sad tidings from up-country. Flight and death. There are many fears lest Lucknow and Cawnpore, with their brave defenders, should be overwhelmed by numbers and famine ere help reach them. No tidings of the fall of Delhi. Today I have felt far from the Lord. I seek his face, and I know that he will look upon me. But it is trying to remain thus, and the flesh takes advantage. I feel what need I have to watch. As proof after proof occurs of the infatuation and obstinacy of the home governors of this country, their neglect of the most ordinary precautions, and closing their ears against the most pointed and reiterated warnings, it is difficult to restrain a feeling of indignation. What suffering and misery they have occasioned by their obstinate adherence to a narrow, selfish, worn-out policy! Their cords were rotten, and yet they stretch them and strain them, till now all have gone at once, and rebellion reaches over all the land, and, like the plagues of Egypt, enters every house.

June 30th. — The Lord has been dealing graciously. Oh that I would but walk more closely with him! I wait on God. No sure tidings yet from Delhi. Fresh atrocities and murders. We are brought very low ...

July 8th. — There is no safety nor peace but in a close walk with God. Cawnpore fallen, and all destroyed. Gwalior in mutiny. God's hand is stretched out still. There are the destitute, the fugitive, the mourning, the dying ... Public affairs still dark, and as yet no gleam of returning light. Want of troops, want of communication, want of energy, want of combination, seem to show that the Lord is hiding his face and holding back his hand. My own future I do not know; but a day in thy courts is better than a thousand. The opening up of one of thy faithful words enriches, and strengthens, and feeds me.

July 27th. — Much has passed since I last wrote. In public the massacre of Cawnpore, the death of Sir H. Lawrence,[1] the beleaguerment of Agra, delay at Delhi, *etc.* Give us peace in this troubled land. Save this town from the danger with which it is threatened. It is but too evident on every hand that the Lord no longer puts the fear of us on these people. We have taken credit to ourselves for their submission hitherto, and now we find them insolent and insubordinate. Lord, help me to eye thee in all things, and to humble myself under thy mighty hand!

---

[1] Some short time before, when our guns were being pointed against the enemy, Sir Henry called out, 'Spare the holy places.' It was a shot from one of these 'holy places' that killed him.

Calm in Troublous Days

Aug. 4th. — *Tuesday.* — Sabbath was one of the days of the *Buchra-Eed,*[1] and a Mohammedan rising was anticipated. We had a body of troops and cannon at the church, and the rest of the town was fully guarded. I enjoyed the day. Yesterday, wearied and sad. Today, quiet and helped. Still things all over the country look dark and menacing …

11th. — A trying, humbling day. I am getting too much engrossed with public affairs. I feel that my only safety in reference to them is to see God's hand in all, even the strange supineness and infatuation of those who are set over us. They are what they are, and do what they do, or rather do nothing, or at least not at the right time, just because God is against us, and withholds good things from us. I desire grace to look more to the Lord …

13th. — English mail come in. Prepare me for tidings, and let not the old man again get the reins in his mouth through worldly excitement …

20th. — After a fortnight's interruption, we have heard from up-country. Things seem improving a little. I trust the tide is beginning to turn, and that the Lord will work deliverance. Delhi still besieged, if siege it can be called, when the enemy is always the attacking party. The fort of Agra still held, and likely to make good its resistance. Lucknow still defended, though in danger. Havelock unable to raise the siege, and returned to Cawnpore. Some progress made in driving the rebels out of Behar.

24th. — *Monday.* — Yesterday was a good day; almost unmingl-edly so. I was helped, and the word remains with me. The town is all guarded, for it is the Mohurrum; and yesterday a body of troops was in the *Madrissa* (college) opposite the church.[2] *30th.* — *Sabbath.* — Quiet

---

[1] A Mohammedan festival — 'the goat's feast'.

[2] In a letter written in August 1857, he says: 'Last Sabbath I preached, surrounded by bodies of troops, two large cannons at the side of the church loaded with canister shot, and other two further down the street. The Free Church is in the most dangerous quarter, being surrounded by fierce Mohammedans. Their college is on the other side of the street, and their chief mosques close by. All our servants, you know, are natives; so you can conceive what kind of a life it is here at present. Yet we have never felt any fear, and we have never lost an hour's sleep on account of it. Our sorrow is for the multitudes who are beleaguered, fleeing, wounded, suffering,

and peaceful. The home letters have come; but they lie unopened, that we may not break God's day, or distract our minds. *1st Sept.* — We have been carried safely through the Mohurrum; but we have gloomy news from up-country. There seems little hope that Lucknow can stand till it is relieved, and so the sad scenes at Cawnpore will be renewed. I feel sad and sick at heart.

September 26th. — *Sabbath morning.* — Many variations of state and feeling. Lord, help me! Make me willing to follow thee in the way of the cross. I am not wise, nor strong; but may seek to walk in thy meekness, patience, gentleness. It was specially in suffering that thou didst accomplish thy mission. May I not despise the passive graces. Are they not the ripened fruit? What dominion self has over me! At every new emergency I pray, and desire to strive that my thought may not be, 'How will it affect my feelings, my intents, my honour?' but, 'How will it affect the Lord, his cause, his people, and my fellowmen?' I pray to be delivered by the cross, the constancy and love of the self-forgetting Jesus, and brought under the habitual, entire dominion of love. May I not live *on* myself *nor for* myself; but live *on* the Lord, *and for* the Lord.

Losing Sight of India

The next entry is October 10th, 'On board the "Hindostan", and *losing sight of India.*'[1]

---

and dying in circumstances of unspeakable horror.'

[1] I do not enter into the circumstances of his leaving India. Mrs Milne's health quite broke down the second time. The medical men were of opinion that she must go to England, and that he must go with her. He gave in his resignation to the Presbytery in March 1857; but remained till October. The following letter from Hawkins (June 1857) to Mrs Milne will be read here with interest: 'I had heard, before I received your letter, of your proposed removal from Calcutta. It did not surprise me, for I did not expect that your health would stand long in India; and another separation, under such circumstances, was not to be thought of. This is but another movement of his gracious hand. I never can regret the part I had in sending your dear dear husband to India. I am as satisfied, as of my own existence, that it was the Lord's doing. I have never had a wavering thought upon that point; and had he been there only as many days as he has been years, I should have thought and felt the same. There his work is now done, and his Master calls him to another

Yet of India he never 'lost sight', all the rest of his life through. He thought of it, spoke of it, wrote of it, pleaded for it, prayed for it.[1] There was a link between him and that land which could not be broken. As his home work and home sorrows had prepared him for India, so had his Indian toil and trials fitted him for his remaining ten years of home work.

Poetic Musings

His voyage home had nothing special about it, and his record regarding it is brief. All goes on smoothly; he preaches and does some work on board; but he thinks it an 'idle life'; he looks home-ward, and wonders what work is awaiting him. Thus he muses in pleasant measures:

> Too long I have been blinded
> By unbelief and sin,
> Too long been earthly minded; —
> The world has dwelt within.
> But now the light has broken
> Upon my foolish soul;

---

part of the vineyard. True, it is a very solemn step; but taken under his guidance, it cannot be a wrong one. It may be contrary to all your desires and hopes; but I need not tell you that these we are at liberty to indulge, and entertain, only so far as they are in unison with his most gracious will. How sweet, at his bidding, to quench every desire, to bid farewell to every hope, and to move cheerfully and unhesitatingly, just as his finger points, or his eye leads! Your dear husband may yet be the instrument of bringing souls to Christ, in Scotland, or some other field of labour. Cherish the thought, for it will cheer and strengthen you.'

[1] Thus he wrote to his friend Mr Mackenzie, on the 7th December 1857: 'It has been, and is a real trial to my wife and me, that we were obliged to leave a country where we hoped to live and die. I shall have much to tell you, when we meet, about India. Only those who have been there for some time, and have seen a good deal of it, can form an adequate idea how little our century of possession has done for it, either in the way of christianizing its people, or developing its resources. We have merely touched it at a few far distant points, and even there have merely grazed the surface. The work is still to do, and will require unspeakable faith, patience, prayer, toil, and, above all, the example and converse of living, holy men, freely intermingling with, and enlightening and quickening, the dark, depraved mass.'

My God in love has spoken,
   His words have made me whole.

I see the strange enchantment
   That led me thus astray,
The hope of full contentment
   Still lured me on the way.
I've toiled in ceaseless action
   For things which never give
True peace and satisfaction
   To those who for them live.

I wish no more to follow
   Those images untrue;
No more may mirage hollow,
   Present itself to view.
Lord, keep me near the fountain,
   Where living waters flow;
And guide me up Thy mountain,
   Away from things below.

And again he sings, as he is sighting the coast of Africa, when about to enter the Red Sea: —

A Friend I have who never
   Forsakes me in my need;
Whose love, continuing ever,
   Is proved by word and deed.
He sought me when, in folly,
   I wandered far abroad;
To Him I owe it wholly
   That now I walk with God.

I often vex and grieve Him
   By sinful unbelief;
And oft forget, and leave Him
   To seek elsewhere relief.

But when my troubles gather,
  And sorrows overpower;
He leaves me not, but rather
  Seems kinder than before.

Though now thick clouds enfold me
  Not knowing what awaits,
I'm sure He will uphold me,
  In all my trying straits.
I know He will my losses
  Convert to heavenly gains,
And He will use my crosses,
  To break my earthly chains.

Chapter 15

1858–1866
Resettlement in Perth,
and Work There

*J*ohn Milne arrives safely in London; and, after spending a week there, goes down to St Leonards-on-Sea towards the end of November. He enjoys the quiet, but longs for work. On the 9th December 1857, he thus writes to Mackenzie from St Leonards-on-Sea:

> We are comfortably and quietly settled here, and I am enjoying the rest. In looking back, as we naturally do in such circumstances, we see much to regret and lament, and are glad to betake ourselves afresh to him who is ever willing to cast his skirt over us, and say, Peace be to you. I trust that Just and Blessed One is becoming better known to you, and growingly precious, as you pass on your way. The under-shepherds come and go, but he ever abides.

Return to Perth

He visits Edinburgh and Glasgow in January. His old Perth flock (with some exceptions) seek his return to them, they being, in God's mysterious providence, at that time without a pastor.[1] Before the call

---

[1] Though his eye turns to his old flock, he refuses to take any step to forward his return to them. 'I am still as of old', he writes, 'the man of peace, and am as fond as ever of peace and harmony in the house of God. I should wish, therefore, to

reaches him, he hears of the desire to secure his return to Perth.

'Professor Bannerman', he writes (Jan. 12, 1858),

> met me the other day, and said — 'So you are going back to your old nest?' 'That's still a question.' 'No, no; you are going back, and you will find it warm yet.' It will indeed be very strange if I should again be settled among you. I quite agree with Mr Burns, that, in our altered circumstances, I cannot expect everything to be quite square and smooth. You sent me away in a kind of chariot of flame, filled with the love of an affectionate people. If I return, it will be in a lowlier guise; and, perhaps, this is the best for us all.

On the 30th of January the call reaches him in Edinburgh. He accepts it. 'A busy but happy month' is his record at this time. He returns for a little to St Leonards-on-Sea. There is some little division among his old people; but he is led to carry out his acceptance of the call, and is settled among them on the 4th of March 1858; 'meeting with much kindness and loving welcome'. He goes to London to bring Mrs Milne home; meets with an old school companion, and hears full tidings about Peterhead, the place of his birth. He congratulates himself that he has not connected himself with the English Presbyterian Church, 'which seems about to divide on the organ question'.

His May journal is brief: 'Life passing on quietly, with many mercies.' 'Kept in peace.' 'Helped in my work, though feeble.' 'I feel the necessity of refusing dark, hard thoughts of God.' Thus he writes his feelings in easy, happy measure:

> Belov'd of Jesus, whence thy fear,
> Thy frequent sigh, thy dropping tear?
> Should not this thought thy spirit cheer,
>   He cares for thee?

---

wait quietly till the Lord clearly point out to me my future field of labour. He has blessed me hitherto, and I know that he will bless me still.'

Thy way, I know, is strange and new,
Thy dear ones gone, thy helpers few;
But still this word remaineth true —
    He cares for thee!

Thy work is great, thy strength is small,
And thoughts of failure on thee fall;
But in thy weakness on Him call,
    He cares for thee!

Whate'er thy tim'rous heart may say,
Whate'er thy feelings, night or day,
Should all seem joining to betray —
    He cares for thee!

He goes with thee, thy steps to guide,
Thy wounds to heal, thy sins to hide;
Then call on Him, whate'er betide,
    He cares for thee!

His love how great no tongue can tell;
He died to save thy soul from hell;
No wife nor mother loves so well; —
    He cares for thee!

Belov'd of Jesus, trust Him still,
Thy lot to choose, thy cup to fill;
Let no dark thoughts thy spirit chill —
    He cares for thee!

Over-work and Its Evils

Settled in Perth once more among his old flock, in which, however, there have been some discords and some changes, he thus writes: 'I enjoy my work, and the Lord helps me. I have abounding cause to love and trust him. Say to me, Lord, as to Abraham, "I am *El-Shaddai;* walk before me, and be thou perfect." I am longing for more POWER. I see that *faith* is *power;* I desire to cultivate faith; to resist and strive against all that would hinder my simple, implicit trust in my God and Saviour.'

Here is a letter to one of his elders, which fits in here:

41, *Bernard Street, Russel Square, London, 3d May* 1858. — MY DEAR MR MACKENZIE, — I ought to have written long ago, and will not attempt any excuse or apology, save reminding you of the dilatoriness incident to a man out of harness, out of usual beat, and quite away from all his old landmarks. I am slowly but reluctantly coming to the belief that I have been suffering from physical causes, — the long overtasking and mismanagement and neglect of the nervous system. Dr Bramwell, Dr Macleod, and Dr Martin all agree in this; and at the mouth of two or three witnesses, this, like other things, must be reckoned established. They all recommend complete repose; and this I feel I have not been taking, even at Ben-Rhydding. The mind was still working in the way of regret for the past, or looking forward to the future. I fear I had too much a lurking idea that I had something in my own power, and that I had only to say, 'I will go out as at other times before, and shake myself.' I feel that I am suffering the retribution, the Nemesis, of former years of unresting, unrelaxing labour. The regular home work, without any weekly rest, and then, when summer came, instead of the yearly relaxation, itinerancies of exciting and threefold labour. There was real folly in all this; it was just, as it were, saying, 'A short life, but a merry one'; and yet, in the end, one finds that there comes a season, neither short nor merry, when the physical, intellectual, emotional, and spiritual all seem expended and worn out, and the unhappy individual becomes a trial and a burden to himself and others. But the ways of the Lord are right, his laws are holy, just, and good; and if, in the well-meaning desire to do all we could, we have overdone, and incurred the righteous sanctions, it is meet to humble ourselves, and say, 'If his law has not been honoured by our obedience, let it be so in our suffering.'

Pray for me now, that I may be enabled to submit, and be really quiet. I have a strong persuasion that when I am enabled, in reference to all this long sore trial, to say, honestly, heartily, and thankfully, 'The will of the Lord be done', then the night will begin to pass, and the morning to dawn. I have said, thankfully; and is not this right? For is it not kind in the Lord to have taken such pains with me? and has not he mingled many mercies in the cup, in keeping the congregation so wonderfully together, and in now bringing among you one who, I know, will be made a comfort and blessing?

I would fain hope that a time of blessing is at hand, both for St Leonard's and Perth. Oh how differently God is dealing with our land — dropping down the beginnings of a pentecostal shower — from the way in which he is dealing with our neighbour nations, on whom the angel from before the altar is casting down the live coals of wrath and vengeance! Perhaps this is the beginning of the end of God's long controversy with those who have hated his truth, and worn out his saints. At the public meetings here, there are constant references to the present crisis; but the constant expression, also, of a deep, heartfelt, universal desire that we may not in any way be entangled or mixed up with the quarrel.

Letter-Fragments

The following fragments are from letters written in this year from different places:

I looked in at the — 's. I spoke a little with them, and then said, 'I am a minister'; took out my little Testament, read, and prayed. I should fancy, from their look, that it rather took them by surprise.

London. — After leaving you I got wrapt in thought, and had some nice thoughts brought to mind, and never roused till we came to the station. There a blind man, who was sitting beside me, got up to leave, and I felt reproach that I had not tried to speak to him. However, it gave me a new idea of the need of 'He wakeneth morning by morning.' Fresh impulse and fresh words are needed every day.

Dundee. — A deserter was at the station in handcuffs, guarded by a sergeant and soldier. I asked to speak with him, and the sergeant took me, and I spoke a little, and prayed. Also, I had some talk with a Jewish merchant. He held that the promises would be fulfilled if the Jews became Christians and amalgamated with the Gentiles. I helped him a little with his luggage, and we parted as friends.

Perth. — The great struggle is to look simply to the Lord, and not look to men's smiles or frowns; but, then, the victory is blessed — peace as a flowing river. What an atheistic state of mind we are often in, when we try to please the worms of the dust! It is very dishonouring, and must be very grieving to the Lord.

Perth. — I think the 'dying of the Lord Jesus' (*2 Cor.* 4:10) is more than the remembrance. I think it is the power of his death; that is, as God, by many instrumentalities — devils, wicked men, his own disciples, the trials of this life, the burden of the sins of many, the sights and sounds of this evil world, and, at last, the cross — bruised him to death; so God is using all occurrences, even the way in which he is leading us in the wilderness, to bruise, mortify, humble, and gradually abolish the old man. And as this death goes on, it makes room for the power of Christ's life.

It is not easy, amid the manifold temptations and consequent heaviness, to be always rejoicing; but I think I should like to be; and I fancy the only way is, Try, try, try again, in the new and living way. 'Let not your heart be troubled.'

He shall hide me in his pavilion, only I must not be always lifting the *Purdah.*[1]

Before the end of this year (1858) his health began to fail, and in January 1859 he had to leave home for change and rest. He went to Ben-Rhydding; — while there, sowing some seed, as occasion offered; reading to the masons, working in the neighbourhood, at their dinner hour. Then he went to London for a while, and returned home in June, far from well, and unfit for his work in consequence of deep depression. Towards the end of the year he rather hastily left home for Liverpool, thinking that he had work

---

[1] Curtain: a Hindoo word.

elsewhere. He then went to Ireland, during the great revival there. He soon after returned to Edinburgh, and then went to Wales for a season; but such had been the extent of his ailment at this time, that he had no recollection afterwards of some of these changes, especially of his visit to Ireland. His head was sorely troubling him. His stay at Llandudno for six months quite restored him, so that he returned to Perth, in February 1860, re-established in all respects. His first sermon was, Job 42:5, 'I have heard of thee by the hearing of the ear; but now mine eye seeth thee.' While resting at Llandudno (in 1859) he could not be altogether idle; but his ignorance of the Welsh language kept him nearly so. In order, however, to sow some seed, he got Welsh tracts for distribution; and he had a few brief sentences translated for him, such as 'O Lord, give me thy Holy Spirit, for Christ's sake'; and

> I am a poor sinner, and nothing at all,
> But Jesus Christ is my all in all.

These Mrs Milne and he wrote on slips of paper, and gave them to those they met with by the way.

Thoughts of a Colleague

In the beginning of 1859 he had begun to feel the undivided pastoral work of so large a congregation as Free St Leonard's too heavy for him, and to think either of a temporary assistant or of a permanent colleague. He thus writes to one of his elders, on the 5th of April, from Ben-Rhydding:

MY DEAR MR MACKENZIE, — I trust you will be guided, wisely and speedily, to one who will be made a blessing to that much and long-tried flock. But it is the Lord's way in which we are going, not our own; and if we are enabled to hold on in faith and patience, we shall certainly reach some blessed landing-place. It is not easy to rest in this while all is dark and uncertain; but they who dwell in the secret place of the Most High can do it. Perhaps the highest honour and the best service we can render to God is to trust him in troublous times. It is then that the flesh is completely mortified, and the soul, in acquiescence and confidence, clings to its Lord. Such seasons manifest and confirm the union between the redeemed creature and its Creator. Paul has gone through much, and looked at the worst that could happen — tribulation, affliction, famine, — ere he could fully realize and make his boast of that union from which he feels that nothing in the height above or depth beneath shall be able to separate.

On the 26th of August, he thus writes to the same:

MY DEAR FRIEND, — My first thought was simply to resign the charge. But this would not meet the present emergency, as, from the dilatory mode of proceeding in such cases, months would probably elapse ere the congregation would be in a condition to make a call. Besides, with the faint dawn of returning mental health there is a revival of old feelings, and a hope that I may yet be able to do something for a people to whom I owe so much, and on whom my return has been the means of bringing so many trials. I therefore feel myself shut up to ask a colleague; and it is a great relief to see the leadings of Providence in the matter so clear. I have therefore enclosed letters to this effect for the session and Presbytery. You might communicate my views and wishes to my friend Mr Cowan. If I should be permitted to return and labour for a season in Perth, there is no one, I think, with whom I should find it more easy and pleasant to co-operate than with him. I shall be anxious to hear how this matter proceeds. Kindest love to all at home, and to other friends. Believe me, very affectionately yours, J. M.

On the 16th of September, he writes to the same:

MY DEAR FRIEND, — As you expected, Mr Cowan has decided to remain at Perth; and this I feel to be a cause of great satisfaction and thankfulness. Though I knew him so little, I have always felt my heart drawn to him in a mingled feeling of hopefulness and esteem; and if

I should be in part and for a season restored to work again, perhaps the spectacle of two taking sweet counsel together, and walking in harmony, may help to repair our breaches, and to promote the cause of God. Our best days in St Leonard's were when William Burns, and afterwards A. Bonar and Mr Cumming, used to take part, and work side by side. But all this is in the Lord's hand, and we must try for the present to leave it there. We know that he will not always chide. I have found it very hard to submit to the dispensation of being wholly laid aside in this season of hope and harvest. But the Lord in mercy still continues the needed discipline; and I have a hope that, in due time, he will bring me to acquiesce, and perhaps enable me even to say, 'Most gladly will I glory in my infirmities.' ... I wonder if there is any place in Liverpool where we could get a small supply of Welsh tracts? We had a parcel of them, but they are gone.

Milne's wishes were speedily gratified, and his anxieties removed, by the settlement of Cowan as his permanent colleague.

Letter to Cowan

Few colleagueships have been the source of so much mutual comfort and assistance. The affectionate way in which Milne always spoke of Cowan showed how highly he appreciated him, and how great was the confidence which he reposed in him as a fellow-pastor and a friend. The following letter will show this:

Llandudno, North Wales, Jan. 12, 1860. — My dear Brother, — I am favoured with your kind letter, and feel that I ought to have written before, to offer our congratulations and good wishes on the occasion of your full entrance on the ministry. But I knew that you would not require words to tell you of the interest which we felt; and I need not say that, in present circumstances, I often feel little inclined for correspondence. Yet I must not complain of this trial, painful and prolonged as it has been. I think light is beginning to dawn upon us, and we are able to say, 'It was needful, and is and will be good.' I believe the Lord is leading us through fire and water to bring us into a wealthy place.

He is showing us that, when he is pleased to shine upon his word, and to shed abroad his love in our heart, we can be happy even in this wilderness, far from work, and friends, and privileges.

Yet the wilderness is to us, as to the Master, a place of much temptation; and the heart longs for the time when he will say, 'Ye have tarried long enough; rise, and take your journey.' We should like to see some clear indication of his will before we take any steps. Pray for us that this may be given, that I may again be set free to engage in his blessed work, in such way and measure as he may see fit. I need strength and grace, and I would fain have the sense of them in my own keeping; but I feel that he is teaching me the life of faith, to feel that I am in myself nothing but sin, and weakness, and poverty; and yet to go cheerfully and joyfully on my way, resting on that word, 'My grace is sufficient for thee; my strength is made perfect in weakness.' This would indeed be the victory over self; and a glorious, blessed liberty.

When one gets a Spirit-bestowed glimpse of the great salvation, — so divine, spontaneous, full, free, and near; how it is shining down upon us like the mid-day light; how it is flooding all around us like a high and resistless tide, — it seems strange that we can remain for a single moment without the fulness of peace and joy! I can see how the Lord should marvel at unbelief, and why that gracious operation, by which it is overcome, should be described as the exceeding greatness of God's power.

I see that you also are tried from day to day; but I trust this only proceeds from the fear of the adversary dreading damage to his cause, and from the wise love of the Master, seeking to make you an instrument of extensive usefulness. It is the worm Jacob by whom he threshes the mountains, and from whom he gets all the praise and glory. The Lord must humble us before he can advantageously or safely exalt us.

We have been thinking of you and the congregation during this week. I am glad that you have these meetings in concert with so many throughout the world. We are with you in spirit, though absent in the flesh.

Here there are united meetings every night among the Independents, Calvinistic and Wesleyan Methodists; but they are all in Welsh, so that we have to be a little church ourselves, pleading the promise, 'If any two of you agree.' Accept our united regards; and longing for your prosperity, and that of the flock, ever very affectionately yours,
J. MILNE.

On the 16th of February 1860, having returned home, he met his people at the weekly prayer-meeting. He told, as he usually did in such cases, of all that he had seen and heard when away: of the work of God in Wales, beginning in one place during the week of prayer; of some striking conversions at Abergele; of the earnest cry of some Christians there previously, 'Is Abergele to be left dry?' He then added,

I dare say some of my old friends here, who can look back twenty years, remember our prayer then, 'Is Kilsyth to get it all? Is Dundee to get it all? Is Perth to get none?' May the Lord's people here thus plead with him till he send the shower! As the people were returning from Abergele Church on Sabbath, they heard voices from a room under an Independent chapel; and some, on looking in, saw seventeen lads, with heads bowed down in prayer, asking for mercy of the Lord. That was said to be the beginning of upwards of a hundred conversions. At Bangor, also, the hand of God was manifest.

Taking Counsel Together

About the same time he writes to Cowan, in reference to the meeting of kirk-session, when the quarterly reports of district visitors were given in:

You will be at the session tonight, and therefore I will not go. You know my mind, that there should be only one will there, and that will should be yours. We can work very well together by mutual counsel and prayer, and show how easy and pleasant all things are to those who live and love in Jesus. Will you make my excuse to the brethren? Say that it is not that I have forgotten our long and pleasant, and often much blessed fellowship, but because the Lord makes me long to see you and them continuing to grow into one another in sweet abiding union, without any interfering influence. I feel sure that you will all have not a little this evening to communicate to one another, of what is hopeful and promising and ground for thankfulness.

In the same spirit, he sends a note to Cowan, in reference to some discussions in the kirk-session:

My dear Brother, — Do you remember that, at the first communion, there was a strife among the disciples? We have often found it so at this time. But we are older and more experienced now. If the subject of helping the psalmody is brought forward, try to get through it smoothly. 'Take us the foxes.' There is a place and work for every one; and every one should be put in their place and put to their work, else there will be mischief. Let us thank God, and use any grace or gift he gives, and not grudge at one another. The God of peace be among you.

On the day after a Sabbath-school *soirée*, he writes thus pleasantly to Cowan:

My dear Brother, — I thought the meeting last night was a great success, and a matter for thankfulness. The speaking that I heard was excellent. The behaviour of the children was all one could desire. I rather reproached myself for being over-stern; and thought, would the Master have checked the little ones in their ebullition as I did? But I thought of old converting days, and was longing for them back again. Let me send an additional gift towards the expenses, which, I fancy, must have been considerable, when I think of the affluence of the good things I saw in the vestry.[1]

In the autumn of 1860, the first of the open-air meetings on the South Inch was held. As soon as he heard the proposal regarding

[1] When intimating a collection, he used to say, 'You know I never beg from you; I only ask you to give the purse-strings to Christ.'

these, he threw himself heartily into the work, and his doing so drew others into it. Those three days' meetings in 1860 were followed by seventy nights of continuous service, when 'many were added to the church.' He greatly enjoyed that time; not the less, because the work was not confined to his congregation, but carried on by ministers of all denominations.

Letter to the People of Perth

The following letter to 'the People of Perth' at this time is as characteristic as it is striking:

MY DEAR FRIENDS, — In the name, and at the request of some of our fellow-townsmen, I venture to address to you a few words of love and kindness. We feel that we are come to a great crisis in our history. After nearly two years of prayer and waiting, the Lord has visited us in unexampled mercy. You are yourselves witnesses of the events of the last fortnight, — you saw the multitudes who gathered together at the open-air meetings on the South Inch, and crowded the City Hall and other places at night. Those of you who mingled with these assemblages, could not but have observed the solemn impression which prevailed, and must also have heard expressions of interest, conviction, prayer, and thanksgiving from many a lip. In particular, at the close of the meeting on the second night, the City Hall presented a scene never before witnessed on such a scale in Perth; it was like a battle-field, a harvest-field; hundreds were seeking the Lord, or rejoicing that they had found him. Blessed be God for such a season; and yet, dear friends, had this been all, we should not now be addressing you. Had the movement stopped at this point, we might have attributed it to the presence and labours of those ministers and laymen from a distance, whom the Lord has so greatly honoured and blessed in other places. But God has shown us the truth of his own word, 'Not by power, nor by might, but by my Spirit, saith the Lord.' After all the visitors had left us, the meetings continued as crowded, as solemn, as earnest as before. It even seems as if the impression were deepening, and growing from night to night.

Oh, dear friends, salvation is near, salvation is in the midst of us! The light of God is shining, and men are awakening; the Spirit of God is come, and is convincing men of sin, of righteousness, and of judgment. Hundreds remain night after night to seek the Saviour, and many find him. Oh! it seems easy at present to be saved. What, in ordinary times, is spread over months or years, seems now compressed into an instant, the twinkling of an eye. Men comprehend at once that they are lost, helpless, without strength, and that the Lord Jesus is all they need. They feel that he is near them, is knocking at their door, is stretching out his hands, and that it is only a look, a cry, an act of reliance, and the day dawns upon them, and their peace begins to flow as a river.

Oh, friends, salvation is near, very near! We can testify of many, who come to these meetings careless, worldly, and influenced only by curiosity, and who yet leave them trusting and rejoicing in the Lord. Yea, we have seen some awakened, converted, and beginning to exhort and instruct others, and all this in the course of a few moments. Beloved friends, there is nothing strange or incredible in this. All Scripture testifies to it. What is salvation? It is just Christ. All the fulness is in him, and God offers him freely to all who will receive him. Does it take long to accept a gift? Does the beggar take long to receive your offered alms? And just so with us; God is willing and waiting to give you his Son. Are you willing to receive him? — *then* he is yours.

Beloved friends, we long for you in the Lord, our hearts are yearning over you. We are happy ourselves, and we wish you to be happy too. Come and see, come and judge for yourselves. Be not influenced by the opinions of men. Do not listen to the suggestions of your own hearts. This is an acceptable time, a day of merciful visitation. The wind is blowing, the tide is swelling high; cut your moorings, and join us in our voyage to Emmanuel's Land.

Beloved friends, you know me; I have been long among you, and have much reason to love you. I left you, and reckoned that, after a short season of labour for my Lord, I should lie down in the dust of a far distant land. But the Lord has strangely brought me back, to gladden me with the sight of answered prayers and fulfilled desires. I hope now to lie down among you, and rest till the Master comes and bids us rise to meet him. And oh! my desire is, that we might all rise rejoicing and singing together our song of triumph, 'O death, where is thy sting? O grave, where is thy victory?' Ah, friends, love not the world, neither the things that are in the world. How poor will all appear in that day when they are passing away as a dream of the night, and when only that Saviour will be precious who is now standing at your door, and pressing himself on your acceptance!

In name of my friends and fellow-labourers, I entreat, I beseech you not to let this season of mercy pass unimproved; night and day we pray for you. — Believe, very affectionately yours, JOHN MILNE, PERTH, *31st August 1860.*

Prayer Union Circular

He drew up also a prayer union circular, with this sentence prefixed:

Perhaps something of this kind might do for next week, if the brethren think good.

Monday. — India.

Tuesday. — Read John 14:15-18, and John 16:7-15. Pray for the Spirit as the Comforter; the Spirit of truth, the remembrancer, the sanctifier, the convincer of the world, the glorifier of Christ; as the Spirit of power, enabling to testify, inclining to testify, so that we cannot hold our peace. Pray for the fruits of the Spirit, the unity of the Spirit.

Wednesday. — Read Psalm 144. Pray for our own town. Confess prevalent sins, growing sins, open sins. Pray for magistrates, that they may be on the side of God, opposing evil and encouraging good. Pray for employers, that they may be considerate like Boaz; and for servants, that they may be diligent and faithful, serving the Lord. Pray for the rich, that they may be liberal; and for the poor, that they may seek things above. Pray for the City Mission, Young Men's Tract Society, all young men's associations, all soul-gatherers, all visitors of the sick. Pray that temptations and stumbling-blocks may be taken out of the way, and that the Lord may visit us again, and make Perth a city of righteousness.

Thursday. — Read Ezekiel 34:11-31. Pray for our congregations. Pray for ministers, elders, deacons, district visitors, schools, Bible classes. Pray for a blessing on Sabbath work, communion services. Pray for unity, peace, growing love; that we may watch over one another, help one another, pray for one another. Pray that the work of conversion and edification may be ever going on among us. Pray that our churches may be missionary, aggressive, seeking to win the unsaved at home and abroad.

Friday. — Read Colossians 3:12-25, and 4:1. Pray for our families, that our houses may be Bethels, our closets Peniels; that fathers may be like Abrahams, mothers like the mother of Moses, of Samuel, of Timothy; that children may grow up in the nurture and admonition of the Lord, seeking early the good part; that servants may do all things without murmurings or disputings, serving the Lord, and like the little maid in Naaman's house. Pray that our dwellings may be little churches, where the world's ways and fashions and vain amusements shall never find a lodgment.

Saturday. — Read John 17. Give thanks for this season of prayer. Confess its sins and shortcomings. Pray for the whole Church of God, the whole family of our Father in heaven, the whole flock of the Good Shepherd. Pray for beloved, but still outcast Israel. Pray for a special blessing tomorrow, that we may be as John at Patmos, that the Lord may bless the provision.

City Hall Meetings

The time of special blessing may be said to have begun on the last day of the open-air meetings. In the City Hall meeting that night there was profound solemnity, as if God were working, and many were aroused. At the close, it was announced that a meeting would be held next evening in Free St Leonard's. Next morning Moody Stuart suggested that the meeting should rather be held in the City Hall. Milne gladly accepted the proposal, went and engaged the Hall, issued placards, informed the other ministers, and made necessary arrangements. Moody Stuart agreed to remain and take part. Seven o'clock came; the Hall was crowded; the audience were deeply impressed, and showed reluctance to separate; some bowed down under a sense of sin, others filled with joy. The meetings and the crowds continued for seventy consecutive nights; and the depth as well as extent of spiritual quickening seemed very great — greater, even, than at the solemn conference-gatherings of later years. 'Many were added to the church'; the dead in sin were raised; the living were replenished with more abundant life. Each day at noon a meeting for prayer was held, and arrangements for the evening made. Milne was able to attend the whole of these noon meetings, and the greater number of the evening ones, being always the last to leave the Hall. He was occupied from morning to night; sometimes corresponding with brethren; sometimes making needful preparations; sometimes smoothing down asperities, or giving explanations to parties, who might think themselves slighted. For the last of these offices, no man was more fitted. The Breadalbane banquet at last brought these meetings to a close, the Hall being required for it.

Two gentlemen were visitors in Perth during these memorable ten weeks, — Christian men from India, but not quite satisfied with what they had heard of such work. One of them, not in the habit of speaking to others on religion, got his lips unsealed, and became so interested that he began to talk to the children around him, and to point them to the cross. He left, thanking God for what he had seen and heard.

Many were the accessions to the membership of the churches at this time; and these added ones have been tested by time and proved genuine. At the following Christmas the *Guizard* boys, instead of singing their usual songs, took to singing 'Rest for the

Weary', 'Christ for Me', and other hymns; — as may be supposed, to Milne's great delight.

Those who have been with him at such times as these, know and can tell the joy that spoke out in his words, and shone out in his face, as day by day brought him fresh news of the work of God.

Dunkeld Meetings

At Dunkeld, that same year, meetings were held in Mr Macpherson's church, not without blessing. Milne took part in them. His methods of 'beating up' for a congregation were too peculiar and too characteristic, not to be given somewhat in detail. There were some five or six ministers expected to take part. After dinner at a friend's house a little out of town, Milne asks them to come by themselves to his room, where he calls on one after another to pray. This done, they set out for the meeting. On the road, before entering the town, they meet a company of masons returning home. M. stops them, tells them of the meeting, its place and hour, invites them, and lest any of them should complain of the halfpenny pontage,[1] takes out his purse, and hands them a sixpence. They yield to his invitation and come. But a number of young women are seen coming along the road from their work. M. stops them, speaks with them, invites them; but does not succeed. By this time the hour of meeting has arrived, and M. is reminded of this. 'Let us run, then', he replies, and quickens his pace. But when proceeding at quick pace, they meet a gentleman enjoying his walk. Too late as he is, Milne cannot pass him. Politely lifting his hat to the English stranger, as he turned out to be, M. asks if he is aware of the meeting in the town tonight? 'What sort of meeting?' asks the stranger. 'A religious meeting, and a most delightful one it will be. Will you go with us?' 'By all means', said the traveller. In a moment Milne's arm is linked in his, and they are hastening to church, where the stranger sat the whole

[1] *Pontage:* toll for crossing a bridge, *Ed.*

time, a deeply interested man.[1] To this period of blessing all over the district, Milne briefly refers in the following entry:

December 31, *1860.* — I look back upon a long season of judgment and mercy, of much sin on my part, and great loving-kindness on the part of the Lord. He has sent from above, and drawn me out of many waters. It has been a year of much spiritual blessing to the town. I have been enabled to rise above private and congregational feelings, and to seek the general good. God has given the blessing, by pouring out on my brethren a wonderful spirit of love, unity, and self-forgetfulness. To this I attribute in a great measure the large and long-continued blessing which has been vouchsafed. In 1840 the blessing was much confined to my own congregation; this year it has been general, every congregation getting a measure of good, and the work spreading to the country all around.

January 4, 1861. — Peaceful on the whole. A good deal of outward work, and less fellowship. Hence a short season of darkness and temptation. But enabled to resist and believe; and the victory has come; and now, help, peace, and joy.

Jan. 8th. — Some changes, but generally helped. I feel that all depends on faith; near Christ; preferring him to all; and doing this *practically* from moment to moment, — this is peace, health, and life. I long to get the selfish element more and more removed. It is the sediment that darkens and defiles the stream of life. Oh that it might subside more and more, and disappear, till Christ be all in all, — motive, power, end! Mary sat at Christ's feet; and then we find her, ere long, honouring him in *deed.* What a directory for every day: sit and hear his words, choose the good part, and then go forth to act!

---

[1] Macpherson gives a reminiscence of a later visit to Dunkeld, in the autumn of 1867: 'He and I ascended one of the heights near Dunkeld (Newtyle Hill). On reaching the outskirts of a wood, he took out his pocket Bible, and proposed that we should read a psalm, and each of us engage in prayer. In the psalm which he read (which, I regret, I cannot recall), was the text from which he first preached; and on which he now made a few comments. Much nearness to God, intensified by the mountain-solitude and the beauty of the scene, child-like simplicity and intense fervour, marked the exercise.'

Jan. 10th. — Still moving on quietly; but feeling the need of continual watchfulness and prayer. I desire growing fellowship, — abiding in Christ, and Christ in me. How important, in the view of heaven, are the daily, hourly occurrences of this life, in their bearing upon the work of God, and the sanctification and comfort of his people! Help me to remember and realize this more, and to walk softly.

Wednesday, 23d Jan. — We have had a very comfortable communion. My desire is that, as a people, we should carry out the two precepts — *pray without ceasing*, and, *in everything give thanks*. Continual prayer would prevail with God; continual thanksgiving would prevail with man. There is a promise of coming blessing; and I desire to expect and wait.

March 3d. — *Sabbath morning.* — I have now been nearly a week confined to bed, and am only beginning to recover. The time has passed quietly and peacefully, though there has been much pain. I feel that I needed this taking aside and breaking down; for, as usual, I was getting away from the Lord, *putting work for him in place of himself*. It is kind in the Lord to arrest the poor backslider in his downward course. He sees the grey hairs here and there, and he is faithful and loving; and so interposes at once. Friends see them often, but false kindness or indifference keeps them silent. He who spared not his own Son in working out salvation, will not spare the rod in applying it to us.

Death of Andrew Gray

On the 21st of March (1861) he thus writes to Glasgow, in reference to the death of Andrew Gray:

My dear Andrew, — I am obliged for your kind and welcome note. Yes; I have been thinking of days gone by, and the time when we used to live and labour here, an unbroken, undivided company. But it is all well. We are farther on, and drawing near the shore. We see eye to eye, and my desire is "Even so come." It was in the end of the week that they thought of having a third sermon, and Mr Duncan came to ask me to preach. It occurred to me that as Dr Grierson and Dr Candlish would likely speak of his public life, it would be better for me to say a word or two of his private life and trials. So I took 2 Corinthians 12:7-9: "There was given me a thorn in the flesh." The idea I had was this, Paul a great worker, and pattern in his conversion, but a pattern also in the discipline to which God subjected him after conversion, and to which, age after age, he subjects those of his servants who resemble Paul in character and work. Then the heads were — Paul under trial; Paul seeking deliverance; Paul joyfully acquiescing in his dispensation. The thorn I regarded as some bodily ailment which was obvious to all among whom he ministered, which hindered him in his work, and gave enemies, spiritual and human, opportunity to harass him. But I shall send you the newspaper. It is not a full report, for I had not my jottings written out to give him. One thing omitted will interest you. On the Sabbath after his last return, Mr Gray gave out the psalm, "I shall not die, but live." He expected to recover. But before the end of the year this hope seems to have passed from his mind. Mr Turnbull, who knew more of his mind than any, permitted me to tell the people that Mr Gray, for months before his death, considered himself a dying man. He put himself into the hands of the Lord, arranged his earthly affairs, set his house in order, and from that time was occupied with things eternal, resting all his hope simply on the finished work of Christ. When he broke the matter to his wife, he put her in mind of the psalm, 'I shall not die'; and then said, 'We must change the text now.'

A letter omitted in its proper niche may be inserted here, as similar in character to the above. It is written in 1848, on hearing of the death of Mr Cormick of Kirriemuir:

DEAR BROTHER ANDREW, — This is a sad stroke. Daniel taken from us without the slightest premonition. I had never heard that he was ill; and found the intimation of his death when I came down this morning. It is some time since we met, in consequence of my reluctance to go from home leading me to shift to another time his invitations. He was last with me. I now wish I had been more with him. It is pleasant to think of having often named him to the Lord. Let us not weary in prayer, but watch thereunto with all perseverance. I feel smitten a good deal with this sudden stroke. Who next? And yet we dare not ask him back.

The journal thus proceeds:

Saturday, 6th April. — There is no benefit in dwelling too much on the sins of the past. It may be done from some remaining love of sin; and this is to be abhorred. Or it may be from unbelief, not realizing the completeness and enduring-ness of forgiveness; and then it is dishonouring to the mercy of God, and the blood of Jesus. We should be seeking to live as those who are free from condemnation, who have come out and are separate, who are sons and daughters of the Lord Almighty, members of the heavenly family, though not yet at home. We should seek to become daily more and more sensible of the least sin, and more and more careful to avoid it, and thus we shall become more and more sensible of sin around us, and concerned for its removal.

Monday, Nov. 4th. — Still moving on in the enjoyment of many mercies. There has been some sickness, and, for a time, cause to fear the return of old and trying ailments. But it is passed, and I have been able to go on with my work. The love of sin is still in the members, and is ever working; and I think wistfully of the power of Christ's death as a means of greater deliverance, even here. Lord, instruct me more fully in this. All things are of God, and he will perfect that which concerneth me.

Home, Home!

To some part of this period the following undated letter to Cowan refers:

Monday morning. — MY DEAR BROTHER, — I was unable to venture out last night, but the servants told me that it was a very nice meeting.

Thank you for the *inbeing* and *indwelling* yesterday. The former term was new to me, but it is very good. There is always life and outflow when Christ is brought in ... Charlie is off this morning.[1] How thankful I am that I have not, like him, to begin life! Home! home! now, is the hope and the cry.

To another he writes, about this time, when from home:

We made an inroad on Mrs — , and got into a most animated conversation with her and another lady, on revivals; in the course of which I took out my Bible, and read the valley of dry bones, with comments; and all this in the library! Wasn't it atrocious?

In 1862 he has a few brief entries:

March 13th. — *Thursday evening.* — I wish more of habitual fellowship. I find that the Lord is willing to meet me when I seek him, to check me when I err. I wish not to be preoccupied with other things, so as not to notice his presence, remark his guidings, or miss his absence ... *April 6th.* — *Sabbath evening.* — Helped last Sabbath at Monzie and Comrie, and also today; but failed during the week to live upon the unsearchable riches of Christ. There must be a higher and more stedfast life than the generality seem to live. I have seen some who seemed to have got into it; a life of faith, a kind of heavenly life on earth. Let me be trying after this ... *April 13th.* — Communion Sabbath. Have had much help and comfort. So also had Mr Cowan. We work most harmoniously together; never, from the beginning till now, the slightest shadow of a difference, either in opinion or way. Praise the Lord!

Letter-Fragments

The following are a few miscellaneous and fragmentary extracts from letters of 1862:

Going to the Infirmary, a number of women were sitting on a high wall, and a man was parading before them, and they were making a

[1] Milne's nephew, to college.

great noise. I said, 'Take care, you are like a city set on a hill.' 'Hech, sirs', said one of them, 'that's true', and they were quite still.

Last night I came upon a group of grown-up lads in High Street, making a nice-looking dog stand on his hind legs and beg. He looked tired. I put my hand upon the shoulder of the one that was conducting the operations, and said, 'That's a very nice dog, and he does it very well; but should you not let him rest on God's day?' They seemed taken aback; but one of them said, 'It's quite right, sir, we should.'

Last evening I strolled to the station. At the further end I found two young men who were commencing their night watch. I spoke a little about the vicissitudes of the place — one moment crowded and full of bustle, and then silent, and feeling quite alone. He said, 'I have often thought of that.' I said there is another way by which we must go alone — no one can go with us. He started, but said, 'I see.' I took his hand and talked a little to him. He wrung my hand most warmly at parting. I think I feel that to be continually nothing is the happiest state. We are then like vessels purged and meet for the Master's use. I wish we were like the skins or parchment of monkish days, where they blotted out one writing to make way for another.

I think we should seek and reckon upon the Lord's guidance and help in everything, however small. We are to glorify him in all we do, and we cannot do this without his help.

I think there should be a constant *retinue* — a holding in and holding back of what is our own. The world likes impulse, — naturalness as it is called, — and you know somebody that likes it too. But I think the Lord is teaching me to distrust it. The world calls those who keep their feelings in check cold and stiff; but the Lord says, 'Watch and pray.' In heaven there will be no need for restraint.

There is a brief entry of March 24, 1863, which I extract, because it carries on Milne's spiritual history: 'Am I counting all things loss for Christ? Am I dwelling in the secret place? Should I be glad if Christ came now? I desire to be often, during the day, trying myself by these questions. Lord, help … I need a continual death and a continual enlivening.'

In this same year he sends this note to Cowan:

My dear Brother, — I enclose a note of Andrew Bonar's. It gives a pleasant definition of your name (*Cohen*, the Hebrew for priest), better than the Celtic one *Chow*, or *Gow*, which connects you with the world-wide family of Smiths. I have answered it; so keep it, and perhaps it may help some future biographer who is inquiring into your *primordia rerum.*[1] I am not up to the mark today; but you know I will work as long as I am able to stand. I seek to rest upon 'my strength is made perfect in weakness.'

From the beginning of 1860, till the autumn of 1866, he was in almost full work, in excellent health, and joyful in spirit. Of this period, however, the records are scanty. On the 1st of January 1864, he writes:

The past year has been one of unusual, peaceful, and equal character. There have been few weakenings of strength and few sinkings of spirit. There have been many lessons and keepings. I look back thankfully on the meetings in January; our stay at Burntisland in June; the communion at Stirling; the conference in September; and a visit to Montrose and Ferryden in the same month. I still feel that my besetting sin is unbelief. I long for obedience to that word, 'Cleanse yourselves from all filthiness', *etc.* Our corrupt nature either cleaves to the dust or soars in the clouds of vanity and high-mindedness. I pray that this may be a year more peaceful and equal than the past. Keep me near thee — thy death, life, blood, and word. For a week or two I have been feeble; but I find that the Lord thus prepares me for some new enlargement; so I try to wait in faith and patience.

On the 5th of this same month he speaks of weakness and sleeplessness, yet of help; and notices the difference between his attempts to keep himself and his being kept by the power of God. He sees deliverance only in the blood of Jesus. It alone opens our way to God, and shuts Satan's way to us. He speaks of 'quiet trust';

[1] 'The beginning of things', *Ed.*

and then again, of the evil of *self:* 'How wretched to be thrusting our shadow upon poor, perishing men, and preventing their looking to God!' Many of his remarks remind us of the words of old Fraser of Brea,[1] regarding himself and his ministry. 'I perceive that I am bound to another kind of life than the rest of the world; to be holy in another manner than they; that as the Lord had set me in a more eminent place, so I should be more eminent in holiness.' He longs so to put on Christ that *he* only may be seen.

Christ's Second Coming

I believe it is so when I come to God, else I could have no access; and now I desire it may be so in all my dealings with my fellowmen. How much has my life been lost and embittered in endeavouring to be something in the eyes of men, knowing all the while that the image I wished to set up before them was not my real, conscious self, but only what I should like them to think me to be! What a miserable ungodliness, deceitfulness, and selfishness there has been in all this, walking in a vain show! I seek now to be delivered from this vain conversation by the power of the Lamb's blood. It will need much watching, prayer, self-recollection, and living and walking in the Spirit. But it can be done by him who maketh all things new.

I should like this week to be much in spirit with the brethren who are meeting in Freemasons' Hall, London, to confer regarding the Lord's coming. I thought it better not to go, though invited, partly because I felt that I was only a beginner on the subject. I believe there was unbelief in this, and unwillingness to go where I could not be something. May I be forgiven. But the Lord can make it up to me and bless me here, and use me, if he see good, in some other way, and at some other time. They have sent me a list of the subjects to be considered night after night, and I feel that it would have been very blessed to be there, and to meet with these loving, gracious men. But

---

[1] James Fraser of Brea, Minister of the Gospel at Culross, whose memoir can be found in *Scottish Puritans, Select Biographies,* ed. W. K. Tweedie (Edinburgh: Banner of Truth, 2008), vol. 2, pp. 89-370, *Ed.*

I feel that I should have been carried away and lifted up, and I believe it is better for me to be here, learning in quiet and silence.

One thought has been occurring to me. Looking back on the New Testament revivals, I think I see a watchword in each: *first,* The kingdom of God is at hand; *second,* The resurrection of the Lord; *third,* Justification by faith without works; *fourth,* Regeneration by the Spirit; *fifth,* The power of prayer and immediate salvation on closing with Christ. What if the next watchword should be a return to the first one, 'The Lord is at hand, the time is short!'...

Thursday, 7th. — I have written to Mr Robert Baxter, suggesting a wide circulation of the reports of their meeting, and the possibility that the next revival watchword may be 'The Lord is at hand'; and thus the Lord may shake the world, and beat out of it what remains of the fulness of the Gentiles ...

Friday, 8th. — Temptation, but rest in Christ. Reading D'Aubigne's *Calvin.* Find it quickening and strengthening. There is a stream of life running through it. I see that some of my brethren suspect the doctrine of Christ's near approach. There is much bigotry even in good men. They judge and condemn without inquiring, and act unconsciously in the very spirit of Popery. I ask help to rest more simply and wholly on Christ, as complete in him, and to mortify and deny the flesh at all times and in all forms.

Jan. 11th. — *Monday.* — Feeble; but helped in preaching yesterday. There is a reluctance to be nothing; but help me to obey thy word, denying myself and looking up to the cross. It is only the blood that makes to overcome.

Not Soon Angry

In another entry he speaks of 'forgetting to watch and pray, and so gave way to *hastiness.'* Hastiness, in the sense of sudden impulse, he did give way to; but hastiness in the usual sense of sudden anger he did not know, or, at least, others never saw. He was so gentle that it was difficult to imagine him provoked. I used sometimes to say to him, 'When were you last angry?' He smiled, and assured me that he really could be angry. I asked the time and the occasion. He could not say; but mentioned something, many years ago, in connection with the beadle's neglect of duty which had much annoyed him. Mrs Milne tells me that the only time when she saw him at all angry, was when the servant had neglected to deliver a message concerning some case of sickness, which he thought ought to have been attended to immediately. With the amount of strong feeling and excitement that was in him, it is amazing how little of 'hastiness' he exhibited, how entirely loving-kindness had overcome all wrath. The next day he writes: 'Feeble, but not fretted nor impatient. Thy will, O Lord, is best. Let me rest in thee. Draw me more and more to thyself. I long to get more into the mind of Christ.' And then, again, he adds: 'Still feeble; longing for revival; yet rest in the thought that Christ is full of life.'

I find several references to his Sabbath preparations on early days of the week, such as Wednesday. He was strikingly conscientious in preparing for the pulpit. This is the more to be noted because he both thought and spoke easily; and could, more than most, have done *extempore* work. But he was careful about his Sabbath services. No sooner was one Sabbath's work over than he began thinking, reading, studying, praying about the next. He did not, during his early years, write his sermons in full, though he always prepared them thoroughly; but afterwards he wrote them more fully, though he never read. He first himself fed on the bread, and then he set to making it ready for others. Those that were much with William Burns in the work at Dundee and Perth will remember this in his case. He did not write his discourses, but he prepared them more than many who did. In one of his visits to Kelso, he preached several evenings in succession. I asked him one forenoon what he meant to give us in the evening. 'I don't know; I have not yet got a morsel for my own soul.' It was with Milne as with him. They first steeped their own spirits in the word, and then they put it in shape for others. This is the truest process of elaboration. And in reading Milne's journals, we are struck with the numerous references, every day of the week, both to the past and the coming Sabbath. His *Sabbath work* was constantly before his eyes; and the results of that Sabbath work upon the souls of his people were matter of prayer, day and night, without ceasing. After writing one Wednesday about help in preparing for Sabbath, he adds: 'I wish to pray more in faith and love for the congregation. I think there is something moving among them, which, if fanned and cherished, may come to a flame; Lord Jesus, help!'[1]

Slumbering and Sleeping

He mentions his reading in the second chapter of Judges, — Joshua's death; the death of that generation of the faithful; Israel's forgetting God; and adds, 'God has in late years added a *third* way among us. Ministers are laid aside, and all seems going asleep. Will the Lord raise up men again, full of power and of the Holy Ghost? I know not in what form, or from what quarter; but I believe they will come.' The following is an interesting fragment from his journal, of January 27, (1864):

Living quietly. Yesterday, languid and out of harness; but a little help at night, when a temptation, resisted and ultimately overcome, gave

[1] I remember once being the means of disconcerting him about his Sabbath preparations. One Saturday evening, before a communion in his own church, I was with him; and after special prayer in reference to the next day's services, I asked him his text. He told me. I asked his exposition of the passage and the arrangement of his sermon. He told me, and added, 'Won't that do?' I said that the sermon was likely to be all that it ought; but he seemed to me to have mistaken the meaning of the passage. We talked over it, and he was persuaded that his exposition would not stand. He was greatly annoyed that night and next morning; and though he preached the sermon, he was not satisfied. So disconcerted, however, was he that he declared he would never tell his text again beforehand to any one; and, so far as I was concerned, he kept his word; always refusing to tell me what he was going to preach upon, and referring to the annoyance of the above Saturday night.

new light and strength. Longing for liberty from world and flesh and devil. Only walking after the Spirit in the light, and dwelling on high, can give it; the Spirit upon us, as it was on Christ (*Isa.* 11), according to our measure, alone can enable us to break through. I get above outward and inward entanglements. I have been thinking of the parallel in Romans 8, — the 'bondage of the corruption', and the 'liberty of the glory'; for this is the right rendering. If we abode in Christ, we should be strong and quiet, and not be preplexed or at a loss at any time. I take this cluster of truths: 'Be still, and know that I am God'; 'Stand still, and see the salvation of God'; 'He who believeth shall not make haste'; 'In returning and rest shall ye be saved'; 'Their thought is to sit still'; 'Is not the Lord gone out before thee?' said Deborah to Barak. This is victory. The King is in the field.

I have been longing for a more simple, unformal, unconventional way of stating the gospel; so that God's love in Christ might come home to men, just as they are from day to day, — in the house, on the street, in their wealth and their want, and even in sin. We find it in Titus 3: 'We ourselves', *etc.*; 'but after that the love and kindness of God our Saviour', *etc.* I have the feeling that if we could live in the light, love, and liberty of Christ, and think of nothing but spreading and extending this on every side, it would be a heaven on earth. I have known a little of this during the days which I have seen of the Son of man; but I think that I did not use it rightly. There was too much of self, of natural enjoyment and exhilaration. I think such seasons come to an end, because we overlook the Author of them, overvalue the instruments, are not sober in our joy and hope, do not watch, give the enemy opportunity, take the blessing as if it were a matter of course, lose the low, adoring, admiring frame with which we at first received this grace of God. I feel the truth of that word, 'If the salt have lost its savour.' If we are to benefit the world, we must be different from it, stronger than it, above its influences; we must break through its trammels, and not be always asking, What will it think? What will it say? How can I keep on terms with it? Let me watch against the flesh. It is always longing for great things, — to be something, to be thought of, talked of, and to pride itself on its own wisdom. But I wish to keep to my measure, and not to stretch myself beyond it, but to wait on the Lord; and if he saw good to enlarge my measure, then it will be safe and blessed. It is the divine *blessing* that is the source of all true good. He *blessed* the Sabbath-day. Christ *blessed* the bread and fishes; he *blessed* the bread and wine; he *blessed* the little company as he ascended.

Fragments

A few fragments are all that I find during the records of the rest of this year. 'I feel as if the kingdom of God were coming to me.' 'I need constant, watching prayer, and looking up.' 'Need a constant restoration, and holding up.' 'Gleams of something better.' 'How good to dwell in the kingdom; to be at home in it; taken up with its interests!' 'The Lord is working in me, if so be he will work by me.' 'It seems spiritually to be a low time everywhere; my "strength is to sit still", to take heed, to turn from self, sin, all my idols, to wait for his Son from heaven.' 'Good to get in to the mind of Christ.' 'Let thy secret be with me; let me not be of those to whom thou canst not commit thyself.' 'Feeble, but sensible of strength not my own.' 'It is the Lord in his free love that comes to us.' 'Let me not look at difficulties and objections, like Zecharias, but to the word of promise.' 'More cleaving to the Lord.' 'A lesson during the day: how little thoughtless people think of their idle words!' 'How few try to be bands, and joints, and corner stones; trying to keep all together, to strengthen and uphold the work!' 'I feel a measure of thy peace which passeth understanding.' 'Let me live out of myself, out of the world; the telescope ever in my hand, beholding the good and glory to be revealed. Why seek the living among the dead?' 'Ups and downs spiritually; conflicts, falls, deliverances. The Lord hath mercy, and so I continue. We have had very much sickness, and many deaths in the congregation since the beginning of the year.

We need greatly a time of blessing and increase. We go to London this week (May 2d). Lord, lead and keep me in thy highway. I am utter weakness; but strengthen, keep, uphold.'[1]

I notice frequent allusions in his journal to his classes. In these he took great interest. He had great influence among the young men;[2] and had, by his kind yet manly address, a way of winning and attaching them, which few seem to understand. He made a point of becoming thoroughly acquainted with them; and he entered most fully into all their plans and prospects. He was so obliging that there was nothing he would not do for them, either temporally or spiritually. He was delighted to be the 'servant of all'.

I remember his class of young men, in the early days of his work. It was a most interesting assembly, amounting, even down to the last days of his ministry, to about a hundred. Interest, intelligence, and warm feeling were marked on every face. His young women's class was no less largely attended. Both of these yielded much fruit, year after year. And down to the very last, his own interest in them remained fresh and fervent. It is not often that we find, at the close of a thirty years' work, as intense a glow of love and zeal as at the beginning. Yet so it was here.

In reference to these classes, Mackie writes the following statement from Warrington, June 11, 1868:

> As one of the young men of the revival period of 1840-41-42, I can say that the decease of Mr Milne evokes the most important reminiscences. To him, and to the Rev. W. C. Burns, scores of the young men of Perth owe all that made them men and Christians. Never can I forget the urgent and impressive exhortations he gave us in his

---

[1] Travelling in a train (1864), he writes afterwards: 'A news-boy was sorting his papers; I said, "I have a newspaper that never grows old." He looked up with such an amazed, inquiring face, "What's that?" I took out my little Bible, and the poor boy felt it.'

[2] In one of his diaries, there is this petition, 'Lord, direct me to the way of obtaining influence with young men.'

Bible class, to be diligent in business as well as fervent in spirit ...
I well remember him saying, at the time of the revivals, that when
the first news of those at Kelso reached him, he was a minister at
Aberdeen; and when, soon after, he opened Old St Leonard's to Mr
Burns, and saw him run after by crowds, he felt the common feelings
of humanity. But he said that he endeavoured to be content, and let
the Lord choose his own instruments; that contentment was to him
great gain. He was a chosen vessel to carry the gospel to many, in
those days, in Perth.

Unwearied in Work

Throughout his diary, both in India and in Scotland, we find constantly recurring references to his *work*. It was more to him than his
daily food. 'Some men', it has been said, 'only work enough to prove
that they are unwilling to work.' Half an hour with Milne would
have satisfied you how much the reverse of this it was with him.
'You know I like to work', are his words in a letter to a friend; and,
certainly, no one who had been an hour with him would question
the statement. Above most men he loved to work, he delighted in
his work. To be idle was irksome. To be restrained from working
was that which most tried his patience. In season and out of season
he would work. He would preach, or visit, or give away tracts, or do
some loving deeds, or speak some loving words. He would throw
himself in the way of work; and you could not do him a greater
favour than asking him to do some piece of Christian service, of
any kind, or to any person. He was strong in body, his only weak
part being his head; and he could undergo an immense amount of
fatigue.

That at times he did far too much, and took too little rest, was
often evident, as we have already seen; but he rallied wonderfully.
Unless when his head was oppressing him, he was most buoyant
and untiring. His alertness of motion and upright elastic form

— though under the middle size — as he moved along, always gave the impression that his life was that of one in earnest, of one who had a great work to do, and little time to do it in.

London Accident

He went to London, as the last sentence quoted from his journal intimates, in May 1864; and while there, he met with an 'accident' which had well-nigh brought death with it. His escape was marvellous, recalling Psalm 91:11: 'He shall give his angels charge concerning thee, to keep thee in all thy ways. They shall bear thee up in their hands, lest thou dash thy foot against a stone.' He was walking with a Christian friend in Eaton Place, in pleasant conversation on eternal things, and had just stepped off the pavement to cross the street, when a butcher's cart dashed round the corner and threw down both of them. Capt. Chapman was thrown to a little distance; but Milne fell under the horse's feet. Before the wheels had touched him the driver had pulled back the horse; but this, while it saved him from the wheels, brought the horse back over him a second time. One of the wheels had been arrested by his right thigh, with which it had come into contact, and in which it had inflicted a broad and deep wound, appalling to look upon, the flesh protruding; but the bone was unbroken. There were hoof marks on one of his hands, the fingers being greatly bruised, and also on his right cheek, about an inch from the eye; and I remember his telling me that the last recollection he had, when thus lying on the street, was of the hoof coming down upon his cheek. He was taken up insensible, carried into a shop hard by, and soon after taken to his lodgings in a cab, having by that time quite recovered his consciousness. His clothes were torn to rags, covered with dirt, as well as steeped in blood. The doctor summoned expressed astonishment that he should have escaped with his life. For some days the extent of his injuries could not be properly ascertained; but he soon rallied, and his recovery, by God's blessing, was very speedy, his excellent constitution and natural fearlessness of character standing him in good stead; and specially his perfect tranquillity of soul, and his happy assurance that all was well, whether death or life were the issue. The following letter, from London to Cowan, contains his own account of it; brief, but graphic.

47, Manchester Street, 15th June 1864. — MY DEAR COWAN, — How solemn are our meetings and partings! My medical man tells me, that another inch one way and our fraternal bond would have been broken, till we meet again before the Lord. On Saturday I went down to visit Chapman, a very dear Christian friend. He is old, very benevolent, and the greatest lover of the word of God that I know. We have found it quickening to see how he lives on the truth, and the truth lives in him. His house is in Eaton Place, one of the districts of Belgravia. We left it to go to see some of his interesting institutions for the poor, a little way off.

We had to cross the street, which is very wide. I remember looking carefully up and down to see that the way was clear, and then pro-ceeded to pass, holding one another firmly by the arm, and engaged in interesting conversation. Just as we had got about a third or more across, one of those wretched butchers' carts came rushing round the adjoining corner, and ere we could move or cry, it was upon us like a thunderbolt. I felt a dreadful blow; my hat went one way, my umbrella another. My beloved friend was happily dashed aside, receiving a stun-ning blow on the ground, and his face and head are much bruised. He still lies very ill. I went down under the horse's feet, which passed over me, trampling on my body. The driver, as he has since told me, horrified at what he had done, drew back with all his might, and so the horse trampled over me a second time. I just remember the hoofs above me, and the wheels beside me.

Captain Chapman was first picked up, and removed to his house close by; then I was extricated from the horse's feet, and taken to a surgeon's house. My clothes were torn in a thousand fragments; my face and hands pouring down with blood; and my thigh quite naked, and a mass of bleeding flesh. But I did not feel any of these wounds at the moment, for I had intense agony, when I breathed or moved, about the chest. The whole muscular and nervous system about that region must have been strangely jarred and shaken; so that almost all my suffering has proceeded from this; and yet no bone was broken.

Captain Chapman made me be taken over to his house to wait till his medical man came. We condoled a little; but it was rather a hallelujah. All is well; it will turn to good. But I would not remain; a cab was brought, and I got home. My dear wife and help-mate behaved nobly. She did all that I told my young friends in the class, about presence of mind, and the meek and quiet spirit.

I am now fast recovering, though I have been suffering much from pain. I am happy; deeply, solemnly happy. So is B. We have just been saying, since your note came, that this must be owing to the prayers of our friends for us. D.V., we hope to be with you this very week. It is a week more than we reckoned upon; but it will be the Sabbatic week, the best of the seven, and none of us will regret it. Sorry not to be with you and the brethren on Wednesday evening; but the Master orders otherwise. Much love to the brethren. Thank all for their prayers.

Queen Victoria's Visit to Perth

This year (1864) the Queen visited Perth, to uncover the statue of Prince Albert. The thought occurred, Could he not do something for her? If she had been of lower rank, he could have given her some suitable book or spoken some special word; but how could he approach Her Majesty? He went to the platform along with other citizens; but it was not to *see* that he went, but to watch for an opportunity of doing something for her. Others might have their curiosity gratified; he was bent on a higher object; for, to be in that crowd, and yet do nothing there for the Master, was to him impossible. He had often prayed for her; could he not get a word spoken, or at least conveyed to her, whatever might be the difficulties? There

was a hymn in which he delighted, and from which he had often
drawn consolation in his sorrows:

> I shine in the light of God;
>   His likeness stamps my brow;
> Through the valley of death my feet have trod,
>   And I reign in glory now!
> No breaking heart is here,
>   No keen and thrilling pain,
> No wasted cheek, where the frequent tear
>   Hath roll'd and left its stain.
>
> I have reach'd the joys of heaven:
>   I am one of the sainted band;
> For my head a crown of gold is given,
>   And a harp is in my hand.
> I have learn'd the song they sing,
>   Whom Jesus has set free;
> And the glorious walls of heaven still ring
>   With my new-born melody.
>
> No sin, no grief, no pain;
>   Safe in my happy home;
> My fears all fled, my doubts all slain,
>   My hour of triumph's come!
> Oh! friends of mortal years,
>   The trusted and the true!
> Ye are watching still in the valley of tears,
>   But I wait to welcome you.
>
> Do I forget? oh, no!
>   For memory's golden chain
> Shall bind *my* heart to the hearts below,
>   Till they meet to touch again.
> Each link is strong and bright:
>   And love's electric flame

Flows freely down, like a river of light,
  To the world from whence I came.

Do you mourn when another star
  Shines out from the glittering sky?
Do you weep when the raging voice of war
  And the storms of conflict die?
Then why should your tears run down,
  And your hearts be sorely riven,
For another gem in the Saviour's crown,
  And another soul in heaven?

Of this hymn he kept neatly printed copies; and one of these, enclosed in a handsome envelope, he took with him, waiting for an opportunity of delivering it. Her Majesty left the carriage, and crossed the platform; but no opportunity occurred. Milne followed to the neighbouring hotel, where she was to lunch. He went to the hotel, told his errand, and being personally known to the hotel-keeper, was politely received, but told that Her Majesty was going to lunch. Nothing daunted, he asked if he could see any of the royal suite? He was told that they were in an ante-room. He asked to be shown thither, which was done. To this room he found his way, and knocked. The door was opened by Lord Mansfield, who, being a Perthshire nobleman, recognised Milne, and received him courteously. Milne, without many words, told him his errand; and said, that he was very desirous that a hymn, which had so com-forted himself, should be put into Her Majesty's hand, that it might comfort her too. His lordship kindly said that he could not present it himself, but that he would take him to General Grey, who was the proper person to give it. Accordingly Milne was introduced to General Grey, and explained his errand to him; telling him how anxious he was that this hymn of consolation should be given to Her Majesty. General Grey was most cordial, and said at once, 'Give it to me, and I promise you it shall be delivered into Her Majesty's own hands.' Milne gladly gave him the envelope with the hymn, and returned home full of thankfulness and hope. Not many would have thought of this; fewer would have done it. But he was always 'devising' such things (*Isa.* 32:8); and he was fertile in expedients for carrying out what he devised. *Nunquam non paratus.*[1] Dr M'Crie said well: 'It is the Christian's cowardice that spoils his fortune.'[2] Of that cowardice Milne knew nothing. Some of us often envied him his boldness and his readiness; especially when we saw it so chastened with meekness, and singleness of eye.

He kept a large stock of such leaflets and little books, and had them always about him for giving to all he met with. I may safely say that he never wrote a letter or note, however short, without some sentence or word, or leaflet, that spoke the man of God; so that you felt, in receiving a note from him, Here is one who cares for me, and is desirous of something more than merely being civil to me. Even when endorsing some notice, or circular, or proof-sheet, he would write some word, or few words, either on the outside or on the envelope, that bore a message for eternity. These little abrupt sentences, verses or half-verses, scribbled hastily as he was about to close his envelope, would, if collected, form a most peculiar little book or tract, whose title might be 'In season and out of season', and whose motto might be Edward Irving's famous sentence, 'Be thou the pastor always, less than the pastor never.' The following is an envelope scrap: 'We were a little sharp upon our brother. I always regret when I let a word slip. Let us have a big blazing fire of love, and plenty of hot coals. That's the way; is it not?' Here is another: 'I rejoice in the prosperity of others; it is the Master's joy, it should be mine.' Here is another on a communion week: 'Pray for me that I may be kept and guided this week; it is often a time of tempta-tion.' A newspaper came from Calcutta to Collace with 'Brethren

[1] 'Always ready', *Ed.*
[2] In his *Commentary on Esther.*

beloved, pray for us', in Greek, addressed, 'Rev. A. H. J. J. & W. B.';
and a note to Glasgow has this postscript: 'The Lord is still near,
waiting to see if we will constrain him to abide.' Another note
closes thus: 'If we earnestly trust in the Lord, *and delight* in him,
what shall we not get?' and another: 'I like the idea of St Leonard's
being a place of resort for every good work'; and another: 'He is our
wonder-working Lord'; and another: 'My future is in Christ's hand,
and I have no thought, will, or plan'; and another: 'Let us wait for
the end of the Lord'; and once more: 'Ah, brother, it is more after
the grain to send a note to Alick Somerville, than a petition to the
king's court.'

Visits to the Sick

His attention in cases of the slightest illness, whether sent for
or not, was remarkable. He would call immediately on hearing, or
write a note, or send a tract, or perhaps his card, with a text upon
it. During the cholera he visited the sick, stayed with them for
hours, as both nurse and pastor; and when urged by the relatives,
on one occasion, not so to expose himself, he said, in his own way,
kindly and earnestly, 'I'm not afraid to die.' He went to another
very infectious case, unsent for (the individual not belonging to
his flock), sat beside the sick-bed, spoke the message of peace, and
received the warm thanks of the dying man. Thinking that the sufferer wanted something to refresh him, Milne raised him up and
offered him something for his parched lips. 'No, not that', said the
dying man, — 'more of the spiritual drink.' The cases in which he
thus went in search of the sick, or the sinful, or the sorrowful, are
innumerable; and his anecdotes of these, his 'spiritual adventures',
were truly interesting.

How he watched for opportunities of dealing with men about
their immortal welfare, and found such opportunities where others would hardly have deemed it practicable, the following letter

written in Glasgow will show. He had been preaching for Somerville, and at the close of the service, which in all likelihood was somewhat late, had hastened away to the house of his brother, then in that city. He writes to Somerville:

What did you say when you got to the vestry and found the bird flown? But I don't regret, or repent a bit, of stealing that march upon you. It was a real, but it was a right act of self-denial to forego the brotherly convoy, though it would have been right pleasant and profitable. Your family needed you,[1] and you needed quiet rest; and so I did right in making the sacrifice. I walked quickly home, and had a nice talk with one of the watchmen, who kept by me till he came to the end of his beat. He thought that a man situated as he was could hardly be expected to be religious. But I fairly turned the tables on him by telling him of a day-watchman with whom I had spoken the other day, who told me that he had to leave his house every morning at six o'clock, but that he never went out without first reading a little of the Bible. I have had several nice talks with young men in this way. I ask a question about the road; they give information; something else follows; they get interested, and once or twice have gone almost to my brother's house. Your city is wonderfully quiet and orderly. I have seen nothing to offend or annoy in all the long line of streets through which I pass, night after night, unless it be the spirit-sellers, who, wise in their generation, have occupied the commanding positions at the corner of the streets; and, with their rounded fronts, seem to command three, or often four streets at once. In Calcutta I used often, in the fine moonlight nights, to take my staff and a servant, and sally out for long long rounds in the native town, and thus came to know, I fancy, a great deal more than some of our friends who have been

---

[1] 'Your *family* needed you.' Do not ministers forget this, and soothe their consciences by thinking that they are attending to their flock or to public duties? Hence the children of ministers lose that special and powerful training which is to be found in the *society* of their father. For this nothing can compensate. The perfect *mould* of character (apart from the mere educational) has a *paternal* as well as a maternal side. If one side of the mould be withheld, the character will be thus far deficient.

there for many years. The European, or west end, is quite detached from the native town, and so one may live long in Calcutta and yet know very little of the natives. There are many bad people there; but I was surprised and pleased to see so large an amount of quiet order, regular industry, and domestic comfort. At night, you know, all is alive and on the move. But I am taking coals to Newcastle; for *ed Io sono orientale.*[1] — Believe me, very affectionately yours, J. M.

The Night-watchmen

Not in Glasgow only did he thus get hold of the night-watchmen. He did the same in Perth; and at late hours might be seen standing in talk with the watchman, or walking by his side. One night he got into earnest talk with one of them, entreating him to give himself to Christ. 'When I marry a couple', he said, 'I say to the woman, "Wilt thou take this man for thy husband?" and to the man, "Wilt thou take this woman for thy wife?" and so the marriage is concluded. Now, I ask you, will you take Christ tonight?' Thus he stood pleading with the man; and then taking out his pocket Bible, which he always carried with him, he asked him to turn the bright side of his lantern so as to flash the light on the page, and thus standing, he read some verses, and parted. Some laughed at such doings, others thought him mad. Yet, if he believed what he professed, could he do otherwise? And if they are mad who take unusual methods of rescuing the lost, what are they who take no methods at all? What are they who believe there is such a thing as a lost soul, and yet meet with or pass by thousands of these each week, without one word of love or of warning spoken?

Another striking incident in reference to this class of men may here be added, to show how, 'in season and out of season', he carried on his heavenly embassy, beseeching men to be reconciled.

It was his invariable practice to accompany his friends or guests

[1] 'And I am an easterner' (Italian), *Ed.*.

to the train when they left; to carry their umbrella, or plaid, or car-pet-bag, and to give them a parting text or little book. He did so once with his friend Mr Riddell of Dundee, who had been preach-ing for him, and who was to start by the late train. On reaching the station they found themselves half an hour too early. 'I'll get you some work to do', said Milne to his companion. He disappeared at one of the entrances, and then re-appeared, bringing with him the watchman of the station, with whom he had been more than once dealing about eternal things. Leaving Riddell with the man, he went home. The man was anxious, but full of doubts. Riddell remained with him preaching the good news; and the light seemed to enter the poor man's heart. On the following morning the newspaper announced the sudden death, from heart-disease, of 'the watchman of the Perth station'. Paul had planted, Apollos had watered, God had given the increase; but the corn thus suddenly ripened was as suddenly cut down.

As he had himself come out from the world, so did he seek with all earnestness to draw others out. Like Noah, he 'condemned the world' (*Heb.* 11:7).

Robert M'Cheyne against Worldliness

Robert M'Cheyne's life and ministry formed a very decided testimony against the world and worldly pleasures. In his private conversations, in his dealings with young people, in his sermons, in his 'fencing the tables', in his after-communion addresses, he spoke out with decision; and some of the most vehement things we ever heard from his lips were in condemnation of the 'lovers of pleasure'. He spoke out against the theatre, the ball-room, the card-table, 'sparing no arrows'. In his younger days he had tasted the world's pleasures, but found them poor.[1]

---

[1] There were few things that M'Cheyne more dreaded than 'worldly amuse-ments' in the families of professing Christians, especially of ministers. Let those

In the beginning of 1838 he had some striking sermons on 1 Peter 1:14–19, the notes of which are now before us. Thus he spoke, and thus he speaks still:

> My dear friends, if you wish to obey the word of God here laid before you, flee from all circumstances, from all places or companies, where you know you may be tempted to sin. Are there not some of you who appear to be awakened and to rejoice in Christ, who yet go, with a bold and daring countenance, into idle companies and places where you know you will meet with temptation? Is this fearing to sin? "Do you wish us to be hermits?" you will say. No such thing. But do you know a company where holy things are slighted, where things are spoken that should not be named, where late, unholy hours are kept, where you have already been tempted to sin? Then, child of God, I charge you not to cross that threshold again, no, not once. I charge you, flee temptation, pass the time of your sojourning here in fear. And here I cannot but allude to an awful provocation of God, which, I have reason to fear, is carried on amongst us. I mean young persons, after the holiest exercises, plunging into the unholiest companies; praying in the house of God, or in a class for religious instruction one hour, and entering into ungodly company the very next. I beseech the unconverted among you to leave off this practice, if you would not have God send some sore judgment on your soul. I charge the children of God among you to leave off this practice, now and for ever. Ah, fear to sin! Flee the world! Flee company! Pass the time of your sojourning here in fear.

---

who think that he was narrow-minded and too rigid, test his views by our Lord's words concerning the world, or by the epistles of his apostles afterwards, especially those of the beloved disciple. 'The extent to which novel-reading, dancing parties, private theatricals, card-playing, luxurious feasting and dressing, loose, frivolous, and profane song-singing, with other exhibitions of utter worldliness, prevail even in professedly Christian families, with the sanction and under the eye of office-bearers in the Church, would hardly be believed. Can we wonder at so many of the children of apparently good men turning out ill, when we know that "Love not the world" was no maxim in their training?' Such is the statement of one who knew something about the ways of 'Christian families'. It was no Puritan who called the world 'an infinite masquerade'. *Risu necat* ('He slays with a laugh', *Ed.*).

Of the same spirit was John Milne. Of the same tone was his ministry. And 'love not the world' came well from his lips; for he lived what he preached. No man could suspect him of loving the world, or caring for its pleasures, or its gold, or its literature, or its company.

Worldliness

It is by being filled with the love of God, and admiration of 'the world to come', that we are made impervious to this world and its attractions. Nothing else will do. Hence the folly of asceticism. It is only before heavenly love and beauty that earthly love and beauty will give way. The world's pleasures: can they co-exist with the love of the Father? The world's religion: is it not poorer even than its pleasures? The world's polish: is it not tinsel, if not rust? Yet an effort is being made by some to reconcile the two worlds and their two masters; nay, to make the religion of Christ in part consist of an enjoyment of the pleasures of life. The construction of a worldly religion, and the enjoyment of religious worldliness, are marked features of the age.

Both these men of God understood 'the world', and recognised in it the adversary of God and his Church, alike in its persecutions and its blandishments. It was not to them a thing of the first century, but of the nineteenth as truly. The theology that teaches men *not* 'to come out and be separate', but to enjoy the world and its pleasures, did not fit in to their system. Worldliness, however refined, was still worldliness in their eyes, because inconsistent with the love of the Father. 'If any man love the world, the love of the Father is not in him' (*1 John* 2:15). Religious worldliness, or worldly religiousness, seemed to them of all things most opposed to the spirit of Christ.

God and the world cannot find room in the same heart now, any more than in former ages. The 'reproach of Christ' (*Heb.* 11:26) is now much the same in England as it was in Egypt once; and 'without the camp' (*Heb.* 13:13) cannot mean 'within'. The attempt

to efface the line that separates 'within' from 'without' can only succeed by the creation of a new Christianity, from which some of the
great features of the old are struck out. The world and the Church
have been found at times not unwilling to patronize each other.
The world has undertaken to be religious, provided the Church
will consent to be worldly. The basis of the proposed compromise
is the mutual understanding that a man may be worldly, and yet a
good man; that a man may be a Christian, and yet not a very bad
man after all.

There was nothing of this compromise in the preaching or the
lives of these two men of God. Separation from the world was what
they taught and lived. No amount of supposed progress, or refine-
ment, or elevation could make the world less the world, or remove
its hatred of Christ (*John* 15:18), or produce the love of holiness, or
supersede the necessity of cleansing by the blood, or regeneration
from above. Certain modern philosophers and poets, in evolving
what they have called the human side of Christianity, proceed upon
the defence or consecration of 'worldliness'. They also assume that
old Christianity, whether of the first or the seventeenth century, is
not suited to an age of progress and intellect like ours:

> Your creeds are dead, your rites are dead,
>   Your social order, too;
> Where tarries He, the Power who said,
>   'See, I make all things new?'
>
> The millions suffer still and grieve;
>   And what can helpers heal?
> With old-world cures men half believe
>   For woes they wholly feel.

The ministry of these two men showed that they had not so
learned Christ. They believed that what man needed was *salvation;*
that the gospel for humanity in all ages is that gospel which is 'the

power of God unto *salvation*' and that this salvation comes not through philosophy, or science, or sacramental grace, or connection with a church, but through the cross of Christ and the Spirit of the living God. Thus they preached, and thus multitudes believed.

Unworldliness

Milne's consistency was as marked as his separation from the world. His conformity to 'the world to come' was as decided as his non-conformity to 'this present evil world'. His relish for it had long passed away, ever since he had tasted the love that passeth knowledge, and known the grace of God in truth. And this disrelish for lower things, and relish for the higher, is our great preservative against worldly conformity. Place Milne anywhere, in any company, his unworldliness showed itself. Place him next a worldly man in a room, in a railway carriage, on the highway, in the course of two minutes' conversation his character came out. It could not be hid. Exceedingly well-informed, gifted with great powers of conversation, and with a most versatile mind, he could take up any topic; and, ere his neighbour was aware, he would imperceptibly give the conversation a higher turn, and, in the gentlest of words and tones, introduce the great question of personal relationship to God.[1] He might meet a mourner in the street; he would go up and speak words of consolation. He might see a sickly person passing; he would go and offer his arm, for the purpose of bringing to him the glad tidings. Many interesting, we might say romantic, stories of this kind has he modestly told us in our quiet walks; for incidents, such as those referred to above, were to him of every-day

---

[1] What the Pagan Pliny said respecting his philosophic friend Euphrates, is in a higher sense true of Milne: *'Sermo est copiosus et varius; dulcis imprimis, et qui repugnantes quoque ducat et impellat. Vitae sanctitas summa, comitas par.'* 'His speech is eloquent and varied and at the same time so sweet that it gains the attention of the most unwilling hearer. He is distinguished by the holiness of his life, and equally by his affability.' Pliny: *Epistles* (1.10.6), *Ed.*

occurrence. He could hardly pass any one without making use of the opportunity of speaking a word, or giving a leaflet or book. In season and out of season he preached, and spoke, and acted. The full heart could not but flow out; and, strange to say, almost invariably without offence being taken, so courteous, so gentlemanly, so kind, so unobtrusive was his manner.

In Season and Out of Season

Sometimes he might get at first a sharp word, but his 'soft answer' immediately turned away the wrath; and as he never took offence, or lost his temper, he soon gained the advantage. Once when he was with me at Kelso for a few days, we went down to the Berwick coast together; and, going into a third-class carriage, we found a good number of passengers, among whom we went distributing some tracts. At the end of the carriage sat a young man in the attitude of resistance. Milne approached him with a tract. He thrust it away, saying, rudely, that he wanted none of these things. 'Very well, my dear friend', said Milne, gently, 'very well; but perhaps you'll change your mind, and if you do, come to me, as I have still some remaining.' We took our seats again in the carriage, and sat, perhaps a quarter of an hour, conversing together, — the passengers quietly reading the tracts, — when we saw the young man making his way to us from the other end of the carriage. 'I've changed my mind, and I'll thank you for a tract', said he. The tract was given at once, and a word in season along with it to the stranger as he left the carriage.

That same day we were walking together along the sandy beach on the south side of the Tweed, just opposite Berwick, enjoying the sea breeze, and watching the fishermen drawing their salmon-nets. We came up to two who were busy on the shore 'mending their nets', or putting them in order. Milne at once saluted them. 'You are fishermen, I see, my dear friends.' 'Yes', said they, 'we are.' 'I'm a fisherman too', said he. They looked at him as if they did not just hear what he said. 'I'm a fisherman, my friends', he said; but without any explanation. They smiled, and implied that they did not quite believe him. 'Yes', said he again, 'I'm a fisherman, and so is my brother here. We are both fishermen.' The attention of the men being now fixed, and their eyes turned on him, he explained himself, telling them that he had come to fish *them*.

When walking out, if he saw a man breaking stones by the road-side, he would often say a word to him about the hardness of his work, and then add, 'Do you know I am a stone-breaker too?' and this would lead to a conversation about the heart of stone.

No one could *mistake* him at any time, or not discover in the course of five minutes 'whose he was and whom he served'. Some of us, when thrown into unpleasant company, prefer remaining silent rather than risk unpleasant collision. Not so Milne. He did not fear being affronted. He did not hesitate to speak, and he had always a word in season, — a mild word too; no sharpness, no dogmatism, no resentment. He seemed incapable of being provoked or ruffled by any amount of opposition; and the 'My friend', or 'My dear friend', with which he prefaced each reply, disarmed and won the opposer.

He bore being railled upon the long sermons of his early ministry with great good-nature, and would pleasantly reply, 'Ah, well, my dear friend, perhaps you are right, I was too long; but, after all, God used the sermon you speak of. I heard of some who were awakened that day.'

With the greatest humility and modesty, — for he did not think of himself at all, — he was one of the most independent both in thought and action that you could meet with. He was equally at home in conversing with the poor or rich; and his uncommonly easy manners found access for him everywhere. His affability prevented any coldness, even among strangers; and the cheerful nod of the head that accompanied his quiet words set each one at ease, as if all had been old friends.

Some are more ready at missing than at making opportunities of doing good. Seldom did Milne let slip an opportunity; often did he make it. He seemed constantly on the watch for some one on whom to let fall a word of wisdom or love. Of the Master it was said, 'This man receiveth (is on the outlook, lies in wait for, προσδεχεται) sinners': Luke 15:2. So was it with the servant in the present case. Before he went out he prayed, in going along he prayed, on coming home he prayed. In answer to these prayers, opportunities, often of the most unexpected kind, were given him. Little, perhaps, did they with whom he thus casually met, think that the word he spoke to them as he passed, or as he walked along with them, was a message in answer to the speaker's prayer.

He entered a friend's house as one who desired to bring blessing with him, not unfrequently giving the apostolic salutation, 'Peace be to this house.' For parents, for children, and for servants he had a word and a look. The following incident is given as fitted to touch the hearts of children. At a brother minister's house once, he was much interested with his host's little daughter, of some four or five years old. He taught her a little prayer — it was, 'O Lord, give me a new heart, for Jesus Christ's sake. Amen.' Some months after, he heard of the child's death, and also, that for some time she had regularly said the prayer; but one day she had omitted it; and when her mother asked the reason she had forgotten Milne's prayer, 'Oh, no!' she said, 'but I have dot it' (got it), meaning the new heart.

If he met a friend in the street, he had some ready word of peace to greet him with. If he went into a shop, he would take occasion, from the articles he was buying, to say a word in season. If he drove in a cab, he would not part from the cabman till he had given him some little book, or spoken some text, or reminded him of his higher calling. Station-masters, guards, porters knew him, for he was so much in the habit of engaging them in conversation wherever he might happen to be. In every man he saw a being on whom a word might tell for eternity; and he acted accordingly. At his own table, or at the table of others, he was the most polite and genial of men; yet with no 'foolish talking nor jesting', no frivolity nor unseemly conversation.

He would speak to the beggar, and, after supplying his need, bid him go to Christ and beg for his soul. He would go up to the servants shaking their mats at the door, and remind them of John Bunyan's room of dust, and how it was laid. He would speak with the same ease to the great; for his natural politeness and presence of mind enabled him to approach anyone, without the slightest awkwardness. He would condole with a person who had met with losses, pointing him to the riches which are never lost; and he would congratulate another on his gains, reminding him at the same time of the world to come, and the better gains.

He would go out of his way to get an opportunity of doing good; nor did he stand on ceremony or dignity in his efforts to win and save. He did not feel that he had done anything undignified when, one evening, in the streets of Perth, he gave full chase to three boys who ran away from him as he was trying to persuade them to come in to his Sabbath school. Nor did he think he had done anything out of the way when he got up on the engine, amid smoke and dust, and drove along for a stage, in order to get a talk with the driver and stoker; or when he marched into church, followed by four soldiers whom he had met as they were going to walk, and persuaded to turn in and hear the word of life.

He sought the outcasts; he sought the Roman Catholics, so that he won the hearts of many of these latter, especially of the children, for whom he had always a pleasant smile and a happy text as he passed along the street, or down the Meal Vennel.

Perth Conferences

It may be well to notice here his connection with the Perth
Conferences. With these he was associated from first to last; for
at the last Conference (September 1868), he being dead yet spoke,
as it was he who drew out the programme. He grudged no labour,
no cost, no trouble of any kind, in making preparations for these
annual gatherings; and a very large amount of correspondence in
regard to it passed through his hands. The preparatory meetings in
Milne's house, in which Mr Macdonald of St Martin's, Mr Grant
of Arndilly, Mr Mudie of Montrose, and others took part, will be
remembered by all present at them for their happy brotherly spirit,
— a spirit to which the loving, well-pleased face of Milne contributed not a little. Here is the sketch of the Conference history, which
he prefixed to the report of 1867:[1]

> The Perth Religious Conference sprung out of 'Evangelistic Open-Air
> Meetings' convened by Colonel Macdonald Macdonald of St Mar-
> tin's. He attended the great open-air gathering held in the summer
> of 1860 in the park of the late Duchess of Gordon at Huntly Lodge.
> He was so affected by the scene and its results, that he came home
> determined, through God's blessing, to have something of the same
> kind at Perth. He called a meeting for consultation; but ministers and
> people were almost all out of town enjoying their annual holiday. Still
> he persevered, though with little encouragement or help. I remember
> that, on the morning of the first day, a number of Christian friends
> met in my house, facing the South Inch, within a stone-throw or two
> of the picturesque spot where, shaded by a clump of trees, the stand for
> the speakers was erected, and a large tent pitched for the anxious and

[1] 'As to the little book [above noted], I have no doubt the Lord has a good reason
for the delay in its coming out; "wait on the Lord, and be of good courage." I liked
very much Captain Trotter's little meetings for prayer [parents for their children].
It was a new but blessed feature. I am so glad that you are seeing fruit, — glad
of the work at Ferryden. The Lord has a favour to that place, and it is interesting
to see how ardently the good Arklays long for blessing upon it.' — Letter to Mr
Mudie of Montrose.

inquiring. There was more fear than faith in that little company; but we did the best thing we could in the circumstances, — we knelt down with one accord, and called on the Lord. One began, another followed in the same strain, and another and another, without interruption, till the supplication went round the whole circle. It was really one prayer uttered by many voices. Somehow, as we went on, we seemed to breathe more freely, our hearts were enlarged, our hopes became buoyant. We rose from our knees, and all turned to the windows; and what a sight met our eyes! Thousands were already assembled, and hundreds were trooping in from all quarters. We felt that the Lord had gathered them, and that he was now going forth with us to the battle. When the service began, it was thought that seven or eight thousand people were collected. Soon came the answer to prayer; the arrows of the King were sharp; the tent was filled with anxious souls; little groups were here and there, all over the Inch, conversing, kneeling in prayer, or praising God for light and salvation. In a little while the adjoining church, conveniently at hand, was opened, and numbers of the awakened resorted to it for conversation.

In the evening, they met in the City Hall, crowded with from two to three thousand persons; and the Lord was present to wound and to heal. The second day resembled the first, and so did the third. But towards the close of the last meeting, the Spirit seemed to come as a rushing wind, and speakers and hearers were alike astonished. One dear brother came home at the end, crying, 'The Lord has come!' another followed, crying, 'The Lord has come indeed!'

It had been arranged that next night, Friday, a meeting should be held in the church, where the anxious had been dealt with at the morning meetings. The minister of that church was sitting next morning at breakfast with a beloved brother in the ministry, when the thought came suddenly with power into his heart, Why should the meeting tonight be in a particular church? Why not in the City Hall, where all could participate? The thought made him start up, and say to his brother, 'Will you stay and take part?' 'Yes', said his friend, 'with all my heart.' After looking up to God, and a moment's consultation with a brother minister in town, the hall was taken for the night, and placards issued intimating the meeting. When we met, the place was completely crammed; and, though the strangers were gone, yet the interest and impression were the same as before. The hall was immediately taken for a week, and then indefinitely, and for seventy nights in succession it was crowded as at the first; and seven or eight hundred persons remained night after night to be conversed with. It was a great harvest; the ministers of the town laboured lovingly together; and each reaped fruit unto eternal life.

Next year similar meetings were held for three days with blessed results. But Colonel Macdonald and his friends began to feel that there was a risk in being in the open air in our proverbially changeable climate; and so, in 1863, all the meetings were held in the City Hall. There were three meetings each day, as at present: forenoon, for short addresses on a fixed subject, and by selected speakers; afternoon, for free conversation on practical subjects connected with the work of God; and evening, for evangelistic addresses, the subjects being left to the choice of the different speakers. At the commencement of this new series of meetings, the name was changed to Perth Religious Conference, this term being suggested by Mr Gordon Forlong, and adopted in imitation of the well-known Barnet Conferences. Mr Pennefather was largely consulted in regard to the arrangements; and he kindly came down to the first meeting to help and countenance. Perhaps it may not be uninteresting to notice the subjects opened up at the forenoon meetings in the succeeding years. In 1863, they were, (1) Love to Father, Son, and Spirit, how promoted and how maintained; Love to Saints; Love to a Lost World; (2) Searching the Scriptures daily; (3) The Believer's position in the world, accepted, working, waiting. In 1864, they were, Progress, Fruitfulness, Holiness; in 1865, Rejoicing, Working, Resting; in 1866, Peaceful, Hopeful, Watchful. This present year Mr Grant of Arndilly presided, as he did in 1865, in consequence of the illness and absence of his friend Colonel Macdonald.

The Lord surely has a favour for these meetings. He has been a wall of fire around them, and the glory in the midst. Untoward things, like frowning clouds, have sometimes appeared in the horizon; but they have speedily changed their character, and become real and helpful blessings. They have been constantly growing in interest and importance. Many look forward to them with desire, prayer, and hope. Some have been converted at them, and others have learned the way of the Lord more perfectly. There have been many testimonies all along from God's people concerning the comfort and quickening they have received. One child of God said the other day, 'We have been in Halleluiah land.' An honoured brother in the Lord writes, 'What will glory be, when there is so much enjoyment in a twinkle of it?' — J. M.

How much we missed him at our last Conference, in September 1868, those who had enjoyed his fellowship at the preceding ones can best say. We missed him from the platform and from the private circle. His fervent voice, his bright expression of face, his pointed petitions, his outstretched right hand in prayer, whether in the congregation or the Conference, were well remembered by many.

John Milne

St Leonard's: 1839-43
Free St Leonard's 1843-53 &
1858-68

Robert Cowan

Free St Leonard's 1859-78

Chapter 16

1866–1867
Illnesses and Labours

*I*n September 1866, he had a severe attack of congestion in the brain, and from that time his strength was perceptibly undermined. His life was for some time despaired of; but in love the Lord prolonged it for a little, and gave him a little more work to do for him here, which he did with his usual energy and gladness, though with diminished power. During this illness he suffered intense agony; the pain in the head being quite excruciating. But his peace was like a river; his patience unruffled; and his sweetness of temper invariable.

After this illness, a friend wrote congratulating him on his recovery, and asking how he felt in the near prospect of death.[1] He thus replied:

> I did think for a little that I was going away, and I felt as if I had nothing to do but to die and be with Jesus. But that soon passed, and then began terrible excruciating sufferings for many nights and days. It seemed as if I had never known suffering before, as if I were enduring many martyrdoms. But the Lord strengthened, and I was enabled to wait quietly the appointed time. I think Jesus helped me to enter into his sufferings in a way I never did before. Also to feel that all I suffered came directly from himself, and was exactly weighed out

[1] See reference to this in a letter on pp. 127-8.

and measured as to amount and duration. Then I began to think of fellow-sufferers, and you often among the rest, and I think the Lord has given me more and tenderer sympathy than before. I had no sleep for ten or eleven nights, but constant racking pain; but I know that the Lord helped me and carried me through. I now see that God is served by waiting, suffering, and striving to say, 'Not my will but thine', as well as by running to and fro, and straining every nerve. I begin to think that patience is the *crowning* grace. You are far ahead of me in this department of godliness, and I may well sit at your feet and learn to cultivate the passive graces. I have a hope that the Lord means to spare for a little on the footstool. Thank you again for this touching, interesting note; and may the God of all grace and peace, after we have suffered a while, stablish, settle, perfect us! 'I will bless God at *all* times. All his paths are mercy and truth.

As soon as he was able he resumed work, and preached on James 1:4. His usual pastoral duties, which he so truly delighted in, he was able once more to undertake for some months. Still frequent changes were necessary. A happy fortnight at the Bridge of Allan, in May 1867, helped to brace him; and another fortnight at Newport, in July. By this time, however, the suffering in his head had recommenced, and there were days of depression. But before taking up this, his last year of work, let us throw together some reminiscences and letters of 1866.

Miscellaneous Notes

He thus writes to Cowan: 'MY DEAR BROTHER, — Go on and prosper. You are making me live my early ministry over again. You will kindly take the session tonight. If the weather permit, I shall be making a good many visits, and tomorrow shall, *D.V.,* be all day at Madderty. Tell the elders how cheery and hopeful our district visitors were.' Again, about May (1866), on leaving for a little rest, he writes briefly to his colleague: 'Good-bye. I missed you when

I got back from the station. I wish we could have had a few quiet moments together; for life is so uncertain; one does not know what a few weeks may bring. Several things within the last month or two have shown me that both mind and body are *run down*, and need a little quiet; and yet I feel it a real wrench at last to leave the objects of daily interest and occupation.' On the 21st of August of the same year he writes to Cowan: 'Thank you, my dear brother, for your welcome note. I should have been beforehand with you, but could not find out your whereabouts. Now I don't let the grass grow under my pen, if such a figure is allowable. It is the first time I ever heard of Enoch Dow; but I shan't forget it. You seem to have fallen on your feet, like Paul at Melita; and the natives seem to be very amiable barbarians. I have a note from Dymock, putting me in mind that you and I are to be with him next Sabbath. Will you go to him in the *forenoon?* and so I shall have the opportunity of intimating your return to our people, and saying that you come as a giant longing to be at work. I trust good days are before us this winter. Let us lie low and look up, and not let him go … Possibly we may take your advice and go away for a little after the Conference.' In October, after the communion, and after his own illness, he writes to Cowan: 'I think we should be very thankful for this communion. To me it has been a blessed time. I thought yesterday, as I sat quiet as a worshipper, that the Master himself was a worshipper in the earthly sanctuary. It was very comforting to me to think that the ever-watchful Shepherd, who knows the end from the beginning, had, without our intending it, made provision for my lack of service.'

Letters

On the 21st of September (same year) he thus wrote from Elgin to my brother:

My very dear Andrew, — We are journeying and meeting with daily, hourly mercies; and we try to see them coming from the upper spring, through the wounds of the bleeding Lamb. We were in the Black Isle, Ross-shire, at B.'s brother, Major Nicolson's, for about a week; and I saw a good deal of the people, both in preaching, prayer-meetings, and roadside talks. There are many bruised spirits in dark, helpless bondage. We are here for a night or two with the widow of John M'Donald, my predecessor in the Free Church, Calcutta. You know how dear his memory is to B., his spiritual daughter.

A few days later, I find the following letter to one of his office-bearers, dated *Perth, 29th October* 1866:

My dear Mr Low, — I was favoured with the minute of deacons' court, which you kindly sent me. I cannot express how much we were affected by the generous and affectionate way in which they were pleased to speak of me. The tie between them and me is now becoming old. I am sure that it is also growing warmer and stronger. I trust that, if not able in future to work so much as formerly, I shall yet be inclined and enabled to pray more for the congregational and individual prosperity of my friends. I observe the strong and united opinion expressed regarding the matter which was brought before the court. If anything could make me depart from the wish I feel, it would be that. But the wish remains unaltered, and, I think, unalterable. I meant it for a little thank-offering for the great kindness which we have at this time experienced both from God and man. I wish the deacons' court to accept this thank-offering at my hand, and to employ it in any way that seems conducive to the good of our common charge, the flock committed to our care. This will be a real relief and gratification to me.

I ask their and your prayers for my brother minister and myself, that we may walk in love, as we have ever done, and that we may be baptized afresh with the spirit of power and devotedness. — Believe me, very affectionately yours, John Milne.

He writes thus to a dear friend, whose son was starting for India:

I should like to shake hands with the emigrant, and bid him Godspeed. I shall bring a note or two with me; but Calcutta society changes very fast; and if I were to go back, I should find myself almost a stranger. I am glad that he goes into so good a house as the Messrs. Mackinnons. I love them all, and the Lord guides and prospers them … Give my love to him. I trust the Lord will give him the 121st Psalm. India is a good country for a man who *is* healthy, diligent, and fears God.

He writes thus to a friend in sorrow:

We remember you and your heart's desire and burden. I trust that at evening time it will be light. I hope Mr M. got the open mouth and found the open door. Nothing is too hard for him with whom we have to do. No solicitude is so interesting, no prayer so prevailing, as that of a child longing for the salvation of an aged, dying father. The long-suffering that has spared so long should fill you with hope and confidence. Somehow, at present, I seem to feel as if nothing will be withheld if we but humbly, trustfully ask.

His Care for Individuals

The following sketch of the Epistle to the Romans was written on the blank leaves of a copy of that epistle which he sent to a friend about this time:

This epistle opens with God as Judge. He sits upon the throne, and the world is summoned before him. Evidence is led, first, against the Gentiles, then against the Jews. The Judge sums up, and the verdict is pronounced. The criminal is speechless; he has nothing to say why the sentence of death should not be executed. This is the state of all men by nature. Oh that all men saw and felt it!

Then the Substitute, Surety, Redeemer is brought forward. He takes the condemned sinner's place; he is willing to do it, able to do it. God accepts this voluntary Surety, and lets him, in the room of the sinner, keep the law, pay the debts, endure the death. There is a complete transference. 'He was delivered for our offences, and raised again for our justification.' Thus God can be just, and yet forgive sinners; for he has received full satisfaction.

This is salvation. God is pleased with it, Christ is pleased with it. *Are you* pleased with it? Do you trust and rely upon it? Then it is yours, with all the blessings which it yields, such as peace with God, access to God, the friendship of God, the assurance of heaven. Your very trials now become blessings, and are cheerfully, hopefully borne, and your whole character is changed and ameliorated. You are peaceful, trustful, thankful; you try to be holy, kindly, living as a child of God, an heir of heaven, a pilgrim on earth, and seeking the good of all about you. It is a thoroughly good and reasonable religion.

Chap. 1:16-32. Evidence brought against the Gentiles.

Chap. 2. Evidence brought against the Jews.

Chap. 3:9-18. Judge summing up.

Chap. 3:19, 20. Nothing to plead in arrest of judgment.

Chap. 3:21-31. The way of redemption free to all by the Surety.

Chap. 4. An example and illustration of faith.

Chap. 5. Benefits of believing on Christ, and taking him as *our* Surety.

Chap. 6. Holiness and new obedience spring from faith in Christ.

Chap. 7. Conflict between the old and new nature.

Chap. 8. Living and walking in the Spirit.

Chap. 12. The holy, loving, kindly life and temper of a true believer.

These notes are written along the margin. To the same friend he would sometimes send a tract, with a word on it: 'I think this will interest you; it is rather a favourite of mine'; or leave a card at his door thus marked: 'With best wishes; John 1:29'; or 'Glad to hear that you are better; John 14:1-3.'

In October 1867, he wrote to the same friend, thanking him for some game, and continues:

I trust you are feeling better, and able to look forward hopefully to the coming winter. I am poorly myself, and so can sympathize with you; but may we both enjoy much of the peace and hope which spring from resting wholly on our loving and glorified Saviour. Dear friend, you know that I love you, and that my desire is, that we may meet at the Lord's right hand.

> Let me in peace resign my breath,
>   And Thy salvation see;
> My sins deserve the second death,
>   But Jesus died for me.

I hope, in a day or two, to call. It will be one of my first visits.

This gentleman was not a member of Milne's flock, but belonged to the Established Church. After Milne's death he wrote to a friend as follows:

I, with all others acquainted with Mr Milne, felt his death much. He was a sincere friend, and a Christian minister, whose whole aim and object was to do good and save souls. While he was always cheerful and lively, he ever had but one object in view; and if he happened to call and not find you at home, he left his card, generally with a reference to some text of Scripture that he wished you to consider. I have often, during my illness, wished I was prepared, like him, for the great change which must soon come.

Anecdotes

Such are some of the letters of this period. Let me now give some miscellaneous fragments and notices connected with it.

In a railway carriage, going a little way from London, an elderly gentleman was our only companion. Some remark was made about the name of a station, and the gentleman said he could give no decided information as he had been long abroad. This opened the conversation; he had been in Italy and Sicily. He described the sad state of those countries, and Mr Milne said, 'What will be the end of all this?' The gentleman replied, 'I ought rather to ask *you* that question, for I see you are a clergyman.' 'Well', said Mr Milne, rising up as he spoke, 'I think the Lord Jesus will come and put all to rights. *That* is my only hope for a sinful, distracted world.' The gentleman immediately stretched out his hand, and cordially shaking that of Mr Milne, said, 'Then we are at one. That is my hope too.' Mr Milne had almost immediately to leave the carriage, and parted with the new acquaintance as with a friend.

During a visit to London, at one of the metropolitan railway stations, while waiting for a train, he was interested with a fine little boy, whose father was pretending he would throw the child on the rails, much to the little fellow's amusement. At last Mr Milne said to the boy, 'Why are you not afraid? If he throws you down, you will be killed.' 'Oh!' said the child, with a shout of laughter, 'he's my papa.' Mr Milne paused a moment, and then turning to the gentleman, said, 'What a lesson your boy has taught us, that, under all circumstances, we should trust our heavenly Father that he will not hurt us!' and then walked on. In a few minutes the gentleman followed and said, 'It is very remarkable that you should have made that remark to me just now. I am now on my way to visit my own father, who is in a lunatic asylum, and I am afraid I have had hard thoughts of my heavenly Father; but — at that moment his train came up, and all he could add was, 'Thank you, thank you.'

An old servant was remarking that she scarcely ever passed him in the lobby without some word to raise her thoughts upward. His study chimney was very apt to smoke, and she was lamenting it to him one day, when he quietly said, 'Oh, never mind, Mary, the fashion of this world passeth away.'

Coming from church one afternoon he saw three women, in a humble rank of life, going out to walk on the Inch. One said to the others, 'Stop, I have lost something.' 'Yes,' said Mr Milne, 'stop; for though I do not know what you have lost, I know what you are losing.' They looked amazed. 'Yes', he continued, 'you are losing your Sabbath;

and if you lose your Sabbaths now, you will lose your souls by and by.' The women did stop and turned back to their house.

Walking in the country, near Bridge of Allan, he met a woman, to whom he offered a tract. She seemed most willing to take it, and he added, 'I hope you can say, Christ is mine.' She hesitated; so holding out the tract, he said, 'I offer you this, is it yours?' She said, 'Not till I have taken it.' 'Well', he said, 'it is the same with Christ. God, by his ministers, offers him to you. Accept of him, and then you can say, Christ is mine.'

Another day, near the Bridge of Allan, a shepherd overtook him, with a dog. Mr Milne spoke to the dog, and remarked that, though friendly enough, he would only follow his master; and then he said to that master, 'He teaches us how we should follow Christ.' He then said, 'Where are you going in such a haste?' 'Oh', said the shepherd, 'three of my sheep went astray last night, and I am going in search of them.' 'That's what the Lord Jesus does', said Mr Milne. 'He is ever seeking and taking care of his sheep. As you go on your way, think of these two lessons, — to follow your Master as your dog follows you; and because you are careful of your sheep, believe in the true Shepherd's care of his sheep.' The man was a Christian, and became much affected. A few words of prayer closed the meeting.

He had preached one Sabbath on 'The harvest is past, the summer is ended, and we are not saved'; and during the course of the following week he saw one of his people walking along with a companion. He went up, and putting his hand on his friend's shoulder, said, '"The harvest is past, the summer *is* ended, and we are not saved" — are You saved?' and immediately passed. His friend's companion said, 'Was not that very forward and uncalled for?' 'No', said the other, 'it is a most important question.' That question led to a true conversion.

One night dining with a friend, the song was sung, 'There's nae luck aboot the house.' Some one admired the sentiments it expressed. Mr Milne did so too, but added, that such expressions in their fullest meaning ought only to apply to the Lord. The singer rather demurred and laughed at the idea; but an interesting conversation followed which arrested all present. Mr Milne used to say that all the Jacobite songs in praise of Prince Charlie, only showed what the Christian's feeling should be to King Jesus. The young man who sung the ballad became quite solemnized, and on his way home, said, 'Well, if I were much with these good people, I think I should become good myself.' The lady, in whose house the party met, says, 'Mr Milne's spiritual tone quite elevated all of them.'

On Sabbath, a Roman Catholic girl was brought to the house in great distress. She had been going to Protestant churches, and her relations threatened to take her life if she did so, while yet she could not stay away, as she felt the life of her soul was at stake. From fear, she was quite ill. She was sent to bed in the manse, and permission was obtained from her mistress to remain for a few days. Two evenings after, the Roman Catholic priest came to the house, and accused Mr Milne of trying to draw away his people. Mr Milne was quite calm, and said, 'Not so, the girl was an entire stranger to me. I never saw her till I saw her in my own house, where she had been brought by one of my people. She was in trouble, and we have shown her kindness.' The priest said something, why had she been brought to Mr Milne's house. 'I suppose', said Mr Milne, 'because my people know that my house and my purse are ever open to them. If one of my people', he continued, 'had been taken to your house, I think you would have acted as I have done. I give you credit for being earnest, and acting up to your light — I only wish that light were clearer. Will you not give me the same credit?' The priest was angry, and asked, Might not her friends see her? 'Oh, certainly', said Mr Milne, 'and she can go away whenever she likes; but no force must be used to take her away.' The girl remained for some days; and though afterwards she lost her reason and destroyed herself, yet she seems truly to have known the Lord Jesus.

One now residing in Canada, but who long sat under Mr Andrew Gray's ministry, writing last year to a friend in Perth, and alluding to his religious views, says: 'Talking of my theology, let me give John Milne justice. My first perfectly clear view of saving truth was from him. "We are saved", said he to me one day in my shop, "*by a person.*" Immediately the truth flashed into my mind.'

He was very fond of children, and almost every child in Perth knew him. Constantly, in the street, he would stop to play ball with one, or throw the skipping rope with another. One writes: 'He used to be so kind to our children one winter, giving them slides; and one day, when he met them going to the post-office, he spoke and passed on, but ran back again, and putting his arm round J.'s neck, walked along, telling him about the little boy in Germany who wrote a letter to the dear Lord Jesus. He did not then know who the children were, for he never asked their names.'

The following extract of a letter from Ontario, Canada, July 1868, to Mrs Milne, may come in here, as containing some incidents of his life:

You can conceive our mutual feelings, when dining lately with a young man converted under Mr Milne's preaching in Perth. I said to him, 'Did you hear of the illness of our friend Mr Milne?' and he replied, 'Did you not hear of his death?' My mother had written me of your precious husband's illness, but my friend had received a newspaper account of his death. Oh how many feelings this sudden news created within me! I cannot call it bad news; for to hear that a Christian has gone to heaven is never bad news.

At the great Convention of Young Men's Christian Associations of the United States and British Provinces, I had the opportunity of telling of the first serious interview I had with Mr Milne, and repeating his memorable words that morning, as he took his watch out of his pocket, and said, "Dear Mr B., I am so glad to see you in this state; but as, when God is saving the soul of a man, he does not require to take the time that belongs to his fellow-man, so it *is* now five minutes to your office hour, and I will not therefore stop to speak to you. One word of prayer first; and then, as the carriage drives you to office, you will be able perhaps to glance at the first page or two of this little book, and be able, even in that short time, to find that as great a sinner as you found mercy; and I will come to see you after office hours." Well do I remember the first letter I wrote Mr Milne, *daring* him to come and see me, unless he got a direct message of mercy for me *on his knees.* Never will I forget the impression his words above quoted made upon me. I saw he was a man who gave God all the *power* and the *glory,* and this made me trust him with all my heart.

The Master's Coming

The incident referred to in the foregoing letter must have occurred in 1854, or quite the end of 1853. Further on, the writer says that he mentions it lest any memoir might be written; as it seemed to him to be a good illustration of Milne's *tact* in winning souls to Christ. The writer has been a consistent Christian ever since. Our readers may be interested by the conclusion of his letter:

> How few seem to receive the comfort of the *first* resurrection in the way Dr H. Bonar views it! Am I mistaken in thinking Mr Milne was a partaker of his views of the pre-millennial advent? How often will you now say, 'No shadows yonder!' May you more and more enjoy the truth Mr Milne once taught me, as he said, 'I love all the 23d Psalm; but the sweetest words to me in it are these, *"He restoreth my soul."*' God be praised, who met me in the way by his dear servant your husband. What a bright crown his must be! He literally turned *many* to right-eousness, and very many more, I doubt not, than he ever knew of. The seed he has cast upon the waters has not been all found yet.

Looking Upwards

Let us now turn to his own journal. We cannot give it fully; but the following extracts will be interesting:

> *Perth, 7th June 1867. — Friday night.* — It is very long since I have made any jottings of the Lord's dealings with me, or of my own spir-itual experience. I know the dangers connected with doing this; but I miss the benefits which used to derive from my poor attempts to

preserve a few spiritual memoranda. I have now entered my sixty-first year, so that my life is drawing near to its close. I have also had some very marked warnings, which assure me that the end of it comes near, and may be very sudden. I seek to live under a happy belief that my Master will come, and may come at any time. I want, therefore, to be more watchful, earnest, prayerful; more happy, holy, and devoted. I know something of my besetting sins, and desire to deny and keep them under. Help me, therefore, Lord, to pass each day in review under thine eye, and so to give thanks, or ask mercy and grace, according to my need. This day has been a varied one; trial in the morning, in which, I fear, I failed somewhat, being taken by surprise from the unexpected nature of the trial. Let me keep in the secret place, and so I shall abide under the shadow of the Almighty, and never be afraid. Some help in preparing for Sabbath, and so some hope that there may be blessing. Peaceful and quiet at the close; but not much girt up, and little spring. I have a hope that it is with me a time between two tides. I know that hitherto I have acted too much under the impulse of self, the flesh, excitement, present things, the sudden view of the moment, man's favour and power. I believe the Lord is delivering me from this; the tide has ebbed away; and I am like a ship that is aground. May I be content; weaned from all that; fearful of being carried away with it again. May I be enabled, in faith and patience, to wait for a better flood, — the river which makes glad the city of God, the life which is hid with Christ in God!

8th June. — Saturday night. — This has been a very quiet, peaceful day, both outwardly and inwardly. I have been preparing for tomorrow, and have desire and hope of blessing. Several things feed this expectation, and I think it will not be disappointed. I am longing for a shower of the blessing which is falling freely in many places both of England and Scotland. It has come very near us on several hands, but has not yet appeared here. — Except in two or three, I see little interest or concern about it. But I know how easily the Lord could rouse the whole community, so I am trying to wait patiently.

June 9th. — Sabbath night. — A quiet day; not much sensible help; not much vigour in my work. I feel as if the Lord were training me to lean more on him, both in preaching and prayer. It is selfishness and unbelief that stand in the way; but the Lord can shine away both these dark shadows. It will be a blessed freedom when they are greatly away. A nice meeting at night, to hear about a work of God in Derbyshire and at Auchterarder. I trust the Lord is preparing us for another outbreak of grace here. Lord, help me this week; make it remarkable for holiness and blessedness! Great help and comfort in thinking of the passages which seem to be suggested to my mind.

10th June. — *Monday night.* — Another quiet day; some trial, but overruled. Enabled to cheer and comfort some. Last night a good deal awake, but finding communion and profitable meditation. The thoughts and texts have passed away, but I was the better for them at the time, and perhaps they will be restored by the Remembrancer. One thought was, that Christ's mediation is the only way in which God can *forget* and *forgive* sin, and in which the sinner's conscience can find a perfect and everlasting rest. I have tried today to cleave to Christ, to abide in the secret place, to have an appetite for the word of God, to care for my fellow-man, and to remember the Master's coming. Lord forgive, bless, and prosper the little note I have been writing. Let it do some good, and not any harm.

11th June. — *Tuesday evening.* — Much at home; writing letters; jaded, but somewhat restored again. It is a great blessing when we learn to stop and turn to the Lord before we are oppressed, and the spirit becomes flat and without spring. Rejoice in the Lord alway. Prayer, the word, meditation, uplift and brace again. The living water springs up afresh.

12th June. — *Wednesday evening.* — Many blessings today; scarcely anything like trial, except the longing to be more lively and spiritual. There seems a divine *couleur de rose* over everything. I feel it a great help to live a quiet, retired life. The Lord prospers me in my desire to avoid being engrossed, carried away, or overburdened. A happy prayer-meeting tonight. Give help and blessing for the coming Sabbath.

13th June. — *Thursday night.* — Helped and encouraged today in various ways. The little note I sent to the — seems to have been blessed, and to have found favour. Dr B. writes very kindly and thankfully about it. I met today with a record of my longings, many years ago, for revival on my soul and ministry: 'That I may preach differently, be more full in setting forth Christ, more fearless in unfolding the law, more faithful in rebuke, more tender in entreaty, more winning in persuasion, have more singleness of purpose, more devotedness to my work, more seriousness in public, less levity in private, more willingness to work, and yet find that work does not weary, nor labour fatigue.' I fancy these are very much my desires today. Perhaps there is little now of the levity of early days. I cannot work now as then. But there is still the desire, and it is a far greater cross to hold in and forbear, than it would be to give rein and rush on. What I desire now is, that it may not be an occasional and passing impulse of grace, but a continuous habit, a walking in the spirit, and so not fulfilling the lusts of the flesh. I think I know now better what I ignorantly asked, — *singleness* of purpose. I know more of the impurity, the subtle mixture, the cleaving of self to all we do. It is the sediment, the dark shadow; but Christ can deliver men from this. I find it a great secret of uninterrupted peace and life not to go on working at anything till the soul becomes jaded, and conscious communion is broken. It needs much watchfulness and self-denial to avoid this. I should stop at once, and wait on the Lord. 'I count all things loss', *etc*. This is the secret. I have been thinking of the infinite originality and variousness of God's contrivances in his works and ways. How wonderful, how admirable is God!'

14th June. — Friday night. — Bless the Lord, O my soul! I never really looked to thee without being lightened. I never waited on thee without getting renewal of strength. I bless thee for this quiet day, and for the pleasant upspringing of hope in my soul. It is the peace which passeth understanding, for I cannot explain it; but the God who has given it now can give it again.

22d June. — Saturday morning. — During the night I thought of Ephesians 6: 'Stand therefore', *etc*. 'That ye may withstand in the evil day, and having done all, to stand.' Stand *before*, stand *in*, and stand

after the fight. This standing is a most important thing. It implies
wakefulness, preparation, watchfulness, determination, faith, and
calmness. The timid and fearful flee; Elijah stands. We stand in grace
before God (*Rom.* 5:2). Am I standing this morning? Then let me hold
on. I suppose this is implied in Gideon's little troop; they stoop down
and lap the water, but are ready in an instant to resume the standing
position; so may I be in regard to earthly things, only stooping for
a moment and sipping a little for refreshment. Yet there is a lying
down. Psalm 23: 'He maketh me to lie down.' But this is safe; we
rise strengthened and hopeful, and he is watching. Help me today to
prepare, and do thou bless, greatly honour.

Quiet Thoughts

24th June. — Monday evening. — Yesterday was peaceful. Some comfort in preaching; but a deep conviction that it is the hand of the Lord,
the Spirit of the Lord, that awakens, convinces, saves. Hear now of the
work of God at Tullibody. No house without some awakened. When
will the Lord visit us? May I, in the power and liberty of faith, seek
this one thing. Let me not *run* before, but wait and renew my strength.
Evening. — Some unexpected encouragement today. Help me to live
for thee, under thine eye. Let me walk in the life and light, and dwell
within sight of the new Jerusalem. Let my days be a jubilee.

25th June. — Tuesday morning. — Trials of faith last night, and failing where I have often failed. But checked, and enabled somewhat
to make head against the evil. I feel this morning how little I know
of the word, and how often I forget and lose the benefit of what I do
know. I look to thee for seasonable help, for watering every moment.
Let the Remembrancer aid me seasonably and effectually. Thy word
is spirit and life.

26th June. — Wednesday morning. — Peaceful yesterday. Help me in
writing and preparing. Yet reminded several times that evil is within
me and without, and that I need the watering every moment. Hold
me in, hold me up, and *so* I shall go on in this way. Quicken me. 'Yet
learned he obedience by the things which he suffered.' Let me learn

in the same way; and may I not cast away my confidence, or faint when I am tried. Help me in preparing for Sabbath, and give courage and hope.

28th June. — Friday morning. — How much we feed, or try to feed, upon ourselves, our own works, plans, feelings, fears, trials! But the Lord says, 'I am the bread of life; come unto me and hunger no more, believe in me and thirst no more.' God is satisfied with him, why should not we? Let me wait for the Lord, so shall I be ever full. Let me not wait for earthly things, for then I shall have constant disappointment.

29th June. — Saturday morning. — I know the Lord is dealing with me in the way of merciful chastisement. In one case he is starving a besetting sin, and withholding gratification. He is taking the work of mortification into his own hand. I kiss the rod; and yet I believe that he will restore these naturally good things, when I can safely enjoy and use them. Let me wait and mark his hand. In another case he has given the rein for a moment to my evil, that I might see how lively it still is, and that I might be stirred up to faith in a crucified Lord, to watchfulness and prayer. David prays, 'Cast me not out of thy sight.' Jonah says, 'I am cast out of thy sight; yet I will look again toward thy holy temple.' Last night reading Dr Marsh's Life; a truly sunny Christian, taught and blessed of God. But I read too long, and had to hurry to bed, and I suffered for it. Communion with the best of God's people will not compensate for the loss of communion with himself. 'Let your moderation be known unto all men.' But we have an Advocate and a fountain. If the blood of bulls and goats gave Israel confidence and boldness to worship in the earthly temple, surely the blood of Christ ought to give us boldness and confidence, ought to give us a good and purged conscience. I wait for God, my soul doth wait.

I feel that I have sinned Hezekiah's sin today. I know not what spirit I am of. Lord, forgive, heal, spare, and make me watchful, self-denying, henceforth.

Night Musings

2d July. — *Tuesday morning.* — Yesterday was a busy day, both in home work and in meeting with friends. It was also comparatively peaceful and happy. But last night, while lying awake, I saw much hollowness in it; a good deal unintentionally of Hezekiah's sin, and little direct conscious fellowship with the Lord. Self sadly interrupts and mars the living with and for the Lord. I like these night thoughts. Peter's 'Lord, save me!' struck me much; also what Paul speaks of, as one end of Christ's death, to take away the middle wall of partition, and make Jew and Gentile *one* new man; and again, John, that he should die to *gather* into one the children of God who are scattered abroad. Satan is the scatterer; Jesus the gatherer: the former breaks down; the latter heals the breach.

6th July. — *Saturday afternoon.* — A short season of darkness, with-eredness, and bondage. It was trying; but I was enabled in a measure to possess my soul in patience. In the morning before I rose, I felt, most unexpectedly, a gracious melting of soul; the cloud was lifted; my soul could again work freely. This has continued more or less up to this time. I am thankful and encouraged, and I hope for good tomorrow. Letters about the Conference. I had hoped to keep out of it, not being strong; and my wife, most dear and needful to me, little fitted at present, from weakness, for the stir and toil always connected with it. Lord, guide; make willing to see thy will and way.

12th July. — *Friday night.* — On Wednesday in Edinburgh, at Moody Stuart's, attending a meeting of ministers for prayer and conference. It was solemn, interesting, useful. Some valuable suggestions, and desire and hope of blessing. Yesterday, help in drawing up programme of Conference. May the Lord guide, help, and prosper! Today busy, but rather feeble, and some temptation. Benefit from reading Dr Leifchild's Life, though it is far from being my *beau ideal.* Give me more and more of thy Holy Spirit in constancy and power. May I not grieve, vex, or quench him.

16th July. — *Tuesday morning.* — Saturday quiet. Sabbath, a temptation in the morning, but enabled to overcome, and the rest of the day strengthened and upheld. Yesterday, weary and somewhat feeble. This morning refreshed, but sensible that sin has revival too, and watches its opportunity. I desire not only to live in the Spirit, but to *walk* in the Spirit. May my heart be ever right and honest with God. How apt we are to think and act as if he were like ourselves; yea, we are more apt to fear and honour our fellow-men than the Lord! How hateful and vile this is!

27th July. — *Saturday evening.* — Still very feeble; a constant growing confusion of head, with pain when I try to think, and great uneasiness and shrinking when unexpected call to effort comes. I have passed through similar trials before; but then I was proud and evil, and so was pierced through with many sorrows. I think, indeed, that the Lord is humbling me, breaking my will, abolishing my idols, and teaching me obedience. Lord, help. Thou knowest how needful thy guidance and support is, when we are going down into the valley. Let not my spirit fail, and the soul which thou hast made; but restore and comfort with thy seasonable, effectual visitations and revivings. Help this day, and give a new song. It seems like martyrdom going on in this weak, helpless state; but thou givest the conquest to the weak. I hear from several quarters that the Lord is with me in my work, and I desire to be encouraged and yet to be humble. 'When Ephraim spoke trembling', *etc.*

The Conflict

1st August. — *Thursday morning:* — *Yesterday* engaged all the day at very blessed meetings with the General Assembly's deputation on the state of religion. Today jaded and cast down. I feel that I am laid aside from active work, and foresee that the trial will be great. But the Lord can enable me to sit still and wait … Several *lessons* today; prayer and patience from Curlie;[1] the evil of giving way to trial, and grieving over it; the blessing of occupying ourselves in helping others. We then forget ourselves, and recover a measure of cheerfulness. Sensible now

[1] The little dog.

and then of a little progress in subduing and putting self away. It is pitiable and ludicrous how it wriggles itself into everything, and the contemptible roundabout, recondite shifts it has recourse to in order to draw attention and give the impression of its importance. It will need much discipline and constant watchfulness to keep it down; but it will never be fully removed till the *coup de grace* is given or the redemption of the body comes.

3rd August. — *Saturday morning.* — Yesterday a very bustling day, visiting the sick, and a great many friends coming in and staying till near midnight. But somewhat kept through all the stir. Yet failed twice, through want of watchfulness and determined purpose. We cannot continue holy except by *constant conscious* fellowship with the Lord. There must be a continual, uninterrupted dying, that the life of Jesus may be manifested in us. How soon we weary and relax! Thus the old enemies get an opportunity, and then shame, doubt, and fear prevail, till the Lord in mercy restores. Keep me henceforth from falling, and present me faultless before thy presence with exceeding joy. It seems impossible at present to realize perfect, everlasting holiness.

5th August. — *Monday morning.* — Yesterday quiet. Now leaving home to go for quiet to Newport for a fortnight. May we have much prayer and meditation there! Keep those who go and those who stay, and give a new song.

7th August. — *Wednesday morning.* — We did not get away on Monday in consequence of heavy rain. But we saw the good hand of the Lord in the delay. Came down yesterday in comfort; stood within a few feet of the spot where Robert Annan went down for the last time. A man who was throwing him a rope, told me that his last conscious effort was to push the drowning boy to the surface, so that he might be taken up by the approaching boat, while he himself went down. He did not live in vain, far less did he die in vain. He was one of heaven's nobles, and his end was enviable. But all the glory was the Lord's, who took the devil's burning brand and made it a pillar in the temple of the Lord for ever. Grant us grace to serve and glorify thee, O Lord, in the perfect quiet of this place. Prepare blessing for Perth.

9th August. — I feel that the Lord is leading and keeping me right, notwithstanding my own blindness, unwatchfulness, and self-willedness. I have many evident proofs of this. I desire never to murmur or despond, but quietly, patiently wait for the end God is working here. I have seen some lately converted lads, the inmates of a bothy. It is another instance of the living kindling the dead. I see that much prayer seems always to precede conversion work. I see also that few can bear to be instruments in conversion, there is such a tendency to become proud and lifted up.

16th August. — *Friday morning.* — I have been learning a good deal since I wrote last. Ups and downs, temptations and deliverances. Give me the abiding use of this; give me a new name, — 'Christ-seeker', 'Christ-pleaser'; take self away, and do it as thou seest best.

4th September. — At home. Many ups and downs since I wrote last; some feebleness of health, but a good deal of heart-searching and divine teaching, and certainly some progress. I have been asking sunny weather for the sake of the fruits of the earth; also a blessing on the British Association, that they may get light from on high, and rise from the lower works to the Creator, Preserver, Redeemer; also for a great and varied blessing on the Conference. I am waiting for the answers, and know that they will come. I feel strangely *kept* and peaceful. These words are meat to me this morning, 'Abide in me, and I in you, and ye shall bring forth much fruit; and if ye abide in me, and my words abide in you, ye shall ask what ye will, and it shall be done unto you.' But how fickle and changeable my heart! If I say, or begin to feel, that by God's favour my mountain stands, I speedily find that I am but a withered leaf, a rolling thing before the wind. Much pleasant intercourse one day with good Mr Hargrove, who stopped with us in passing. His has been a strange history; but he has learned very much, and, like a stone in constant motion, has become smoothed and rounded. He thinks love the way to men's hearts. May my heart be more full of love to souls, and my words more dipped in love! I must be dead, and Christ must live in me that I may be truly useful to my fellow-men.

Preparing for the Conference

9th September. — *Monday morning.* — Still moving on; a good deal of occupation in preparing for the Conference; but strangely kept and guided. I wonder and admire the long-suffering of the Lord. I feel that I am in the border land, — not the near but the far border; not the banks of the Red Sea, but the banks of Jordan. I feel the cross proving more precious; that wondrous cross, where God and man meet, righteousness and peace meet, where things in heaven and things on earth meet. Lord, lead and guide all through the week, and prosper and bless. May there be much prevailing prayer!

19th September. — *Thursday morning.* — The Conference has come and gone. I enjoyed it at the time, and the benefit remains. It has been the best we have yet had, and I have got more personal good from it, and not been much wearied. There were things that threatened evil; but they have been turned to good, and, I hope, great and lasting good. Thanks and praise be to the Master of assemblies! I feel that his goodness and loving-kindness are humbling me to the dust, and making me more and more his own for ever. Let the old things wholly pass away; let self and love of sin be wholly gone; and let me anticipate growingly the full redemption, the deliverance from the bondage of sin, and the being brought into the glorious liberty of the sons of God. Felt, in studying the 69th Psalm yesterday, in a way I had never done before. There was the sense of union with Christ in his sufferings. I had fellowship with him. I find this very healthful.

26th September. — *Thursday morning.* — I have had much and profitable teaching from day to day; much to humble, quicken, and make me watchful; but a growing sense of the Lord's love and care. He seems very near, and I feel that his eye is upon me, and I like to have it so. That word, 'I the Lord thy God am a *jealous* God', seems to be getting a hold upon me, and, in connection with this, the word *duty.* I feel my chief concern in anything should be, not, How will this look? How will it tell upon my interest and comfort? but, How will it affect my Lord? Will it please, honour, serve him? May this abide and grow till God becomes all in all, and it be my meat to do my Father's will, and help on his glory!

2d October. — *Wednesday morning.* — Moving quietly on, and getting teaching both night and day. Saturday morning some brokenness of heart, yet a measure of self in it. Sabbath some help, but over-driven. Monday night called out, after I had undressed to go to bed, to see a girl dying apparently, and in deep despair. Her cries for mercy were very affecting. Tuesday morning found her exhausted and quiet, and, I believe, the cloud passing away. May what we saw and heard that night be blessed to us all! I have been thinking about the office of the evangelist. It is Christ's gift to the church, and yet it is neither recognised nor much used. Teach me, and lead me into the truth concerning it. May they not correspond to the judges in old times, sent forth immediately by God? 'It is not in man that walketh to direct his steps.' We err by running when we should sit still, and sitting still when we should run.

3d October. — *Thursday evening.* — Weary and jaded yesterday, and so tired I found that nature and the flesh take advantage, and so old sins and stumbling-blocks return. But also divine kindness, help, and deliverance, and so I desire to bless the Lord, and to hope continually. Give me constant guidance, and teach me to seek for it, and expect it.

The Religion of Patient Waiting

9th October. — *Wednesday morning.* — Weary, jaded, but quiet, and not cast down. I must sit still. This is religion at present. Nature and the flesh would drive me out. But this is a temptation; it springs from unbelief, and looking to man. Christ's yoke is easy; just sit still. Several deaths of friends. Great loss of property at Dundee by fire. Our Town Council, against the remonstrance of a faithful minority, resolve to restore the drunken booths on the Inch at the races. Prosperous drink-sellers, holding office, and having influence in the Church! Calamities to my old church at Calcutta. Mr Pourie very ill, and Mr Don obliged to leave charge of it, at least for a time. Few among us, I fear, thorough and simple on the Lord's side. Self-interest, fear of man, and unbelief largely rule; but the Lord ruleth. He doeth his will, he leads the blind by a way they know not, he tries and strengthens their patience. It is good to wait on the Lord, and to hope in him. I would learn to be wholly given up to him. I find by experience that this is very blessed. I have been trying to get my way most of my life; and had I got it, I should have been destroyed long ago. I see ceaseless, marvellous mercy and patience, and I desire to close my eyes and say, Lead, Saviour, lead.

14th October. — Monday morning. — Still kept in the house by illness; but enabled to preach yesterday with real comfort, and so thankful and peaceful. Still a prisoner, and obliged to give up thought of going to Mr Riddell at Dundee on Thursday. I gratefully feel that I am much changed in these things, and can quietly, hopefully say, 'Not my will, but thine be done.' Lord, teach and help me to count all things small and little in comparison with thyself. Write thy law upon my heart; let me supremely love and enjoy thee; and let all creatures be enjoyed in thee. It is thy blessing which gives the enjoyment of any-thing. God gives a heart to enjoy, else our possessions are only vanity and vexation of spirit. Without thee we cannot think, do, speak. 'It is not ye that speak, but the Spirit of your Father that speaketh in you.' 'Let your speech be alway with grace, seasoned with salt.' We can only pray truly in the Holy Ghost. We cannot see, cannot hear, without the Spirit. Lord, teach me in all things, and help me continually to realize it; so shall I be contented, thankful, looking only to the Lord, and waiting only on him.

18th October. — Friday forenoon. — Feeble in body. Bad influenza; but able to visit the sick yesterday, and to walk out a little today. Very happy in the Lord, who is literally loading me with benefits, and making me ashamed of doubts and fears. It is the race week; but I am unable this year to do anything. The little book about the Conference is published, and selling well. I am not sure that I have ever felt a real solid sense of bodily weakness till now. There was always a feeling of latent strength which had only to be called out, and it would appear. It seems as if this did not exist now; so I fall back upon the Lord, assured that 'as the days, so the strength.

20th October. — Sabbath evening. — Helped today in preaching, and peaceful, but still very weak. Help, Lord, in preparing for coming communion. Give suitably, seasonably, abundantly, both in body and soul.

22d October. — Tuesday. — Have heard of good received from the sermon of Sabbath. I feel encouraged, and thankful. Met with a man who has long been doltish and stupid, as if he had not a soul. He is now ill, and appears awakened, and, I trust, really calling on the Lord. I have hope of another man, a stranger, who seems dying. These things stir me up to hope for great blessing on the coming Sabbath, our communion.

30th October. — Wednesday morning. — The communion seemed a blessed time. I felt it helpful and strengthening. The Lord blesses and helps in various ways. But I am sensible that my head needs complete rest for a little; and I hope to get it. I think the Lord is drawing up and fixing my thoughts upon himself, as on a centre and focus. I trust this will go on, and that I shall be enabled to say, 'My heart is fixed. I have set the Lord always before me. He is at my right hand, I shall not be moved.'

1st November. — Friday. — Last night was our special meeting of workers, and seems to have been hearty and useful. The Lord seems to have guided and overruled, and I believe it will help to quicken, encourage, and knit together. It was a trial to be absent; but I saw the Lord's will in it, and I had a very peaceful night while B. was at the meeting. Surely the Lord is teaching and training me.

11th November. — Bridge of Allan. — Monday. — We have been here since last Monday, and have much enjoyed and been benefited by our stay. Both soul and body are better. We are very quiet, alone, very much with God, and hope to be more rooted, grounded, and settled than we have ever been. Many thoughts have been occurring, and subjects opened up; and I trust the Spirit, the remembrancer, will bring them seasonably back when they can be followed out and made useful. At any rate, it shows me what riches the Lord has to give.

23rd November. — Home. — We returned on Monday, better for a season of quiet and rest. The Lord seems to be blessing the flock.

There have been some interesting meetings, and both minister and elders are hopeful.

Faint Yet Pursuing

27th December. — Friday. — I am still utterly weak and feeble. My head refuses to think fixedly, and becomes confused and pained the moment I begin to urge it to act. There is no freshness or upspring. It seems dead, dry, useless. I suspect that this is going to be a longer and sorer trial than I have yet suspected. The trial is increased by being in the midst of my usual work, and yet absolutely incapable of taking part in it. My rest will begin when I am able to say, 'It is the Lord'; he is taking his own way, and who could turn him back — who could wish to turn him back? I would not, I do not. I want to be as clay in his hands; and I only ask strength and patience to resist the suggestions of the devil, and the words or looks of ignorant, unsympathizing men. I am sure that God is dealing with me in kindness, and leading me in a right way. Close my eyes and say, 'Lead, Lord.' Let me leave off struggling, and quietly accept the chastisement and the teaching. I have been delaying the blessing by my efforts to be what the world calls *'myself'* again. I believe the Lord means I should never be myself; and I am losing the desire to be myself again. I want to cease from the past, and be a new creature, a new vessel, the handiwork, and, perhaps in some way yet, the glory of the Lord. I pray that I may be enabled to accept my dispensation, to sit still, be of no strength, be helpless, even though some will say it is sloth, self-indulgence.

Ministerial Power

In all these journals, as in his letters, the single eye is manifest. He left home for *one* object; he went to India for *one* object; he lived in Calcutta for *one* object; he returned home for *one* object; and this *one* object shows itself in every page he writes. Toil, reproach, suffering, self-denial are nothing to him if he can serve Christ and win a soul. Power with God, whereby he may assail the fortresses of the Evil One in that land of idols or in this land of worldliness, is what he seeks. And the life he lives, so high above the common rate and the common level, tells how thoroughly in earnest he is. He meddles with no politics, he mingles in no strife, he seeks no promotion. If he approaches the governor, it is to plead for missions. If he goes into a merchant's counting-house, it is with his Bible in hand. If he sits down at the tables of the rich, which he but seldom does, or at times joins their society, it is as Christ's minister. To win souls is his object — his passion; and to this everything must bend. He has got firm hold of the great Bible truth that *salvation* is his message, his mission; that everything short of this is failure, — eternal failure; that 'necessity is laid upon him' to deal with men personally about their immortal welfare; and hence he goes out and in as one believing all this. He goes into his closet, and he comes out of it, as one to whom life was nothing, save as the opportunity for serving the Master and winning souls. He knows, too, that every soul won to God is not merely a sinner saved, but a citizen gained, a new element of peace and order and love infused into the constitution of the realm, a new security found against mutiny in India, or lawlessness in England. Mutinies abroad may not be over, revolution at home may not be far off. The dread of a dark future is coming down upon many, who would rather not prophesy, if they could help it; and the one hope for ourselves, and for our children, lies not in what men call progress, or culture, or the diffusion of science, but in THE REGENERATION OF INDIVIDUAL SOULS BY THE POWER OF THE HOLY GHOST.

We dwell on this, not simply because the power of the pulpit is a question of the day, but because both Church and world have crossed the line of a new era, and are passing into a new phase of thought and action. Materialism is in the ascendant, — materialism, either in the form of that rationalism which rejects the spiritual, or of that ritualism which accepts the sensuous. The supernatural is pronounced incredible; and for this reason it is denied by scepticism and welcomed indiscriminately by superstition. The human is dislodging the divine, the visible the invisible. The ministry of the Holy Ghost is being supplanted by the ministry of the human intellect. Formalisms and ritualisms, — the one the embers of Judaism, the other the dregs of Paganism, — will not serve Satan's purpose much longer. They are repulsive to modern thought. They lack reality and robust manliness and coherent life. They are productive of no literature; they only emasculate and degrade. Yet man, instead of betaking himself to the one oracle of truth, is falling back upon his own 'intuitions', — upon that 'internal revelation', with which mysticism and infidelity are feeding his pride, and beguiling him away from the inspiration of prophets and apostles. The 'verifying faculty' which Rome placed in 'the Church', is now placed in the individual intellect; in both cases to the exclusion of the Scriptures and the rejection of the power of God.

Jerichos are thrown down by rams' horns. Red Seas are severed by a rod. Giants are slain by the sling and stone. So was it before the 'foolishness' of the gospel that the gods of Greece and Rome fell down, — a gospel not elaborated by Plato nor embellished by Demosthenes, but simply preached by one whose 'bodily presence was weak, and his speech contemptible'.

The power to please may be found anywhere; but the power to seize the conscience, and bring the sinner face to face with his own worthlessness and condemnation, must be had where John Milne, and William Burns, and Robert M'Cheyne sought and found it, — in simple faith and happy fellowship with God. The 'lightnings and thunderings and voices' that are to shake the world, must come 'out from the throne' (*Rev.* 4:5), and the illumination of the race must be from 'the seven lamps of fire, burning before the throne' (*Rev.* 4:5). Other lights are sparks of human kindling (*Isa.* 1:11), and go out in darkness; other voices are but as 'sounding brass or a tinkling cymbal'.

Chapter 17

1868
His Last Months

*W*hen speaking of Christ's second coming, John Milne said once and again, 'I may have to lie down a little before he comes.'[1] It was to be even so as he said.

Of this he seems to have had some forebodings, for, at his last communion, in October 1867, at the close of his sermon (on *Heb.* 2:14, 15, Death and Deliverance) he said, 'Should I not live to another communion, I wish you to know that I am quite happy.' After this he only preached three times. His last sermon was on the transfiguration.[2]

---

[1] In one of his last note-books he has the following broken thoughts as to the Lord's coming: 'Nature and grace cry for the glorified Christ to complete his work, to rectify disorders. All proclaims and demands his return, all but the unsanctified heart of man. There alone no voice is heard to welcome the mighty Stranger. Dawn is contemplated with hatred, horror, and dismay. Hearts united to the world's corruption, how will they hail an immortality of meekness, simplicity, and love? Whole hopes, prospects, and calculations bound up with the fortunes of the world, how will they bear to have him personally and visibly holding the reins? We marvel that he tarrieth so long. Numberless schemes of prophetic chronology, while they keep thoughts engaged on it, yet serve by differences God's purpose, and show that no absolute certainty is yet vouchsafed. Sure of event, uncertain of time, — knowledge and ignorance. Dimness of light leaves us in a state more suitable and profitable than either absolute ignorance or perfect knowledge, — awakens feelings which former would fail to excite, and latter would quench as they arose. But the very certainty which was meant as perpetual stimulant to watchfulness is abused to security, just as invisibility of God, which is perfection, leads to atheism.'

[2] On leaving for Edinburgh, he writes to his colleague: 'I send you the list of the class of young men. I told them last night that I am going away, and that you would

In the beginning of January 1868 he went to Edinburgh for medical consultation. Both his head and his heart were found to be affected; but his chief suffering was from the former. His depression was great. The following is his own statement:

Edinburgh, 57, Queen Street. — Friday, 17th January. — We have been here for more than a week. Professor Henderson says that diseased action of the heart is the cause of the fearful headaches from which I have been suffering. He enjoins absolute rest and abstinence for three months, at least, from all duty and brain work. I fancy I am beginning to improve a little under his treatment; but there are many backgoings and sinkings of heart. There are many and sore trials: sitting still when I used to be active, silent where I used to speak; being misunderstood by friends who see the outward appearance of health, and know not the inward sufferings, the aching, confused, and powerless head, the inability to think, speak, or write for a few moments, with the loss of power to do anything. It is a great trial, and during last night it seemed as if I were going to faint and give up the conflict. But that word at length seemed to be fulfilled, 'Thou hast delivered my soul from the battle which was against me.' I am more cheerful and hopeful today, and desire to go in the strength of the Lord. I need the shield and buckler, I need the powerful upspringing of the well of living water. I ask these things for thine own glory, and for the help and comfort of my dear wife, who has suffered and is suffering so much.

Forebodings

Shortly after Milne came to Edinburgh, I met Dr Henderson, who had been consulted medically as to the case. I remember the

take them up. It is a sore pang to leave them, for I am sure that there is among them the "making" of a number of good men. We shall ever remember one another in our diverse circumstances. We go to Edinburgh first; thus far we seem to see the Lord leading; where, afterwards, we cannot tell. It is a school of trial; but we have been in it before, and we have always found that the Lord is very gracious and merciful. I think the congregation is in a very living, loving, hearty, workful state. The Lord be with you.'

day well. It was a gloomy, wet, winter twilight, as I was returning home, between four and five o'clock, along the South Bridge. I learned that the case was a very serious one, hopeless so far as return to ministerial work was concerned; but holding out the possibility of prolonged life, if great care were taken, and entire rest secured. I saw that it was not a mere return of one of his old low moods; but that some deeper evil was at work in his system, — the original cause of these depressions now developing itself in a more decided form, the stroke received fifty-six years before now working out its long-resisted results.

Gatherings from a Ministry

I walked onwards with sad thoughts, wondering if now John Milne was to be taken from us, and if so, was there to be any record or memorial of one whose life had been so signally useful, but who, in the shape of authorship, had given nothing to the church but scattered papers written in various periodicals, likely soon to be lost sight of.[1] It was then that I thought of collecting into a volume these scattered articles. Being thus minded, I went to him next day and laid my plan before him. He evidently liked it; but modestly

---

[1] The following entry, in one of his Indian journals, touchingly records his own feelings on this point: 'While speaking with B., a dart, as it were, pierced my heart. The sudden thought that all my ministerial life I have given myself to visiting, preaching, dealing with souls, instead of studying systematically. I have prepared nothing that can outlive me, and my work must cease with myself. I shall be like a bubble on the water. It was bitter; but I think I was willing, after a little, to be a hewer of wood and drawer of water, a doorkeeper in his house. Lord, in mercy forgive, wash, sanctify, use me as thou seest good.' But even though he had not given us his 'gatherings', his life will live after him, and his works do follow him. His service is not yet done. His voice is not yet silent, and his last sermon is not yet preached. To show how he was cheered by the thought of usefulness through the press, I quote the following note to Professor Smeaton on the 4th February 1867: 'MY DEAR BROTHER, — Thank you very much for your kind, cheering words. I don't know how I have got so much connected with *The Revival* [magazine]; but your note encourages me to go on. I regret, with you, the strong and frequent advocacy of female preaching, which I regard as an unwomanly, unnatural, and unscriptural thing.'

said that it would not do, the book would not sell, the thing would be presumptuous, he could not venture on such a volume. I told him, however, that I would undertake to get the whole thing done for him, if he would just give me his consent. He did so, and we resolved to proceed. Mrs Milne had carefully preserved copies of all the periodicals in which the papers had been inserted, so that there remained no difficulty. He was quite willing, though still diffident, to let me go on with the arrangements for publication, and felt that it would be a pleasant work for him to carry the volume through the press, and that it would almost make him feel that he was still useful, and still able to speak. Thus he wrote to me, when sending the papers:

> MY VERY DEAR HORACE, — Here are my wife's gatherings. But I am quite out of all regard for them, and think it would be presumption, and probably serious loss, to promote them to the honour you spoke of. I only send them because you asked me to do it. It is kind of you to glance at them. Just let them lie beside you, and we can pick them up the next time we come to you. We enjoyed our visit so very much, and were greatly the better for it. Pray for us that we may be strengthened unto all patience, and especially for B., who suffers more than I. But we should both like to quit us as the followers of a crucified Saviour. Very much love from us both to you all. — Very affectionately yours, J. M.

I did *not* let them lie beside me, but set about arranging them and preparing them for the printer. They were printed without delay, and form a most handsome volume, which has met with warm acceptance in many quarters, and presents as authentic a specimen of the preaching of Milne as can be done through the press, in a case where the voice and the tone and the manner contributed so much to the power of the preacher's message. He cared little about elaboration and style, but poured out his full heart and well-stored mind in words which critics might carp at, but which admirably expressed the speaker's meaning, and never missed the mark. If point, and directness, and vigorous English, and vivid illustration, and well-expounded truth be the main elements of pulpit power, Milne possessed them all. He had no time to polish, and he had no wish to divide his hearers' attention between the figure and the truth. He spoke right into his hearers' eyes and hearts, using great plainness of speech, yet speaking oftentimes with amazing power, as if discharging a whole quiverful of arrows.

> Ambitious not to shine or to excel,
> But to treat justly what he loved so well.

In the message the messenger was lost sight of. The word was everything, the speaker nothing. Yet Milne, had he chosen it, could have embellished and elaborated; for he was a student, and a scholar.

But he eschewed 'the wisdom of words, lest the cross of Christ should be made of none effect' (*1 Cor.* 1:17). He was illustrative, no doubt, in his preaching; but he knew the difference between figures that *enforce* and figures that *supplant* truth. The truth was foremost and uppermost, the embroidery was subordinate. With what power those direct, keen, vehement, yet loving appeals came home, those can best tell who have heard them. They were resistless, because so natural, so spontaneous, so unstudied, yet so devoid of everything that was coarse or unpleasant either in manner or in language. For his voice and tone were thoroughly *natural*. No one could accuse him of simpering, or whining, or speaking in a falsetto voice. That voice, even when most vehement or most tender, was always his own. I give here some fragments for ministers contained in one of his latest pocket-books:

> Placed on the bank of a mighty river, which bears multitudes of perishing, our business is to ply net and drag to extricate. Gracious promises of success. Leave all. Take heed. Watchman! … Want of call. Not waiting for word of Lord. Not knowing and not declaring whole

counsel. Sloth, fear of man, restraint of prayer, want of Spirit, because not in sympathy, not tending flock, not dealing closely ... Ministers should be able to show register of spiritual birth and of divine call to office. Have mind fully made up to live to God's glory, to live faithfully to Church; go into the kingdom himself, and carry many with him; purify himself as Christ is pure. Should go about work with Christ's fortitude; be much among his flock; and not suffer himself to be discouraged. When things go heavily, it may profit ourselves, keep from presumption, make acquainted with selves, humble before God, much in prayer ... Heart filled with Christ's love will make lively and active, bold and ready. Let not complaining, or anything else, choke up the inexhaustible springs ... As a landed proprietor will often put into court a protest against some invasion of his rights, though he knows that no immediate good will result from it; so a minister should persevere in bearing witness to the truth, though he cannot see what good it will do; for seed cast upon the waters may be found after many days; and, meanwhile, he has delivered his conscience.

His First and Last Volume

On sending him afterwards a copy of the volume as soon as it came to hand, when he was at Morningside, he wrote to me briefly, thanking me, but still expressing fear that he had done a presumptuous thing. I expected that he would be cheered by it, as he had several times asked me when it would be ready; but he was rather dull, and took it quietly. He was disappointed that I had not written a preface. He would not write one himself, but had urged me to do it. I could not bring myself to do a thing which seemed as if I were recommending one, from whom it rather became me to receive recommendation. Besides, a sad foreboding haunted me that this was the close of his work on earth; and to write a sketch or commendation of him before the time seemed unbecoming, — as if anticipating his decease. The book came forth without a preface; but, in truth, it needed none. It will become, I trust, a fireside volume in

Scotland; and perhaps India too may lovingly accept the last messages of one who took so profound an interest in her welfare to the end.

During the winter I saw him very frequently; for, though we dwelt at opposite ends of the city, the distance was not great. I found him ever the same, — as a friend, a Christian, and a minister. He was sometimes low in spirit at first; but ere ten minutes had elapsed he seemed to rise out of his depression, and the visit ended with prayer and thanksgiving. Many a pleasant hour did we spend together. At our ministerial meetings at Moody Stuart's, he was able once or twice to be present, and to take part. He was anxious also to be present at our prophetical meetings at Captain Shepherd's, and had fixed to accompany me one evening, but found himself unable. His note of apology is as follows:

> 57 *Queen Street.* — *Friday, January* 10, 1868. — MY VERY DEAR HORACE, — I fear that, after all, we must deny ourselves the cherished pleasure of being with you on Tuesday night. It is the only kind of meeting that we should care to be at; but it seems clearly the Master's will that for the present we should abstain from this. He seems desirous that we should learn brokenness of will, and obedience, by withholding from things which are to us good, and profitable, and enjoyable. I am sadly weak, both in body and mind, and possibly my case is worse than we yet know. But the Lord is with us, and we know that he careth for us, and manages all for us, from hour to hour. Pray for us, that "the blessed hope" may have a more constant, habitual influence upon us. Then will there be no more feeble minds and sorrowful partings. May you have earnests and outshinings of the coming Lord in your meeting. United love to all at the Grange. We hope soon to reach you. — Believe me, very affectionately yours, J. M.

On the 9th of January he writes to Cowan:

> MY DEAR BROTHER, — We got here on Tuesday night, and on Wednesday we went to see my old and valued friend Dr Henderson. He came to the same conclusion as our friend Dr Bramwell, that body

and mind are completely worn out, and that a considerable season of entire rest is absolutely indispensable. Will you kindly make this known to my dear people, and also to the brethren of the Presbytery, and ask from both their sympathy and prayers? It is not the way we should have chosen, but the Lord knows best, and we hope to learn obedience, as he himself did, by the things which we suffer. Remember especially my dear wife, who, in clinging to her broken-down husband, has to leave behind her interesting home-duties and work. I grieve to throw such burdens upon you from day to day. But you are young and hopeful, and many prayers and encouragements will cheer and support you. I know the Lord is loving and all-sufficient, and I trust we shall yet be spared and brought back to labour with you in the Lord's vineyard. You will see from this brevity that I am already taking up the yoke.

Only the Rock

On the 16th of January he writes to the same:

We shall be with you in spirit at this time, all through. I trust you will have a very refreshing and encouraging season … I must walk softly with the Lord. We both find the Lord teaching and upholding us, and hope to gather fruit in the valley … What a life this is! — the tossing of a troubled sea; but the rock remains firm amidst it all.

On the first Monday of each month, last winter, there was a social gathering of all Free Church undergraduates in the Presbytery Hall, under the care of Mr Main of St Mary's. There was a large attendance of students; several ministers and elders were present. Addresses were delivered; conversation took place; and the young men were then introduced to one another, and to Christian friends in Edinburgh. Milne felt the deep importance of the meeting, both as bearing on the present interests of the students, and on the future welfare of the Church. No such interest was taken forty years ago in the spiritual welfare of our young men. They were wholly neglected;

left without any spiritual superintendence in the midst of a great city. Milne expressed his desire to be present at one of those meetings, though unable to take part; and he had agreed to accompany me one evening. But he did not appear; and next day he sent the following note:

> 57 *Queen Street.* — *Tuesday.* — MY VERY DEAR HORACE, — I was too weak to venture to the meeting last night. But I thought of you and tried to pray. I trust that it was a place of decision; a Bethel meeting, with the ladder in the midst; and many a young dreaming Jacob had his eyes opened to see, and his heart turned to choose a better world. I trust that parents' prayers were answered, and that trembling hearts will be encouraged by the results of that meeting.

Prophetical Meeting

Finding himself tolerably well in the beginning of April, he ventured to our prophetical meeting at Captain Shepherd's. It was a very solemn and profitable evening. Milne felt it to be so, and enjoyed it exceedingly. He took part in the conversation; and, as usual, threw in something fresh and spiritual, both in interpretation and thought. He conducted the closing services, and proceeded some length in a most interesting exposition on the last three verses of the Epistle of Jude, till I had to remind him of medical orders, and to request him to spare himself. I have seldom done anything with so much regret; but I felt it was due to himself. In former days, when sitting behind him in the pulpit, I had often, when he had got the length of an hour, or perhaps an hour and quarter, without compunction tugged the gown, to intimate that it was time to stop, and had been answered, with a pleasant nod, 'Just a few minutes more, my dear friend'; but now he yielded at once, knowing that the excitement of speaking might be fatal. I was satisfied that I had done a right thing; but

I never look back on that blessed evening without regret, feeling as if I had been the means of closing his lips ere God had closed them, and had stopped him in the middle of his last message. The prayer with which he summed up will not be soon forgotten by those who heard it.

Feeling himself worse latterly; often borne down with unaccountable depression; afraid of what this might end in, and, at the same time, not unhopeful of restoration if properly cared for, he desired to be put under partial restraint for a time. I saw him more than once at this time, he calling for me and I for him. Though perhaps a little dull, he was just the same in other respects; and we walked together, talked together, prayed together as usual.

Fragments of His Last Days

The following extracts are from letters of this period. They are touching in the extreme, some very beautiful:

I suppose this is the youthful lesson in obedience which was omitted in my early education, but which must be learned by all the members, old and young, of the heavenly family. I wish I could submit to it in this light. If I were peaceful and happy again, I see already that there are not a few I daily meet to whom it would be easy to speak a word of peace and comfort from day to day. There are many broken, bruised hearts, some in absolute despair. If one could speak heartily, effectually, of the blood and righteousness, it would be easy to gather a harvest.

I try to anchor myself on that word, 'for the present grievous, yet *afterward* it yieldeth the peaceable fruits'; and so I hope that this will turn out a seed-time both for here and hereafter.

I got good from the 25th Psalm today. Also from *Daily Light*, and *Here and There*. It is pleasant to think that if, soured, mortified, disappointed by the creature, we hunger and thirst for God, we shall be satisfied. I have seen a lark in a dark close garret singing so cheerfully on its little bit of turf; why cannot I? But it won't do, for I am a sinful man. Grace, conquering grace, can, and I hope will, do it.

I did not sleep much last night, and was afraid that it was going to be a trying day; but I was agreeably disappointed. About breakfast time the Lord seemed to come in love and favour to my soul, and continued with me to the end.

I was happy; everything prospered; I had many opportunities of reading and speaking with people. It was the best day I have had for months. 'The Lord's hand is not shortened.' Let us trust and not be afraid. My dark thoughts are away, and I am again hopefully and joyfully pressing on to the city which hath foundations, and the gathering together of the saints unto the Lord. I am thankful for this affliction, and am sure that in no other way could the Lord have done me the good which he has intended me from eternity. Covenant mercies are sure mercies, though they are sometimes long hidden and hindered; but wait, and they will spring up and ripen. My head is not strong, will never be; we shall be poor and afflicted; unfit to shine in the concourse and clashings of men; but we can pray and keep Christ's word, and he will come to us and make his abode with us.

Yes, I know weariness, intense weariness; but I try to think of him who knew it too. I am often inclined to say, Wherefore hast thou made all things in vain? But I know this is my infirmity. He will not always chide, and the captive exile shall not die in the pit. I find much scripture opened up and brought home; the passages serve their purpose, and then pass away. Thank you for reminding me of Joseph. I have often thought of him; like him the iron enters into my soul. But if we learn obedience, we shall never regret the schooling. We shall wonder, adore, and praise the patience and care of him who takes so much pains to train and educate us.

Yesterday Horace and Andrew Bonar called and were very kind. Just now I have a parcel from Horace, containing a few books, one of them my own, which I suppose will be out immediately. May the Lord take it up! I feel like the Jewish matron, when her son was born, — 'Ichabod.'

I have been reading a valuable book from Dr Bonar, *Saving Truths of Christianity,* by Luthardt, a German professor. It is very good, except that it is Sacramentarian. Also another book from him, *Man's Renewal*, by Austin Phelps. But I find my head very feeble, and fear this is to be my thorn and trial, till thorns and trials are done away in the world of rest ... I enjoy so much the 30th Psalm; it just suits me. I am not anxious how we shall get on, when I am able to return to social life. I have confidence in God, and am sure that He will make all smooth and easy. It has been a new and sorrowful experience; but I think I have learned many things which, *afterward*, will turn to profit.

I try hard to think that all that has happened is the opening up of the covenant, and it is a comfort. 'Be of good courage', *etc*.; 'Be glad in the Lord', *etc*., suit me today. God is seeking to humble us, and we must try to be meek and lowly.

I have a solemn feeling in the thought of returning again to society. I tremble at the thought of going again into the vortex. But 'My grace is sufficient', sustains me, and the thought that it will not be long. May we have a little gleam of pure, domestic, heavenly peace, ere we are parted again!

Grace, mercy, and peace be with you. May the Lord dwell in us both, rule in us both, minister to us both, and then we shall be truly one, though still divided! I believe this will be a profitable time to us both, though for the present there is often weariness and heaviness. But it is one of the 'all things'.

Forgive the blots in the former page. I have just been thinking that if we are temples of the Holy Ghost, we ought to do everything thoughtfully, carefully, worthy of God.

I pray that the Lord in mercy may give a quiet season in the earthly home, ere he takes us to the true home.

I am longing to know a little of 'being made perfect by suffering', and becoming a partaker of his holiness. My life has been a sadly broken, intermitted one; but I know I have a complete and perfect life in Christ. When the Lord turns my captivity, he will show us what to do. He never does things by halves. Look at the end of Job, Nebuchadnezzar. The valley of Achor is a door of hope. The Lord is with us, and will appear for our help in due time.

I see from many things that God's word is, 'Rest, be still', and I try to submit and obey. I used to *run;* I must learn now to *walk.* My heart's desire is, that the Lord's will may be done, and that we may both be partakers of his holiness.

Sad Thoughts about the Church

Here are some scraps of notes, written during his stay in Edinburgh, to his colleague:

I remember you continually before the Lord. Pray for me, that I may not fret or grow weary, but be enabled, with my dear wife, meekly to bear the affliction of Christ, for his body's sake. This view is what really best reconciles to trial, and carries above and through it … I like one of your helps 'for the Church'. I fear our well-meant attempt at union is going to cause wide and bitter disunion among ourselves. Let us pray daily for the plentiful rain that would restrain and quench these embers, no longer *suppositos,* but open and manifest, which are causing already suspicion and estrangement among dear friends. *There will be a middle party, crying for delay.* Pray for us; we need faith and patience. Help, Lord! I should like to share your danger and labour, at least among the sick … *2d March.* — You are right. I often long to leave this sevenfold heated furnace of restraint and self-denial, and fly back to Perth. But the Lord is teaching me to say, 'Not my will, my way.' Or, if I try to presume, the rod soon reminds me that I am in higher and better hands. For instance, that audacious step of going to the forenoon meeting of Presbytery [Edinburgh] cost me too much to venture on a repetition. Yet I was thankful to see for myself the spirit which is prevailing. It is very bad, very sad; and I fear the worst. Our friends are too hot and excited calmly to meet and pray before the Lord, and ask the sending forth of his light, that they may see how little reason there is to quarrel and devour one another. But the Master knows it all, and will in the end get all the glory … I think the Lord is teaching me a little; and I hope he will spare me for a little to help in his work. But *compelled inaction is, I think, the sorest of all trials.* Yet the Lord can strengthen for this.

Resting in God

On Monday, April 26th, my brother Andrew and I spent a most pleasant hour with him, partly walking and partly resting; nor would he have us part without prayer. On coming home, I sent some books which he had asked for, and, among others, his own new volume, which had just arrived. He sent me the following note:

Tuesday. — My very dear Horace, — Thank you and Andrew very much for the kind visit of yesterday; also for the books. The 'gatherings' are very handsome; but they want the only thing I cared for, — your introductory brotherly word. Had I been well, I dare say I should have been pleased with the volume; but now I can only say, Ichabod. I have been reading *Faint Not* with profit; but this affliction is so universal, deep, and crushing, that I find it hard to realize and rest in the Father's love. But I know it is all right. I see reasons for it, and perhaps by and by may be able to rejoice in it. Thank you very much. Love and best wishes for you all. — Yours very affectionately, John Milne.

On the 1st of May he began a new diary; but the entries in it are few. The following are some fragments. They show the same spirit of faith and love as in all the previous journals, but they exhibit more of the depression which was settling down upon him:

I long for the seeking, trustful heart, concerned for the glory of the Lord. Show me thy ways, teach me; but, above all, *lead me.* Remember thy mercies; remember not my sins. Thy mercies are older than my earliest sins. Let me encourage myself in the Lord. He is good and upright; he will guide the meek, and all his ways are good. 'The secret of the Lord', — this is for friends. David got it, and it comforted him in trouble. I greatly need to be assured that all my present afflictions are the evolutions of an eternal counsel of love. Strengthen me to wait meekly and patiently for the end. If I become partaker of God's holiness, I shall to all eternity rejoice and praise. But the heart rises and rebels, and I fret, and try to take myself out of God's hand. Lord, help me to lie passive. I have seen the lark, in some dark, close hovel, sitting on its little handbreadth of turf, and singing its cheerful song. Why should not I be such? Now, Lord, help me this day. I lift my soul to thee, not to man. I expect all good from thee. I wait for thy time and way.

May 3d. — Perfection is the goal towards which God is tending in all his dealings with his people, — likeness to himself. For this end he chose them in Christ, gave them to Christ, redeemed them in him, in due time calls and severs them to holiness. Already they are perfect in his sight; but he stirs them up to become actually so. Let me be diligent; ask God to search; use the blood. Holiness is happiness. Start at once in the upward course, and hold on. The blood cuts the connection with the past; don't return to Egypt. Christ has taken charge of that (the past); it is in his tomb; don't seek to bring it back. Resist the devil, doubts, darkness, accusations. Keep your heart; keep out error, keep in truth. Lose not your peace, your crown, your life. Be more concerned to be really good than to do great things. It is the greatest of mercies when our house on the sand topples down, and we escape, naked, bruised, covered with shame, from its ruins. The Lord sometimes sensibly delivers men up to the devil for a season, that they may grow in grace. He did it to Job; he sent his people into captivity that they might know the difference between his kingdom and the yoke of the enemy. I have long felt the duty of laying aside every weight, of cutting off the right hand; but I have delayed and procrastinated. But now the Lord has done it for me. May I get grace to see God's loving, wise hand in this, and embrace the opportunity of entering on a new and higher life. Clear the way, and let me start fair; let me run for the crown; let me wrestle, watch, labour; and let none come between me and the crown. Let me never forget for a moment how unstable I am, or how strong is the hold of the power of darkness … Pride and self-will are like the law; they drive on without mercy, and give no help nor support. Christ leads gently, and supports.

There is a fulness of time and ripeness in all God's ways; and happy are they who patiently wait for it. But this is very hard. We are doing nothing; perhaps see no progress; and our heart sinks. Soldiers find it the hardest part of the battle just to stand still and do nothing. Our hasty soul cries, 'What shall I do?' and the answer is, 'Be quiet and wait.' This is the trial of trials. Abraham knew it; Christ knew it. But look to the Lord; expect from him; search the promises; in due time they will speak, and not tarry.

The rest of this little manuscript volume is chiefly occupied with brief extracts from some books which I had lent him, one of which was *Man's Renewal*, by Austin Phelps. I need not quote these extracts; but I give here a short fragment written about this time in connection with Christian responsibility:

I must be faithful — to men — to my trust. I know not why God may have been pleased to place me for a single hour in connection with others. Their happiness for eternity may depend on that hour. Waste no hour. Be about my Master's business. Seek not self. Lord, what have me do? my question in every crisis and relation of life. Many temptations to be unfaithful: indolence, selfishness, worldly distraction; much sinful and low example. Let me waste no more of my Master's goods. Realize responsibility. Have to give account. Let house and heart be in order. Every day's work finished. Soon judgment-seat, where we shall meet souls with which we have been connected.

If I remember right, the last day I saw him was Wednesday, 20th May. He called for me in the afternoon. We had some pleasant converse alone in the study first, and afterwards with some friends who were calling. We walked out together and enjoyed some fellowship. He talked of the past, — his own early years; and then of his present trial. He was anxious to get back to Perth. I saw him that same evening in an omnibus, going into town. He left the omnibus at Charlotte Street, and bid me good-bye with his own expressive nod and kindly smile, I saw him no more. Nor shall we meet again till the resurrection morning.

His last *public* service was in the Barclay Church. After the Tuesday's lecture, he was suddenly called on to pray. The prayer impressed many who heard it. It was the breathing of fervent desire for the Lord's coming; the utterance of earnest petitions that time, and years, and every obstacle might be 'shovelled out of the way.' The effort, however, excited him greatly, and he suffered for it.

Preparations for the Conference

On the Tuesday before his death he attended a meeting in connection with the Religious Conference at Perth, suggesting the subjects for the ensuing one, which was to be held on the first, second, and third days of September. On the following Friday he filled up the texts suitable to the subjects; forwarding the needful papers to others, as he felt that he had no prospect of being able to take that part in the Conference, or in preparation for it, which he had hitherto done.[1]

---

[1] We give the programme thus drawn out by Milne: —

Tuesday, 1st September — Forenoon.

FAITH.

Eph. 2:8: 'By grace are ye saved, through faith.' Heb. 12:2: 'Without faith it is impossible to please God.' Rom. 5:1: 'Being justified by faith, we have peace with God.' Acts 15:9: 'Purifying their hearts by faith.' Mark 9:23: 'If thou canst believe, all things are possible to him who believeth.'

AFTERNOON AT TWO O'CLOCK FOR FREE CONVERSATION.
Subject — *The Gift and the Ministry of the Spirit.*

Luke 4:17, 19: 'The Spirit of the Lord is upon me.' Acts 1:8: 'Ye shall receive power after that the Holy Ghost is come upon you.' 2 Cor. 3:6: 'Ministers not of the letter, but of the spirit.' 1 Thess. 1:5: 'Our gospel came to you, not in word only, but in power and in the Holy Ghost.' Zech. 4:6: 'Not by power, nor by might, but by my Spirit.'

Wednesday, 2d September — Forenoon.

HOPE.

1 Tim. 1:1: 'Jesus Christ who is our hope.' 1 Pet. 1:3: 'Begotten again to a lively hope.' Eph. 2:12: 'Without Christ, having no hope, and without God in the world.' Rom. 15:13: 'The God of hope fill you with all peace and joy in believing.' Heb. 6:2: 'We desire that every one of you do show the same diligence, to the full assurance of hope unto the end.' Titus 2:13: 'Looking for that blessed hope, and the glorious appearing of the great God, and our Saviour Jesus Christ.' The whole creation

His Last Week

A few days before his death he was calling for a friend, who expressed a hope that he would soon be better. 'Thank you', was the reply; 'weeping may endure for a night, but joy cometh in the morning, and *it won't be long';* referring, as he often did, to the Lord's appearing, and our gathering together to him. He lived, latterly, very much under the power of that blessed hope. He did not speak much of it to those who differed from him; for he thought that the Lord only could give them the seeing eye, and that their seeing how it comforted and strengthened him would impress them more than words. Yet he often said that he could not understand how people did not see the pre-millennial advent in Scripture, and that, since he had got that key, he had found his way into many an obscure text. This was after his return from India; for, in the earlier part of his ministry, he was somewhat opposed.

On the Friday evening he strolled with Mrs Milne through the Grange Cemetery, and returned to his lodgings at Spring Valley, Morningside, certainly not worse. Plans were formed for going abroad as soon as possible; and these thoughts occupied him on the following Saturday. He was in town during the day, and returned home in the omnibus in the afternoon. As usual, he began to converse with the passenger next him, who happened to be one

---

waiteth and groaneth for this hope. It sanctifies — it is an anchor — a life-buoy — a helmet — a light in a dark place.

AFTERNOON AT TWO O'CLOCK FOR FREE CONVERSATION.
Subject — Mutual, brotherly, co-working of Ministers with other labourers, who may come, or be sent to their aid.

Thursday, 3d September—Forenoon.
LOVE.
1 John 4:16: 'God is love.' John 3:16: 'God so loved the world that he gave his only-begotten Son.' 1 John 3:1: 'Behold what manner of love the Father hath bestowed upon us, that we should be called the sons of God!' Verse 2: 'If God so loved us, we ought also to love one another.' Verse 19: 'We love him, because he first loved us.'

connected with my own congregation; true to his Master to the very last, and carrying out to the end of his busy and consistent life the principle on which he had acted from the first, of speaking some word for Christ to every one whom he could possibly reach.

These words in the Morningside omnibus, to the stranger sitting next him, were his last spoken in the Master's service.

On coming in, he said to the servant that he was hungry, and asked if dinner were ready. She brought it in, and waited till he should give the blessing. Instead, however, of the usual kind of blessing, he said, very strikingly and solemnly, 'Blessed are they that hunger and thirst after righteousness, for they shall be filled.' And truly such was his life; that hunger and thirst increasing more and more, and manifesting themselves with greater intensity during the last months of his course.

On Saturday, the 30th of May, he thus wrote to Cowan, and this was the last letter he wrote:

Miss Aird's Lodgings, Spring Valley, Morningside. — MY VERY DEAR BROTHER, — You have been a brother indeed in this time of trouble. I thank you for your sympathy, your prayers, and many substantial acts of kindness. You have been a helper and comforter to my dear wife, and, best of all, you have been feeding wisely and prosperously the flock of God which he hath purchased with his own blood. I am better, but not strong, and we are living quietly here for a little, till the Lord opens up our way. We have been passing through great and sore adversities; but it is the Lord, and we seek to be dumb. I thank you for your ever welcome letters, by which I have been kept informed of what was passing among you, and have been trying to be thankfully, prayerfully present with you in spirit. It was peculiarly gratifying to find that we were so constantly and lovingly remembered and mentioned by our friends in prayer, both in public and private. The Lord return to you all abundantly, even 'into your own bosoms'. The annual report was very encouraging. The Lord continue and increase the prosperity, both spiritual and material, of dear St Leonard's a hundredfold. How easily he can do it, if we will but open our mouths wide! The fountains are full and overflowing, and he is ever ready to open the sluice. 'He hath *given* gifts.' … How quietly the Assembly seems to be passing away! When the Lord gives peace, who can cause trouble? Let us thank him for his kindness at this present time, and leave the future to his wisdom and love.

The General Assembly

The above reference to the General Assembly leads me to add a brief remark on that subject, which was so much upon his mind — union between two of the Presbyterian bodies in Scotland. Up till 1867 he was decidedly in favour of the present union scheme; and I find in his journal one or two expressions of dissent from myself personally in this matter. But in the beginning of 1868 he became persuaded that matters were not ripe for union, and that it ought to be postponed. He wrote his views at some length in March; but afterwards destroyed what he had written, which I regret. Not that they altogether coincided with my own; but they were the words of a man of peace. Delay, and prayer, and brotherly conference were the things he wished to urge. He spoke to me very freely upon the subject; but I would not venture to give what might appear to some a one-sided report on so delicate a matter. 'I see it won't do, my dear friend', was his frequent conclusion. He was thoroughly a man of peace, and his leanings were towards union; so much so, that at the time of the revival in 1860, he took part in a meeting in one of the Established churches of Perth. On the 2d of March 1868, he thus wrote to one of his elders: 'What is going to become of our poor Free Church? I fear we are on the eve of a disruption which will rend us in pieces, ruining our usefulness, and making us a scorn in the earth. It is sad for all lovers of peace. We need to pray much, that the evil spirit which has already begun to work may be cast out, and that we may be preserved from consuming and devouring one another.'

His Death

On the morning of his death (May 31, 1868), he rose between five and six for prayer, as he frequently did; and then, on returning to bed, asked his wife if she knew what psalm they were to read that day; they being in the habit of reading the same portion of Scripture daily. It was the 57th, a great favourite of his:

> Be merciful unto me, O God,
> Be merciful unto me;
> For my soul trusteth in Thee,
> Yea, in the shadow of Thy wings will I make my refuge
> Until these calamities be overpast.

He then asked her if the Lord was with her this morning, adding, 'You know I cannot be happy unless I *feel* the love of God.' Soon after he rose to dress in the adjoining room; but after a little returned to say something that would tend to her comfort. He then went back into the other room, and within a quarter of an hour afterwards a groan was heard; the servant went in; he was found lying on the floor on his back, not having finished his dressing but his dressing materials all neatly put aside in his own careful manner. He had passed away. From prayer he had gone to praise.

His Bible lay on the bed, open at Ephesians 3 and 4. He had been kneeling in prayer, for the bed was pressed down on each side of the Bible, as by his arms; suddenly his heart had ceased to beat; he had fallen backward; his eyes open as if looking upward; his face entirely placid, as if there had not been a pang or a struggle.[1]

[1] In connection with the death of those who have thus died *alone*, such as Dr Chalmers and John Milne, the exquisite words of the great pagan historian Tacitus, regarding the death of his father-in-law Agricola, have often occurred

He died not at home, but in lodgings, and when just preparing to move elsewhere. He died within a few minutes' walk of the house where Dr Chalmers fell asleep, twenty-one years before. He was buried in the Grange Cemetery, on Friday, June 5th; not far from Chalmers, and Tweedie, and Cunningham, and Bannerman, and M'Intosh, and a band of others, like-minded with himself, whose memory is blessed, and whose names are household words. It was a bright sunny afternoon when we laid him down, and spread the green turf over him. Moody Stuart, in that memorable prayer offered up ere we left the house of death, had dwelt on these words of the Lord, 'Father, I will that they whom thou hast given me be with me where I am, that they may behold my glory'; and we could not but feel, as we stood in that graveyard, how much better it was with him who was taken, than with those who were left. To have the Lord 'with us' here was much; but to be 'with him' was more and better far. And then the promises summed up the whole: 'Thy brother shall rise again'; 'Them that sleep in Jesus will God bring with him'; 'They rest from their labours, and their works do follow them.' In one of his last sermons he spoke these words: 'You are troubled about that thing death. Well, he has the keys of death; he is himself the door; he will open it, and when you are at the other side you are WITH HIM.'

Faithful unto Death

Some men God raises up for a certain work, and then sets them aside, like broken vessels; some he uses to the last. So was it with Rutherford and Whitefield and Chalmers; so was it with John Milne. He was made use of to the last. 'I began my ministry', he said, 'amid revival; so amid revival may I pass away.' He had feared

---

to me, though he was one of those who 'sorrowed as those who have no hope': *'Paucioribus tamen lacrimis compositus es, et novissima in luce desideravere aliquid oculi tui.'* 'With too few tears you were laid to rest, and in the light of your last day there was something for which your eyes longed in vain.' Tacitus, *Agricola*, (ch. 45), *Ed.*

a period of uselessness; he was spared that. God took him in the midst of his work.[1]

After his death his purse was found full of sixpences and fourpenny pieces, meant to be given away to the poor. All his life through he was noted for his generosity; and so strong did he feel the temptation to giving, — sometimes indiscriminately, as he was conscious, — that he was afraid to carry a purse at all. He could not say 'No' as long as he had any money in his pocket. He denied himself many things that he might give the more away.

I close with a few extracts from letters. The first is from Somerville, one of the few remaining members of that happy brotherhood, of which the first who left us was Robert M'Cheyne:

> Christ's garden on earth has been deprived of a flower of rare beauty and sweetness of odour. A more unselfish and pure spirit than that which our late friend possessed it would be difficult to find. Christ glowed in the man as well as in his preaching. This gathering away of John Milne, James Hamilton, and William Burns, within so short a period, warns *us* to be ready.

The second is from a Calcutta civilian, not connected with the Free Church:

> Calcutta will long remember your husband. I doubt whether it ever saw a Christian of equal attainments. Certainly it has not seen many such. His memory is green amongst us all. For ourselves, we shall ever think it one of the choice privileges of our lives that we knew him. He was one, in many respects, greatly favoured of his Master. I never saw a more loving, earnest, unselfish Christian.

---

[1] Since Milne's death, a friend writes: 'Having to travel several times up and down between Perth and Edinburgh, one of the railway guards was always very attentive to me. At last I one day said to him, "You are not one of the St Leonard's people?" "Oh, no", he said. Then I added, "You must have known Mr Milne?" "Oh, yes", he said in the most tender way, "almost as long as I have known myself; and I am so sorry for him." "Do you know Mr Milne's Master?" I ventured to say. The man hesitated, and then said, "No." "Oh", I said, "why don't you seek him? Why not try to trust in him? I am sure Mr Milne must have told you to do so." "Told me!" said he; "Ay, MANY A TIME he told me."'

The special characteristic of a river is its *onwardness*. Not its clearness, or depth, or breadth, or volume; for in these each stream differs from the other; but in that *onwardness* which is common to all. From the time it leaves its source till it reaches the sea, it is *moving on.* Such is the man of God. Such was John Milne. Through much warfare, sorrow, change, — still moving on pressing towards the mark; often weary *in* the work, but not *of* the work; faithful unto death.

I know thy works, and charity, and service, and faith, and thy patience, and thy works, and THE LAST TO BE MORE THAN THE FIRST.

Chapter 18

Various Years —
Miscellaneous Gatherings

*W*hen the news of his death reached Perth, there was sorrow in many a heart. Men of all churches and creeds felt the blow. Outside his own flock there were many who loved him, and who had, in their hearts, looked to him as the man to whom, above all others, they could betake themselves in the day of sickness or grief. His departure had suddenly made a blank in the city.

Tribute to His Memory

Many were the testimonies which flowed in, respecting him; from the pulpit, the press, and the private letter. These were so numerous that I shall not undertake to name them, far less to print them at length. I merely give one which strikes me most. It is from a London friend, Mr J. Calder Stuart, to his brother, of Scone, in Perthshire:

> Oh that I had fuller and more constant intercourse with you, my own beloved brother! But *for you* — and just *one or two* like-minded followers of our dear Master, whom occasionally meet in the city, I can open my heart to — I should really feel as if dwelling in Mesech, and sojourning in the tents of Kedar. All 'the good people' I have to do with seem to be *satisfied* with the discharge of their outward services, which are of undeniable importance; but I can't win my way into anything like spiritual intimacy with any of them. Cold water — a

chilling assent, even to a proposal of an occasional meeting in private for prayer, so that the idea drops lifeless! Isn't that sad? I feel this just at this moment more acutely (or I would not hurt you by saying what I do) because I only learn now — today — the death of that precious man Mr Milne. Your paper, with its touching tribute to his memory, reached me this morning, and gave me the first news of his death.

My opportunities of personal intercourse with that dear saint were comparatively few, *but* each of them left on my inmost soul an abiding impression of the most elevating kind — a sacred and inexpressible exaltation of spirit into an upper, heavenly atmosphere, full-charged with all that could stimulate love and devoted perseverance in following the Lord, and serving him.

The very last time I saw dear Mr Milne was at his lodgings in town here some years ago, when on a visit with his excellent wife, and her aunt, Mrs Jackson. Very pleasant indeed was the converse ('Such as God approves.'— *Cowper*) at the tea-table; and I remember perfectly some beautiful and affecting words of his on the parable of the Prodigal Son. My time was limited, and I found it suddenly exceeded. I had, therefore, to leave abruptly. He showed me to the door; but, somehow, we could not part; and he ran back for his hat, and accompanied me out on my way home; but we turned back repeatedly, perhaps for an hour; and never have I in my life had such an hour of heavenly intercourse with any one. I remember perfectly saying to myself, when reaching home, 'What a place must heaven be, when such blissful converse can be enjoyed on earth!'

Some very remarkable thoughts of his are well remembered by me, with regard to the twofold work of the pastorate: some ministers gifted and appointed, as it were, by the Lord to the express work of winning souls to him; others to the distinct work of edifying and building up the converted. He expanded the theme by showing its applicability to Christians, as *individual* witnesses and labourers for the extension of the Redeemer's kingdom.

A Fool for Christ's Sake

John Milne was content to be 'a fool for Christ's sake'. His was a very unworldly course; and many had the impression that he was not at all a thinker or a scholar, whereas he was both. His was a life of great intensity and simplicity, yet full of cheerfulness and love. It was the life of one to whom the world to come was much; this world very little. Yet wherever he went or was, he made worldly men feel that he was a friend, that he loved their souls, and cared not what they might say or do to him, provided he could win them to the Lord. 'Not soon angry', never ruffled, careless of praise or blame, he went about upon his work, taking an interest in every being he met with, man or child. Some of the things which looked peculiar in him, were the doings of a humble and unselfish man, who thought himself almost unfit for any service, and would, therefore, throw himself into work which others might think beneath their dignity; for he was always willing to take the lowest place and to do the hardest work. Both at home and in India we find the same consistent, unworldly, unconventional life; the life of one 'not conformed to this world'. 'We try', he writes from India, '*to live separate from the world;* and yet we seek to gather round us those who fear and seek the Lord. This is a very worldly place; and it is a blessed, though a difficult work to live holily and self-deniedly . . . Dinner here is late, about eight o'clock; but we never go to dinner parties. I laid down the rule from the first, and stated it openly, in answer to two or three early invitations; and so we are now free from that danger of distraction and worldliness.'[1]

[1] '*Facile contemnitur clericus, qui, saepe vocatus ad prandium, ire non recusat. Nunquam petentes, raro accipiamus rogati.*' 'That clergyman easily comes to be despised who, being often asked to dinner, never refuses to go. Let us never seek for presents, and rarely accept them when we are asked to do so' *Ed.* Jerome to Nepotianus, *Works,* Letter 52. We remember a minister, called 'evangelical', above forty years ago, whose accepted dinner invitations averaged five a week; and another, respecting whom it was said, 'If you want a visit from him, you will have to ask him to dinner.'

He often said that he thought Luke 14:12 was quite opposed to the party-giving and feasting of the present day, even among Christians; not merely because the luxury of the table has become so excessive, but because the Lord here points to something else than personal gratification in such cases. As the thirteenth verse could not easily be carried out in its literality, he sought to act upon its spirit by giving gifts at the New Year, and such times, to those whose means shut them out from such comforts. He was often saddened by hearing of some, whom he believed to be Christians, going to the world for amusement and relaxation. The enjoyment of the good things of this world did not seem to him the same as joy in God. The true human side of Christianity to him was that in which he could follow the man Christ Jesus, denying self and bearing the cross. He did not need the world to fill up any void in his being. The length to which the luxuries of dress, and food, and furniture are carried, he felt to be inconsistent with Christian simplicity and self-denial. In the midst of these the salt loses its savour, the witness for God becomes dumb, and the ambassador of Christ returns home with a heavy heart, feeling that he has not been able to let his light shine, or win a hearing for his Master.

Yet he was a thoroughly social man, and could not find himself near a single human being without entering into pleasant talk. The society of Christians he delighted in; Christian conversation in company he tried always to cultivate; and he succeeded in this above most. Hence he felt the difference between Calcutta and Perth. 'I think', he writes from India,

> the feeling of isolation here makes me think more of the family of God, — the Church militant throughout the earth, sometimes also of the Church triumphant. One in this way gets into a large place, away from the coldness, indifference, defects, and often follies of those near us. It helps one also to bear the slow progress of God's work in our particular neighbourhood, when we think it may be going on

prosperously elsewhere, and that God has his hidden ones whom he can at any time bring to light.

He was afraid of too much *religious work,* too many religious engagements, too much religious bustle. Societies' committees, 'social meetings', Bible-readings, are good things, but they may be unduly multiplied. 'I should like to get nearer the Lord', he says.

I feel the danger of becoming absorbed by religious as well as worldly work. Nothing can make up for the withdrawal of God's gracious presence. His favour is life. How kind is it of the Lord to restore us from time to time! Without this we should go down altogether. I am quite sure that it is indispensable to spiritual health to maintain a thankful, hopeful, cheerful spirit in all circumstances.' And again: 'I should like to shut the eyes of sense, and to cut the sinews of carnal feeling, and try to be wholly the Lord's. Why do we allow *anything to vex us that would not vex him, or to please us that would not please him?* When shall we be able to say, in regard to all connected with our fallen estate, I am dead, nevertheless I live? How would *he* feel, act, and speak, if he were where we are, and as we are?

His desires after higher attainments thus get vent to themselves: 'I long to be holy, and to see others holy. We must live nearer the Lord. Nothing will compensate for intercourse with him; and yet we daily barter it for things of nought. We must try to cultivate *attachment* to Christ. It may be cultivated, it may grow; and then our religion would be a more living, happy, actual thing.' — Again:

Oh that we had more nearness to him, more full and manifest communications of his glorious grace, both in private and public! Tell me something about your own soul, and your flock, and also what you are thinking of our prospects at present. If we could boldly say the mighty God is on our side, we should not heed the rising storms; but I fear our heart in many things condemns us.[1]

[1] Letter to Somerville.

His teachableness and readiness to judge himself by what he saw in others, thus show themselves in another note to the same:

I have just been at a meeting of my Sabbath-school teachers. I wish you would tell me what you do to encourage and strengthen the hands of yours. When do you meet with them, and what do you do on these occasions? I am going to be a great deal more amiable, since I saw your affectionateness with your flock. 'Take us the foxes, the little foxes that spoil the vines.' Do you find use for this prayer? I shall remember you tonight, and find good in doing so.

His constant, child-like reference to God in everything, was remarkable. In going out and coming in, he consulted his heavenly Father. If some blessing had come, he would at once give thanks. If some difficulty had occurred, he would turn to those who were with him, and join in seeking higher counsel. Few realized so fully these words of grace and duty, 'In everything, by prayer and supplication, let your requests be made known unto God.'[1] In private, his prayers were striking for their minuteness of detail; they took in everything, great or small. Even in public this was carried out by Milne to an extent which few are able to do. His ready sympathies, his

---

[1] Here is a remarkable letter to Mrs Sandeman, regarding the list of girls for whom and with whom she had prayed, dated December 1865: 'I was much affected by that list of hundreds of names. It seems to me a very solemn and encouraging document. How many souls we have all met with in the course of a few years! How have we felt for each of them? What have we done for each of them? What influence have we exerted over each of them? Few of us, I fear, know; few of us have kept any count. You have; and there is your register. How many of these were never spoken to, prayed with and for, till you did it! Thank God for it all. It is very encouraging, for it shows the truth of that word, "To him that hath shall be given"; and if we try to enter in at the open door, it will be opened wider, and no one can shut it. Sow on, pray on, love on, and soon the harvest will come, and the crown. You speak of being solitary. I know it. So was the Master, so was Paul; he says: "I have no man like-minded who will naturally care for your state; for all seek their own, not the things which are Jesus Christ's." But there is sympathy in heaven with the Father, Son, and Holy Ghost, with ministering angels, and with the redeemed, who now know the value of souls and the Saviour's love in a way they never did on earth. — Very affectionately yours, JOHN MILNE.'

quick apprehension of the case, his easy, natural language, enabled him to give utterance, before God, to feelings which all assembled shared in, but which hardly another man could have expressed. So irrepressible was this spirit of intercession and consultation, that it came out in strange places and circumstances; on the road as well as in the room, in the railway carriage or the waiting-room, yet always without obtrusion or ostentation. He felt deeply when he saw or heard of brethren deliberating or planning without this. In one of his notes to Somerville, this sentence occurs: 'I was surprised and grieved, on Tuesday night, at the strange difference of opinion that existed; and perhaps, also, that there was so little desire to look up for counsel.'[1]

Samuel Rutherford, and the men of his day, both in Scotland and England, frequently, in subscribing their letters to friends, added an expression significant of the conscious common bond between them and their correspondents. Whitefield and his followers did the same. In Robert M'Cheyne's letters this was frequent, though not invariable, — as, 'Yours till glory dawn'; or 'Ever yours till Jesus come'; or 'Ever yours in the gospel'; or 'Ever yours in Jesus'. Generally his letters ended with 'Yours affectionately', or 'Yours faithfully', in the usual way. In William Burns' letters we find more of this 'peculiarity'. Here are some signatures from his old letters, now lying before us: 'Yours in the Beloved'; 'Wishing you conformity to

[1] There are one or two very brief notes to Cormick of Kirriemuir, referring to the state of religion at that time, which may be here introduced, though a little out of place: 'I feel much as you do with regard to the state of religion. The fault lies a good deal with ourselves. Who shall raise up Jacob, for he is low? The Lord seems to have poured on us a spirit of deep sleep, and we are willing to have it so. How many means the Lord has used to prevent this! but when all fails, He at length says, "Sleep on now, and take your rest." Which of us is not meriting the rebuke, "What, could ye not watch with me one hour?" I find help in my ministry, and a considerable degree of peace in my mind, and a few tokens that the Lord still is working some souls, and not leaving himself without a witness. But my heart fails when I think of the general appearance of things. There seems a great and growing backsliding, and I don't know where it is to end.'

the Son of God, yours always'; 'Yours always with brotherly love'; 'Yours in haste, with the affectionate desires of a cold heart'; 'Yours in Emmanuel'. A letter to me, dated June 9, 1847, off Portsmouth, on board the 'Mary', for Hong Kong, ends with 'Yours ever in JESUS our hope.'

For this 'peculiarity', Burns was called to account by some of the members of the Aberdeen Presbytery in 1841, when the committee, appointed by that Presbytery, examined him as a witness in reference to the revivals of that period. The matter is thus put before him: 'Do you not think, with reference to this letter, and another to the convener, dated April 13, 1841, that signing letters "Yours in the Lord", and "Your humble servant in the gospel", thus introducing sacred words and names, contrary to common usage, and in connection with words which in themselves are not matter of fact, but are notoriously matter of mere compliment, does not tend to edification?' Burns' answer to this interrogation is as follows: 'I do *not* use the words, "your humble servant", to which you allude when you say "words of mere compliment", in the manner which you here suppose; and as to the expressions, "in the gospel", "in the Lord", I may just say, that though these expressions are not in *general* use, yet they have been, and still are not unfrequently used by the ministers and people of God; and though there is undoubtedly a great danger of our using them without good ground, or if on good ground, yet with formality and lightness, still I do conceive that their use cannot be universally condemned.'

These expressions Milne seldom used. His letters, long or short, generally ended with 'Yours faithfully', or 'Yours affectionately', or some such natural utterance of warm love to the friend he was writing to.

His thoughts were those of a fresh and ever-working mind; but, still more, of a spirit in continual fellowship with God, and sympathy with his word. They were thoroughly artless, without effort, without desire to say a striking thing, or to win praise for himself. His conversation was most lively and genial; no frivolity, yet no moroseness; always attractive, often quite original; full of interesting illustrations, both of story and of figure, interspersed with choice adaptations of Scripture to the points conversed over.

Sometimes he would advance an opinion, or state a case, quite expecting your concurrence. You differed from him very decidedly, and could give good reasons for differing. He would not argue nor resist. He was not in the least ashamed to give way. He listened to you; gave the due force to your statement; and in his own quick, decisive way, said, 'You're right, you're right, my dear friend; I see that I was wrong.' How pleasant the memory of these conversations, ended generally with prayer, and carried on with such ease and frankness!

One night (many years ago) we drove together from Perth to Collace, about seven miles. It was dark, but the stars were bright above us. He spoke of their beauty, and wondered how anyone could doubt that they were inhabited. He was asked for proof, and he gave for this the simple fact that they *existed*, asking, what was their meaning if there were no dwellers. On the road we passed several houses; and without referring directly to the previous part of the conversation, he was asked whether these houses were inhabited. He replied, that he did not know. 'What is their use, then?' he was asked. He saw at once the point of the question, and acknowledged the difference between the 'inhabited' and the 'inhabitable'. The stars were 'habitable' in all likelihood; but are they now inhabited? We did not attempt to settle the question; content to set it on its legitimate basis, and to use it as the subject of some pleasant mirth in after days, and other walks or drives. No one entered more heartily into such pleasantry than he, whether to take, or to give the retort. One communion Sabbath he preached on Elijah's despondency (*1 Kings* 19:4), a most solemn discourse throughout, but without that exhibition of the grace of God at the close, which was fitted to meet such a case. The brother who assisted thought he saw a deficiency, and in his table service ventured to supplement at some length what had been left out, trusting to the well-known frankness and forbearance of the minister, with whom he had taken such a liberty in his own church, and before his own people. He had not sat down before Milne grasped his hand, and exclaimed, in no undertone, 'Thank you, thank you; you're right; I was wrong.' Not one minister out of a thousand would have borne such supplementing, however needful, or would have so cordially thanked the supplementer. Often, in after days, did he refer to that scene, and repeat his thanks. So little did he seek himself; so desirous was he of being set right; so devoid was he of that pride that leads many of us to defend a false position, or at least to be anxious about being let down softly.

During the last six months of his life, when laid aside from public service, he felt very deeply the trial of not being permitted to speak or work. And yet, instead of envying his stronger brethren, who were still toiling in the field, he rejoiced unfeignedly in them and in their work. Any work that he heard of done by others, when he was thus laid aside, cheered him, though it sometimes called forth a sigh. Every word he was himself enabled to speak, every tract he gave, every letter he wrote, helped to cheer him, as making him not feel wholly useless. The proposal to publish the volume of 'Gatherings' was a gleam of sunshine to him; and his 'notes' on the inside of the envelopes, as he returned the proof-sheets to me every second day, showed that he was cheered as he went along. Here is one of these many envelope snatches:

Thank you very much. I thank the Lord often for the large door he has set before you. I find it good to try to rejoice in the prosperity of others. It is the Master's joy, and should be mine. (March 13, 1868.)

Inside the envelopes in which his sermons for the *Christian Treasury* used to come to me, there was not only some loving word, but some line of hesitancy or fear: 'Do I *bother* you with my sermons?' 'Am I not writing too much?' 'Tell me if I should stop.' 'Do you think I am doing any good?' 'Shall I send you any more?' Such were the messages that used to come from month to month; thoroughly characteristic of the writer, and expressive of the feelings of the moment. His childlike happiness on being told of good done by these sermons, or on approbation being expressed by Christian friends, was no less characteristic. It was not elation nor vanity; it was not any idea of the excellence of what he had written; it was *the pure joy of having written something that God had owned*, of having been made the channel of conveying a drop of living water to thirsty lips. Many were the letters which he got, thanking him for his words in season, and great was his gladness in receiving these; nor in that gladness did there mingle any element of vainglory. Besides these, he has left in several notebooks fragmentary remarks, criticisms, and imperfect jottings. They are set down in no order; some at the end, some at the beginning of a book; some in ink, some in pencil; some fairly written, some crossed and almost illegible. They are very like what used to come out in conversation; never tame or stiff, often happy and suggestive; seldom in the line of other people's thoughts, even when not striking.

We number them for the sake of order; but they are gathered from a score of different manuscripts and letters, unclassified, and generally undated, often but broken snatches of thought:

1. To see the eternal across the temporary! Live on; pray on; hard by Jordan.

2. What a view! God hanging on a cross. Hating sin, loving sinners.

3. Submission to the will of God is the end or object of repentance. If the sinner, by the power of the awakening Spirit, reaches that point

in five minutes, he is ready just then to receive mercy, as much as if a lawwork of five years had gone before.

4. We can only get Christ's grace by getting himself. He and his benefits are never separated.

5. We are hindered by the leaven of self-dependence. We put vows and resolutions in the place of believing.

6. It is more blessed to give than to receive. But we grudge God the blessedness of giving. We want to put him in our debt by bustling and running to and fro. There are hundreds of Marthas for one Mary.

7. How much (the name) "Son of God" implied, may be learned from the hatred and opposition which it excited in the scribes and Pharisees.

8. He (Christ) is the meeting-place of heaven and earth (*Eph.* 1:10; *Col.* 1:20). They were to be no longer two, as sin had made them, separated and estranged; but friendly, in loving intercourse. This was to go on from age to age. Children of men, yet citizens of heaven. Prayers and answers, graces, blessings, gifts, heavenly help — these make up Christ's golden clasp that binds all together.

9. Joseph and Christ (*Matt.* 1:19). Joseph fancies, Christ knows. Joseph would not expose, Christ hides for ever and takes away. Joseph purposed to put away; Christ says, Return again to me. Joseph is betrothed, Christ married; the Lamb's wife.

10. The seventy return (*Luke* 10:17), saying, 'Even the devils are subject unto us.' They were sent to *heal;* but even in efforts beyond their commission succeeded. There was exultation, yet peril in this. Nothing is more perilous for a man than his discovery that spiritual powers wait upon his beck. Therefore they are warned. There is a safer and truer joy; without self-satisfaction and self-elation.

11. When weak, then is the need of divine help; when weak, Satan tempts; when weak, God is very present.

12. The 'fearful' (*Rev.* 21:8), or 'cowards', are not those who *fear* to come short (*Heb.* 4:1), or *who fear to* disbelieve (*Heb.* 11:7), or who *fear* to be too bold or presuming (*Mark* 5:33). But those who dare nothing for Christ; not valiant in fight; who fear them that kill the body; who sway with the times; afraid to fight against lust, and to deny the flesh.

There is the fear of the evil servant (*Matt.* 25:25); of those who are lazy in holy duties; who see a lion in the way; who will not venture to suffer anything for Christ. The 'unbelieving' are not those who are weak in faith, but who never believed at all; who never closed with Christ's offers.

13. They shall 'see *his face'* (*Rev.* 22:4); Moses saw only his *back parts* (*Exod.* 33:23).

14. Walking one day, I saw an aged person. I asked, 'Is Christ yours?' She hesitated. I said, 'Here is a tract; I offer it, give it. Is it yours yet?' 'No, for I have not yet taken it.' She then stretched out her hand, and took it. 'Now it is mine', she said, shedding tears. See here why so many gospel hearers are unsaved. Salvation is offered, given, pressed; but *never taken,* and so does not become theirs. What I did to that woman, I am doing here in God's name tonight. As a fellow-worker, I *beseech* (*2 Cor.* 5). I show you the *grace* of God; tell you of *peace* with God. He has *made* it, and offers it to you. Be reconciled. Look no longer at your sins. Believe; become friends; come join hands. Do it *now.* Put away doubts, fears, suspicions; become a child, a friend of God. Receive not the grace of God in vain.

15. Let us put away our own ideas and plans, and let the Lord work when and how he will. Let us look away from difficulties, unlikelihoods, impossibilities, and rest simply on the Lord. This honours him; and he will honour us. How much has faith done! How much it still will do!

16. They constrained him (*Luke* 24:29); they took hold of him. Yet this would not have done it. But their heart took hold of him, clung to him. So we love, value, find blessing; want more. Stay with us, we say, and complete what thou hast begun. This prevailed then, and it always will. The Lord wishes to be loved, valued, needed, held fast. So he blessed them, and sent them to bless others.

17. Supplies of animal spirits or intellectual vigour will not do; it must be spiritual strength to do and suffer; constant and seasonable; the flesh swallowed up by the Spirit. This leads to heavenly promotion (*2 Cor.* 4:17); brings into sympathy with Christ; fellowship of suffering;

makes us able to bear the weight of glory. Less of glory on earth; more of glory in heaven.

18. The Holy Spirit is not intermittent; not limited to revival seasons. Parents give good gifts at all times; and more so God. We are commanded to do all duties in the Spirit; to live, walk, pray, work in the Spirit. We should not be blamed for sloth and carnality if the Spirit were not always attainable. God is not impoverished by the abundance of bestowment. Like the sun, he is never exhausted.

19. I have hope that the Lord will so show us the worthiness of his Son, that we shall ask, expect, and receive greater things than we have yet known. I feel as if I had been an idler. We should try to keep up the continuity of grace. Our good frames are usually like spring-tides, that swell high for a season, and then shrink back, leaving our deformity and fruitlessness to appear.

20. I have a growing impression that we do not lean enough on the Lord while we are preaching. We are apt to trust to our sword and our bow. Of course it would be folly to go to the field with an inefficient sword or bow; but even when the weapons are at the best, they do not form the chief or essential element of success.

21. Why are we poor and needy, when he who came to seek and save us is rich and bountiful? Are we enough alone? Do divine things get time to soak into our souls, and get at the roots and principles of our life?

22. I wish you would teach me how to feed constantly on the hidden manna; but flesh and blood cannot reveal. Why are we weak and empty, when Jesus is entered into his rest, and *is* ever overflowing?

23. I enjoyed preaching last Sabbath on Popery very much. It is a controversy into which, I think, I shall be enabled to go with all my heart and strength. It is no fragmentary, corner question that is mooted; but life or death, Christ or Satan. I should like to wear out in the storm, rather than rot in the stagnant calm. Only the Spirit lift up the standard.

24. I give you a text: 'Surely in the Lord have I righteousness and strength.' How humble, and yet how bold; how weak, and yet how

strong, we should be if we could act on this principle! These, I suppose, are the wings that make the 'liers among the pots' 'mount up like eagles.'

25. Our sins hinder us from seeing the glory of God.

26. We see how any supposed or real offence mars and hinders intercourse with one another. What, then, must it be when sin comes between us and God? How vain our attempts to be as before! Let us hasten to the Advocate and the blood.

27. I desire to humble myself to thy will, and to be crushed and broken at every hand.

28. How dreadful if sin went unpunished!

29. 'I was daily his delight.' Let not this slip from my mind. Oh how blind and wicked I have been, in seeking or making vain substitutes for this blessed portion both of God and man!

30. God's service is honour, blessedness, true liberty.

31. He redeems with his blood. He became a sacrifice, a curse; was made under the law. What should I be for him; and what should I be willing to do and suffer for his elect's sake, which is the church?

32. Let me know thy love, in its reality, tenderness, sweetness, more and more from day to day.

33. Leviticus 25:36-38. The redemption from Egypt is given as a reason for the willing performance of difficult duties. Lord, keep me ever under the power of thy dying love.

34. It does not matter much, whether it be the work of the world or the work of God in which we are busy. *Self* can be as active, and perhaps more secure in the one, than in the other. O Lord, save me from this leprosy!

35. I never noticed till today, the *negative* character of the commands regarding the Holy Ghost. Resist *not;* quench *not;* vex *not;* grieve *not;* seeming to imply, that if we do not restrain and force him away, it is his blessed disposition to abide, and spring up as a well of living water.

36. I accept my punishment in the cross of my Lord, and desire now to fill up the measure of my afflictions.

37. *Judge angels*! Do we not do this already, when we examine Satan's suggestions, and resist, and reject them? Is not the daily life of the thriving child of God, a judging of the god of this world, and condemning him?

38. Hold up, hold on, hold out; the longest earthly trial will come to an end.

39. When we try to please men, we fall into a snare; but when we please our blessed Lord, all goes well.

40. Living near the Lord is the secret of peace. Why should we walk among briers, and get entangled and torn, when we might mount as on eagle's wing? Sometimes we have not the wing, and then it is sad enough. But I believe that if we wait quietly and thankfully on the Lord, he will soon pity us, and send from above, and take us, and draw us out of all our troubles.

41. It is a duty to cultivate a holy cheerfulness, hopefulness, and trustfulness. It is not easy, and it is not common among good people. But it is surely right, and it is possible. Sorrowful, yet always rejoicing: that, I suppose, is the joy of the humble, yet hearty believer.

42. Letters from home. Thankful for manifold expressions of kindness from afar; but, Lord, thou alone art my portion. Weary, yet seek to fall back on my heavenly, never-failing Friend.

43. Compare the end of Psalm 2 and Revelation 2, and Psalm 110 and Isaiah 62, and one cannot help feeling that there is a more than possibility that the millenarian view is right. Let me search and wait and pray. Be thou my teacher, and let me not, from a desire to escape from the burden of an unconverted world too easily, receive a system which, if it is true, helps to explain the present state of things. Our supineness, unbelief, selfishness, miserable divisions, account for the little progress in spreading the gospel. But a universal preaching of the gospel would not amount to what is promised. Christendom *is* not Christian.

44. In a little while the wickedness of the wicked and the follies of the righteous will come to an end. The first will pass away, and the latter will be made straight. Should it be according to *our* mind?

45. Let us brace ourselves for trials. I see they are unavoidable here. The fickleness, the ceaseless change, the gathering and scattering, must be a constant trial. I see no hope of rest but in the crucifixion of the flesh, the ceasing from pride and self-will, and learning meekness and lowliness as the yoke-fellows of Christ. The Lord has been taking us apart to train us himself. Let us learn *fast,* that our task may be the sooner done.

46. Our own soul is our worst counsellor, and our own heart our worst comforter.

47. I was much struck today with the morning light. A cloud suddenly broke in the east, and there was in a moment a glorious burst of radiance. So, sometimes, the truth works quietly in the heart, and then suddenly breaks forth, and the happy man knows that the kingdom of God has come. So it will be with the Beloved. Sometime, when all seems dark, the heavens will rend, and the sign of the Son of man will appear. May we, in coming joy and sorrow, be able always to say, Amen, even so come, Lord Jesus!

48. Why are we cast down at the indifference and hostility that prevail to the kingdom of our Lord? The real truth is that He REIGNS! He has many loyal subjects. He has a dominion on high. Why do we not rather rejoice that we belong to such a glorious, mighty, prevailing, and everlasting kingdom? We must not stand, shamefaced and craven, like Israel before the vaunting Goliath; but rather go like David, rejoicing in our glorious Lord, and speaking of the greatness of his kingdom, and the might of his power. Do you think we live on earth as citizens of the new Jerusalem?

49. I have been thinking of the necessity of having a thorough bent to good. No one can do good to his fellows without it. I suspect those who are to be of large usefulness, must get that bent early, and cherish it, and strengthen it.

50. I am so accustomed to realize the minute providence of God, that I think I see his finger in the minutest matter — a look, a word, a manifestation of temper. But I have not often, I fear, the comfort of this, just because I do not pray enough to this all-ordering Lord.

51. May the Lord take the guidance of our affections, as of all else!

52. Don't you think we need to bring our highest principles and motives to bear on hourly little things?

53. Our great business should be to keep up the life of God in the soul.

54. How sad that it should ever be an act of violence to ourselves, to come near to God! yet we should be oftener doing this violence.

55. Let me in all things take up the cross.

56. A little trial; but it passed away. How wrong it is, at the appearance of every little cloud, to cry, A storm! a storm! Let me ever see the rainbow in the cloud.

57. My sun and shield, the lifter up of my head, I feel some longing to be with thee!

58. Prosperity leads to pride, and trouble to heartlessness. In every way there is sin. But in thy presence is purity and peace.

59. Help me to think more of those who are neglecting the pleasant land.

60. There must be clouds and darkness; but the Sun of Righteousness is above them all.

61. I see that nothing is really terrible but the wrath of God. Other troubles can be borne, triumphed over, and made to work for good; but the wrath of God withers and destroys. Who can bear it?

62. When Satan sifts, he raises such a commotion that nothing is seen but the dust and chaff.

63. I wish we were home, when the members, as well as the head, will be able to say of one another, 'Thou art all fair.'

64. This is not our rest. 'Thy will be done', is the thing that comes next to it.

65. I see it would be the highest wisdom to let all go to wreck and be lost, a thousand times, rather than commit a single sin.

66. Submission and patience is the way of peace.

67. To look forward to the Lord's coming, when he will rest from his labours, be fully glorified, fully gladdened, when the whole body will be gathered in, — that is the true Christian spirit.

68. I have been thinking of the Lion, Ox, Eagle, and Man. How all meet in Christ! Dignified, diligent, disinterested, divine! How much we fail in one or other, and too often in all!

69. Look at Ezekiel 29:16. There are some sins which, if we fall into them, bring all past sins up again into the memory of God.

70. There are but two great springs of action in the world, — selfishness and love. How very much of our life has sprung from the former, and so is sin, and therefore worthless!

71. I think one great want — the want of the age — is a deep and real persuasion of the punitive judgment of God.

72. The godly man's darkness is better than the worldly man's sparks and fires.

73. Human temporary ties are of little value anywhere; but we see this here specially. Yet God is forming a body for his dear Son, and none of the members thereof shall perish.

74. The close of a year is like the deathbed of a benefactor. A friend, who has been long with us, and brought us many mercies and opportunities, is going away.

75. I have been thinking that the Lord's coming is strangely overlooked by most. It seems as if Satan contrived to spike the battery.

76. If we could cease from self and outward things, we should always have comfort in the Lord. Food in our hunger, strength in our weakness, and hope in our darkness.

77. Accepted in the Beloved, we have only to try to do God's will on earth, as they do it in heaven, not as servants, but as dear children.

78. 'I will come again' — sooner than the world wishes, but not too soon for those who love his appearing.

79. Injuries and wrongs God is using to detach our hearts from the world, and to loosen the roots which bind affections to earth.

80. God is striving to make the inheritance meet for us. How sad that we should be so loath to be made meet for the inheritance!

81. I have been thinking of that verse, 'His fruit was sweet to my taste.' Don't we try to live on our fruit, instead of getting life, strength, and joy from the tree of immortality?

82. I think Satan hates peculiarly Messiah's *crown*. 'Yet have I set my King upon my holy hill of Zion.'

83. I desire especially to put myself into thy hand for guidance, in regard to the way of conducting my work.

84. I am aware that I would fain live low, and walk by sense. Lord, make me willing to be trained to a higher life.

85. May love to thee kill discontentment, ambition, and unbelief.

86. I find it easier to count all loss, than to be counted loss.

87. How easy it would be to walk through the shadows, if we kept the eye fixed on the opening door, and the coming glory!

88. I think I should like to be in a multitude, clapping their hands to God with the voice of trumpet; and yet there might be a great deal of mere sympathy in this, and carnal feeling.

89. I can sympathize with those who cry, 'Lord Jesus, come!' Oh, quickly come, and take the kingdom to thyself.

90. Trials should only exercise love, and make it grow. I feel this, and really wish that each day I might become brimful of grace and kindness, and forget myself altogether, and go about seeking to do good. Let us try to be cheerful, and thankful, and loving to all, and to bound over obstacles, and smooth over asperities.

91. I have been at a funeral. It was a most dreary morning. I think one would almost like the sun to shine upon one's grave.

92. I am persuaded that unbelief is *the* root of bitterness. There are others, doubtless; but that is the root of all evil. Even the love of money springs from this; for if we had faith in God, we should not care for a stock of our own, but would be content to leave all in the hands of God.

93. We should be thankful for trials. What should we be without them? There may be people that do not require them. I am not of that number.

94. We should make a distinction between being faithful and loving; but I doubt if they can be separated. If love is wanting, it is bitterness, not faithfulness.

95. I long for the purged conscience, the *kept* heart, the humble

mind, the girded loins, the crucified flesh, and the lip and life of truth.

96. To hold habitually any truth which is above nature, and above the state of mind of those with whom we mix, requires increasing watchfulness, self-recollection, and prayer.

97. I fear few can habitually say they possess and enjoy the better part. Now and then I see some who seem to do it. You know it by their meekness and quietness of spirit under all trials.

98. I have been thinking of the high state of a man in Christ. Everything that lights upon him really lights upon Christ, and he may well let it pass, assured that the Lord will take it up in due time. I think this is the secret of Christian meekness, and almost indifference to the mockings of the Ishmaelites of this world.

99. If we had a better idea of the evil of sin, and how deeply and strongly it is rooted in our nature, we should be less surprised at the frequency and severity, and sometimes singularity of our trials.

100. God makes his people's sins work for the advancement of his work in one another; just as he makes Satan and his seed the Gibeonites in his temple. But no thanks to them for this; the glory be to the Lord.

101. We need much grace to be able to see the kingdom of God, where man sees it not. Christ goes down into his garden, and he finds wonders there — the patience of Job, the Canaanite's great faith, the Magdalene's much love, and he is satisfied; but nature is like the Pharisee — 'This poor publican'; or like Simon, 'If he had been a prophet', *etc.* And so, till we have the mind of Christ, and only so long as we have it, do we see the beauty and value of grace.

102. Faith is a paradoxical creature; so strong that he can pull the treasures of heaven down, and yet so weak that a little of earth's dross can quite crush him.

103. I am more and more persuaded that holy love is the very element of true blessedness. I wish we could live in this frame, excluding selfishness, both in its religious and its sinful forms. Have you not often noticed how we can, as it were, form for ourselves a kind of new

creation? If we are in a dissatisfied, selfish spirit, we see only what is dark and faulty; but in a thankful, cheerful spirit, we see only what is bright, and cast a kind of robe of beauty over all we meet.

104. A weak faith cannot do much, but it can receive a whole Christ.

105. Christ's smile is better than all knowledge or self-work.

106. I am sure that to keep near the Lord is better than all other knowledge; but it is necessary to keep pace with what *is* doing in the work of God.

107. Satan will try by bad things, and, if that fails, by good things, to turn us away from the Lord.

108. I feel so strongly that no work stands but God's; that one word spoken in his Spirit is worth ten thousand of our own; and that the little finger, when he wields it, can do more than ten thousand men without him.

109. I have been noticing how easily our vain minds are diverted away from Christ, even while we are endeavouring to hold communion with him. Surely we do lightly esteem him, when every trifle can draw us away. But he has those in the world who do cleave to him with full purpose of heart, and count all besides, in comparison, dross and dung.

110. Mercy and judgment are twin sisters, that came hand in hand, and hitherto have continued walking together, or if one sometimes goes before, the other speedily overtakes. The finishing of the mystery will terminate this sisterhood; for heaven will not need, and hell shall not enjoy them.

111. The best way of winning souls, is *not* by trying to get people's love and confidence for ourselves, but trying to lead them to give their love and confidence to Christ; trying *not* to get them to attach themselves to us, but to lead them to attach themselves to Christ; trying *not* to get them to think well of us, but putting ourselves out of sight, to lead them to think Christ the chiefest among ten thousand. This seems a roundabout way, but it is the true way, for the souls we bring to the Lord become ours by a tender and everlasting bond.

112. I wish we could be so *in* him that self would be forgotten, and we should not think of what we do or suffer. Could we become as the blind that see not, and the deaf that hear not. We have been long thus insensible to the things of God; would it not be a blessed revenge to crucify the flesh, and now be as insensible to all its corrupt affections and passions?

113. How can we think anything that befalls us hard or strange, after the manacled hands, and the smitten, insulted face of the Lord of glory? Isn't it a beautiful little trait of John that, when he tells how the caitiff struck the Lord, he adds, 'Now Annas had sent him *bound*' *etc*. So that Jesus was defenceless, and this struck the disciple as a touching aggravation of the foul deed.

114. How adorable and admirable was Christ's human life! The constant self-possession, the readiness to meet and go successfully through every little emergency, the hearty, earnest entering into the little details of each passing hour, his tender sympathy for the afflicted, his reproof and warning of the proud and worldly, his stedfast ongoing amid difficulty and discouragement, his frequent retirement and prayer. Why do we not love and glorify him more, as the chiefest among ten thousand, the perfect Man, and the everlasting God?

115. Don't wonder at occasional castings down. The Bible would not be so full of 'Comfort ye's', and 'Fear not's', if God's dearest did not need it.

116. Did not get near God in the morning, having to go out; so failed all the day.

117. When shall I have an entire, loving faith, that will construe all God's dealings kindly and favourably?

118. Some trials, but scarce worth the name. If I were more meek and poor in spirit, I should not feel them.

119. What I need is more living on Christ.

120. Men are everywhere fearfully turned away from God. Lord, save and deliver!

121. Hold me *in;* hold me *up;* hold me *back;* and grant me this day to see the dead hearing the voice of the Son of God.

122. Resting on Christ; his work, his care, his government, his grace.

123. Fill me with the Holy Ghost today.

124. Watching unto prayer; with thoughts of him and his coming.

125. Draw me, keep me, possess me, and be my all in all.

126. Keep me this day feeding on thy fulness and glory.

127. Trust in him, my soul, with all thy might.

128. Keep me from every earthly selfish impulse, waiting quietly on thee, of whom and through whom are all things.

129. I desire to dwell this day among the eternal things.

130. Jesus in greatest darkness saw the coming glory. His *holding* (*Luke* 22:63) is our freedom. His *blindfolding* is our light. He held us, though storms blew. Let us hold him through tribulation. He held us amid mockery and spitting. Let us hold him amid shame and contempt.

131. When I would see myself by nature, I would look to the garden, judgment hall, Calvary; when I would see myself in grace, I would look to God's right hand.

132. Obedience can only be known through suffering. If what we have to do is altogether agreeable to us, then we may do it, not so much from a regard to the will of another, as to our own. Selfishness may have place in such a case. We may be doing things to gratify ourselves, not to please or serve another. But when we do things irksome, humbling, painful, this is obedience.

133. In seeking some recommendation in yourselves to come to God, you are dishonouring his justice in thinking you have anything fit for its acceptance, dishonouring his grace in thinking he cannot love and save freely, and dishonouring his Son's blood in thinking it cannot cleanse from all iniquity and make a full atonement.

134. Apostles stand amazed at the greatness of salvation; they do not attempt to tell how great; but simply say, '*So great salvation.*' What manner of love!' 'So loved.'

135. More consciences are slurred with flagrant sin than we know of, and the stain remains within when it is blotted from the book of heaven. But the sad memory is a cure for worse things than itself, a

perpetual antidote to pride, an ever-ready reproof to discontent, a good help to patience and self-renunciation, and makes the heart run over with thankfulness.

136. It is our pride, our delicacy, our earthly-mindedness that are anxious. God has not promised to provide for them, and therefore we cannot trust him with their concerns.

137. 'He that made me whole, the same said', *etc*. I never questioned, but believed it right. He is a God to me; what he says I unhesitatingly do.

138. What have they seen in thy house? Silver and gold — natural; it is a King's house. But what have they seen? A lately endangered, delivered man. Have they seen the records of thy thankfulness for divine mercy? They have seen ostentatious display of earth's grandeur; they would see that at home. What is seen in my house? When a stranger comes, what does he see? Where is thy God, thy religion, thy peace? Unseen.

139. Earth's best unions and fellowships are poor, shadowy, and unsubstantial in comparison with that which the gospel introduces.

140. The Holy Ghost so works in us that he works by us. If we do nothing, he does nothing. 'Go', he says, 'and I go with you.'

141. Christ is the King excluded from his dominion while a usurper occupies his throne. The believer is a loyalist in the kingdom during the usurpation. What can he join with in the world? His heart is with his absent King, his hopes all centred in his return. The whole course of the kingdom has but one character in his eyes, as not knowing him whose right it is.

142. A walk by faith seems to the world void of common sense.

143. Colossians 2:3. Secular as well as divine. Satan seeks to separate knowledge from Christ its Source, and then to set it in antagonism to him. He calls the laws of nature, God. Every new discovery in science of heavenly or earthly things is put in the witness-box of infidelity, as an evidence against revealed religion.

144. Seek such light and faith that you may see as clearly the folly and absurdity of going contrary to moral as well as to natural laws. We see the folly of walking on water or through fire; but should we not also see

the madness of transgressing any of God's laws? God can contravene physical laws; say to fire, Burn not; water, Drown not. But he cannot say to sin, Hurt not; bring not desert of death.

145. Death through sin is dreadful, here and hereafter. Death to sin, blessed, holiness. Death from sin, everlasting rest.

146. When we are at the lowest, his help is nearest.

147. Broken volcanic mountain-ranges tell of physical convulsions; fortresses and defences tell of political; denominations and sects tell of moral and religious.

148. The green leaf, full of sap, displays little of the skill and care of God, compared with the same leaf when withered and turned into the skeleton of its former self.

149. Grace and corruption, love of Christ and love of the world, are the centripetal and centrifugal forces acting on the child of God, and their relative force determines his place and conduct.

150. What portion is best? That which induces a habit of daily dependence, and an exercise of daily faith in the Author of every good and perfect gift.

151. Sinners returning to the Lord are like lines converging from the circumference to the centre; they not only meet with God, but also with one another. Near to Christ, near to one another.

152. Years are the waves of Time's tide.

153. There is a cataract in the eye of unrenewed nature, and God alone can couch it.

154. God has prepared magazines for his army on the road. Hagar's bottle of water is spent; but God's fountain comes to view. Light against the time of darkness. In a railway carriage, we scarce observe the lighted lamp in the roof, feebly twinkling. But all at once the whistle sounds; and in the darkness of the tunnel we rejoice in the considerate provision which cheers us, until we again emerge into light of heaven.

155. Matthew 14:5. Herod. Those who are kept back from evil only by outward restraints, will, ere long, break through. The fire burns, grows; and some new fuel throws down the barrier.

156. Popery and Puseyism both claim a monopoly of the water of heaven; but they cannot prevent the rain from falling where God will.

157. What we need is pointed, penetrating, discriminating application. Argument breaches the wall; application storms it.

158. Discharge your gun among a covey, and you probably kill none. Aim at one after another, — insulate, — and you probably get all.

159. The earth has internal heat, whence come volcanoes, earthquakes. It receives heat from above; hence life and fertility; *flesh* and *spirit.*

160. One earnest Christian in a place is like a pebble thrown into water; the circle widens, and includes many.

161. In the experience and actings of a Christian, everything depends upon the place which God occupies in the heart. If our thoughts of God are low, the standard of judgment and conduct will be low.

162. We do not sufficiently live in the atmosphere of God's holiness and grace. Our conflicts, sorrows, and experiences come between us and God, and shut him out of our mind; and then we lapse into legalism and religiousness of nature, or worldliness and moral evil.

163. He only can bear to know all that is in his heart who can say, 'Thou hast cast all my sins behind thy back.' When thus prepared, the nearer we approach to the knowledge of our all, the nearer we come to the knowledge of God's all.

164. We are like the king who smote thrice and stopped. We do not know the value of prayer.

165. Hezekiah. The king of Assyria, with an army, was overcome. The king of Babylon, with a present, overcame. Hezekiah was off his guard. The plausible Gibeonite is more dangerous than the rugged sons of Anak. He had much to tell about God, but he only speaks of himself.

166. From the first moment of spiritual awakening to the close, precious in the sight of the Lord is the death of his saints. Our power to refresh and gladden the mind of Jesus is fully, freely owned in God's word. But the affection that can be gratified may also be wounded.

167. It is humbling to know that the heart left to itself cares not for

the Lord or his glory. It sold him for a mess of pottage, for a herd of swine, for thirty pieces of silver; and would still for anything.

168. As a general rule, the more deeply religious men become, the calmer and more stedfast they grow. Joy of feeling is direct, but often turbid, temporary. Joy of calm, stedfast doing is safer; steals gently in, and is 'I am with thee.'

169. There have been *Great Discoverers.* — Christ brought life and immortality to light by the gospel. *Great Conquerors.* — Christ spoiled principalities and powers. Some have left their high state to do good to others. Christ left the throne of glory and took the form of a servant. *Great Sacrifices.* — Christ died on the cross. *Great Architects.* — Christ made all things.

170. Can I thank God heartily when, in his sovereign grace, he pleases to use another in his service, my inferior in standing, in talent, in intelligence?

171. Diversity of opinions, and mutual kindly expression of them, is the sifting or ventilation that elicits truth.

172. The smallest thought of good, such as, This is sinful, This is selfish, is the Potter's hand touching you, to break you off the lump. If you persist in going on, in what he has begun to convince you is sin, or folly, or even not quite right, then you resist. Refuse not.

173. Suppose Barabbas had said, 'It is impossible that these tidings can refer to such a criminal as I. It is absurd.' Or, 'I will not leave my prison till I become another man, and prove my repentance.'

174. A young Christian thinks that he knows everything. He advances a little way, and finds that he knows not the half of what he thought he knew. At last he says, 'I know nothing as I ought to know.' He begins to fight with the idea that nothing can overcome him. He ends with the conviction that anything will throw him down without Christ's grace.

175. Finite being has no peace to enjoy or to confer; it is the gift of the Father, the purchase of the Son, the creation of the Holy Ghost.

176. Fear not to meet the assembly of the first-born; they are little children, humble and loving.

177. Habits go with us to eternity.

178. 2 Timothy 2:10. Prayer is one of the ways of enduring hardness. We need self-denial and resolute effort to get even *time* for prayer; and we must endure conflict with Satan and self ere we are able to continue in prayer. Away from company, from books, from study, from work, let us give ourselves to prayer far oftener than we have done. Let us be prepared to meet with few sympathizers. Though the labour of the mind may find many to appreciate it, yet the labour of the heart — prayer, who will regard this? Let *us* endure this disregard.

179. Knowledge of God. Works help; the word more, but Christ most. If an angel came to earth when first created, what would he have looked at to know God? Not sun, sky, garden, but man — this his image, his likeness. So Christ is the image of invisible God.

180. Titus 1:2. In hope of eternal life. Thinking of my own habitual state of mind, I am grieved to observe how little this great object is present and influential on my mind. I seem to live in and for present things, the daily duties, occurrences, and trials of life. But I feel that the future life should be the great object in my heart, and that the thought of it should stimulate, comfort, support, and guide me.

181. Titus 1:7. The steward of God. I feel as if I had not sufficiently thought of my office in this aspect of it. What has the Lord committed to me? What conscious possession have I of the unsearchable riches? And what am I dispensing? whom am I feeding? and with what? I think my mind fixes more upon the idea of the Shepherd, and only on one branch of this, the literally pastoral, dealing with individuals, following and exerting a somewhat mechanical influence over them. Lord, help me to think of my office in all its length and breadth, and manifold ministrations and responsibilities.

182. If we are prepared to shine, God will find the candlestick; if we are prepared to work, God will find us something to do. Only be ready and willing for anything.

183. The baptism of fire would recall Abraham's smoking furnace, the burning bush, pillar of fire, shekinah, coal of fire on Isaiah's lips,

Ezekiel's visions, and teach the approach of a new manifestation of the power and presence of God.

184. The spring of the clock represents the inner life; the pendulum, outer life. The pendulum will not go without the spring, and yet the spring will go to wreck without the pendulum.

185. When my body, that played so great a part in my temptation, sin, and shame, and was the busy and eager servant of my depraved spirit, is restored to me incorruptible, what a triumphant proof that I am wholly redeemed!

186. God takes our Christian friends; but he will give them back, after a season, worthier than before.

187. Do you not observe exuberance and overflowing in some of God's gifts? Light for all, though blind; for those who close their eyes, and live in deep mines, and never benefit by it. Yet there it is, if they would use. So fulness in Christ, though multitudes never avail themselves of it. Free to all, sufficient for all.

188. I feel that it is only by being full of faith and of the Holy Ghost, that I can hope to hold on with any comfort.

189. I long for more of direct, conscious, happy fellowship with the Lord. I know that this can only be by faith.

190. Gave way in the morning to unbelief, as if the Lord could not keep and prosper me, notwithstanding obstacles and enemies. I suffered, in consequence, all the day, going haltingly, and easily overcome. Help!

191. A quiet day, yet feeling ungirded, and in danger.

192. Past suffering is a possession.

193. When so fully as when we see him as he is, shall we mourn the pierced one? Happiness is not exclusive of sorrow.

194. Trials were once stumbling-blocks; now a causeway to heaven.

195. I am my own night. Christ is my day. When I walk in the day (in Christ), I stumble not. When I walk in the night (in self), I fall.

196. I ought to hate sin; all my experiences should make me hate it; but I have no true hatred of it, but what I get from God. I seek to live in communion with him *for this,* as well as for peace and joy.

197. Work, Lord, in and by and around me.

198. Amazed at the extent of human depravity, the weight of divine wrath, and the intensity of Satan's malice.

199. Unbelief cannot sleep; nor self-will; nor love of earthly things. God gives his beloved sleep.

200. No thorns on the rose of Sharon.

These unstudied fragments may fitly close the life of one whose mission was to work and to speak, more than to write; whose ministerial course developed an originality, a *uniqueness,* such as makes us, now that he is gone, ask, Who shall step into his place, or do that peculiar work which he did so well?[1] 'By the grace of God he was what he was'; and anxiously do we look for another to fill up the blank. His life would take up large room in true Church-history,

[1] While correcting this sheet for the press, a letter has come in, which must not be omitted. It comes from a Free Church manse: 'From an early period my only desire as to a profession was that I might be permitted to serve God in the gospel ministry; and I do not remember anything which led me to think of even reconsidering that choice until the month of April 1853, when I was seventeen years of age. At the close of the session of the Edinburgh University in that month, I was fortunate enough to receive three prizes, — the second in the Senior Greek, the first in Sir William Hamilton's Logic, and the gold medal in the Natural Philosophy; and on the day on which I brought them home I was strongly tempted to abandon the purpose of preparing for the ministry, by the thought that in so doing I must forego both the exclusive pursuit of studies in which I found singular enjoyment, and the possible attainment of distinction, which I coveted with ardent ambition. After spending the day in perplexity, by reason of the conflict between newly awakened feelings and former resolutions, I went in the evening to Free St Luke's Church to hear Mr Milne, who was then about to leave for Calcutta in a few days…The text on which the discourse was based, was the language of Saul of Tarsus when Jesus met him on his way to Damascus, "Lord, what wilt thou have me to do?" To me it was "a word in season". The question which had agitated my mind during the day I was now brought to consider in the right frame of spirit, submitting the decision of it absolutely to the Lord; and when the claims of Christ on the service of his people, the necessities of perishing sinners, and the happiness and honour of labouring in the ministry of reconciliation, were set forth with a fervour and eloquence doubly impressive because of the circumstances of the speaker, so soon to bid farewell to his native land, I felt constrained to give myself anew and unreservedly to the Lord, and came home freed from every doubt as to the path of duty, and from every desire to do otherwise than devote my life to the blessed work of preaching the unsearchable riches of Christ. I have seldom read or heard the name of Mr Milne since that time without recalling, more or less vividly, the critical occasion on which his preaching was so blessed to my soul.'

though his name may be unnamed in the annals of a world which chronicles, not the harvests and the calms, but the famines and the convulsions of earth.

Yet it is the *unsensational* that is the effective and the abiding. For as days are not measured by the number of storms or rainbows, but by the still hours that go by unheeded; so the life of a divine workman, quietly busy at his immortal work from hour to hour, is to be estimated, not by the modern rules of sensation, and show, and bustle, but by its silent activities, and their everlasting, though at present invisible, results.

Inscription on the Monument of John Milne.

JOHN MILNE,

MINISTER OF
THE GOSPEL OF CHRIST.

CHRIST SENT ME TO PREACH THE GOSPEL.

'WE ARE AMBASSADORS FOR CHRIST,
AS THOUGH GOD DID BESEECH YOU BY US:
WE PRAY YOU IN CHRIST'S STEAD,
BE YE RECONCILED TO GOD;
FOR HE HATH MADE HIM TO BE SIN FOR US,
THAT WE MIGHT BE MADE
THE RIGHTEOUSNESS OF GOD IN HIM.'

HE LABOURED
FOR TWENTY-FOUR YEARS IN PERTH,
AS MINISTER OF ST LEONARD'S CHURCH,
FIRST IN THE ESTABLISHED,
AND THEN THE FREE CHURCH,
AND FOR UPWARDS OF FOUR YEARS
IN CALCUTTA.

BORN AT PETERHEAD, 26TH APRIL 1807.
DIED IN EDINBURGH 31ST MAY 1868.

St Leonards-in-the-Fields, Marshall Place, Perth, was built in 1885, 17 years after the death of John Milne. It replaced the 'inconvenient and uncomfortable' Disruption building in Victoria Street. Interestingly, the foundation stone of the new building was laid by Horatius Bonar, Milne's old friend, fellow worker, and biographer. Two stone inscriptions, which bear eloquent testimony to the congregation's old Free Church heritage, still greet the worshipper on the approach to the main door: 'For the Lord is our judge, the Lord is our lawgiver, the Lord is our king; he will save us' (*Isa.* 33:22) and 'The Lord our God be with us, as he was with our fathers: let him not leave us, nor forsake us' (*Isa.* 8:57). The building has belonged to the Church of Scotland since 1929, at which time it recieved its new name.

Appendix I

Extract of the Minutes of the Presbytery of Turriff, Licensing John Milne as Preacher of the Gospel[1]

Turriff, 24th *November* 1830. — The Presbytery met, and having been constituted. *Inter alia,* —

Mr John Milne, student of divinity, who lately came to reside within the bounds of this Presbytery, from the Presbytery of Aberdeen, produced a certificate from said Presbytery of Aberdeen, bearing that he had undergone preliminary trials, with approbation, on the 21st of July last, that circular letters had been addressed to the Presbyteries of the Synod, and that the Synod had allowed him to be taken on probationary trials. The Presbytery of Aberdeen having transferred his trials to be completed before this Presbytery, there are now prescribed to Mr Milne the following pieces of trial: An exercise and addition on Romans 5:1-5; homily, Matthew 6:33; lecture, 110th Psalm; popular discourse, Matthew 5:8; and exegesis,

[1] Mr Geddie of Banff, in forwarding the above extract to Cowan, adds: 'In his note, Mr Abel says, I may state that the moderator who licensed Mr Milne was Mr G. R. Davidson, now of Edinburgh; and that of the members of Presbytery then present, two others are still living — *viz.* Mr Finlay of King Edward, and Mr Manson, now residing in Banff.'

Quae sunt criteria divinas revelationis? [1]

Turriff, 30th March 1831. — The Presbytery met, and was constituted. *Inter alia,* —

Mr John Milne delivered a homily, lecture, and popular discourse
on the subjects prescribed him.

Fyvie, 4th May 1831. — The Presbytery met, and having been
constituted. *Inter alia,* —

Mr John Milne delivered an exegesis, and exercise and addition
on the subjects formerly prescribed. The Presbytery, considering that
Mr Milne had undergone the several pieces of trial required by the
laws of the Church, now took a retrospective view of the whole, and
having had much reason to be satisfied, Mr Milne was called in,
and having returned satisfactory answers to the questions to be put
to all candidates for licence, by Act 10, Assembly 1711; and having
subscribed the formula *coram,* the Act against simony was read to
him. Whereupon the Moderator, in name and by appointment of
the Presbytery, licensed Mr Milne to preach the gospel of our Lord
Jesus Christ, and directed the clerk to grant him an extract to this
effect when required.

Extracted from the records of the Presbytery of Turriff; on this
and the preceding page, by

JOHN ABEL, *Presby. Cl.*

---

[1] 'What are the criteria of a divine revelation?' *Ed.*

Appendix II

Reminiscences of John Milne, by One of His Elders

I became a member of Mr Milne's congregation before the Disruption, and left Old St Leonard's, which had been the hallowed scene of many precious services, and of the revival under the late Mr W. C. Burns, along with Mr Milne, and the great body of the congregation, in 1843. I have known him from that time down to the present, and during a great portion of that time I knew him intimately, and had the privilege of being admitted to his confidence.

I wish now to state a few brief impressions regarding him.

His Spirit and Aim

No one who was privileged to sit under Mr Milne's ministry, or meet him in private, could fail to be struck with his holy zeal and earnestness. The unhappy contrast, which so often is felt to exist between the spirit exhibited in the pulpit, and that exemplified in the private intercourse of life, did not apply to him. On the contrary, his spiritual life was so distinctly marked and vigorous, that it was impossible to be in his society, for however short a time, without being impressed with the conviction that you were holding communion with a holy man of God, whose walk was 'a walk in the Spirit'. This rendered his visits very precious, however brief, whether to those in health or in sickness. The writer has often felt stimulated and rebuked by a short visit, amounting to scarce more than a salutation, because of the spiritual savour which accompanied the few warm words he spoke.

His Visits

He greatly excelled in congregational visitation, and spent a large portion of time in this work. He knew all his people, old and young alike, thoroughly. When any were absent from church, he made it his business to inquire about them. As a general rule, every Sabbath evening was spent in visiting those unable to go to church from sickness; and if it proved to be from indisposition, however trifling, he almost invariably made it the occasion of a call. He seemed to attach great importance to this, as if it were with him a maxim, that where God in his providence was working in any special manner, it was his duty, as a worker together with him, to be following hard after, to seize the opportunity of sowing precious seed in soil already prepared for it. No time was allowed to elapse between the knowledge of sickness and his calls. The iron was struck when the impression could best be made; the mould of the word was applied when the soul was most impressible. Many, in consequence, were brought to the knowledge of the truth as it is in Jesus in this way, and God's people found such visits very helpful. On one occasion, one of the members of his congregation was confined to bed by one of those short illnesses which operate as a withdrawal from the bustle of the world, so needful to save the soul from the crust of worldliness. Mr Milne made a brief visit. Before leaving, he quoted, without note or comment, that word, 1 Timothy 4:6, only changing the 'she' into 'he:' 'He that liveth in pleasure, is dead while he liveth.' The word was felt to come with the power of the Spirit to the heart, being truly a word in season.

His Mode of Confirming Young Christians

He regarded it as a fundamental principle, that, in order to proper growth in the spiritual life, there must be work for Christ. He invariably, therefore, sought out some occupation for converts, according to their capacity. The Sabbath school, tract-distributing, visitation of the poor, or similar work, was found for them; and he carefully kept his eye on them, giving them all needful counsel and encouragement. Many in this way were trained up to become useful and confirmed Christians, and could testify, if necessary, to the benefits they thus received. The writer was early enlisted in this way, by Mr Milne, as a Sabbath-school teacher; and he believes that, under God, this was the chief means of preventing him making shipwreck of faith amid the temptations incident to an anxious and harassing profession. The study required for the Sabbath school, from week to week, kept his mind in close and living contact with the word of God, and with God in Christ, the treasure hid in this field; and he cannot but thank God that he ever was invited by his departed servant to engage in this good work. His experience, however, is only, he is persuaded, that of many others.

His Work in the Sabbath School

He took a special interest in this department of Christian work. Before going to India, when his health was good, he almost daily visited the Sabbath school, often addressing the children, and — frequently going from class to class, cheering the teachers and scholars alike, by his evident interest in their work, and by the seasonable words which fell from him.

His Session

As he delighted in pastoral visitation, so he succeeded in getting his elders to perform a large amount of congregational visitation. They visited their districts before each quarterly communion, and, as far as circumstances permitted, conducted a religious service in each house by reading the Scriptures and engaging in prayer. They reported the result of their visitations quarterly; and at the meetings for this purpose it was very interesting to hear the reports, showing the variety that exists in human experience, and the value of watching for souls as they that must give account.[1] When a difference of opinion arose on any point, he discouraged the idea of putting it to the vote, but got the session to allow it to stand over for consideration to another meeting, at which unanimity was generally secured.

His Pulpit Work

This was characterized by great warmth and earnestness. A predominant desire was the conversion of souls, especially in the early part of his ministry. The Lord seemed to lay this on his heart more

---

[1] The Session agreed to the following heads of inquiry, to be put to the elders individually, at a special meeting to be held for the purpose previous to each quarterly communion: — *1st*. Have you endeavoured to visit and converse with all under your charge as an elder since last communion? *2d*. How are your visits generally conducted? *3d*. Are there any in your district under suspension, and if so, what means have you employed for their recovery? *4th*. Have you had occasion to know of any good being done in the way of awakening, conversion, or special upbuilding of God's people!

Appendix II 407

than the edification of believers. As might be expected, his mode of handling divine truth was not in a cold or didactic manner, but in a warm and experimental way. He had a remarkable richness and variety of thought and expression, both in his sermons and prayers, and not seldom rose in both to the point of genuine eloquence. He had read extensively; and having a good memory, he was never at a loss for an illustration. Some of these were of the most homely kind; but what would have looked vulgar or undignified as coming from some ministers, seemed appropriate after passing through his mental alchemy. On one sacramental season, when speaking of the Church's desire for communion with Christ, he quoted the lines of a well-known ballad:

> His very foot has music in't
> As he comes up the stair.[1]

His mind was cast in a decidedly poetical mould, and this was very apparent in all his services, not excepting his prayers, in which his soul oft-times was carried away in soaring, rapturous flights, like the chariots of Ammi-nadib. He quoted freely from the sacred poets, both in his sermons and his prayers. The following lines amongst others were often quoted:

> And a heart *at leisure from itself*
> To soothe and sympathize.
>
> Nothing in my hand I bring,
> Simply to Thy cross I cling.

He used often to remark that 'Each man had his own stroke of work;' that 'A congregation was not unlike an *hospital*, and therefore the members should deal kindly and gently towards each other.' Like other ministers, he had his favourite passages of Scripture. We note a few of his at random. The commendation of the Syrophenician,

[1] It was *exquisite;* but he was horrified when reminded that he had been quoting 'There's nae luck about the house.'

'O woman, great is thy faith!' The saying of the dying thief, 'We indeed justly.' That prayer, 'O the Hope of Israel, why shouldst thou be as a stranger in the land, and as a wayfaring man that turneth aside to tarry for a night?' The promise, 'I will make them, and the places round about my hill a blessing', *etc.*

HIS KNOWLEDGE OF HUMAN NATURE

He had a good insight into character, and combined the wisdom of the serpent with the harmlessness of the dove. He instinctively knew the men on whom he could rely. He knew how to bear with the infirmities of those who were weak; and this he would do over a period of years, and at last conquer by love. In this respect he often acted towards the wayward as John Newton dealt with Scott the commentator, and at last had his reward. One of his members and office-bearers was of a rather prosaic turn of mind, and craved, above everything, a didactic, exegetical exposition of Scripture. He often complained to Mr Milne that he failed in this respect, and these complaints were listened to without the slightest irritation, and so far from leading to estrangement, laid the foundation of lasting friendship. So far from discouraging the statement of his difficulties, he encouraged it, knowing that, whether well or ill-founded, they were honest. Let one example serve for all. On one occasion the person referred to said to Mr Milne, 'When you select a text from the prophets you often divide it into heads, and proceed to expound it without explaining the context. I can't listen with any profit to such a discourse. I must see that the foundation is properly laid before the superstructure is laid.' Mr Milne gently answered, 'But, my friend, there should be that bond of confidence between a minister and his people that they will trust him that he has studied the context, and that he gives them the result in his sermon.' The reply was, 'I beg your pardon, but I cannot subscribe to this doctrine. A minister is the ambassador of Christ. He should show his credentials, which he can only do when he clearly opens up his Master's commission; and woe then to the man that refuses to listen to his message!' Mr Milne tapped him on the shoulder, and, with the utmost frankness and kindness, said, 'You are quite right, friend; you are quite right.'

His Removal

His removal has caused a great blank in Perth. He was the centre of all evangelistic movements there, and a bond of union among all Christians, smoothing away difficulties, and bringing them together. His loss is universally deplored, and many and deep are the regrets that we shall see his face no more.

Appendix III

Mrs Milne's Memoir

*W*e should gladly have given the whole of the interesting record of the first Mrs Milne's deathbed, but we can only find room for the closing pages:

A few days before, she had said to her friend, Miss Sandeman, 'I feel willing to go for myself now, but how shall I bid them all farewell, and how will they stand it?' Miss S. advised her not to burden herself with such thoughts, but to trust that the Lord, who had done so much for her already, would care for her to the last. This comforted her; and her joyful smile, always when taking leave of us, showed how her confidence was not misplaced. Once John said to her, 'We shall miss you very much, but you shall not miss us.' She calmly replied, 'No; I don't think it.' He said, 'I just hope not to be long after you.' She replied sweetly, 'Well, you know I cannot now be anxious that you should be very long left.' The thought of leaving her baby never seemed to disturb her. Once, when she heard him crying, she looked up, and said sweetly, 'My little lamb bleating'; adding, with a smile, 'but I doubt I'll not be his dam.' On one occasion, when speaking of unbelief, it was remarked, What a dreadful sin it is! She replied, 'Yes, we see that when it is past, such presumption for a worm to doubt the Creator.' Towards evening she said to her husband, 'You will return thanks to the people for their prayers, for I feel I have been much indebted to them.' At one time John said, 'You feel quite easy.' She said, 'Yes, very easy; but it is not always so easy, it is just in keeping with all the rest of his dealings to me.' She delighted to recount her mercies, and said, 'It was kindness to let me come home, when I had such a wish for it.'

A little later in the evening she asked to have read to her a passage out of Welwood's *Glimpse of Glory*, and was able to listen with enjoyment to many pages of it. When asked if she was not tired, she said, 'Oh no; if mamma is not tired, I think it is very cheering.' Some time after she asked for it again, and seemed to enjoy it much. She said, 'It is just my supper.' When told next day was Sabbath, she said, 'It is long since I had a comfortable Sabbath here.' Then, alluding to the near approach of the communion, she added, 'By the time your communion comes, I'll be drinking the new wine of the kingdom.'

At another time, when the Sabbath was spoken of, she said, with great animation, 'Oh, I wish we could all spend it on high!' and again, she said, 'I dare say you will often be envying me.' The same night she said, 'I am the best off tonight, for we are all very wearied; but this will be my last bad night.' After lying quiet, she said, 'I'll be going home, after all, tonight, and I am not sorry to go home.' We repeated many passages, to which she smiled assent, and often finished them herself. With an emphasis we can never forget, she said, 'I will trust, and not be afraid, for the Lord *Jehovah* is my strength and my song.' Also, 'Today shalt thou be with me in Paradise.' She began to repeat, 'He gives the conquest to the weak'; and when we said, 'O death, where is thy sting!' she took it up, and added, 'Thanks be to God who giveth us the victory'; and again, when we repeated, 'I am my Beloved's, and his desire is towards me', she said, over again, 'Is towards me.' After dozing a minute or two, she started up, and said, 'Who is to go with me?' We said, 'Jesus is with you, dear', which quite satisfied her, and she quietly lay down again. She often said, 'I am ashamed of my unbelief'; and when reminded of the verse, 'That thou mayest be ashamed, and never open thy mouth any more', *etc.*, she said, 'I must just take this sin and lay it where all my others are.' She had before this sent a message to one of her particular friends, when I said, 'I would deliver it.' She said, 'Oh yes, and you will tell her what I have been feeling; but don't make too much of it, as if there had been anything wonderful about me.' I said, *'His* dealings have been wonderful to you.' 'Oh yes', she replied; 'you can't make too much of *his* dealings to me.' After this she said, 'I feel getting very weak, and in a few minutes I think I shall not be able to speak; you'll explain it to John when he comes in.' [Her husband had left the room to rest for a little.] In a little while she added, 'I think I'll soon be going now, and I am not able to speak, only *I am with thee,* as Miss Sandeman always says.' Adding, as she turned round, with sweet consideration, 'Tell that to Mary.' In a minute or two she again said to me, 'Come, dear, I think I am just entering, say, "When thou passest through the waters", and perhaps I'll be over before you have finished.' At another time she said, 'Do you think I am in the dark valley? for, if I am, there is not a dark spot in it at all.' And again she said, 'Remember, if you love me, you are not to mourn for me.'

Once, when much exhausted, John said to her, 'Jesus will soon come and carry you safe home.' 'Oh!' she said, 'if I was once fairly off earth, I know I would not be long.' At another time her husband came into the room as we were giving her a little restorative; she turned to him and said, 'I was feeling a little nervous as if I would cry.' John, fearing she was troubled in mind, said to her, 'But Jesus will keep you.' 'Oh,' she said, 'it is only bodily; I have nothing now to do with preparation for the journey; my clothes are all ready', alluding to the casement of salvation with which she was adorned.

A little after twelve o'clock at night John said, 'The Sabbath is begun now.' When she replied, with emphasis, 'Ah, endless Sabbath!'

During the night she had a season of quiet triumph, which seemed to inspire her with new strength. She exclaimed, 'Oh, I cannot tell you what I feel! I am not able to speak to tell you what God is to me. Oh, *love* him, *trust* him, *serve* him!' Then, raising her hand, she continued, 'He is just bearing me up on eagle's wings.' One of us was inclined to lose composure, and was reminded any sound might disturb her; upon which she smiled brightly, and said, 'Oh, nothing can disturb me just now; I feel the everlasting arms are behind me.' With an emphasis we can never forget, she repeated —

> Were the whole realm of nature mine,
> That were an offering far too small;
> Love so amazing, so divine,
> Demands my heart, my LIFE, my all.

Some one said to her, 'You would not change with any one just now, Robina?' 'Oh, no!' was her joyful reply; 'I would not change with all the kings of Europe. It's worth being born just to die, that I might see this; and it's grand.' After this she said, 'I feel quite revived and strengthened with this.' John said, 'Grace is sustaining even your body; grace is keeping you from dying.' With a sweet smile she replied, 'It is all the same, if I enjoy heaven upon earth.' After this she was quiet for some time, but was still able to hear and often to repeat some favourite texts. Once she repeated that one, 'I knew that thou wouldst deal very treacherously, and be called a transgressor from the womb'; adding, 'I like that.' Another that was often on her lips was that, 'Into thy hands I commit my spirit, for thou hast regarded me, O Lord God of truth.'

On Sabbath morning she had a season of intense suffering. Her bodily agony from suffocation was dreadful to witness; and, at the same time, her great enemy, knowing that his time was short, was seeking to wound her sorely with his fiery darts. 'Oh!' she cried, 'this is a sore disappointment.' We repeated, 'Underneath are the everlasting arms.' She said, 'Oh, I trust they are; but I don't feel them. Oh, pray for light; pray that he would come quickly for me.' While we were praying, she cried out in anguish, 'It is an empty cry; it will never reach.' She was reminded how God's own Son had been left to cry, 'My God, my God, why hast thou forsaken me?' but her bitter reply was, 'But he was God.' This suffering continued some time, and her mind seemed quite settled for some time after, from the severe agony through which she had passed. Afterwards she said, 'Oh, I am really ashamed of all this; I did not understand it.' She spoke of it as a dreadful conflict, an awful time, and said, 'I thought everything was to be annihilated; it would have been relief to have felt sure even that there was a hell. I felt as if time and eternity, heaven and hell, were all melting into nothing. It was an awful struggle, and I got quite confused. Oh! I am very much ashamed.' John said to her, 'Jesus is not ashamed of you.' 'Well', she said, 'I hope not; but I am very much ashamed of myself.'

She wandered a good deal after this, and seemed much confused at the remembrance of the past conflict, but with sweet lucid intervals. John said to her, 'You love Jesus.' 'Oh, yes!' she said; 'I love him very much.' He again said, 'He is precious to you.' 'Oh!' she quickly replied, 'He is very precious.' She was very anxious to have her mind cleared up in reference to what had perplexed her; but when we said, 'Never mind; just wait a little, and you will understand all about it in heaven', she sweetly replied, 'Oh, very well; I can wait if I will know about it in heaven.' Once she laid her hand on her head, and said, 'Oh, I have done very wrong.' We repeated, 'He that is washed, needeth not save to wash his feet', which seemed quite to soothe her. Shortly after, in full consciousness, she said, 'Wondrous views I have got'; and again she said, 'Oh, I am ashamed of my presumption.' Then, bending her hand, she said, 'My soul was just bent over with presumption.' She was much exhausted, but said, 'I don't think I can get any more sleep; but I will soon be where I'll not need to rest day nor night.'

Often there was much sweetness even in her wanderings, as on one occasion she insisted on having us all before her, that she might show us a treasure; and then, with a smile, said, 'Some of them have been much troubled today with unbelief, and I want to give them a sight of Christ.' At another time she said, 'I was nearly across, and I saw one who had got on wonderfully well.' When asked who it was, she replied, 'I think it was Mrs Milne.' Another time she fancied she had been at Bethany, telling us it was just across the hill. John remarked to her, 'Jesus loved Martha, and Mary, and Lazarus, though Martha had some idols.' 'Oh!' she said, 'everybody has something — husband, or bairns, or something.' John said, 'You have been taught to say, "What have I to do with idols?" and in heaven there will be no idols'; to which her peaceful smile was a sufficient reply. Shortly after, she said to John, 'Did you think I would get deliverance in that dreadful struggle?' He replied, 'Yes; I was sure of it.' 'Where from?' she quickly inquired. 'From the Lord', was his reply. 'Oh, yes!' she said, quite satisfied; 'I was afraid of any presumptuous trust.'

After this she was not able to speak much, but could repeat verses, word by word, after John. Amongst others: 'Fear not, for I have redeemed thee.' 'This God is our God; he will be our guide even unto death.' After some pause, she very slowly, and word by word, said, 'If — he — had — not — given — himself — for — me, — I — am — sure — I — never — would — have — given — myself — to — him'; and these were nearly her last conscious words. After she was speechless, she took up her handkerchief, looked stedfastly on it, as if she saw some beauty she was unable to describe, and constantly turned round her face, lighted up with heavenly joy, as if to invite those round her to share in her peace.

John stooped down, and repeated, 'The robe of righteousness, clean linen, which is the righteousness of the saints'; to which she sweetly smiled assent. Often she looked round, recognising each with her well-known smile; then would lift her eyes upward, and smile again, as John remarked, 'It was now the little child putting her hand on the cockatrice den.' She never spoke again; and, at twelve o'clock noon, she entered into that rest for which she had so longed, and for which, through grace, she was made so meet.

Appendix IV

Letters From India

TO THE REV. A. A. BONAR

22, CHOWRINGHEE ROAD, CALCUTTA,
15th June 1853.

MY VERY DEAR ANDREW, — I was reading at family worship this morning the chapter that speaks of Ahimaaz and Cushi, and I told our friends here how a sight of your handwriting was always to me like a sight of Ahimaaz. Is this the only sight I am to have till we meet one another before the Lord? You are dearer to me than ever, and oftener in my thoughts, and my heart warms at every remembrance. I suppose Lizzie has let you know some of the occurrences of my voyage. Save a few days of severe illness between Aden and Ceylon, it was a very happy time; and I never look back to it without thankfulness. Unfortunately I could not land at Madras, being too weak, though fast recovering. And now for Calcutta. As a city, it exceeds in magnificence any idea I could have formed. The largeness and manifold comfort of the houses; the number, variety, and richness of the equipages; the multitudes of attendants; and the noble plain, along one side of which runs Chowringhee, where I am living, and am to live; on another side the fort, government house, *etc.*; and on a third, the broad rapid Ganges, covered with large ships from all countries, forms quite a dazzling and overawing scene of Eastern magnificence. I do not find the heat particularly trying. I rise soon after four, and walk a little on the plain, then home before the sun rises; get a cup of tea, read, write with fuller energy than at home; am shaved, bathe, dress; and breakfast at nine. At ten I get into my garree, a very handsome affair, with coachman, harkaru or messenger on the box, and a nice-looking syce, or tiger, behind, and visit from ten to two. This is quite a novelty. I go with my Bible in my hand, read and pray; go to the offices and warehouses of the young men, read and pray, and hear a little of their state of mind, and enjoy it vastly. They seem so astonished at the idea of my seeking them out, and tell me affecting stories of the sad conse-quences of the absolute neglect of pastoral work in all denominations. You could not easily believe the warmth of affection and fulness of joy with which they welcome the manifestation of ministerial love and concern for their welfare. If I am spared, and enabled to go on, there must be a revolution in this matter by and by, and I shall not have come in vain. There is a great increase in Sabbath attendance, prayermeetings, and considerable numbers beginning to ask me about becoming members of the church – I mean communicants. I do trust there is a softening and expectation. I was admitted on Sabbath last, and on Monday evening we had a very solemn prayer-meeting for a blessing. Dear Fordyce closed it in a most touching, refreshing way. He has passed through revival times; and how marked is the differ-ence between such and those who have never witnessed anything of the kind! I have had no care, nor fear, nor sadness of any kind since I came, till today — the anniversary of my dear Rue's departure. It is curious that, when I went to visit a large hospital for Europeans, which I mean to do once a week, the first object I saw was a young widow in great affliction for the death of her husband, the chief officer of one of the large ships in the river. I had seen him the week before, and hoped to find him convalescent. This a little tried me; but I am better, having just returned from the weekly prayer-meeting, which I felt strengthening and refreshing. Ewart, Fordyce, and Morgan of the Parental Institution are the men I shall cling to. We seem already of one heart. The Institution is really a noble thing; and the crowds of fine, intelligent, hearty lads, are greedy for information, and every way accessible. I never feel so happy as in the midst of them, starting with the subject of their studies, and then getting to the truth, and appealing to heart and conscience. How far this may please our scholastics, I do not know, and desire to wait on God. I am hinting a slight fear, which may be groundless, and Andrew will only mention it to our Lord. I do think the door is open, and that some crisis is at hand if there were hearty, united, unjealous working. A restraint on us is the necessity of keeping the young converts *en famille*, so that great prosperity would be an alarming thing, — many new mouths, and nowhere to put them, and nothing to feed them with. This is a trial at present. But I think it should not be. Prejudice is breaking fast, and by and by parents will acquiesce in their Christian children continuing to reside under their roof. Also, situations in common life will open up more frequently for the converts, and only the choice of them will look to the ministry. There is a large number of institutions connected with the different religious bodies, with some of which I am already getting acquainted. Mrs Ewart has a very important school for native girls. Like her husband, she is one of the excellent of the earth, most devoted, laborious, thankfully abounding in the work of the Lord, and yet little known. Mrs Hoeberlin, one of my people, has a school for higher-class native girls; she is an experienced Christian, but restrained by the constitution of her school. I have met with almost all the missionaries and mission ministers. We have a monthly prayer-meeting, and then a meeting for prayer, breakfast, and conference next morning, in one another's houses. I think I shall like it. Perhaps I would desiderate more fervour, spirituality, and aggressiveness; but I do not yet know the effect of this climate. The old bishop keeps a good many nice men about Calcutta, and they have welcomed me with great kindness. They are doing real good here; but, alas, what a scattering if a Puseyite gets the see! I am picking up a little Hindostanee, having begun to try from the first day, and so I jabber a little. I am interested in the domestic servants, they are so kind, so watchful of our comfort, and yet I fear the vast deep of deceit, sloth, and want of natural affection is underneath their gentle demeanour. I have had some curious little talks. Also I am much interested in the East Indians, and hope to contrive some way of reaching them. There is no city mission yet in action in Calcutta, though they have been long talking and contriving. I may, perhaps, be able to get a congregational one set agoing very soon, and so give the example. But the climate is a great hindrance, and also the long business hours, and the severity of the application to their work, which makes those who would be willing to take interest in such things quite jaded before evening, so that they are fit for nothing but to drive about the plain, or on the strand. Your poor friend must plead guilty as to this, for every night I drive out for an hour or more. But, you know, 'Wait on the Lord, be of good courage.'

What I miss in the missionaries, I see, is that glow and warmth and stirring of spirit you see in Paul to the very end. May I live fast and get an early grave, if one must, after a time, thus cool down! But good-bye, dearest A. How kind is the Lord to give me one I love so much! Write to Horace and John and James, and tell them that my heart is often with them. Remember me to the little prayer-meeting, Wilson, W. Greig, M'Donald, Bain, and especially to my brethren of the Presbytery. I shall write to Mr Gray soon. Say to him that I don't shirk the yoke here, but am taking my place at the different committees, and that kind of work. At home there were so many better able than I, that I thought I might stay away; but I owe a duty here to the church, whose only ministerial representative I am, and so take up the cross, and my proper share in these public matters. Warmest love to I., and the infantry. I am six weeks or more behind the flow of events, and know not private or public affairs. — Believe me, your very affectionate brother, JOHN MILNE.

TO THE REV. A. A. BONAR

1, SOUTH COLLINGA STREET, CALCUTTA,
16th Jan. 1854.

MY VERY DEAR ANDREW, — Did I write as often as I fondly think of you, many a letter would you get; but procrastination prevails here as at home, and our doings are seldom up to our wishings and intendings. I got your very welcome letter, as also a briefer but welcome one from Horace. Will you thank him for it, and say that I shall write soon; for B. loves you both as much as I do, and, I dare say, if she were at home, would be a greater favourite, for you and she have an inner character in common, into which I have not yet been able to penetrate. I dare say you will smile, and say, Wait awhile; you are in good company. Truly one feels here the need of some great evolution of divine power; for all that our missions are doing, seems like a handful of men labouring to level the Alps. But 'Thou shalt arise, and mercy yet.' I am fully and variously employed, and am about as happy as I can expect to be in such a world, and with such a body of sin and death. My wife and I try to hold up as high a standard as we can of spirituality, devotedness, and consistency. Pray for us, dearest brother, that we may be upheld and prospered. A holy, stedfast life will tell in time, even in the most worldly place, and we shall gather about us those who fear the Lord. Ask my sister Polly some day, and she will tell you what are the desires of my heart in reference to this place; and I do hope to see them realized ere I die. But I am only writing a little chit, just to keep up brotherhood, so I will not enter into details. I should like to hear what is doing at home. I see you gave the series of lectures you spoke of; I like the subjects. Some one sent me a copy of the *British Messenger,* from which I saw that the Lord appeared to be visiting both Collace and Blairgowrie. Tell me all about this. I have just been writing to W. Burns. I hear of him occasionally from people who see him as they visit China. Of course my heart has been often with him since I became his so near neighbour. What changes seem to be on the wheels for that great land! and what a noble field for dear William, after all his humble, patient, and laborious waiting! *He* is a good Master, as you well know, and we never have cause to regret any effort that we make in his service. Let us be strong, and of good courage. Yet I think I often feel like Job, 'I would not live alway.' There is little to desire or expect on earth except times of refreshing, or, as you and my little Puss beside me would say, waiting, like Simeon, to see the Lord's salvation. Tell me about Collace, and Perth, and the doings in the Presbytery, and what new work you are bringing out, for you are never idle. How pleasant it is to look back on the days that are past, and to think of the time when we shall meet in the presence of the Lord, unchanged, except that all flaws and defects will then be gone! B. joins in love to her sister Isabella. Tell us of the children. My love to all at York Place, Kelso, Greenock, and London. — Believe me, very affectionately yours, JOHN MILNE.

TO THE SAME

24, RUSSELL STREET, CALCUTTA,
26th October 1856.

MY VERY DEAR ANDREW, — I was favoured, through Bombay, with your ever welcome letter, which made me remember many things far from these Hoogly banks and sun-scorched plains. If through grace I am preserved and carried through to meet you on the mountain of myrrh and the hill of frankincense, do you think memory will go back, as I find it does now, to scenes gone by? I still remember our first meeting in the old Presbytery, and where I was sitting when you came in and shook hands; and then R. M'Cheyne and you coming in to me at 14 Rose Terrace, and laughing at my *carte blanche* to Miss — to collect a staff of lady Sabbath-school teachers; and then our next meeting in the vestry of Kinnoul Street Church at the scaling of the forenoon meeting, where you ministered to the wounded and grieved in spirit; and then in the evening 'he went on his way rejoicing' [the text] in St Leonard's, when for the first time it was lighted up with gas; but the light from the heavenly city was gathering many in. Shall we ever see these days again? Nothing but a work of this kind can raise up a true church here, and our converts have not the life, or fire, or sense of sin, and spiritual experience that are needful in those who would be the light and leaven to their fellow-men. There is a tameness and want of enterprise, and an absence of anything like spontaneous, heaven-wrought desire and effort for the salvation of men. I only know of one, Shib Chunda, who has something of what one would like in those who are the hope of India. Everything here seems to stop and come to a stand. We catch the spirit of the country, get into ruts, and round and round we go in a round of perfunctory duty. We would need a constant influx of fresh men, relay after relay, to keep the machinery in motion, acting and enlarging. Yet you must not fancy that I regret coming here. I am never permitted to do so, though the heart often thinks of former opportunities, and privileges, and happy fellowships. I feel that I have a place and work; and, as time passes, the Lord, I believe, will enlarge them. I think, dearest A., that our system of keeping such numbers of the best and holiest of the earth accumulated in one spot is not according to the design of him who said at his first creation, 'Replenish and subdue it'; and at the setting up of his second creation, 'Go ye into all the world.' Should we not be a little jealous of ourselves on this point, lest we close our eyes to the pointing of the Lord's finger? We know that all our predilections are in favour of home; this is our rest, here we will stay; and even the multitudes who come here in civil, military, or mercantile occupations, come only as birds of passage, and live as such, always looking forward to their return as the one great end and joy of existence. So I hope there will be a watchful eye and listening ear, and a standing on the tower in the library at Collace, and a saying, 'Lord, what wilt thou have me to do?' and a 'Lord, send me'; and then some day I will be calling for the creels, and the tent will be unfixed, and following the pillar. You may come hitherward, and, you know, B. and I will welcome you, and share and share alike. What say you to this? Don't forget to bring old Trusty with you. I should like to see his sonsy face again.

Thanks for all your kindness in providing me with healthful pabulum. I have more time for reading here, but fear I don't make all the use of it I might. I saw, lately, Bishop Smith from China. I was interested in him from some of his papers on late movements. He knows W. Burns, and admires him. He still looks hopefully on the Insurrectionists, and is strongly opposed to the Imperialists. He says the Jesuits are at work to prop up the old empire, because they dread the idea of Bible-readers and iconoclasts getting into power. He seems a good, devoted man, and not very churchy; but he is in feeble health, and I should hardly look for any very bold, energetic course of action from him. He said they were taunted often with their cowardice in keeping to the coast, instead of going, like the Popish missionaries, into the interior. But, he said, we cannot tell lies like them, masquerade like them, and be smuggled through the cordons as they are. I also met the new Bishop of Labuan, Macdougall. I fancy he is a friend of Patrick's, the professor, for he asked about Auld Reekie. I should think he was not a spiritual man, but he is full of energy, animal spirits, health and strength, a great friend and admirer of — , with whom he lives, free from Churchism, and having many qualities and gifts to fit him for being a breaker up of the way. He thinks Borneo will soon have a story of its own, and be a light of that Archipelago. I liked him, and I hope to see him again ere he goes. Good-bye, dearest A. I think God does not leave himself without a witness. Now and then he works by me here. But it is only a day of small things. I expect to have all the news of the manse next mail from B., for she was coming to you again. I fear Oban has done her no good. Warmest love to I. and the infantry, and the elders and deacons and Sabbath-school teachers. Tell them Collace is a household word here. Remember to Horace, John, James, and William, I wish B. could meet them in London. I think it probable she will winter there. Remember me at Glendoick. I owe a letter, and will not forget. Thanks for remembrance at the monthly meetings. Keep a seat vacant for me, and I shall be with you in spirit, perhaps some day in body again. — Yours ever very affectionately, JOHN MILNE.

TO THE SAME

4, RUSSELL STREET,
7th March 1857.

MY VERY DEAR ANDREW, — This paper has been folded up in its envelope for nearly a month, for I had reckoned on being able to write sooner. But I know that you are clement, and will bear long with brother John, who has still, as of old, too many abortive purposes to mourn over. The two young men have found their way to the Calcutta Baboo, though theirs has been a hair-breadth escape. They came under charge of Samochan Mookerjee, who embarked in the Duke of Wellington. She was an old ship, heavy laden with iron-work for the railway; and in a storm which they met at the mouth of the Bay of Bengal, the vessel stranded, her seams opened, and the crew had to take to their boats. Samochan put on his best clothes, putting your packet into one of the pockets, and they tossed about the ocean till some ships picked up first one boat and then another, and Samochan was carried to Singapore, then Moulmein, and at last arrived here. My two friends, who are admirably like the originals, are now framed and hung up beside old M'Donald, preaching in the tent at the Ferintosh communion. Thanks for the mindfulness which has given me a starting-point for many a pleasant backward, and sometimes forward thought. Thanks for all the other nice things, and, above all, for the warm love Collace Manse bears to my far-off wanderer. Keach and his accompaniments, a goodly store, has not yet made his appearance, and I am a little afraid that he may have gone to the bottom in the Duke of Wellington. I have made inquiry of the consignees, who say there was no entry in the ship's manifest, which was brought from the wreck. B. and I keep up our journalizing, and our letters reach from thirty to forty or forty-four pages; and she tells me now and then of a book from you, and a letter from Isabella. By the way, do our two erudite help-mates reciprocate in alternate Hebrew and Greek? In a specimen of elegant Grecian orthography, which came lately from Hastings, I thought I could recognise the style of the learned clerk

of Collace. Does not one of Shakspeare's heroes somewhere say, 'We
are now past the noontide [winter] of our discontent?' and so, since
we began the new year, I have been feeling that we have crossed the
meridian of our exile, and are now, like Ovid's charioteer, galloping
down to the western goal. But there is some tough work before us yet.
We have just entered on what seems likely to be a very hot season,
and you can little conceive the trial of sweltering days and restless
nights, and then the rains, with their dreary dampness and hindrance
to our meetings. These try me most; but the promise is, 'When thou
passest through the waters I will be with thee, and through the fires.'
I feel it a blessing that India is not my earthly all; that I have dear
remembered friends at home to whom my heart so often turns. And
yet, even here, I am meeting with not a few, with whom I shall meet
if I am privileged to enter the rest that remains. There are many dear,
devoted, holy souls here, in the world, but not of the world, whose
calling was usually very striking, and whose onward course has been
stedfast, unquestionable, and beneficent. There is a ceaseless flux and
reflux here, which brings all kinds of people about us. It is the gate
of the East and West, and there is a constant coming and going; and
somehow the Lord brings me into acquaintance with very many
of his dear ones. Were I at your fireside, I could tell you not a few
interesting stories of grace. And the Lord in mercy has given me some
jewels here. I feel that I have not come here for nought. Pray for me,
dearest A., for I am still the unturned cake; but yet, amid not a little
to try and humble, I often feel, in the review, nothing but praise and
thanksgiving to a gracious, merciful Lord. As one said when she was
departing, we shall all find voices when we get to the mountains of
myrrh and the hill of frankincense. By the way, I have not got hold
of your spikenard yet; but I am seeking after it, and hope to send you
some. I have written through a godly man, Colonel Smith, to Madras,
to see if it can be got there. Dr Duff is with us, and wonderfully well.
He came on a Saturday night, and next morning preached for me, on
'The righteousness of God', a very noble experimental sermon, full
of power and unction. He is laying himself out in all directions, and

will, I trust, be a great blessing. At the conference of missionaries last Tuesday, he gave out this question, 'Whatsoever ye do, in word or deed, do all in the name of the Lord Jesus' — what principles does this embody? and how far are they at present carried out by professing Christians? I love him very much, and I think the feeling is reciprocal. I have not forgotten, I hope, the lesson I had to learn seventeen years ago, and would be willing to twinkle while a brother shines. We have got our new Governor-General, Lord Canning. No one knows what he will be; but if he seeks grace and wisdom from on high, he has a noble field before him. Lord Dalhousie went last night about five. An hour before he sent me a letter, written, he says, in the midst of hurry, with 200 rupees for the mission. On a former occasion he gave me 500; but would not then give me his name, being tied up by state considerations. Poor India! Many are the obstacles to her regeneration. But the Lord is gathering in one and another there, and perhaps this is all that he intends till the days of restitution. Dearest A., my heart is pouring out in me as I think of former days; but, as I was reading in Jeremiah today, perhaps we may yet rejoice together even on earth. So Horace has actually cut his moorings and become a rolling stone! The proverb will for once find an exception; for, doubtless, he will bring many notes with him, and pictures too. I heard of him at Malta and Cairo. Love to I., and the bairns, and to all friends. — Yours very affectionately, JOHN MILNE.

TO THE SAME

CALCUTTA,
December 20, 1857.

MY VERY DEAR ANDREW, — Who is to blame for this long silence? I will plead guilty, and without more ado begin my amendment. My dear wife and her aunt arrived safely nearly three weeks ago, and both wonderfully well. They are now living with me in my lodgings, but we hope next month to have a home of our own. You and Isabella, quiet, stay-at-home people, cannot fancy what it is to meet again after so long a separation. The pleasure, however, is purchased at so dear a price, that I hope I shall never have to go to the market again for such a commodity. We have had many a pleasant talk about you both, and the infantry, and Collace; and I have felt as if I were once more at home. Thanks for all your brotherly kindness to my dear wanderer. It is pleasant to me that my dearest friends have become equally dear to her. How strange the scattering which a few years have made! I saw in a Perth paper sent me, the account of the Presbytery proceedings; and now I see by the *Witness* that you are fairly settled at Finnieston. I know the place quite well. There was once a work of God there, in which I remember I was interested at the time, and now it will become to me a Kebla, where heart and mind will often turn. The Lord be very abundantly with you in this new part of the valley to which he has taken you. 'To the poor the gospel is preached', marked out the Elder Brother, and, I suppose, still marks out those who come nearest to him in spirit and character. Keep a deacon's place for me, and if B. and I are driven out of this trying land, we will come and cast in our lot and labour with you. I think I growingly see that place and circumstance, and frames and feelings, are but very secondary things, and that God in Christ, God in covenant, is our all in all. Faith, direct faith, alone will make us walk upward and carry us through. The Lord has a people here, scattered up and down, and some of them are choice Christians, simple, scriptural, and devoted. Living often alone, and forming their opinions for themselves, they are often what we should call odd, and do not keep step with our train-bands at home. I doubt if some of my dearest friends would pass muster with — and some others; but they are true men for all that, and walk with God. The Lord is adding to the number of his people in this land, now one and now another, and this comforts and encourages me. Pray for B. and me, that the word of the Lord may have free course. We do a good deal in the way of correspondence, getting acquainted with young men as they pass through, and then following them by letter to their distant and often isolated stations. In this way there is a large and open door. I hope to move about more than I have done. During the late rains, I went up as far as Benares, and thus saw a good deal of the country, and made many pleasant acquaintances. It is a land made up of many different tribes and people, in very different states of civilisation. It strikes me that we have committed an error in our missionary work, in beginning with the more learned and conceited, and passing by the simple, outlying tribes, who are more ready to receive and obey the truth. I cannot say I see my way to any large work of conversion here in Bengal. Education is extending in Calcutta and some of the chief towns; but it is only valued as the means of obtaining a better livelihood, and does not usually make them more favourable to the gospel. Without the full assurance that God's counsel will stand, and that in his own time and way he will bring it to pass, it would be unspeakably sad to live among these perishing millions, and see how little has been done, or apparently can be done for their deliverance. You see in all this only the fulfilment of Isaiah 26:17-19. By the way, dear A., how will you get on among these western men? Won't you be like a turtle living alone, and every one giving you a peck? But good-bye. Warmest love to Isabella, Horace, James, John, and all friends. I shall leave B. to add a P.S. — Yours ever very affectionately, JOHN MILNE.

TO THE SAME

4, RUSSELL STREET,
22d August.

MY DEAR ANDREW, — You will be glad to hear that, amid all the dangers and horrors that have been occurring around us, we are still safe and well. You, at a distance, can form little idea of the state of this country. You have read of the feeling of insecurity which people experience amid a succession of terrific earthquakes. Just such is the feeling here. We are encompassed on every side with the natives, and our old secure confidence in them has been completely destroyed, so that we cannot tell when or from what quarter death may come. I

cannot help seeing in all this a righteous retribution. We have been
unfaithful to God and his truth; we have fraternized with error, and
have protected it; we have, as it were, entered into a compact with the
Prince of Darkness that, if he will preserve our dominions, we will do
what we can to preserve his. And now God has risen in anger, and the
reed on which we leaned has broken, and pierced us through. We have
had several panics here in Calcutta, and, at times, have been in real
and imminent danger; but the Lord has graciously interposed to arrest
or avert the threatened blow. Perhaps he wished to keep Calcutta as
a place of refuge for his many destitute and fugitive ones, who have
been flocking in from all quarters. The enemy still have possession of
the country, and we have only a few beleaguered places here and there,
some of which, we fear, will fall ere they can be relieved, and so suffer
the fate of Futteyghur and Cawnpore. But I do not think the Lord
means to drive us out. He is chastening us sore, but he will not give us
over to death. I would fain hope that a stronger and more Christian
government will take the place of that, which is passing away. A revolution is a sharp and sore remedy, but it is a thorough one, and does in
a day the work of a century. Pray for us that better days may dawn on
India, and pray for us also that while we remain, we may be kept and
blessed. God is driving in the ploughshare wide and deep; and we have
abundant opportunity of ministering to the sorrowful, the destitute,
and broken-hearted. Perhaps the Lord will give us a harvest. Pray for
this. I have lost many friends, and some, I trust, spiritual children, in
these sad calamities. I preach under military protection, — soldiers,
volunteers, and cannon are at the side of the church, which is situated in the most thoroughly Mohammedan district. How little mere
external means can do! At first one is solemnized, then they grow
accustomed, and then feel as if they could not live without the excitement of these extraordinary events. Providence, even in its strangest
evolutions, is but a handmaid. It is the Lord that adds to the Church
such as shall be saved. Yet I trust that he will appear at this time,
and build up Zion. B. is not strong, but she struggles on, and does a
good deal with her pen in the way of correspondence. The Greek also

flourishes, and you may look for a nice edition of the καινη διαθηκη[1] with choice comments. United love to I., and all friends. — Yours, very affectionately, JOHN MILNE.'

TO THE REV. DR HORATIUS BONAR

CALCUTTA,
4th August, 1853.

MY VERY DEAR HORACE, — I know I need not to tell you how often my heart has been turning to you since I have been 'alone in the world', and yet 'not alone'. I have seen much of our Lord's mindfulness and faithfulness since I left our common earthly home. But for a rather sharp, though short feverish attack, which I rather think I brought upon myself by roaming about on foot in Alexandria and Cairo, I might almost say that the voyage was, all through, a kind of pleasure excursion. I found it a season and opportunity of active usefulness, and look back upon it with thankfulness. Since I came here I have met with not a little to encourage. My people are kind, cordial, and united; and there is an *esprit de corps* springing up. They are also increasing, and perhaps there are some quickenings and touchings of the heart. If, through your sympathy and prayers at home, I continue to maintain spirituality, liveliness, and a holy activity, I cannot doubt but that I shall be used here. I see already many ways in which, if I were a really holy, wise, and earnest man of God, I might be greatly useful in gathering and building up a true church, in helping the passers-by, and those who are at a disadvantage in the cut-stations; and perhaps also in quickening my brethren around me, who, from the effects of this sad climate, and our engrossment in the routine of translation and education-work, may have forgotten Paul's and Martyn's rule, 'I count all things loss', and so have suffered damage in their spirituality. I rather think if I had known, as I now do, the extent and importance of the work, I should have shrunk from coming here; but, you know, 'I

---

[1] 'New Testament', *Ed.*

will lead the blind in a way that they know not', and so I think it has
been with me all through this affair. I must set my heart to my work.
I must set my heart to my work, and wait on him who gives power to
the faint, and who can make my hands sufficient. I found pleasant the
other morning, 'Out of the mouth of babes and sucklings'; and just
now I have been reading, and I have been quickened with this word
— 'All *filled* with the Holy Ghost.' It is just what is needed here, where
I think they look too much at the stone on the grave's mouth, and are,
perhaps, too much enslaved by human plans and policy. Oh for the
liberty of the Spirit! the noble daring and uncalculatingness of those
who, in seeing him who is invisible, can see nothing else. Fordyce is
a great comfort to me, so is Morgan. You have some who love and
follow you here. I have lived since I came mostly with the Nicolsons,
one of my elders' families. Miss Nicolson, I find, is one of you; and I
was amused to find that she was quite afraid of me, for she thought
I was a regular David Brown man. Dear Horace knows how far I am
from that, though not just quite so far as he would like, and sometimes
hopes to see me. It seems our friend — of — had written to — the
missionary, giving a kind of bird's-eye view of their future minister;
among other things he said this: 'He is the friend of the Bonars; he
is *no* millenarian.' Mrs Ewart, the wife of our best missionary, and
herself the carrier on of an important female school, is also at one
with you. We have a monthly missionary conference made up from
all the bodies. Our question on Tuesday was, 'Is the Church prepared
for a large work of Gentile conversion?' Mr Smith opened. He rather
ran down the Church at home, and fell foul of you millenarians. You
know I always defend you, and so I did. Also, I said, the Church at
home will rise to the occasion, and will rejoice at a work of God here;
but are *you* prepared? And I fear I was somewhat sharp and warm.
Fordyce was grave, and following, took up the cause of his friends. It
was an animated discussion. At length Mr Cuthbert, secretary to the
Church Missionary Society, and a man I greatly like, avowed himself a
millenarian, and Smith and he had a short conversation on the subject.
I really hope for good here. I wish I had the power of clairvoyance

— to see you and be seen by you, in my new and strange abode. I walk a good deal on the roof, morning and night, looking out on a noble plain, the Corso of Calcutta, and as crowded and animated in the evening as Hyde Park in the season; for every one here has a carriage. Were it not that I am so far away from you, and that I suffer sad torture from a thing called Gurmee, or prickly heat, just like wearing the shirt of Nessus, I suppose I should be bound in truth to say that I am very much at home, and like my work. This same prickly heat, it seems, arises from an over-robust and healthy constitution that will not succumb to the climate and prostrate itself in the seasoning fever. So you may judge of the amount of sympathy which my torments call for. But it is, dear Horace, a sad climate; and you must pray for me that, till my work is done, I may be borne up in body and spirit. My love to Mrs Bonar and my well-remembered young friend; also to Collace, Greenock, and York Place! The old lady, — is she well? How ripe in years and grace![1] — Believe me, dearest Horace, your ever affectionate brother, John Milne.

TO HIS SISTER-IN-LAW, MISS STUART

Calcutta,
17th October 1853.

My dearest Lizzie, — Many thanks for your ever welcome letter, for I can heartily respond to you, and say, that when the letters come, the first that always catches my eye and thrills my heart, is the one that says, 'I am from Lizzie.' You will see that I have had some ongoings since I last wrote, and I can truly say that word is true, 'Yea, what is good the Lord will give.' Your new sister's heart and mine seem strangely attuned to one another. How blessed it is to be one in Christ, and one in his work! Our prospects of happiness and usefulness seem bright; and even if the Lord should see fit to appoint otherwise, yet it

---

[1] My beloved and honoured mother, to whose calm faith and holy life a family of seven sons and four daughters (the greater part now with the Lord) owe so much. She fell asleep in Jesus, at the age of eighty-one, on the 29th of August 1854.

is good to have such a season as we are enjoying together to look to. I wish you and Polly would come and see us. I think the house would, in many respects, remind you of Leonard Bank, for the same lady-like taste and elegance govern here as there. Though very different from our house at home, you would find it very comfortable. I like the openness all around, which lets the air sweep through; and the Purdahs, or hangings which form the doors between the rooms, often remind me of the pictures in the Arabian Nights, and I look up expecting to see a corner lifted and a face looking in. In the compound behind is a quantity of poultry, and a huge black goat which gives delicious milk for tea. I think B. proposes having another, so that we shall have quite a farmyard. You would be amused with the number of servants, and how each contrives to keep to his own work … I think I should have liked a little stroll with you on Rothesay shores. It is sweetly embalmed in my memory; and even the Kyles, the lochs, and the straits beyond, all the way to Oban, only make me think how our God leads the blind in a way that they know not. It is a complete change, a new life; and yet I think I am happier and better than I should have been at home. The modes of operation here are different, and there is little for sense to rest on; but it is a vast field, full of the seeds of great events, and I am trying to help on the harvest. I feel that I am growingly finding my feet, that doors of usefulness in various directions open, and God gives me now usually grace to hope and wait. Again you know, 'Yea, what is good —.' He is a rewarder of them who diligently seek him. How good it is to get hold of a principle that will never fail us, and on which we can rest for time and eternity! Your favourite word, my little sister, has often comforted me when I was ready to faint; and now I put to a new seal.

Half-past Five. — At this hour last week we were entering our house for the first time. It has been a very happy week, and we have had much joy in one another, and still more in the Lord. I do feel that he has been with us in reading, in prayer, in converse, and I feel that godliness is profitable for the life that now is … — Remember us in prayer, and believe me, my dearest L., ever most affectionately yours, JOHN MILNE.

TO THE SAME

1, South Collinga Street, Calcutta,
2d December, 1853.

My dearest Lizzie, — This is Friday morning, and we have had our little meeting from ten to eleven. The passage was Matthew 25:36-46; and, after speaking a little, we read your favourite 'Gethsemane' ... I feel that I am in my place here. I am half-ashamed of the dark views I took a little while ago; but you know your brother, and would not be surprised. I think God is with us, and so everything prospers, and our peace flows as a river. The congregation grows, and will in a little while, I trust, be quite a new one, both in members and in the spirit of its members. The Sabbath school has become very large. B. and I always move about a little, calling at the door here and there before the evening drive, and so we are getting quite known in the district round the church. The children come running to the carriage, or gather round me, as I walk of an evening. Everywhere we have people about us here, often passers-by, and we try to make our house Bethel. Remember us, my little one, that we may be enabled, in all our walk and conversation, to show how holy and happy, God can make poor sinful worms when he is pleased to raise them up from the dust. We are always busy, and find the day and week too short. I find the Lord enables me to hold on, with less of the casting down than I almost ever used to suffer, and I do trust that, through the help of your prayers, the Lord will be pleased to use us for good to this land. Somehow I have a hope, and so has B.; and you know, when two agree —. I am going through Genesis at night on Sabbath, and I have reached the birth of Isaac, and the casting out of Hagar. The people seem interested. On Wednesday evening I am going through the Acts, and have just reached Pentecost. I will tell you another time about my young men — European, East Indian, and Hindoo. Surely the Lord is willing to pour out his Spirit, and make the wilderness to prosper. Is not his time at hand? Let us try not to give him rest. I heartily agree with you in all your longings for usefulness, and for deliverance from selfseeking, self-trust, and self in every form. Why are we not more self-forgetting, self-renouncing, self-loathing? What wrong self does to that loving Lord, and how it grudges and is narrow-hearted to our fellow-men! But I trust there is some progress, and that late events have helped and will help us more. For myself, I feel as if the Lord were showering burning coals upon my head, and bent upon overcoming my vileness by his good. And won't he do it? Who can stay his hand? Why do we not remember that he is as resistless in grace as resistless in judgment? He will subdue our corruption. He will cast our sins into the depths of the sea. It is strange how completely the world seems put out of my heart. I seem not to have a thought or care about earthly things. The Lord seems to have realized my idlest dreams, and in every way to have exceeded what seemed my most foolish wishes, so that I seem out of the reach of temptation in that quarter. Aunt Jackson took all these burdens on her, and now B. has taken it up, and I need only give myself to prayer and the ministering of the word. I think I sometimes, for a moment, feel how sweet it would be eternally to delight and rejoice and glory in the Lord! Thanks, many thanks, for your long, most welcome letter.

We greatly need to be upheld by prayer, for there are hindrances here which you do not know. But, as you say, all things are possible with him. It will need great grace to make the Bengalees a zealous, holy, earnest people. There is a languor, carnality, and want of enterprise which are disheartening. But, again, all things are possible. I remember the girl — very well. They have been a very unsatisfactory family; but I have long thought the Lord had hold of them. I should like to hear the result of your dealing with her. I shall write to J. C., but not by this mail. Poor fellow! I fear lest that word comes to pass in him, 'He who, being often reproved', *etc*. Poor Mrs D.! What a long passage hers has been! but she will reach the end, and enter the wealthy place. Remember me very kindly to her and her husband … The Episcopalians took offence at my reading and praying there at my first visit. Three of their ministers came making complaint, which I heard of from Mr Wylie. However, Lizzie knows that her brother will not care much for this. B. and I unfold the banner wherever we go, and my little Psalm Book, which I got from Mrs Trotter, is always on these occasions in my waistcoat pocket.

I am glad you speak of K. I have sent an extract of your letter regarding him to his mother, who will be much gratified. I wish you would write to the girls. I think R — a worthy, kind-hearted man. Pray that the Lord may make my being here a blessing to him and his family.

I see cholera progresses. It is no stranger here. Last Sabbath morning, about 8 o'clock, I got a hasty note from A. B. M'Intosh, C. Stewart's cousin, saying that his brother — had been seized about 4 o'clock in the morning, the most dangerous part of the twenty-four hours, and was quite despaired of. I hurried off with my sola hat and chatta, not waiting for the carriage, which B. sent after. Above expectation he rallied, and is now better. May you all experience the safety and the comfort of the 91st Psalm!

Mr Wylie has told us of Dr Gordon's death. Good-bye, my dearest Lizzie. Love to M., B., H., K., and all friends. — Yours ever very affectionate, JOHN MILNE.

TO THE SAME

1, South Collinga Street, Calcutta,
30th March, 1854.

MY DEAREST LIZZIE, — No word as yet of the steamer; but I am at home tonight, and so take time by the forelock, *for once*. Our hot weather has fairly set in, but as yet I have not found it very trying, as we have had a succession of showers, which has every now and then cooled the air. You would be alarmed at first by our north-westers. The most brilliant lights, then thunder, as if the heavens were crashing to pieces, and all earthly things about to share the convulsion; then an outburst of wind, and torrents of rain. I have been a little poorly for a day or two; but have kept the house yesterday and today, and am better almost again. Barbara and I are sitting together in the little drawing-room; we have had a north-wester, so the room is all shut in. It is about 8 o'clock, and we have had tea, and are set down for the evening. I wish I could give you a bird's-eye view of our snuggery; or better, I wish I could introduce you to your new sister. Had I been quite well, I should, at this time tonight, have been gone to the house of two of our people, Cameron and Galbraith, where a number of them meet to practise sacred music. Over their work they have a very large room, which is nicely fitted up as a drawing-room, and we sit round the table. One plays on the seraphine, and all the others have their music-books. I begin with prayer, then give out psalms which are to be sung on Sabbath, giving a little explanation, and then, at the end, pray again. It lasts an hour, and I think I shall enjoy it, and find it useful. The telegraph has now been finished up to Agra, and we get news by the way of Bombay before our steamers arrive. We have just heard that war is not yet declared, but that troops are embarking for the East. Tomorrow, or next day, we shall get our letters, and hear, I trust, that you are better, and all the rest well … However, Paul and Peter were satisfied with being servants of Jesus Christ, and so am I. If that dear Lord would arise and plead his own cause, these partition walls which divide Indian society in many sections would melt like snow before the sun, and the many little apartments would become one large room, like Mr Cameron's big drawing-room. The Lord is not leaving himself without a witness near here. He seems to deal with souls here and there, awakening them to concern about eternal things. I trust, as we become better known, we shall hear of these things of-tener, and perhaps be used, by the Lord in counselling and encourag-ing these young ones of the flock. Perhaps there is more openness in speaking and writing about these things than at home. When people are worldly here, they are thoroughly so; and consequently, when they begin to reflect, and change their course, the alteration is very marked. Thus far I had written on Thursday night, when I suddenly left off, and went for the first volume of Jonathan Edwards, Polly's friend, and read about Mrs Edwards' experience to Barbara, who had never heard it. I always enjoy that narrative; it makes me cry, 'Restore unto me the joy of thy salvation.' Oh, how easy it is to triumph over all our ills and sins when God's grace is shining on us, and he is pouring into our hearts his gracious Spirit!

Did you ever think of it as a Christian duty — 'Be filled with the Spirit?' Surely it is a duty; it comes out of the law, 'Love the Lord with *all* thy heart'; and so our whole heart ought to be full of him. I remember at one of our meetings at Andrew Bonar's a long inquiry, which came to little, as to what was meant by being 'filled with the Spirit'. Had some praying servant girl come in, she would have smiled at our difficulties; or if the Lord had come in, would he not have said, 'Are ye masters in Israel, and know ye not these things?' I think our great hindrance in spiritual growth is want of continuity. We are inconstant, and, after a little tension, we break off like a deceitful bow. After spiritual employment, and perhaps some comfort and light, if we would watch, deny ourselves, and hold fast, we should not be always in poverty, living from hand to mouth as we are.

No word of the steamer yet. I think I told you of my nice Arab. Well, I rode about a great deal; but horses here are not like horses at home; they are not so tame and broken in. Also, Arabs never lift their feet; they shovel along, which I don't like, as I want to daunder about, and think of many things — maybe Annat Lodge — instead of taking care of my beast. My good horse, also, was apt to shy and go off in an instant, like an arrow. However, we kept together *pretty* well, till one morning, when, after bidding salaam to Aunt Jackson, who always walks on the housetops from five to six o'clock, I was riding smartly off, when a lumbering garree came by, and, ere I knew where I was, my friend went off like a bolt, and, ere I could recover my seat and draw it up, I went clean over its head. You would have laughed to see brother John stretching out first a leg, and then an arm, to ascertain the extent of the injury, and then rising and calling to stop the poor animal, lest he should get home riderless. It was sent off and sold, and I am to get a Cabool horse from the hills, which will be sure-footed, and answer my purpose better; for I should like to ride about the lanes of a morning and evening, and make my observations and calls. How many outward mercies and comforts are we surrounded with! and yet these are not a man's life. 'Come unto me, and I will give you rest.' There is no really valuable happiness but that which has this for its foundation. I hope to hear that you have good accounts from the West Indies. Cholera is at work here, and will grow worse as the heat continues and increases. On Monday night I thought for a little that I had got it. Here it is a terrific disease, and is infallibly fatal if not arrested in time. A sudden chill will occasion it. Are we ever to meet on earth? My work and my heart now are here; but I sometimes think I should like to see the old house once more, and pace up and down my old walks. Who can tell? God's ways are not as our ways. We may all meet yet under the same roof. And yet how short these meetings are! Let us rather dwell on the eternal meeting in the presence of the Lord.

We are labouring on much as usual — sometimes hopeful, and then a little cast down. Barbara, I think, enjoys her hope of Christ's near appearance. After seeing a little of the sad state of the world, and the manifest inadequacy at present of the existing Church to do *almost everything* to remedy it, one cannot help feeling that there must be some great change, in order that the faithful promises may be accomplished. The Gentile dispensation, the times of the Gentiles must be near an end; and yet how little has been done, how much once gained has been lost! Let us exhort one another, for we know not what may be at the door. May we be found with loins girt, and busy at our work. This is the 1st of April; and this day last year, Saturday, about this time, I was leaving Huntly Lodge for Perth. I remember the walks down the avenue, for the ground was covered with snow, and no conveyance could approach. I remember the heart filling as I thought of leaving friend after friend; but I strode on, and then, at the little bridge, turning round to take one look, I saw the butler posting after with the large muffetees. How little kindnesses endear us to one another! But good-bye. Give love to the Cunninghams, Cornfutes, Rosses, and all other friends. The heart warms to many around you, because it knows them best, and thinks old friends better than the new. — Yours very affectionately, J. M.

3d April. — You must get fast better, else we shall send for you to try the effects of a warm sun. God bless my little sister! Let us try to keep near the Lord. There is nothing really valuable but his favour. I rather think we should be more meditating on the word of God, 'If ye abide in me, and my word abide in *you*', I would like to be *uncareful* without being *careless,* and contented without being stoical or indifferent. I shall be anxious till I hear from you again.

TO MR J. AND A. CORNFUTE

BENARES,
15th September.

MY DEAR JAMES AND ADAM, — You will see by the date of this, that I am far from home, and this will account for any interruption in our hitherto unbroken interchange of papers. My long, close confinement to Calcutta, the trying rainy season, and loneliness, had begun to tell on me; and, in order to arrest the progress of the evil, I got into one of the inland steamers, and came up here for a week or two. Look at the map, and I will tell you a little of my journey and my adventures in the Moffussil. On the afternoon of Saturday, the 23d August, I embarked, and found a large number of passengers — civilians, military, railway engineers, and merchants and indigo planters. I was, of course, pleased at this, for the angler cannot have much success where there are not plenty of fish. We got off before it was dark, and threaded our way through the crowded anchorage till we got up into the open river, which was running with a mighty current, and against which even the powerful steamer could hardly make way. At nightfall we anchored opposite Serampore, formerly belonging to the Danes, and where Carey and the other Baptist ministers took refuge when they were persecuted by the East India Company. They have still a large institution there, though it is now more a trading than a missionary establishment. The best newspaper in India, the *Friend,* which you know, is published here; and I wanted to go ashore and see the editor, Mr Townsend, for a little; but the stream ran so fast, that though the captain said he would man the long-boat for me, yet he urged me not to go, as there was danger. So you have got no *Friend*, for they have gone to Calcutta.

Next morning we went on, and soon saw the effects of the long rainy season. The country was flooded on both sides as far as the eye could reach. Think of a mighty sea of fifteen or twenty miles, spreading all around, and the steamer sailing over fields and villages. The houses of the poor people are built of mud, like the bothies on the Strath; and so, when the water reaches, down they go; and we saw many, many a most harrowing scene. The population had mostly wandered far away; but here and there we saw crowds of people, with their children in boats, or gathered together on some slight elevation, with the poor cattle, starving like themselves. I often would have liked to stop and give rice; but it was impossible, as we should have been carried away by the stream. There is incalculable loss, the crops being destroyed; and after the water subsides, there will be malaria and abounding famine and diseases. This is the country to see misery in every form. Rich, gorgeous India has a wretched, miserable people. Brahminism, like Popery and Mohammedanism, impoverishes and degrades. We had service in the cuddy after breakfast, and I preached. I tried to get a psalm sung, and a young Scotchman sung while I read the line; but the success was not such as to lead me to make a second attempt. So, ever after, I shortly prayed, read a psalm, had prayer, read a chapter and preached out of it, prayed and pronounced the blessing.

We sailed along the region which B. and I had coasted about the same time two years before, when we went in a budgerow for her health, and, of course, I had many memories rushing into my mind. I felt my way with my companions, and got a Bible class established in my cabin, where from five to eight regularly attended, and we soon became exceedingly attached to one another, and formed a kind of little church or brotherhood in the ship. We read 1st and 2d Peter, and 1st John, ere we parted, and talked over it, reading a chapter each morning. Altogether it was a happy party, every one in the ship seeking to please and be pleased. Look in the map and you will find Cutwa, where B. and I stopped two years ago, and turned back. But now we moved on and reached Berhampore, which was formerly a great military station, but is now greatly deserted on account of the damp and bad health. It is all bounded or embanked towards the river, and the water, when we were there, was said to be seven inches higher than the land. It is the great silk district. There is an Independent Church mission, which I visited; one of the missionaries, Mr Hill, being an acquaintance. Here, as everywhere, they complain of deadness.

We sailed on till we got to Moorshedabad, where the old Nawab, or king of Bengal, has two palaces. It was his ancestor that perpetrated the enormity of the Black Hole of Calcutta. He is now a pensioner of the Company, getting about 10 lacs a year, or £100,000, which he miserably misspends, though the Government has an office whose business is to overlook the expenditure. Like all the other knights and grandees of this country, who subsist on the bounty of their conquerors, he is a miserable, licentious wretch, who poisons the whole neighbourhood. One thing, however, he did, which was not so bad. He gathered the learned Brahmins and pundits to a great entertainment. They came from far and near, and were royally entertained. After the feast was over, and they were all talking, as is their wont, on such occasions, of the savouriness of the curries, and the tenderness of the pillaus, and the abundance of the entertainment, the royal blackguard summoned the cooks, and, to their horror, they found that they had been eating victuals prepared by Mohammedans, and that cow-flesh and other pollutions had formed their feast. They rose with a cry of horror, ran out of the palace, and were never heard of again in that part of the country, for they had all lost caste, and become more despicable than the meanest soodra.

We passed on, still in the midst of fearful flood, to Bhangulpore, the scene of the Santhal insurrection. You will see that we had now left the Bhaguretty, and entered on the mighty Ganges itself, which is at all times a noble flood, but this season seems literally a shoreless sea. One morning, at sunrise, we saw the snowy tops of the far-off Himalayas. At Bhangulpore we landed at night, and, accompanied by my young friends, struck into the country. We had a good deal of talk with the natives. A crowd came, and I found that none could read or write except the Brahmins. So, by the help of my friends, who are fluent speakers in the language, I urged upon them that, as they were supported by the villagers, they ought in return to gather the chokras, or boys, together, and teach them. But these comfortable gentlemen patted their stomachs, and said, 'We get plenty without doing any work, and why should we trouble ourselves?' Some of the old people also remarked that their fathers had fed their cattle very well without reading or writing ; and, kiswasti, what was the use of it to them? So it was no go, as they say. But the schoolmaster is abroad, and we found that Government is to establish a school here.

We went on to Rajmahal, and came upon the incipient railway, and sailed along near it, and the grand trunk road, all covered with water. The hills here skirt the river, and are very beautiful. It is redolent of home for a drooping exile from the land of heather to be here, and I found it quite reviving. They are a long, fine range, running off from the Himalayas as the Ochils run off from the Grampians, and they are covered with jungle up to the top, the haunt of the tiger, leopard, bear, wild buffalo, and snakes. One of my young friends had killed two tigers in one week, and another seven panthers in four days. This is their pastime; for they are busy, energetic men, carrying on extensive mercantile concerns. One of them belonged to the Greek Church; but, as he read the Bible, he became a Protestant, and we had many nice talks; and I have a confident hope that four of them will stand firm, and that, if I am saved, I shall meet them in heaven. The Santhals are a fine, manly race of savages, strong, active, truthful, living on their little bit of reclaimed jungle, and hunting the wild beasts. But they fell into the hands of the Bengalee mahajuns, or usurers, who deceived and oppressed them, and so they were maddened into the commission of many barbarities. They are now quiet, and Government is anxious for their improvement.

The country of Behar, along which we sailed for a day or two, is high, and so has suffered little from the inundation. It is quite

English-like, — green fields, interspersed with topes or clumps of trees, and full of herds of buffalos. They are what they call the gwala, or cow-feeding caste, and they make ghee, which is a kind of coarse butter. The buffalo is not at all a pleasantlooking animal; and in our evening walks — for the steamer always stopped at sunset — we had to dodge about to keep out of their way; for it seems they do not like strangers, and have a peculiar predilection for hunting a black coat, so that I felt I was rather a dangerous companion for my friends. One of them had once been saved by a faithful dog, which flew at the furious creature, and hung on his head till his master had contrived to make his escape. We saw crowds of crocodiles, which were more afraid of us than we were of them, though one would not care to meet them in their own element. At one of our coaling stations a serpent-charmer came, with a number of large cobras in small vessels. He took them out, and irritated them and made them bite; and then a little wretch of a boy, a mere child, took them and twined them round his neck, and there they hung. It was horrible and disgusting, and I turned away. As a missionary's wife told me, there are no children among the natives; they are men and women ere they cease to be infants; precocious, and matured in all evil.

Moughyr, which you will see, is a nice town. Here they excel in all kinds of cabinet work. Patna is a great Mohammedan place, ten miles long, and often compared to the 'lang toun of Kirkaldy'. It is one of the most turbulent places in India. Dinapore is a large military station close by, to keep Patna in check. I knew some of the officers, and went ashore. Patna is famous for all kinds of cloth, and Dinapore for slaves. Here I was visited by Mr Brice, a merchant missionary. He seems a good man. He came out for missionary work, but has engaged in trade; but says he would never advise any one to imitate him. No; but I wish we had missionary merchants — men who would do their worldly business diligently, and yet try to be epistles of Christ, seen and read of all men.

After we left this place we had two severe storms, which kept us awake for two nights. Fortunately the wind and current were in opposite directions, else we should certainly have been sunk or driven on the shore. It is a curious river, the Ganges, shifting its channel constantly. It rises and falls many feet with amazing rapidity. One evening the steamer in which I was sailing anchored in deep water. Next morning she was lying high and dry far inland, and it was six or seven months ere they could make a canal to get her down to the distant river.

We now got up to what are called the N. W. Provinces, and reached Gazipore, a fine town. There stone is used instead of the ceaseless red brick of Bengal. I went ashore — it was Sabbath afternoon — and stopped a little with a friend, Major Ottlay, who, with his wife, are good people. We arranged for evening sermon in the English church, as there is no chaplain; and tidings were sent round the cantonments. It is a very fine church. Mr Hamilton, a civilian, read the English prayers, and then I preached. I don't know that our friends in Princes Street would be so liberal. The Lieutenant-Governor, Mr Halliday, had just been visiting this place. We met him going down. He is not a religious man; on the contrary, he lately published a proclamation, declaring that he had nothing whatever to do with missionaries or their doings. But the natives cannot understand that a man can be really ashamed of his religion. So they thought Mr Halliday was playing a deep game, and that he had some plot to make them all Christians. Their idea was, that he would invite the whole place — many, many thousands — to a great burrah-connah, and make them eat with him, and so break caste. So there was a great consternation. Some of us are not sorry that his attempt to gain favour by a supererogatory liberality has had such a result.

We came to Buxar, where there is a fort, with a fine view from the ramparts of a green, well-wooded, English-looking country. Here the horses for the cavalry, and the country generally, are bred at the huge Government studs. It is a fine sight to see hundreds of these creatures running unbroken, and at perfect liberty, like the wild horses of South America. Captain Macdonald, Margaret Maclean's husband, is connected with the stud, and lives in this neighbourhood, but too far off for me to reach them. I have a nice long letter from her, wishing to know my movements.

We came on to Benares, when I left the steamer, which goes on to Mirzapore and Allahabad. I went to stay with Mr Tucker, the commissioner of the district, a man very high in the service, and one of the best of men. It was the Mohurram, a Mohammedan festival, lasting for a whole week; and Mr Tucker has taken me about to everything. He is next to the Lieutenant-Governor, and has in his district 40,000 villages, 500,000 distinct holders of land, 10,000,000 of people. Why, it is a great kingdom; and as he moves about, making his progresses in the country, he comes into contact with every part. His management seems admirable, and he labours from morning till late at night. What a responsibility! They are a delightful family, and I have felt myself in a kind of little heaven during my week's stay. Mr Tucker gives all his large income to the Lord. He writes, or gets prepared, great numbers of works in the vernacular for the natives. He has made quite a library. He visits, assists, and encourages all the missionaries without any partiality, though himself belongs to the English Church. He has begun a noble normal school, where he gathers together the best young men in the district, and maintains them at their studies for six months, and then sends them home to benefit their neighbours. Government abstains from teaching Christianity in their institutions; but he says, 'I must do what is right'; and so he pours in Bible knowledge with all his might.

Another interesting school of his is for the sons of men of the highest rank. These men say, 'We will not send our sons to a common school or college.' So he called them together, and they came readily; for he is the great man of the quarter. Then he spoke to them of the progress of knowledge among the poor, and that their children would fall behind. They said, 'We must have a school of our own.' He said, 'Very well'; and turning to one of them, he said, 'Give me that empty house of yours.' The Baboo did not like to say no. So the school began. It is a most interesting sight; fine-looking, noble-looking boys, elegantly dressed, with jewels, and huge armlets and necklaces of solid

gold, their servants standing behind them, and all so full of animation, and thirsting for knowledge. Why, it will quite revolutionize the
palaces and harems of Benares. One could almost take the bright little
fellows to one's bosom. They came crowding round to shake hands
as we left. Poor fellows! if this attempt fails, they will soon be lost
and degraded like their fathers. Mr Tucker pointed out boys whose
fathers are worth four millions of money. Benares is the headquarters
of Hindooism; and the city, like Athens, seems quite given over to
superstition. Everywhere are temples, idol-shops, weavers weaving
the names of the gods, stalls with flowers for worship; and it is Shiva
— the obscene, abominable — that is everywhere served.

Mr Leupolt, an English Church missionary, took me round a great
deal one day. We set off from Mr Tucker's before six in the morning,
and soon reached the large mission-house, where Mr Tucker left me.
Then Mr Leupolt drove to Jainarain's College, a large building of
which I must tell you. Jainarain was a Bengal noble. Being ill, he made
a pilgrimage to Benares, as they always do, either to get better in that
most sacred spot, or, if he died, assuredly be blessed. He continued
ill, however; but heard of a merchant living near where I lived, who,
it was said, could tell him how he might be cured. He went to him.
The merchant was a good man, and said, 'I know one that can cure
you. What would you give?' Jainarain said, 'A lac of rupees.' 'No, that
will not do.' 'Four lacs of rupees.' 'No, He will take nothing but your
heart.' He gave him some simple medicines, and showed him how
to pray; and he went away and soon recovered. He came back to ask
what he should do in gratitude. The merchant said, 'Build and endow a
school.' He did it. The good merchant afterwards became embarrassed
in his affairs, and then took the head-mastership of the school, and
all prospered. But after two years he died. Jainarain was at a loss what
to do, for it went back. But he heard that there was a good chaplain
that loved the natives and sought their good. So he began to pray that
this good chaplain might come to Benares. One morning some one
came in, and said, 'A new chaplain has come.' 'Who?' said Jainarain. It
was Corrie, the very man he was praying for. He hastened to him, and

Corrie advised him to hand the whole over to the Church Missionary Society, which he did; and now it is admirably managed. When we went in, one of my old scholars at Calcutta came up to me. He said, I read Bunyan's *Pilgrim's Progress* with you. He went on the railway as a clerk, but feeling not at ease, came here, is now a teacher, and has lately been baptized. Two others of our Calcutta young men came up to me, both teachers here, and valued.

We went from this to a girls' school for the higher classes, conducted by Mrs Smith, wife of the valued missionary. We examined them. She says they are soon taken away on account of their early marriages.

We went into town, meeting dromedaries and elephants. After a little we were obliged to leave our buggy, and walk, for the streets are very narrow. We came to a mosque, built by Aurungzebe, with two very lofty minarets, one of which was ascended with not a little fatigue; but were repaid by a noble prospect. The city is built of stone; the houses four, five, and six stories high; the narrow lanes all paved with flag-stones; an excellent sewerage; everything clean and orderly; and I quite blushed for Calcutta. I often asked, Where are the houses for the poor? When I got down, my legs were bending and trembling under me; but I was ashamed to say anything, for my companion seemed not to feel it. So off we set on foot, in the sun, with our sola hats and a chokra to guide us to explore. I was much interested with the narrow, crowded lanes and lofty houses. We came to a temple called Veshishwar, the centre of the world, and the most sacred spot in the sacred city. There is a well, down which the god jumped when the Mohammedan conquerors were testing his godship by firing cannon balls at his idols. Very proper, was it not, to get out of the way? I looked down the well, and saw quantities of pretty little flowers thrown in as offerings. Then we went into the temple — a strange scene, where many were mad on their idols. They go about the work seriously, as if it were the great business of their life. Indeed, there seems no other business, except religion and banking — Benares being the Lombard Street of India.

A priest of the mosque here gave Mr Leupolt and Mr Smith a good lesson soon after they came out. They were preaching, and Mr Smith began exposing the obscenities of the Hindoo gods. Then Mr Leupolt began, and spoke harder still. The priest rose with calm dignity, and salaaming, said, 'Sahibs, gentlemen, we came here, not to listen to the misdeeds of the Hindoo gods — we know these better, perhaps, than you do; we came to hear of something better, how we may be saved.' He salaamed again, and sat down, and they felt quite abashed. This man was a mighty adversary; and Mr Leupolt says he went to preach with fear and trembling, for he always took him to task. He evidently studied the Bible in order to refute him. One day he said, 'Show me where it is said that the Holy Ghost spoke, and I will no more object.' Mr Leupolt opened his Bible, and pointed to the beginning of the 13th chapter of Acts. The man took it, and read, 'The Holy Ghost spake and said, Separate me Paul and Barnabas.' He read it again, as if he were confounded, like Paul on the way to Damascus. He closed the book, and never objected again; on the contrary, took their part. He died, and they refused him Mohammedan burial, for they found his Koran covered with refutations and notes, that showed his Christian leanings. The missionaries would have given much for that Koran; but it was burned by his bigoted countrymen.

Here, in a niche, I thought I saw a statue covered with dust; but it turned out to be a fakir, quite naked, who had sat in that position for years without moving. If any one puts food into his mouth he eats it, but never speaks or moves. I spoke to him in vain. Mr Leupolt told me of another, who had sat in the same spot for thirty years without moving, and was counted prodigiously holy, far above the possibility of passion or emotion. Mr Leupolt was building a preaching place close to his seat, and one day a small stone fell down and struck the saint smartly on the back, and up he started with a howl of rage, and his righteousness was for ever gone.

We then went to an observatory, old, and very extensive, where all the astronomical instruments for making observations and calculating eclipses are built of stone, huge circles and gnomes and quadrants, and all sorts of things. But I see I cannot tell you, though I wrote for hours, all the wonders I saw here. The river front is very grand; the whole consists of noble ghauts and temples built by wealthy men; it is in the form of a half moon, or crescent; as you float down for a couple of miles, it is a grand panorama.

I went back to the mission-house to a very late breakfast. Then worship in Hindostanee; visiting missionaries; the Christian village. It is a stirring scene; and I was amused to hear the infantry in the compound saying one of their marching songs or hymns to the tune of 'There's nae luck aboot the house.' It quite made me start, though, you know, I never took my diploma in music. There seems to be a great deal of hopefulness and unanimity among the missionaries here. It will interest Mr Gray to tell him that, visiting the great Sanscrit scholar, Dr Ballantyne, principal of the Government College here, I found him busy putting into Sanscrit our *Shorter Catechism*. He said he wanted a succinct, comprehensive body of divinity, and this he thought the best. He put each question as an aphorism, and then compares Buddhism, Brahmanism, *etc*. with it. He is, I suppose, the best Sanscrit scholar in the world. Tell your dear father that I got his packet of 'Voices'. How great and many have been his kindnesses to me! James Young is quite full of all the kindness of your family and my Perth friends.

Appendix V

A Help to Self-Dedication

I give here, for the purpose of preserving it, one of his earliest publications, which has been found very useful both in this country and in India. It was written in March 1841, for a Bible class. Milne announced from the pulpit that he had prepared such a paper, and that copies would be given to all present, and he would be glad if they would prayerfully consider it, and after doing so, that all who could truthfully say it expressed their desire, would attach their signature to it. A lady, now in Edinburgh, has one of the original copies, with her signature affixed, and she says she cannot tell what a comfort it has been to her, in times of darkness, prayerfully to go over the different items and renew her dedication. She speaks of the communion seasons as so remarkable. She says that ten years she sat under Milne's ministry, and that it was really to her like heaven on earth. Her family circle being a very united one — three sisters and a brother — all like-minded.

> *'I the Lord, will make an everlasting covenant with you'* (Isa. 5:3).
> *'One shall say, I am the Lord's, and another shall subscribe with his hand unto the Lord'* (Isa. 44:5).

Lord God of Hosts, thou didst enter into covenant with Abraham, as he waited beside the sacrifices which he had prepared (*Gen.* 15:18), and thou art now graciously waiting beside Jesus, the sacrifice which thou hast prepared, in order that sinners may come and enter into covenant with thee (*2 Cor.* 5:19). Father, I have sinned against heaven, and in thy sight, and I am no more worthy to be called thy child; but thou, in thy rich mercy, art willing to receive me, and I, through thy grace, am willing to be thine. I lay all my sin (*Isa.* 53:6) — the sin of my nature (*Psa.* 51:5), the sin of my heart (*Jer.* 17:19), the sin of my life (*Job* 33:27), the sin of my lips (*Isa.* 6:5), my secret sins (*Psa.* 139:3) — I lay all my sins, and iniquities, and unrighteousness, and transgressions, upon Jesus, the Lamb of God; and, cleansed by his blood, and made acceptable in his righteousness (*Eph.* 1:6, 7), I desire now to give myself to thee (*2 Cor.* 8:5) in an everlasting covenant, never to be broken (*Jer.* 32:40).

I am not my own, I am thine (*1 Cor.* 6:19). My heart is not my own, it is thine; I will endeavour to keep it for thee, and to make it Bethel, a temple for the Holy Ghost (*2 Cor.* 6:16). My thoughts are not my own, they are thine; I will cultivate godly and heavenly meditations (*Psa.* 1:2, and 63:6). My words are not my own, they are thine; I will avoid all idle, unprofitable, vain-glorious, flattering, uncharitable discourse (*Eph.* 4:29; *Col.* 3:8, 9); and I will seek to have my conversation always savouring of Christ and heaven (*Deut.* 6:7; *Matt.* 12:34-37; *Col.* 3:16). My eyes are not my own, they are thine; I will withhold them from looking upon sin and vanity (*Hab.* 1:13). My wealth is not my own, it is thine; I am only thy steward; I will therefore lay it out prudently and faithfully for thee, avoiding all unnecessary expense upon myself (*Deut.* 24:19-21; *Job* 29:12, 13; *Prov.* 3:9, 10; *Matt.* 25:5, 36; *Luke* 21:2, 8, 4). My time is not my own, it is thine; I will employ it for thee, doing all I do as unto the Lord, striving every day to grow in grace and in knowledge, and to make myself useful to my fellow-men; I will redeem my time from too long or needless visits, idle imaginations, fruitless discourse, unnecessary sleep, and more than needful care about my worldly affairs (*Eph.* 5:16; *Col.* 4:5). I desire to commit all I have to thee; my friends, my family, my health, my business, my esteem in the world. I am willing to receive what thou givest, to want what thou withholdest, to relinquish what thou takest, to suffer what thou inflictest, to be what thou requires!, and to do what thou commandest.

Lord God of Hosts, I desire, deliberately, cheerfully, and with full purpose of heart, thus to surrender myself wholly and for ever to thee; I feel that this is my duty, my interest, my privilege, my glory; — I believe that thou wilt receive what I thus give (*2 Cor.* 6:17); I believe that thou wilt keep what I have thus committed to thee (*2 Tim.* 1:12); — I will trust in thee for temporal provision (*Psa.* 23:1); I will trust in thee for support under daily cares and labours (*Isa.* 26:3); I will trust in thee for pardon of daily sins (*Ezek.* 36:25); I will trust in thee for growth and fruitfulness (*Hos.* 12:5); I will trust to thee for strength in the hour of death (*Isa.* 43:2). If I sin, may I grieve without despair; if I walk uprightly, may I rejoice without pride.

Lord Jesus, I take thee for my Prophet, my Priest, my King, my Life, my Light, my Rest, my Joy, my Glory, my All in All.

Spirit of Adoption, that proceedest from the Father and the Son, I desire to receive thee into my soul, that thou mayest abide with me. Convince me of sin, convince me of judgment, guide me into all truth; take of the things of Christ and show them unto me; be as the dew and the rain of heaven to my soul, causing the word of life to take root, and grow, and bear the fruits of peace, joy, love, gentleness; enable me to mortify the flesh with its affections and lusts — when the enemy comes in like a flood, do thou lift up a standard against him; be in me as a well of living water — be in me as the earnest of the inheritance, as the first-fruits of heaven — sealing me unto the day of redemption. Holy and blessed Spirit, help me to distinguish between thy voice and the voice of the evil one — between thy suggestions and the impulses of the flesh — between thy leadings and the frowardness of my own heart. I will labour not to resist, nor grieve, nor dishonour, nor quench thee; but, with a humble, broken, mortified, self-denying spirit, will endeavour to fall in with thee in all things, and to think, and speak, and act in thee.

Free St Leonard's Manse, Perth.'

I wished to have inserted a few more letters, and also more of the hymns scattered through the pages of the Indian Journal. But the volume would thus have swelled out unduly. Indeed it has only been by the exercise of considerable self-denial, that I have been able to keep it within moderate bounds. What I have given, however, is sufficient to show the man at all points, and in all these points the same single-eyed, consistent man of God, and minister of Christ.

In another page [p. 399] will be found the inscription on his monument in the Grange or Southern Cemetery; and I may add here, that on the wall of the new hall, belonging to the Perth Young Men's Religious Tract Society, a memorial slab of marble is in process of being fitted up for him, as well as another for Burns. The Grange memorial is in the obelisk or pillar form, of white marble, with choice texts, and an open Bible above his name; and she who erected it closes a note to the author of this memoir with these words, — words which all of us who knew him will take as expressive of their own feelings: 'I love to think of him now as a pillar in the temple of our God.'

> *Him that overcometh will I make a pillar in the temple of my God, and he shall go no more out: and I will write upon him the name of my God, and the name of the city of my God, which is New Jerusalem, which cometh down out of heaven from my God; and I will write upon him my new name.*

THE END

Victoria Street, Perth, as it is today. The original Free St Leonard's Church stood on the right, about half way down the street.

The old Disruption church, which was opened in 1843, occupied the site on which these flats now stand.

In 1885 the congregation of Free St Leonard's moved to their new church building in Marshall Place, two blocks away to the south. The foundation stone of the new structure was laid by Dr Horatius Bonar, the author of this biography of John Milne.